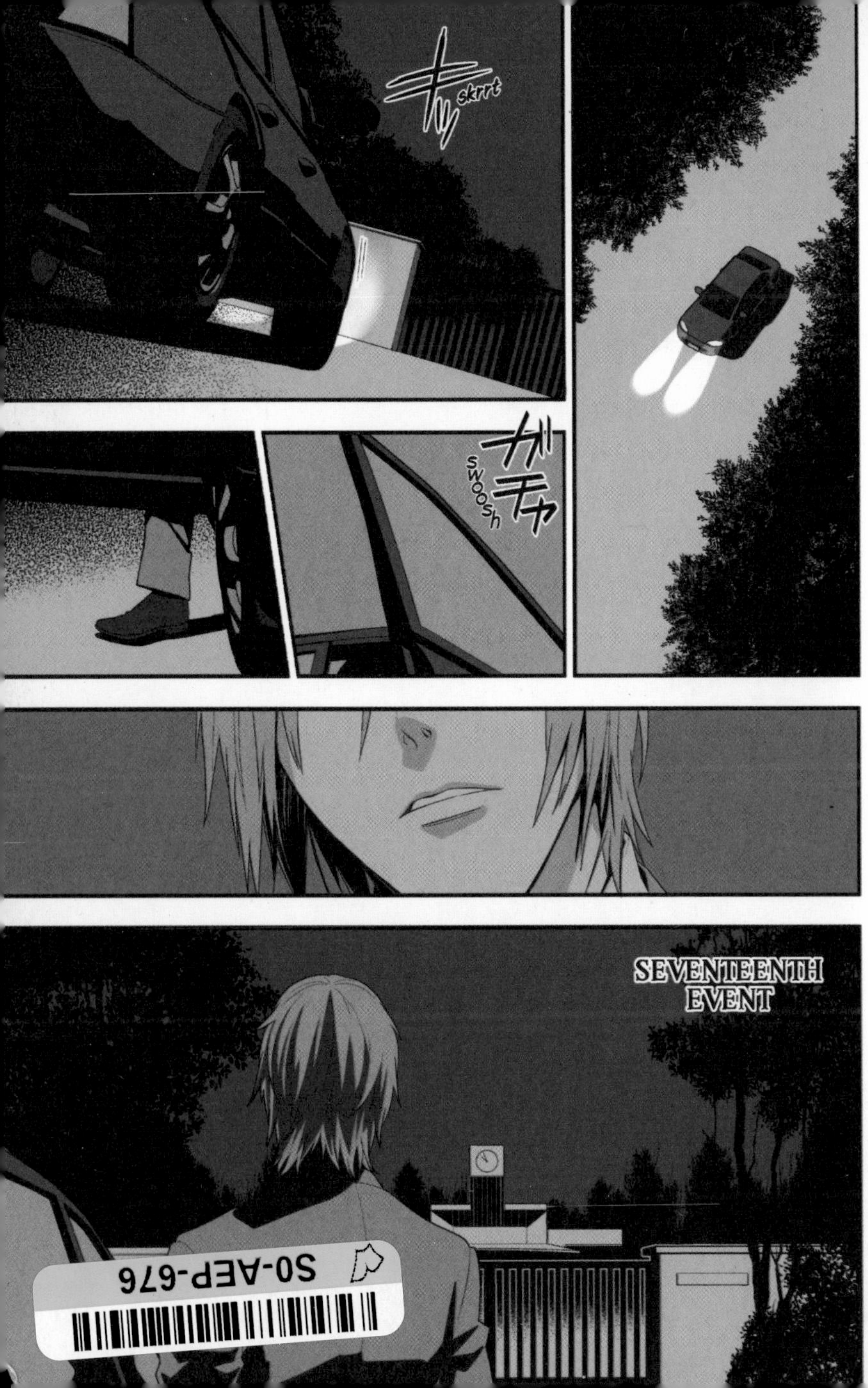
キッ
skrrt
ガチャ
swoosh
SEVENTEENTH
EVENT

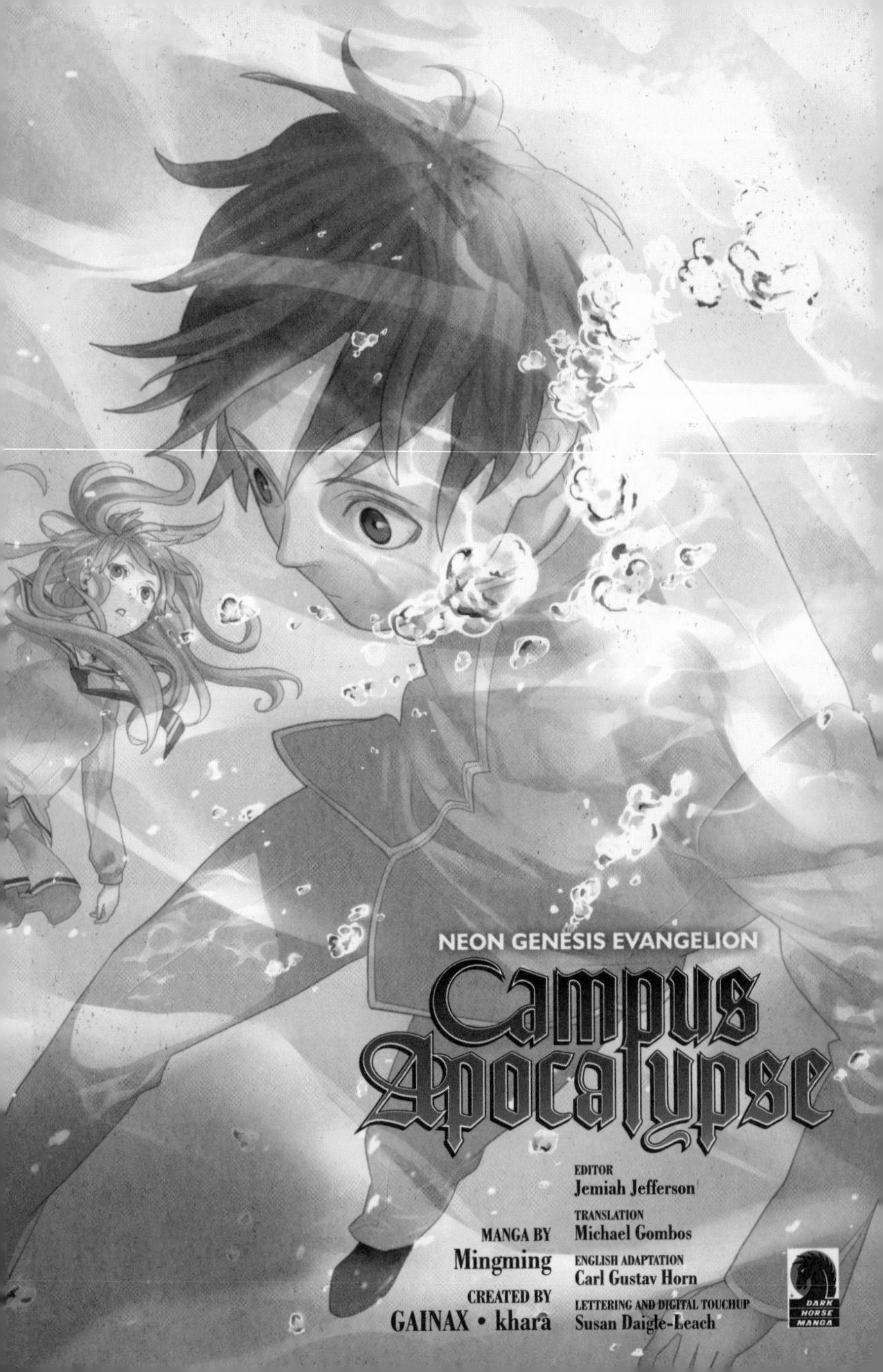

NEON GENESIS EVANGELION

Campus Apocalypse

MANGA BY
Mingming

CREATED BY
GAINAX • khara

EDITOR
Jemiah Jefferson

TRANSLATION
Michael Gombos

ENGLISH ADAPTATION
Carl Gustav Horn

LETTERING AND DIGITAL TOUCHUP
Susan Daigle-Leach

DARK HORSE MANGA

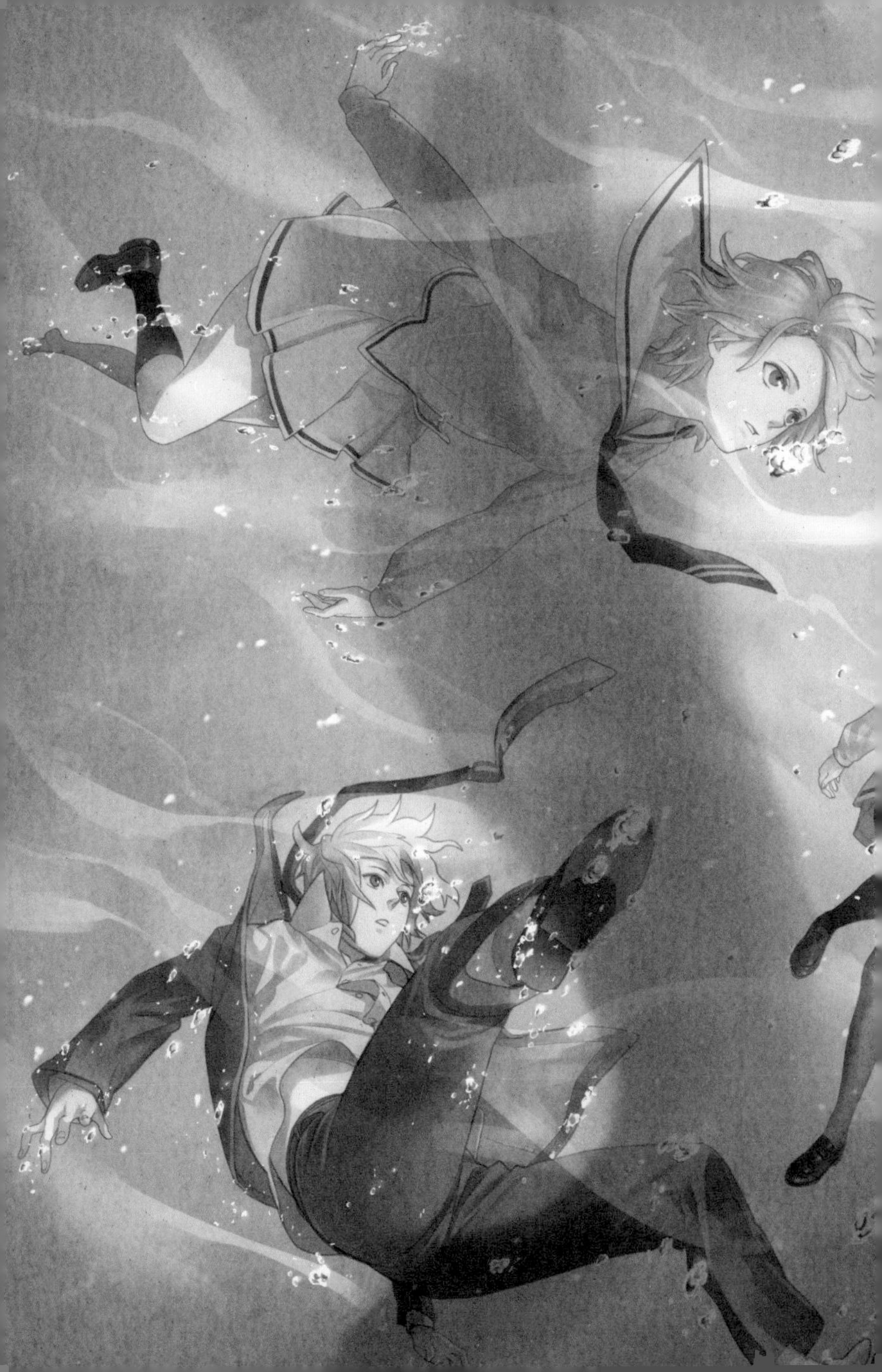

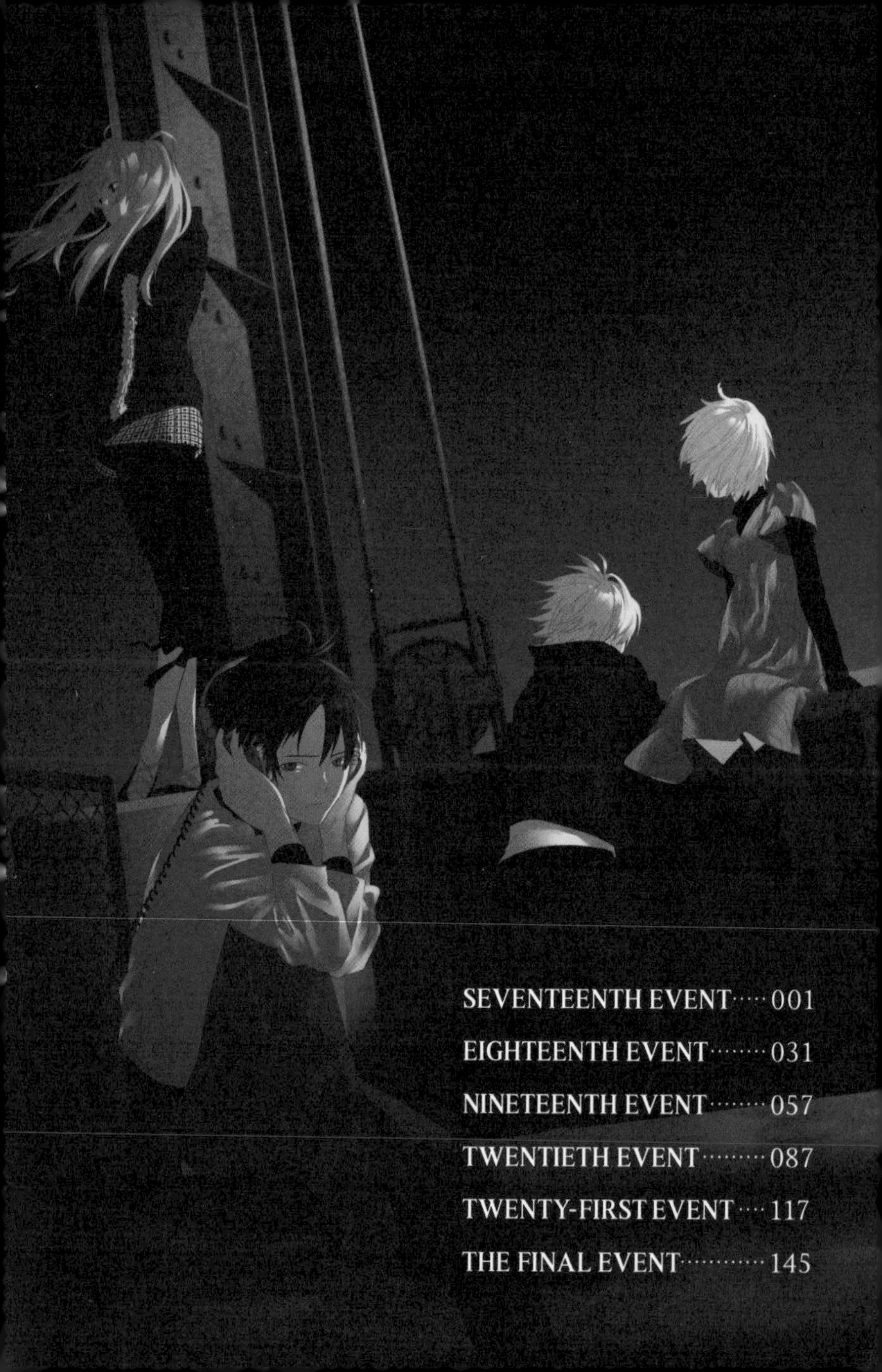

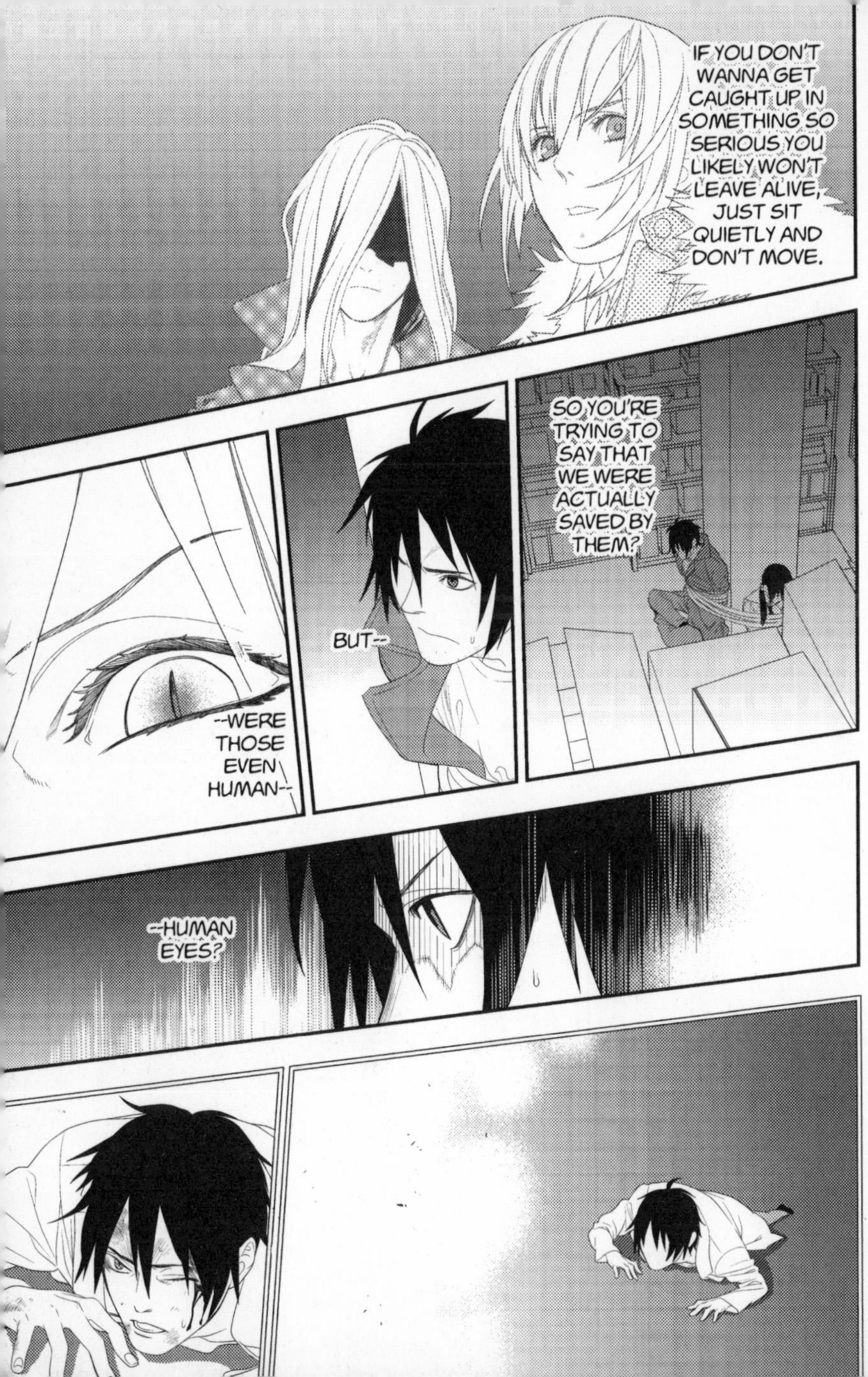
IF YOU DON'T WANNA GET CAUGHT UP IN SOMETHING SO SERIOUS YOU LIKELY WON'T LEAVE ALIVE, JUST SIT QUIETLY AND DON'T MOVE.
SO YOU'RE TRYING TO SAY THAT WE WERE ACTUALLY SAVED BY THEM?
BUT--
--WERE THOSE EVEN HUMAN--
--HUMAN EYES?

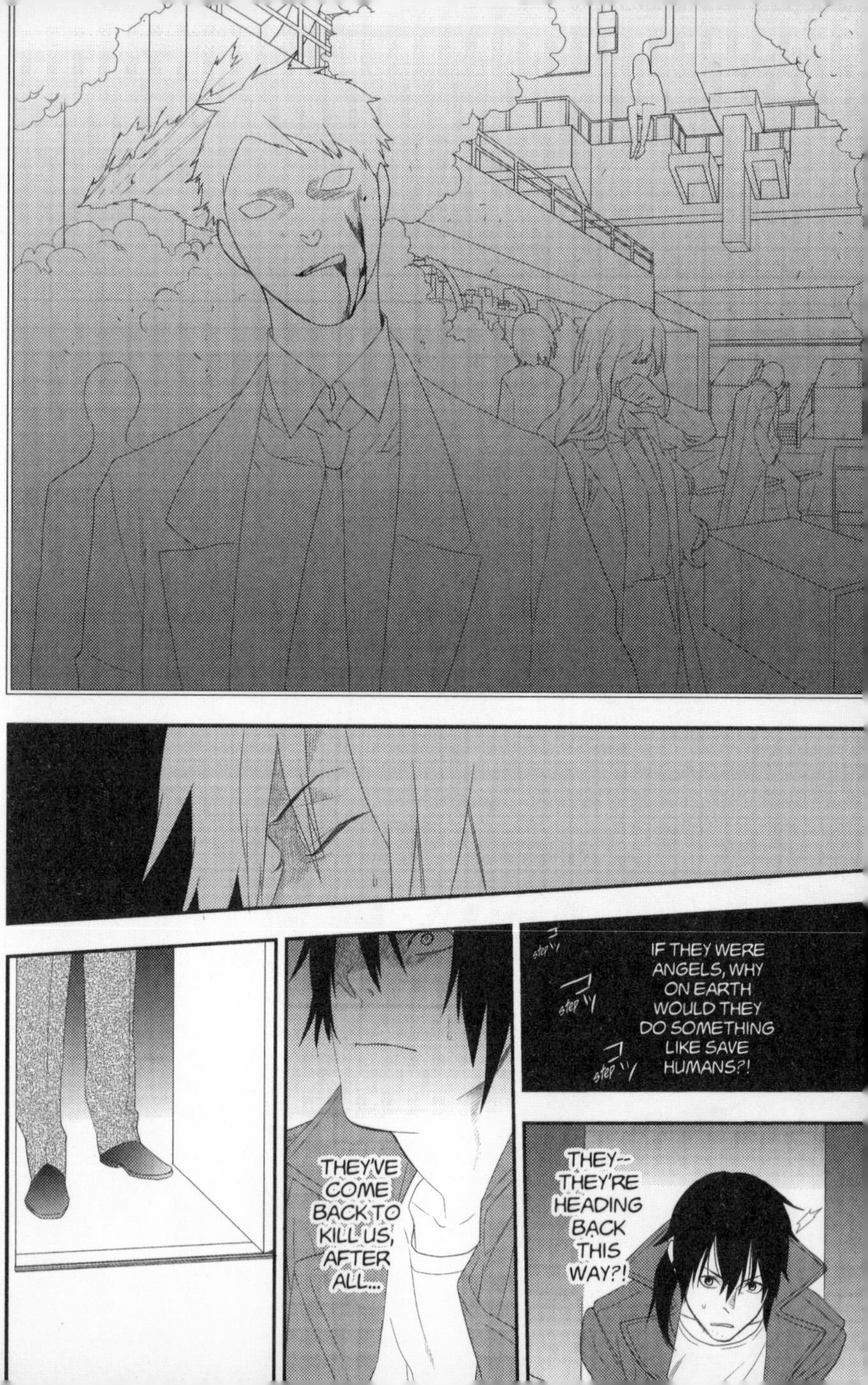
step
step
step
IF THEY WERE ANGELS, WHY ON EARTH WOULD THEY DO SOMETHING LIKE SAVE HUMANS?!
THEY-- THEY'RE HEADING BACK THIS WAY?!
THEY'VE COME BACK TO KILL US, AFTER ALL...

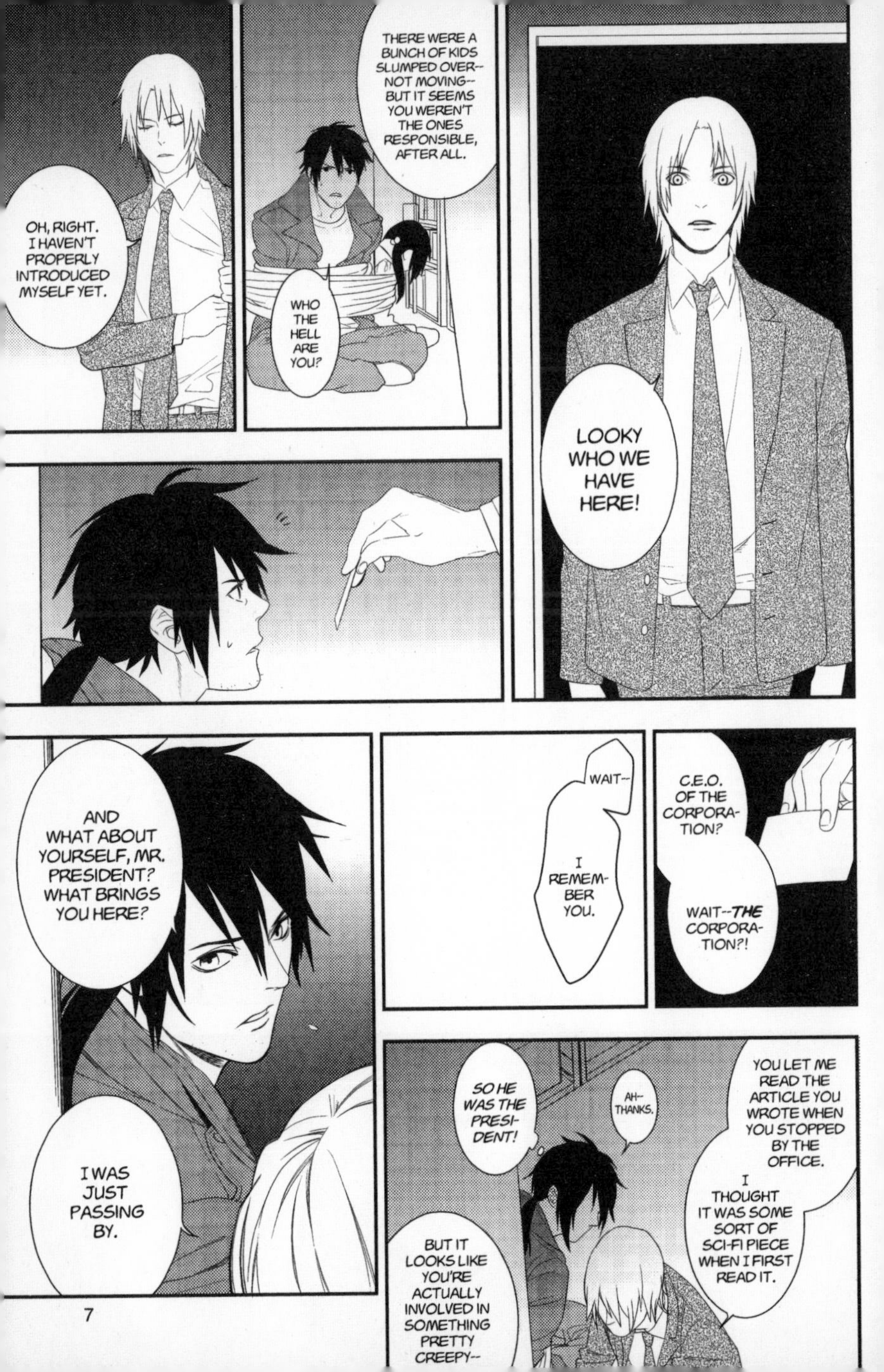
LOOKY WHO WE HAVE HERE!
THERE WERE A BUNCH OF KIDS SLUMPED OVER-- NOT MOVING-- BUT IT SEEMS YOU WEREN'T THE ONES RESPONSIBLE, AFTER ALL.
WHO THE HELL ARE YOU?
OH, RIGHT. I HAVEN'T PROPERLY INTRODUCED MYSELF YET.
C.E.O. OF THE CORPORA-TION?
WAIT--*THE* CORPORA-TION?!
WAIT--
I REMEM-BER YOU.
YOU LET ME READ THE ARTICLE YOU WROTE WHEN YOU STOPPED BY THE OFFICE.
I THOUGHT IT WAS SOME SORT OF SCI-FI PIECE WHEN I FIRST READ IT.
AH-- THANKS.
SO HE WAS THE PRESI-DENT!
BUT IT LOOKS LIKE YOU'RE ACTUALLY INVOLVED IN SOMETHING PRETTY CREEPY--
AND WHAT ABOUT YOURSELF, MR. PRESIDENT? WHAT BRINGS YOU HERE?
I WAS JUST PASSING BY.

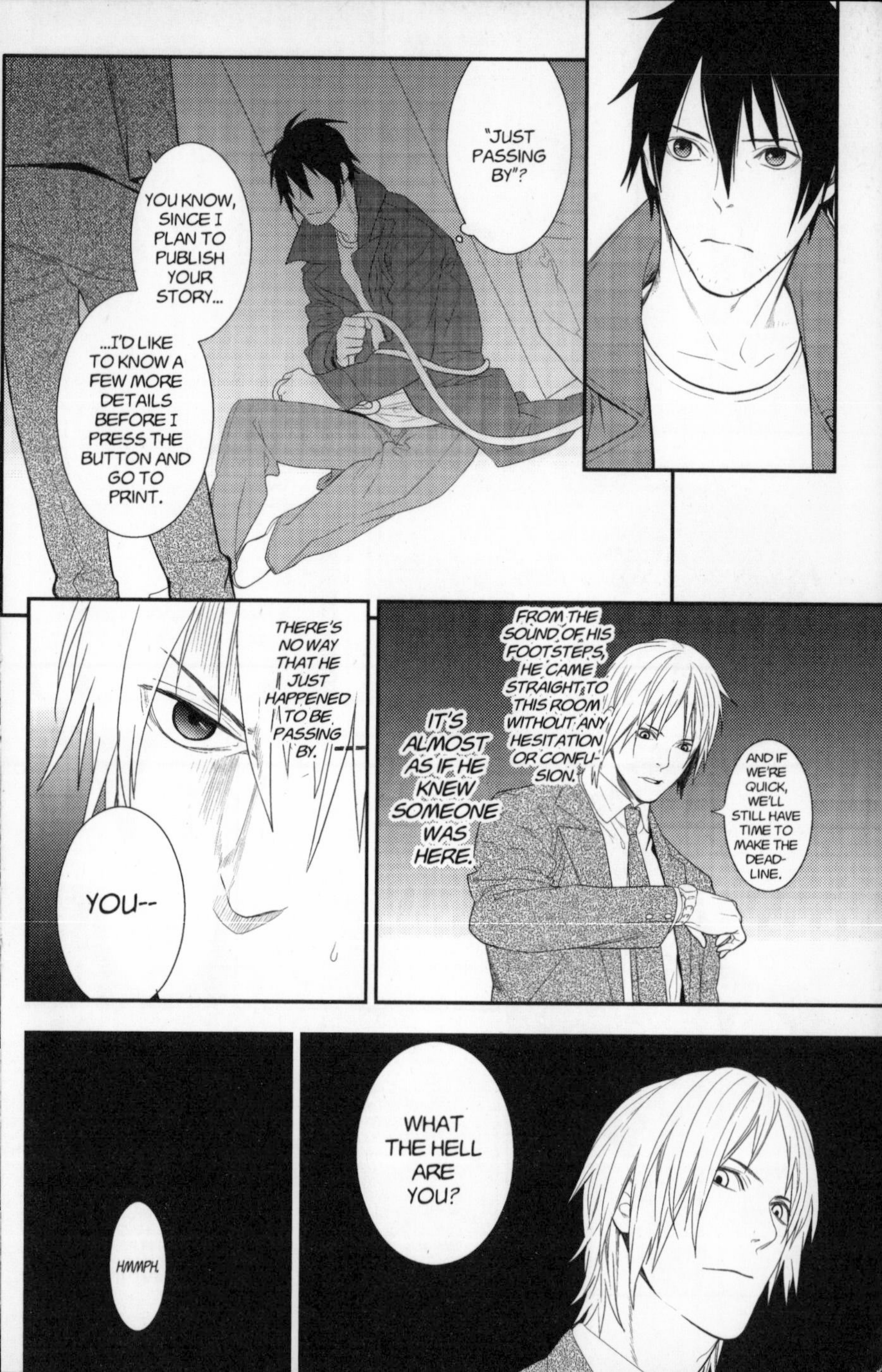
"JUST PASSING BY"?
YOU KNOW, SINCE I PLAN TO PUBLISH YOUR STORY...
...I'D LIKE TO KNOW A FEW MORE DETAILS BEFORE I PRESS THE BUTTON AND GO TO PRINT.
FROM THE SOUND OF HIS FOOTSTEPS, HE CAME STRAIGHT TO THIS ROOM WITHOUT ANY HESITATION OR CONFUSION.
AND IF WE'RE QUICK, WE'LL STILL HAVE TIME TO MAKE THE DEADLINE.
IT'S ALMOST AS IF HE KNEW SOMEONE WAS HERE.
THERE'S NO WAY THAT HE JUST HAPPENED TO BE PASSING BY.
YOU--
WHAT THE HELL ARE YOU?
HMMPH.

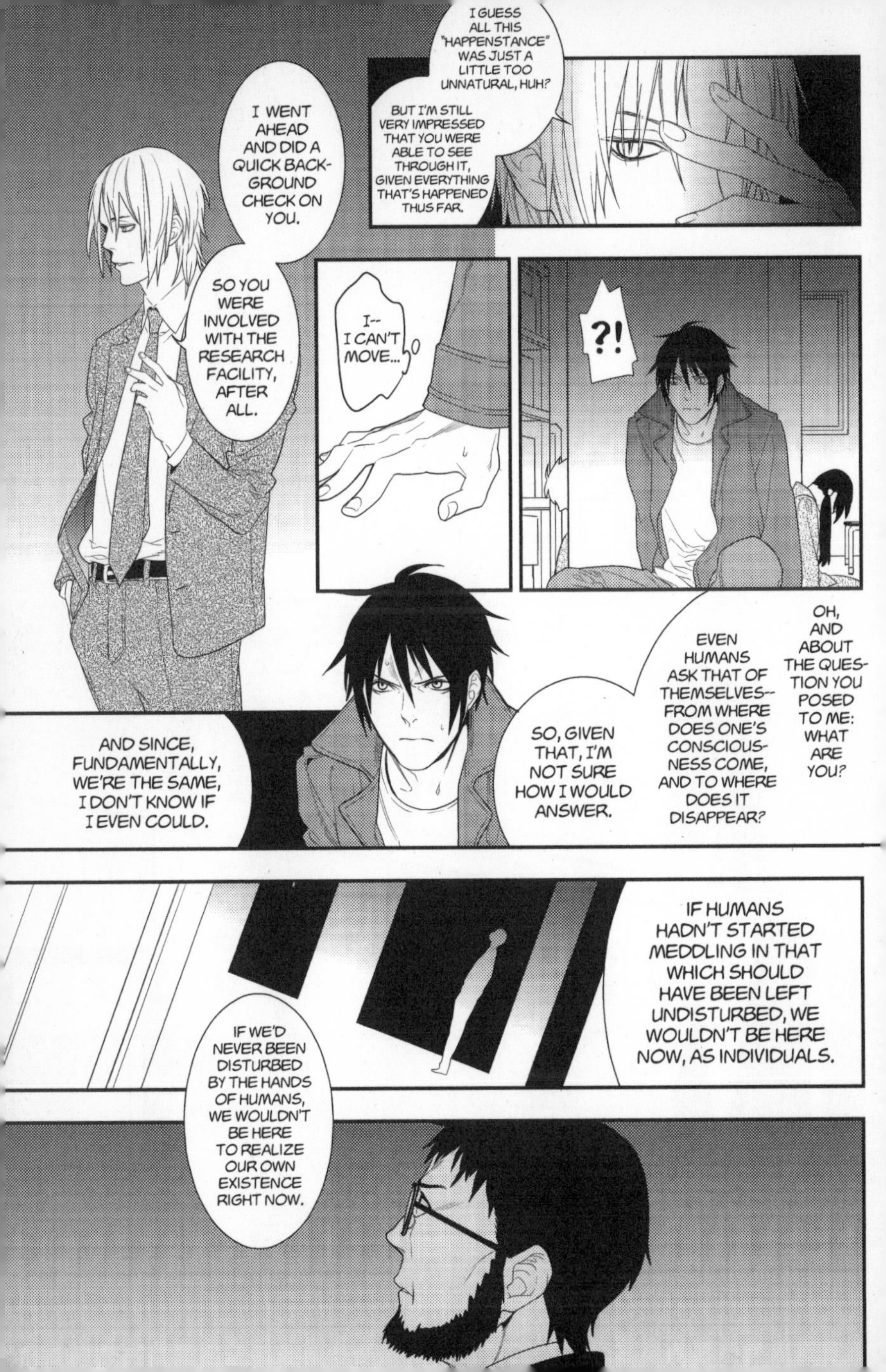

I GUESS ALL THIS "HAPPENSTANCE" WAS JUST A LITTLE TOO UNNATURAL, HUH?
BUT I'M STILL VERY IMPRESSED THAT YOU WERE ABLE TO SEE THROUGH IT, GIVEN EVERYTHING THAT'S HAPPENED THUS FAR.
?!
I-- I CAN'T MOVE...
I WENT AHEAD AND DID A QUICK BACK-GROUND CHECK ON YOU.
SO YOU WERE INVOLVED WITH THE RESEARCH FACILITY, AFTER ALL.
OH, AND ABOUT THE QUES-TION YOU POSED TO ME: WHAT ARE YOU?
EVEN HUMANS ASK THAT OF THEMSELVES-- FROM WHERE DOES ONE'S CONSCIOUS-NESS COME, AND TO WHERE DOES IT DISAPPEAR?
SO, GIVEN THAT, I'M NOT SURE HOW I WOULD ANSWER.
AND SINCE, FUNDAMENTALLY, WE'RE THE SAME, I DON'T KNOW IF I EVEN COULD.
IF HUMANS HADN'T STARTED MEDDLING IN THAT WHICH SHOULD HAVE BEEN LEFT UNDISTURBED, WE WOULDN'T BE HERE NOW, AS INDIVIDUALS.
IF WE'D NEVER BEEN DISTURBED BY THE HANDS OF HUMANS, WE WOULDN'T BE HERE TO REALIZE OUR OWN EXISTENCE RIGHT NOW.

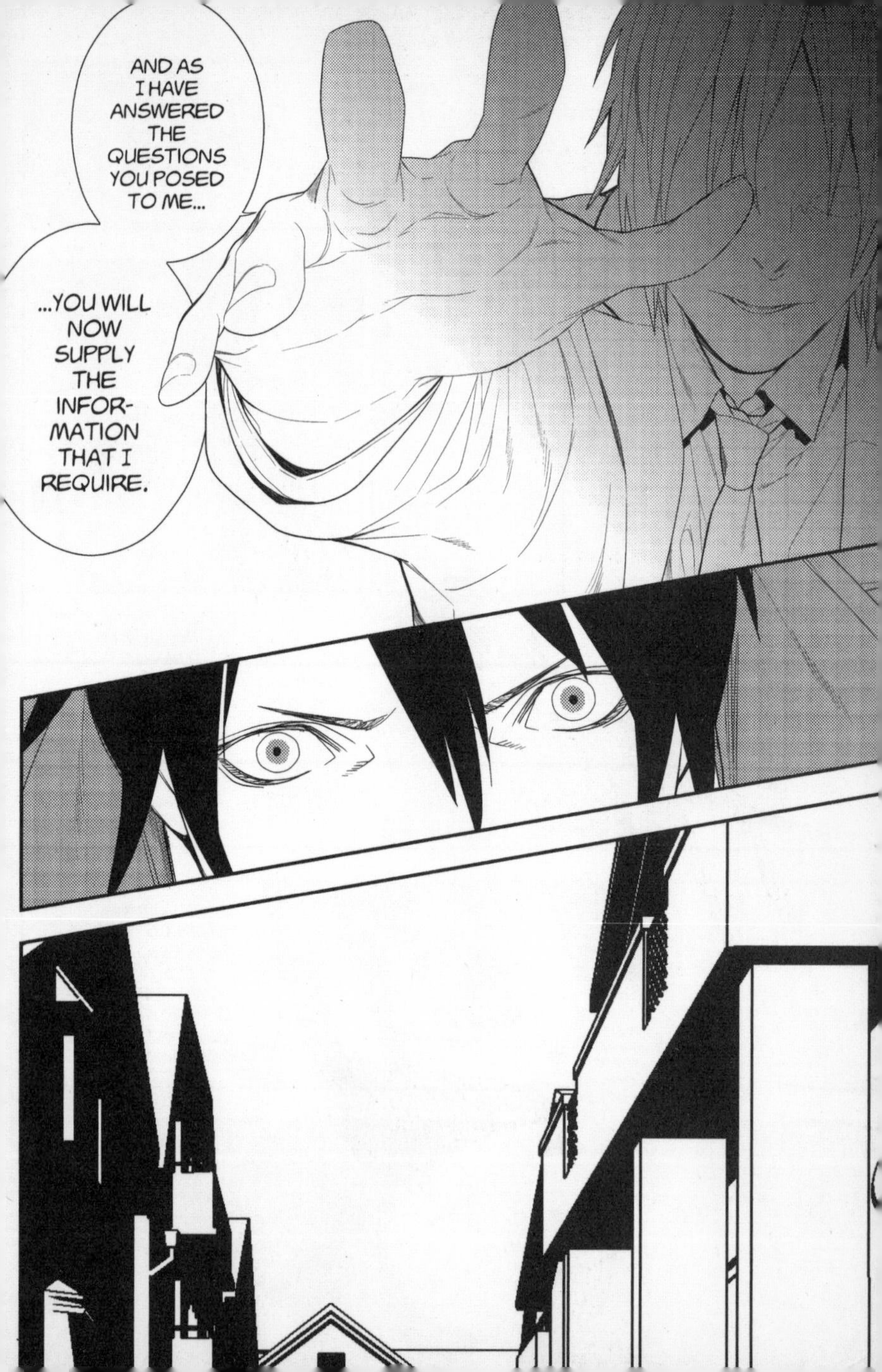
AND AS I HAVE ANSWERED THE QUESTIONS YOU POSED TO ME...
...YOU WILL NOW SUPPLY THE INFORMATION THAT I REQUIRE.

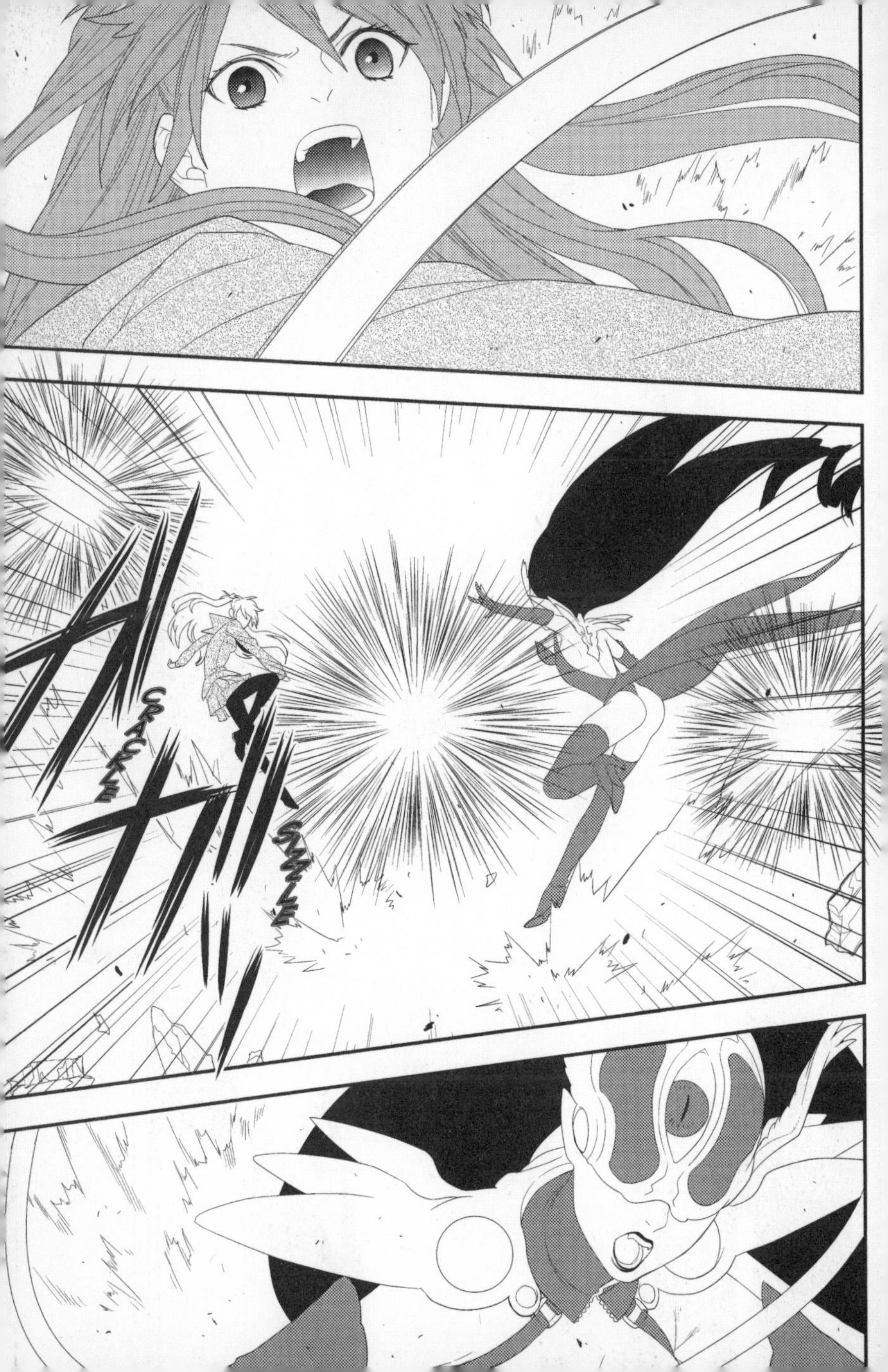
SIZZLE
CRACKLE

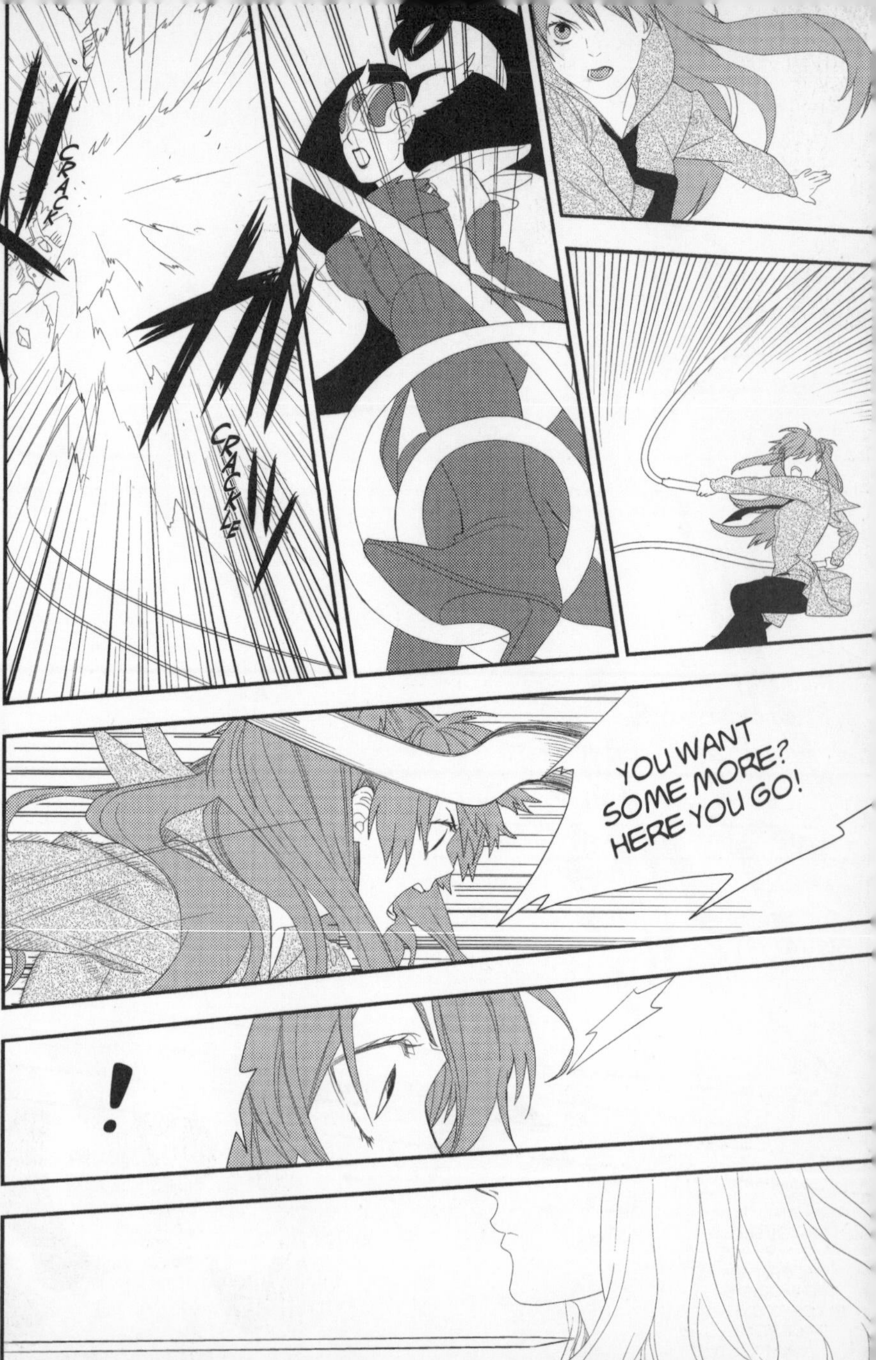
CRACK
CRACKLE
YOU WANT SOME MORE? HERE YOU GO!
!

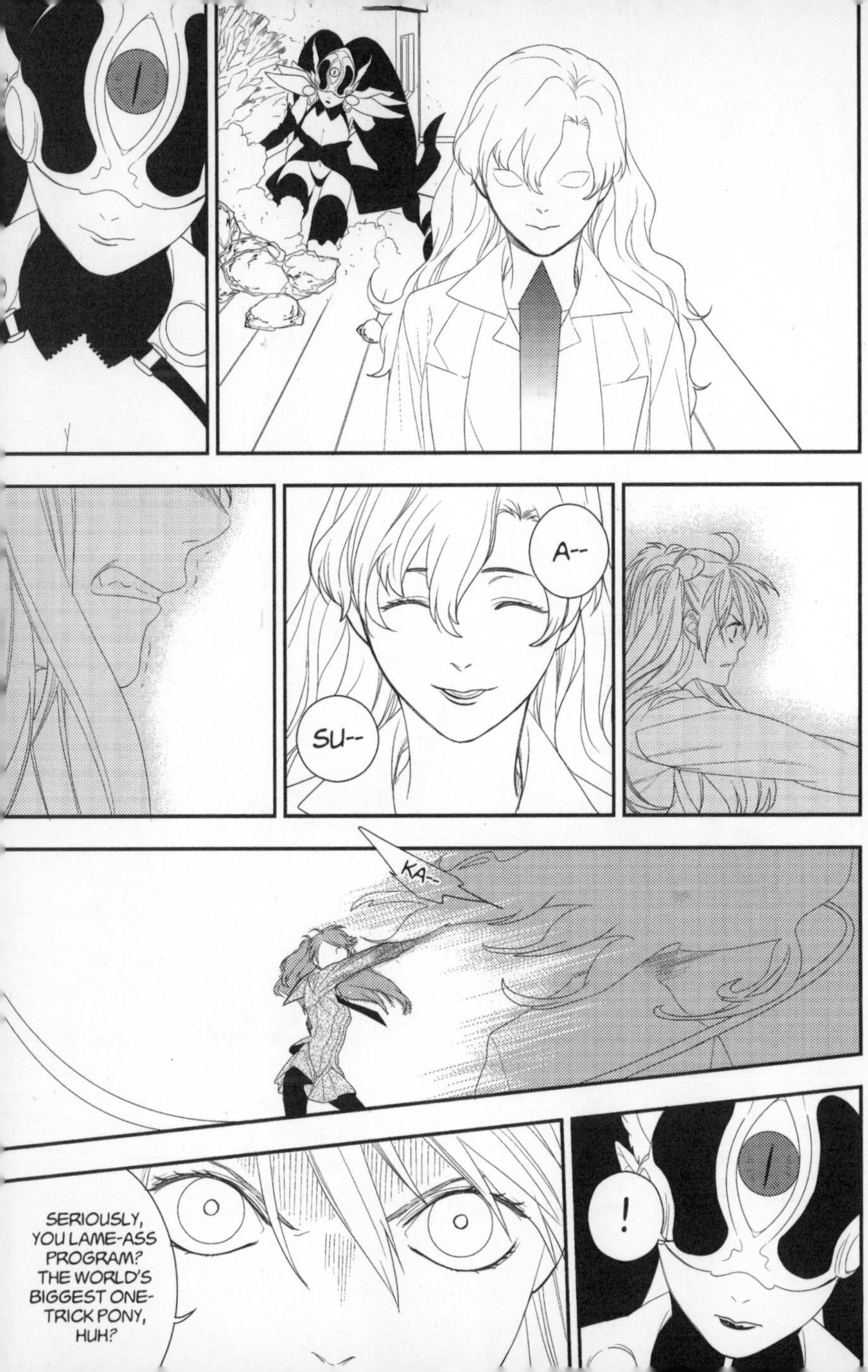
A--
SU--
KA--
!
SERIOUSLY, YOU LAME-ASS PROGRAM? THE WORLD'S BIGGEST ONE-TRICK PONY, HUH?

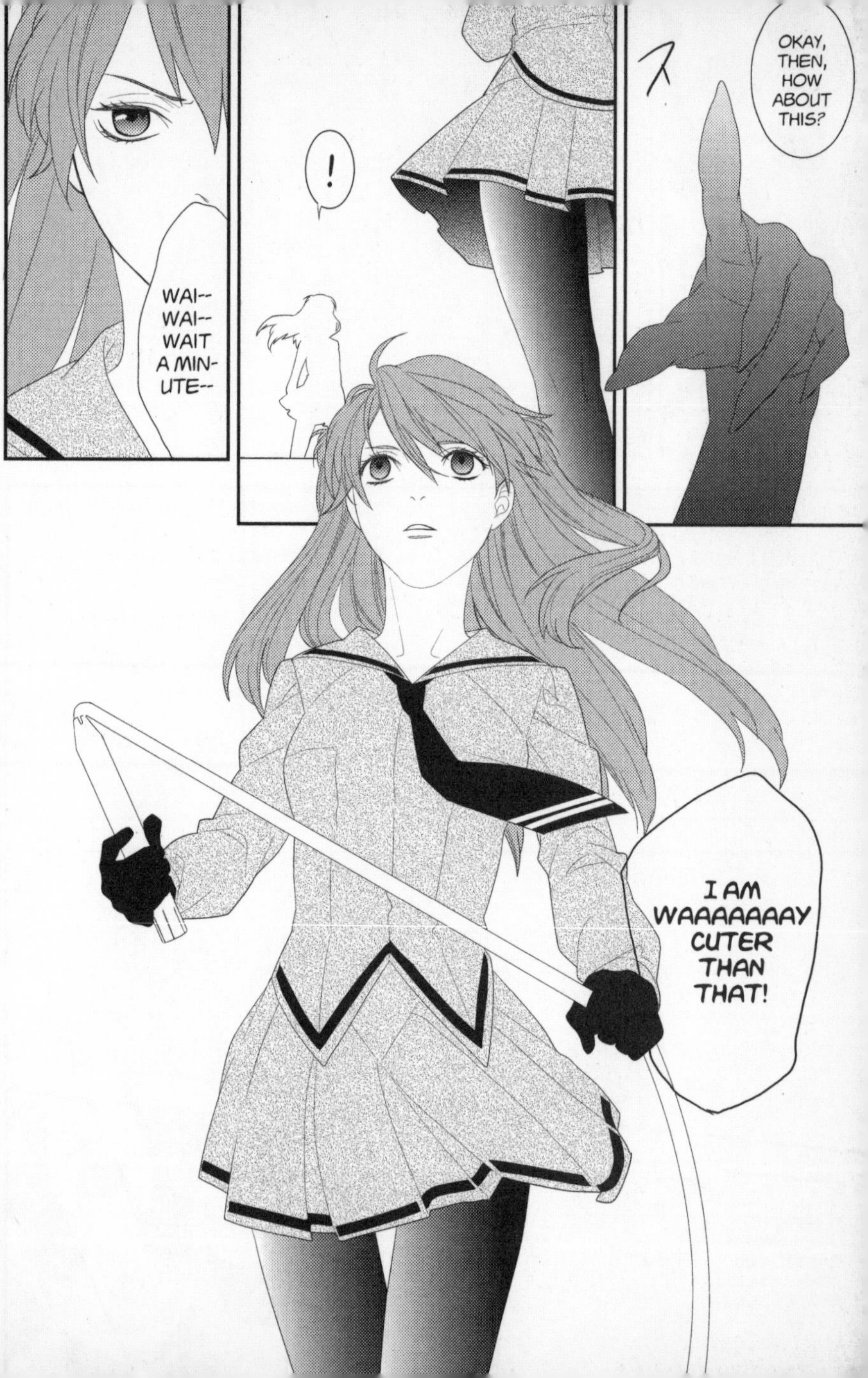
OKAY, THEN, HOW ABOUT THIS?
ス
!
WAI-- WAI-- WAIT A MIN-UTE--
I AM WAAAAAAAAY CUTER THAN THAT!

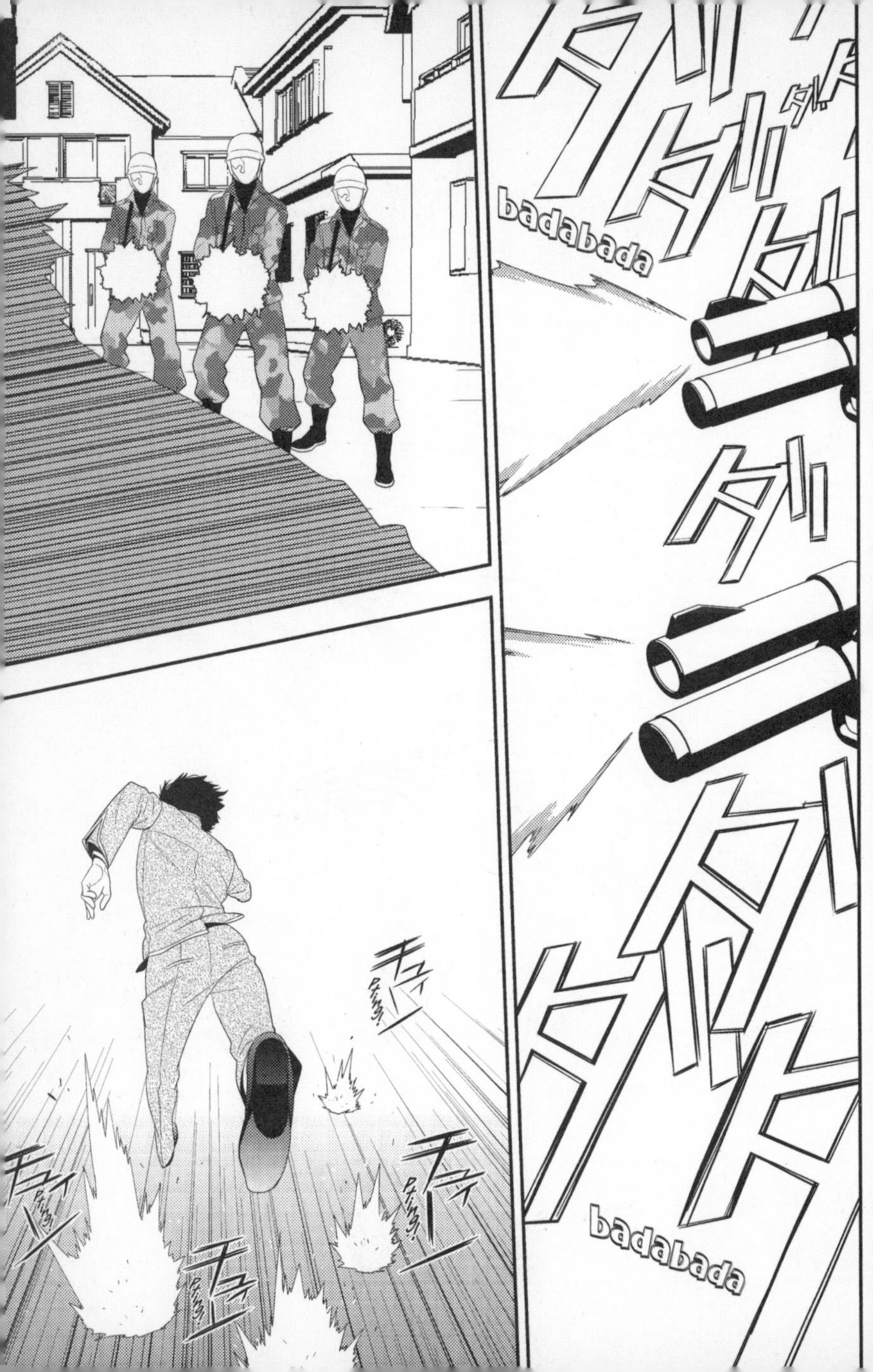
badabada
badabada
PTING!
PTING!
PTING!
PTING!

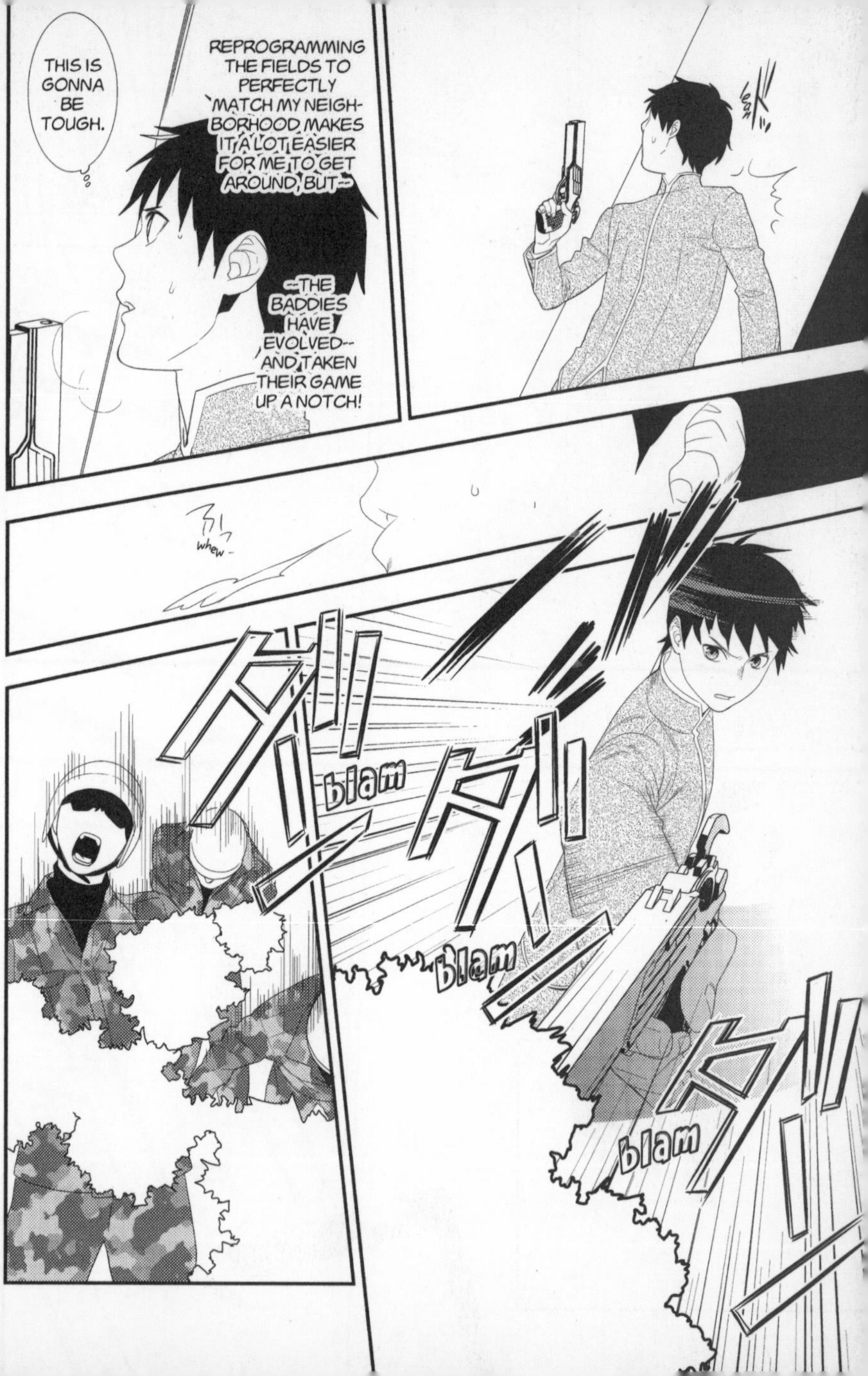
lean
THIS IS GONNA BE TOUGH.
REPROGRAMMING THE FIELDS TO PERFECTLY MATCH MY NEIGHBORHOOD MAKES IT A LOT EASIER FOR ME TO GET AROUND, BUT--
--THE BADDIES HAVE EVOLVED--AND TAKEN THEIR GAME UP A NOTCH!
whew -
blam
blam
blam

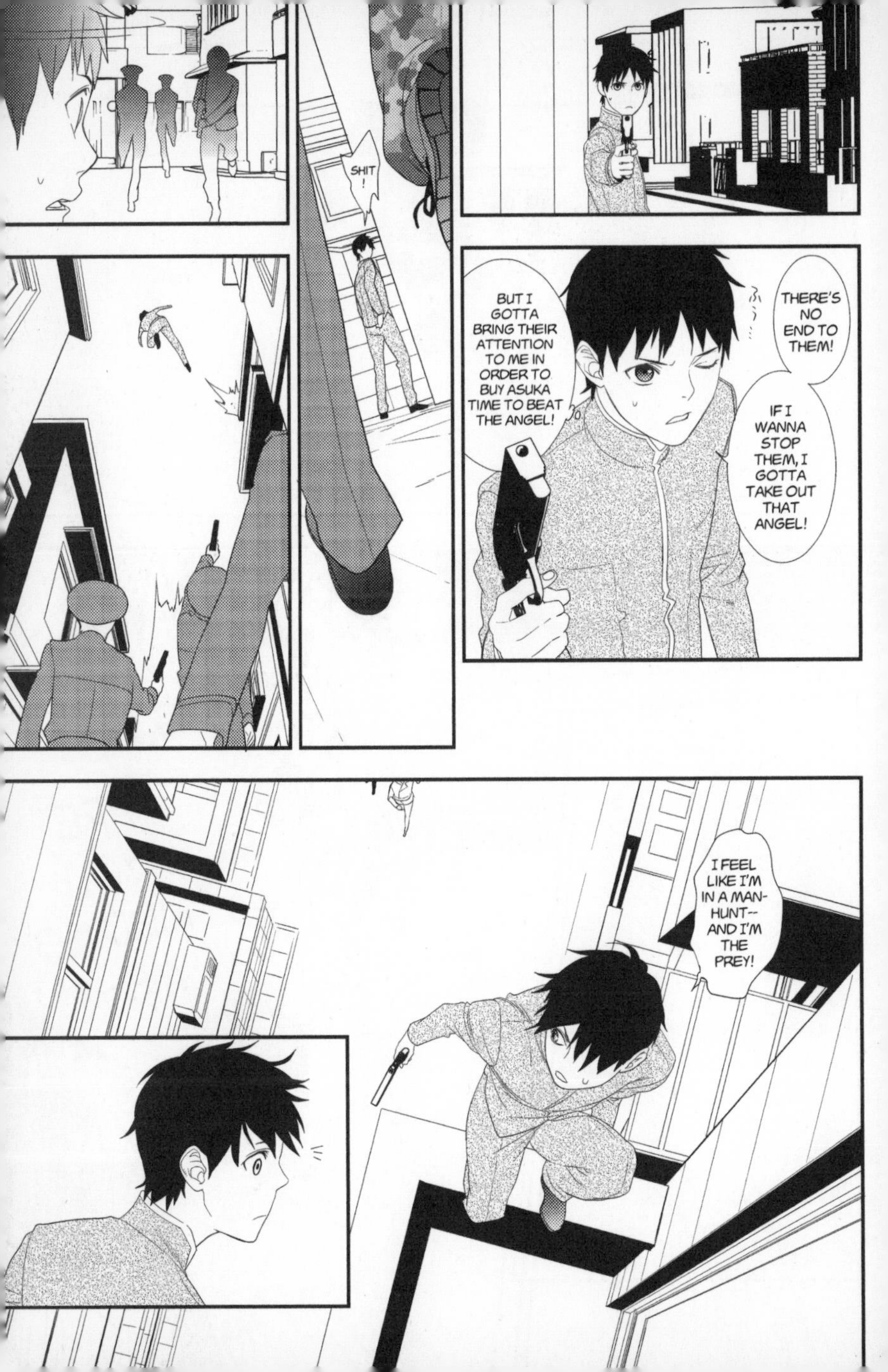
THERE'S NO END TO THEM!
IF I WANNA STOP THEM, I GOTTA TAKE OUT THAT ANGEL!
BUT I GOTTA BRING THEIR ATTENTION TO ME IN ORDER TO BUY ASUKA TIME TO BEAT THE ANGEL!
SHIT!
I FEEL LIKE I'M IN A MAN-HUNT-- AND I'M THE PREY!

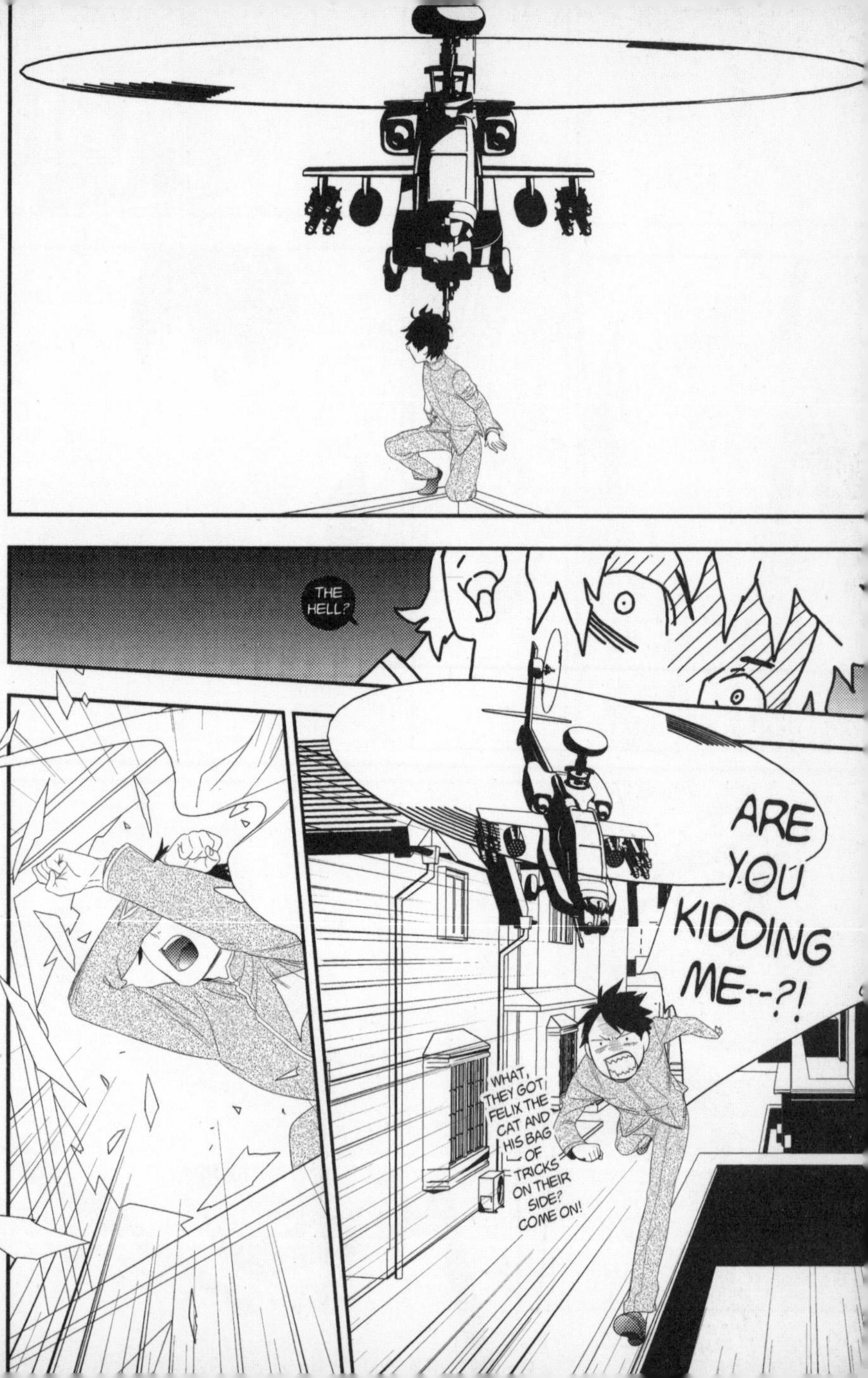
THE HELL?
ARE YOU KIDDING ME--?!
WHAT, THEY GOT FELIX THE CAT AND HIS BAG OF TRICKS ON THEIR SIDE? COME ON!

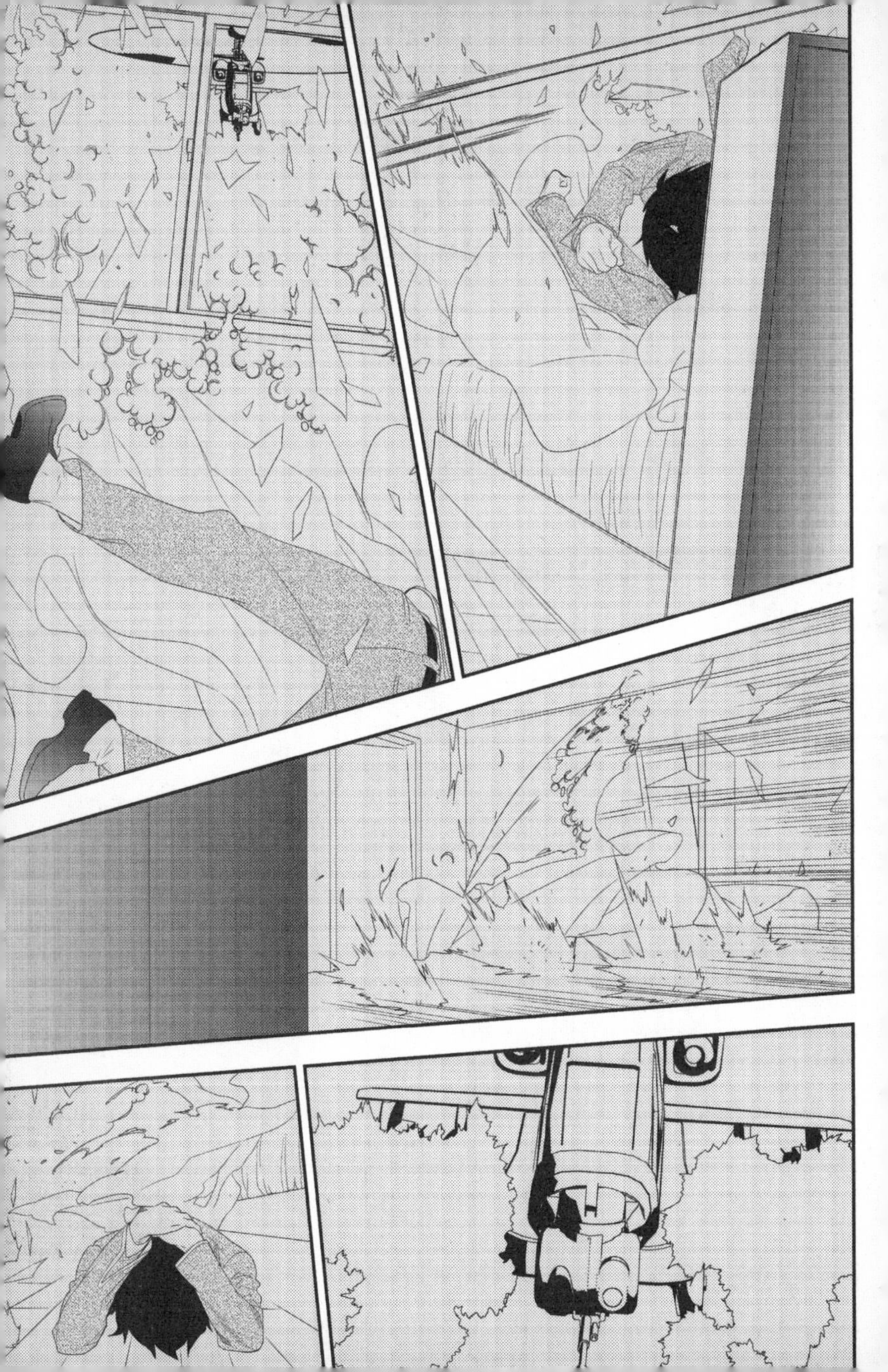

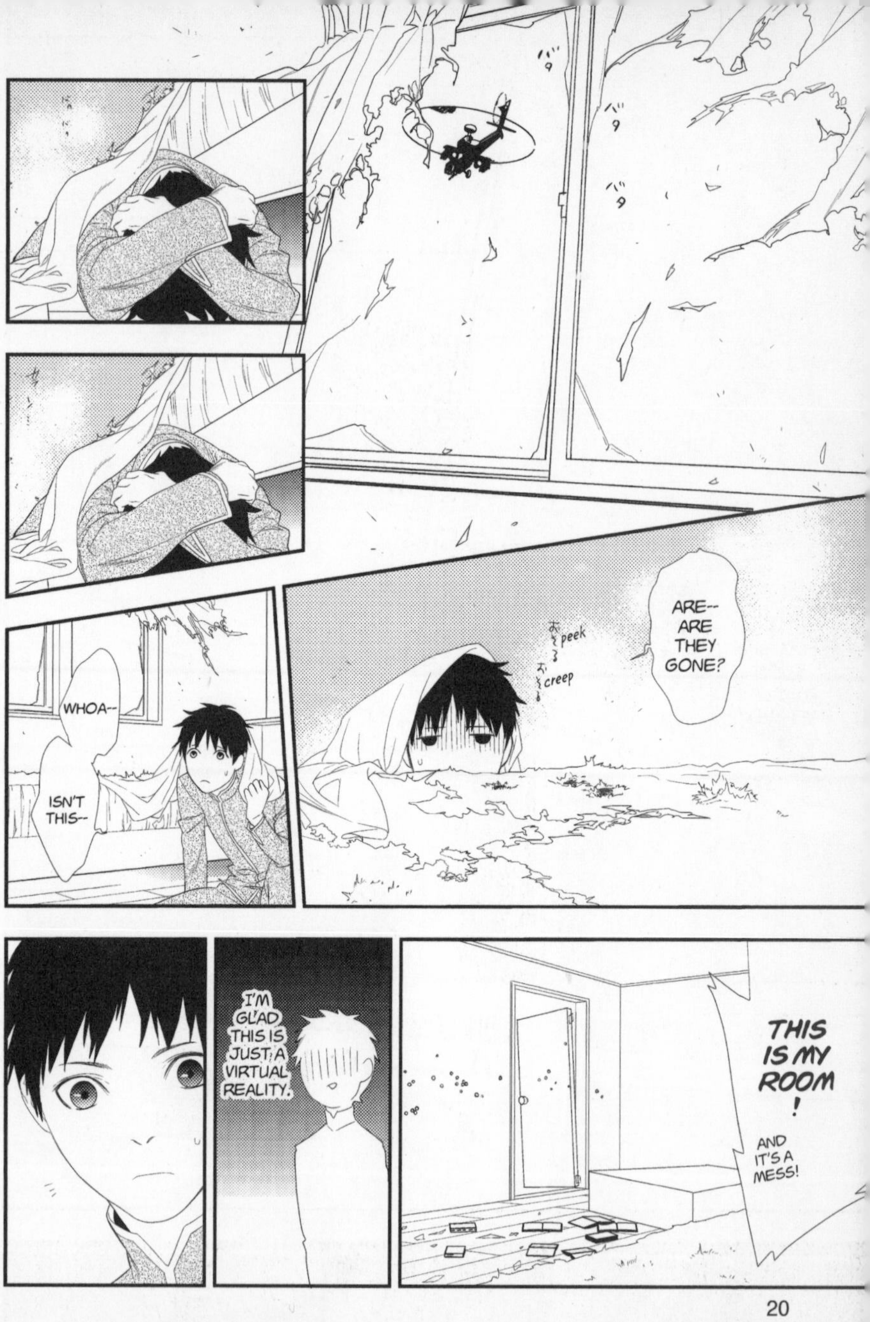
peek
creep
ARE-- ARE THEY GONE?
WHOA--
ISN'T THIS--
THIS IS MY ROOM!
AND IT'S A MESS!
I'M GLAD THIS IS JUST A VIRTUAL REALITY.

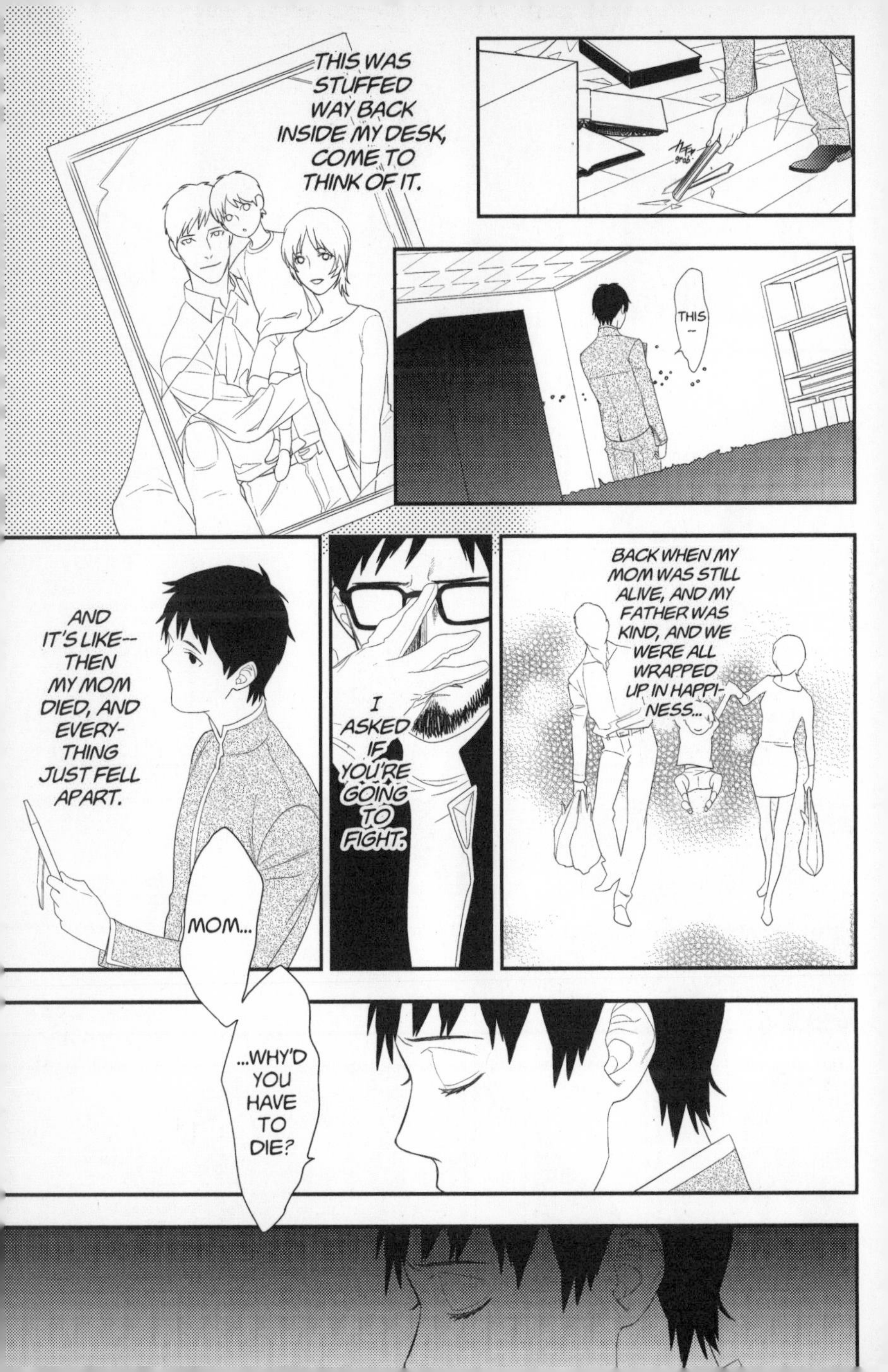
grab
THIS —
THIS WAS STUFFED WAY BACK INSIDE MY DESK, COME TO THINK OF IT.
BACK WHEN MY MOM WAS STILL ALIVE, AND MY FATHER WAS KIND, AND WE WERE ALL WRAPPED UP IN HAPPI-NESS...
I ASKED IF YOU'RE GOING TO FIGHT.
AND IT'S LIKE-- THEN MY MOM DIED, AND EVERY-THING JUST FELL APART.
MOM...
...WHY'D YOU HAVE TO DIE?

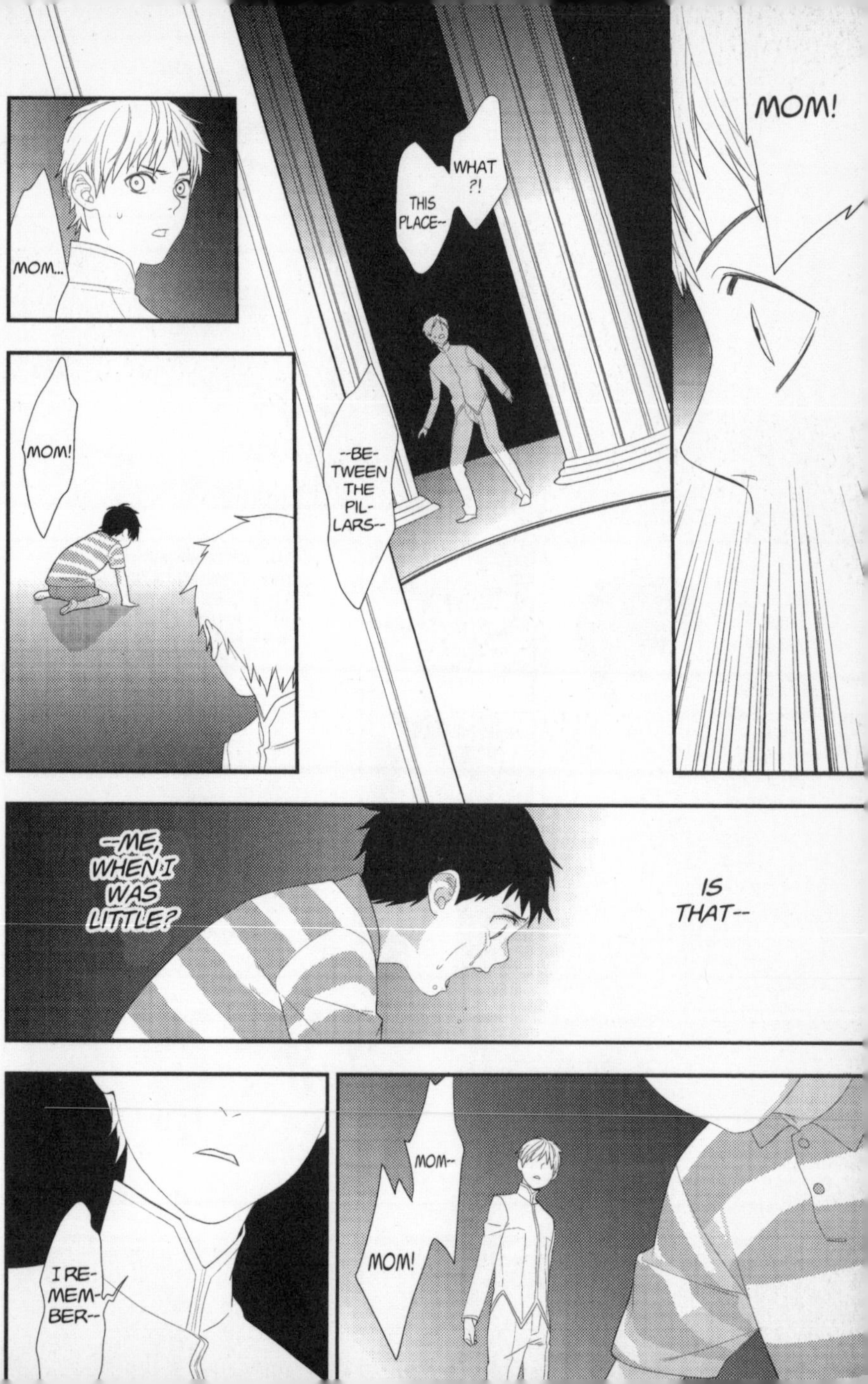
MOM!
WHAT ?!
THIS PLACE--
--BE-TWEEN THE PIL-LARS--
MOM...
MOM!
IS THAT--
--ME, WHEN I WAS LITTLE?
MOM--
MOM!
I RE-MEM-BER--

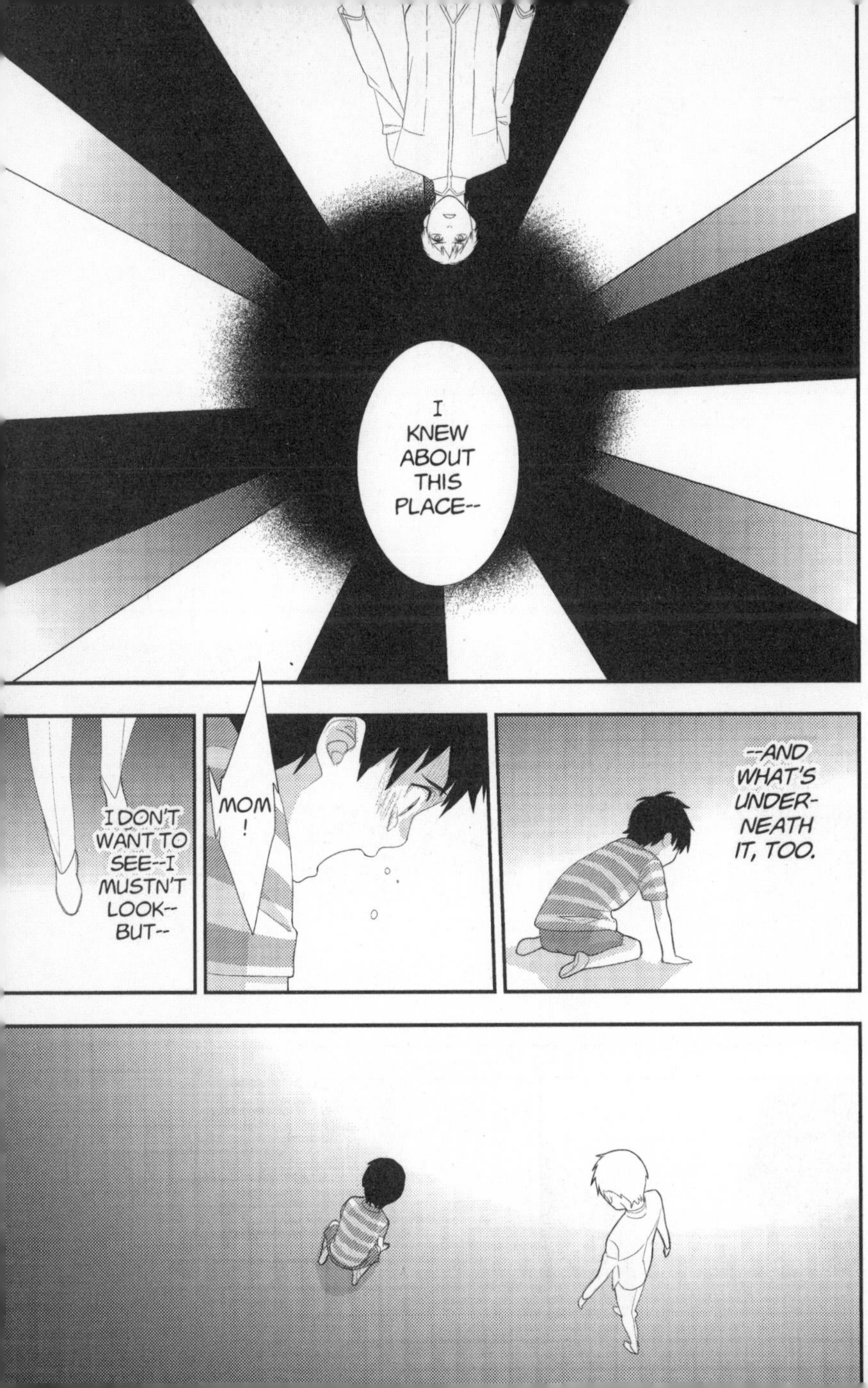
I KNEW ABOUT THIS PLACE--
--AND WHAT'S UNDER-NEATH IT, TOO.
MOM!
I DON'T WANT TO SEE--I MUSTN'T LOOK--BUT--

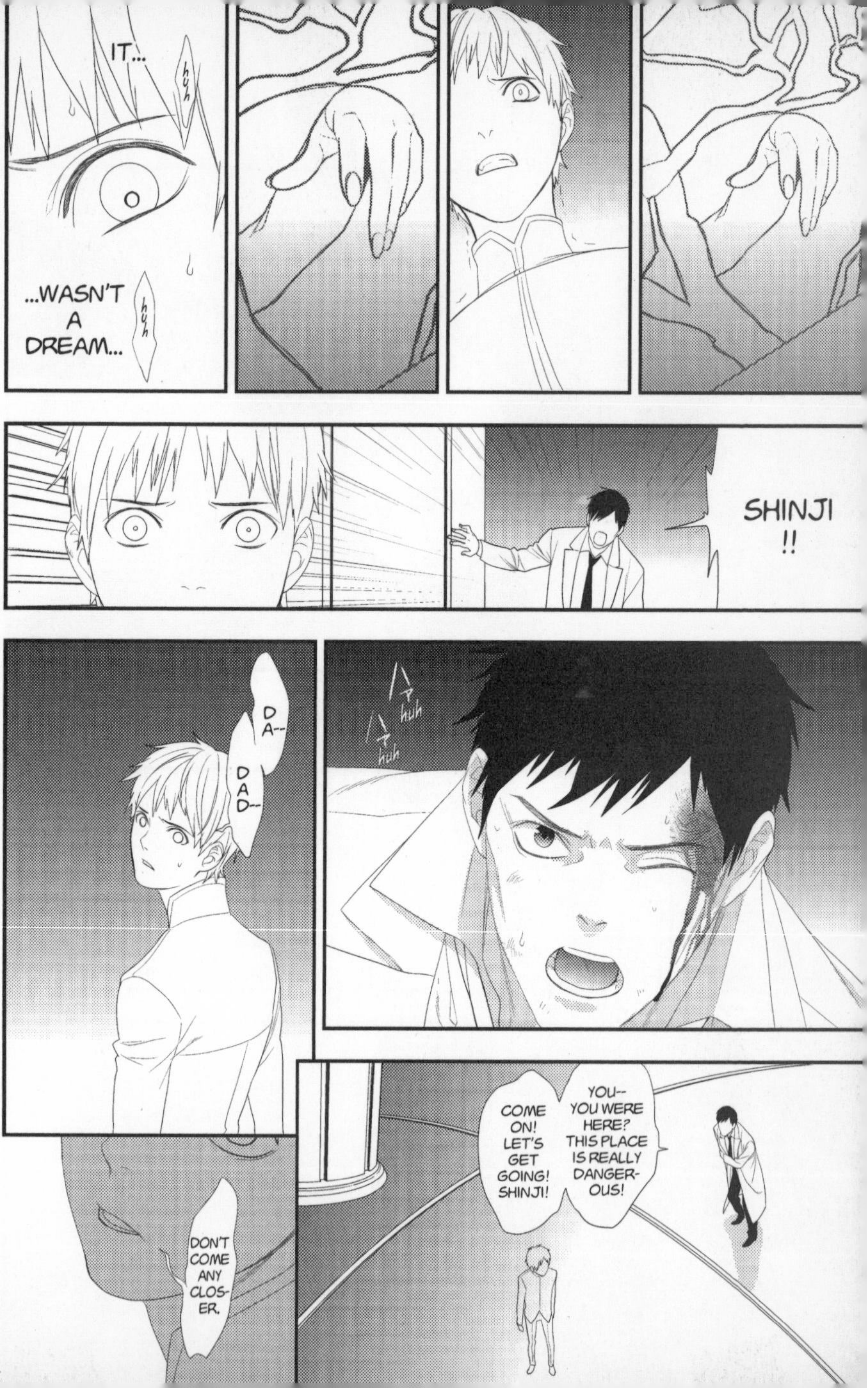
IT...
huh
...WASN'T A DREAM...
huh
SHINJI !!
ハァ huh
ハァ huh
DA--
DAD--
YOU-- YOU WERE HERE? THIS PLACE IS REALLY DANGER-OUS!
COME ON! LET'S GET GOING! SHINJI!
DON'T COME ANY CLOS-ER.

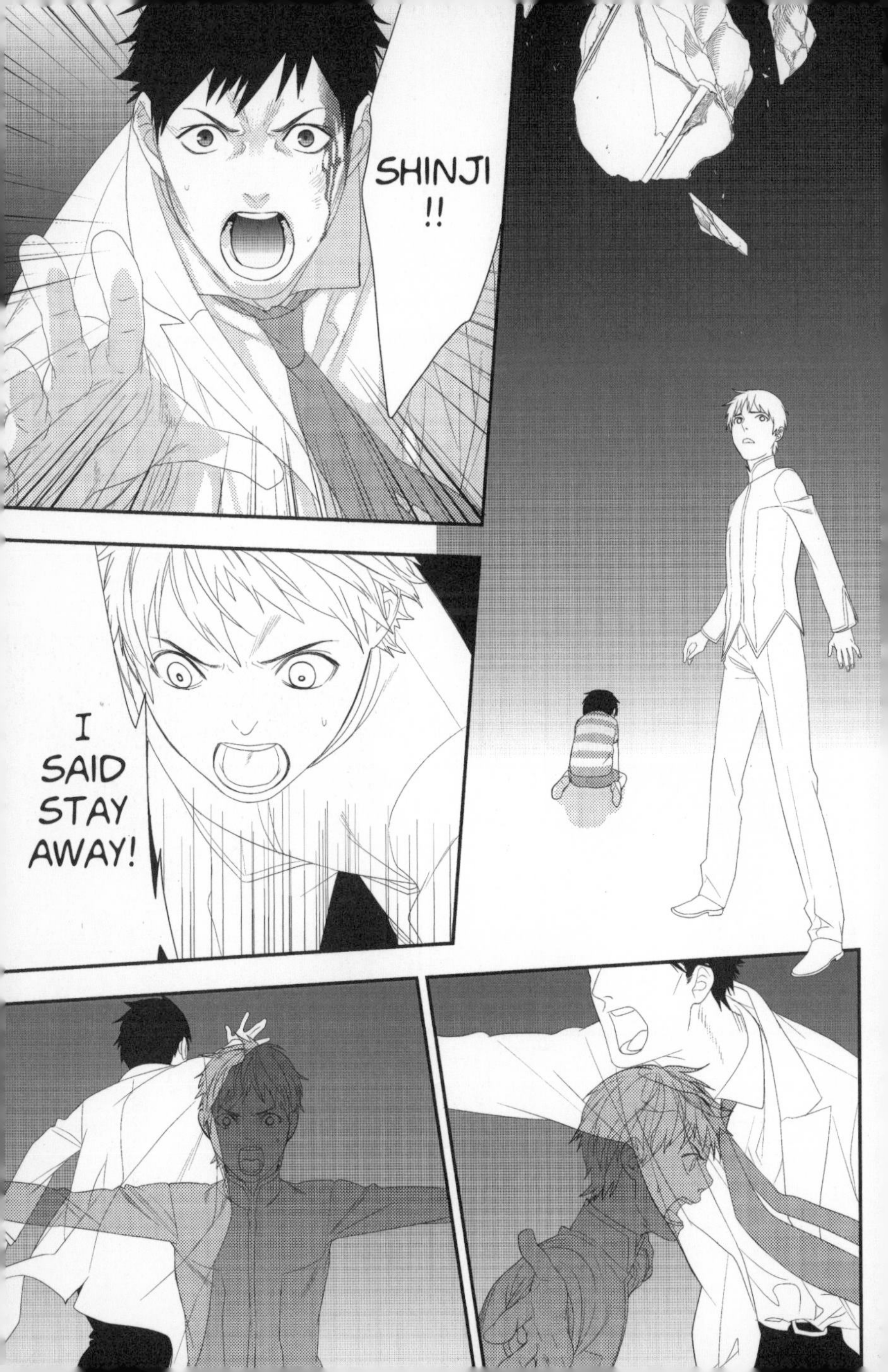
SHINJI !!
I SAID STAY AWAY!

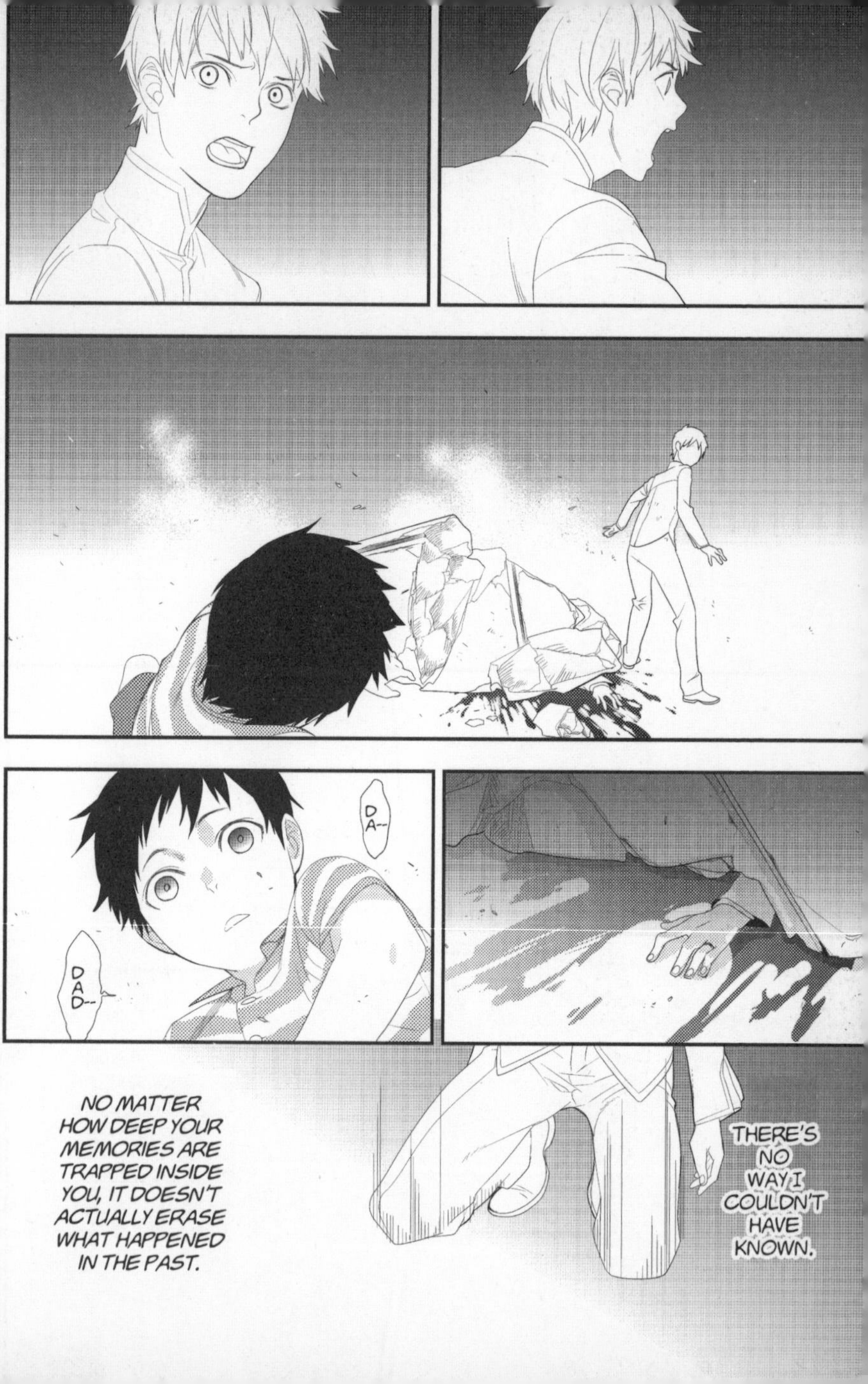
DA--
DAD--
THERE'S NO WAY I COULDN'T HAVE KNOWN.
NO MATTER HOW DEEP YOUR MEMORIES ARE TRAPPED INSIDE YOU, IT DOESN'T ACTUALLY ERASE WHAT HAPPENED IN THE PAST.

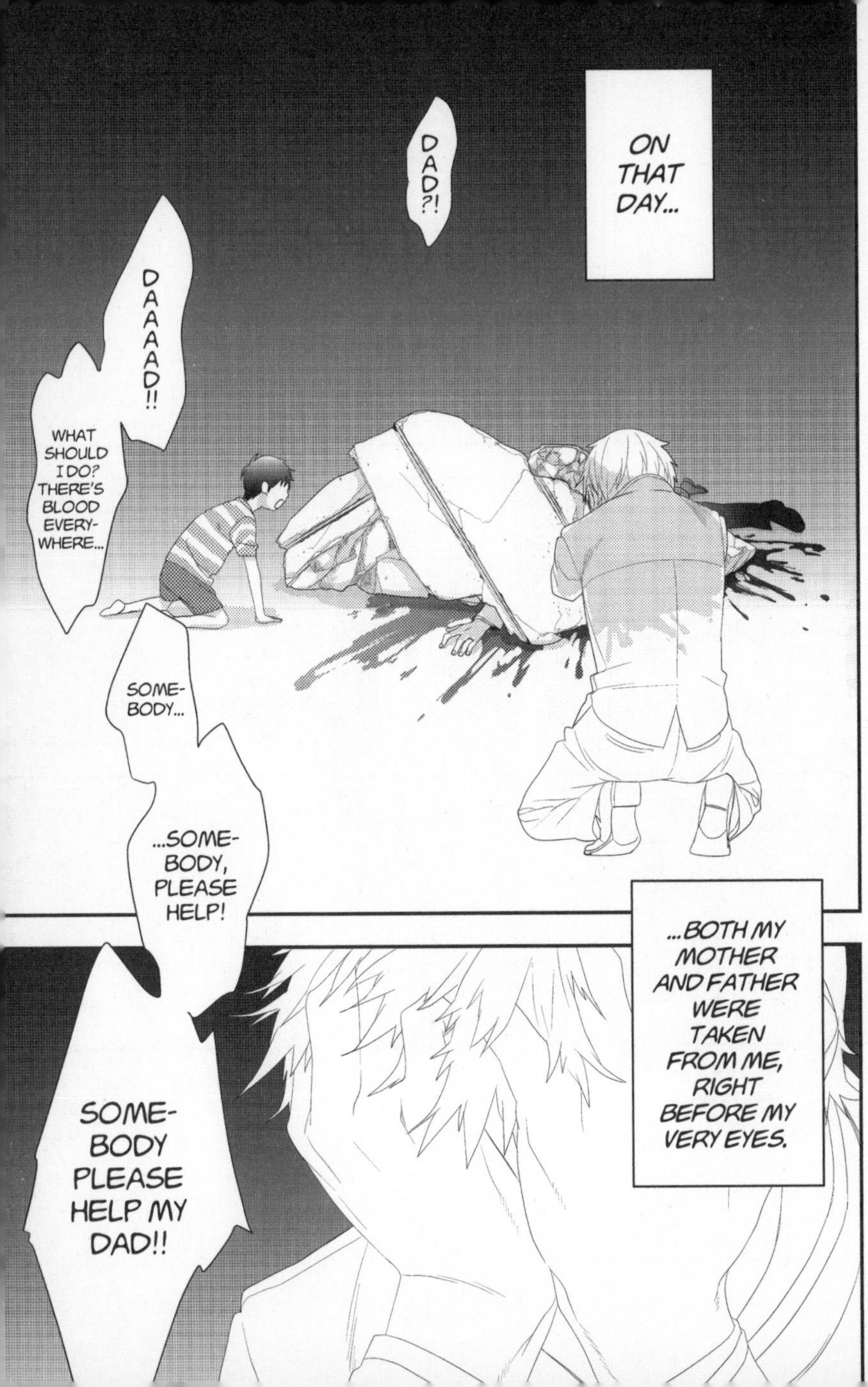
ON THAT DAY...
DAD?!
DAAAAAD!!
WHAT SHOULD I DO? THERE'S BLOOD EVERY-WHERE...
SOME-BODY...
...SOME-BODY, PLEASE HELP!
...BOTH MY MOTHER AND FATHER WERE TAKEN FROM ME, RIGHT BEFORE MY VERY EYES.
SOME-BODY PLEASE HELP MY DAD!!

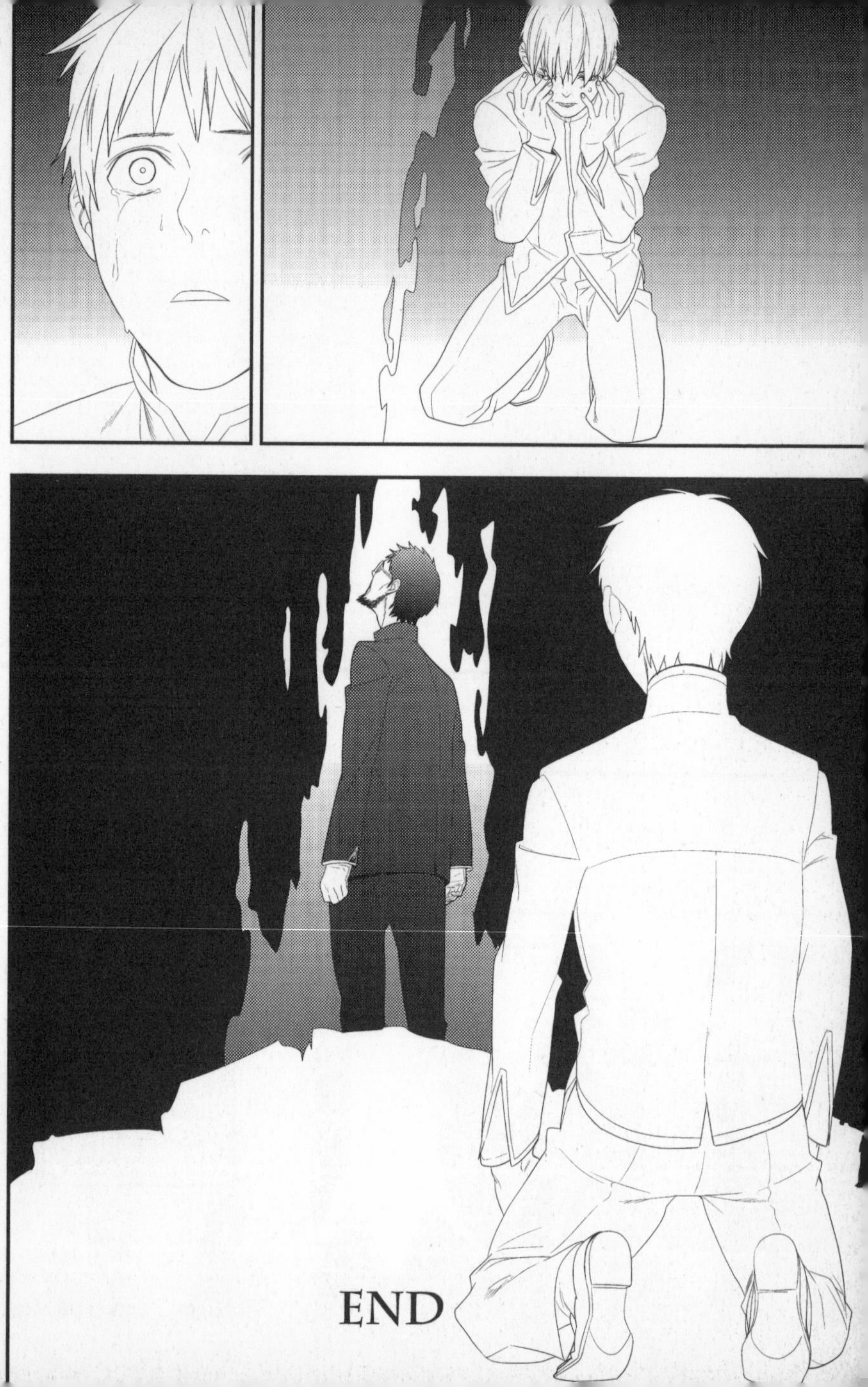
END

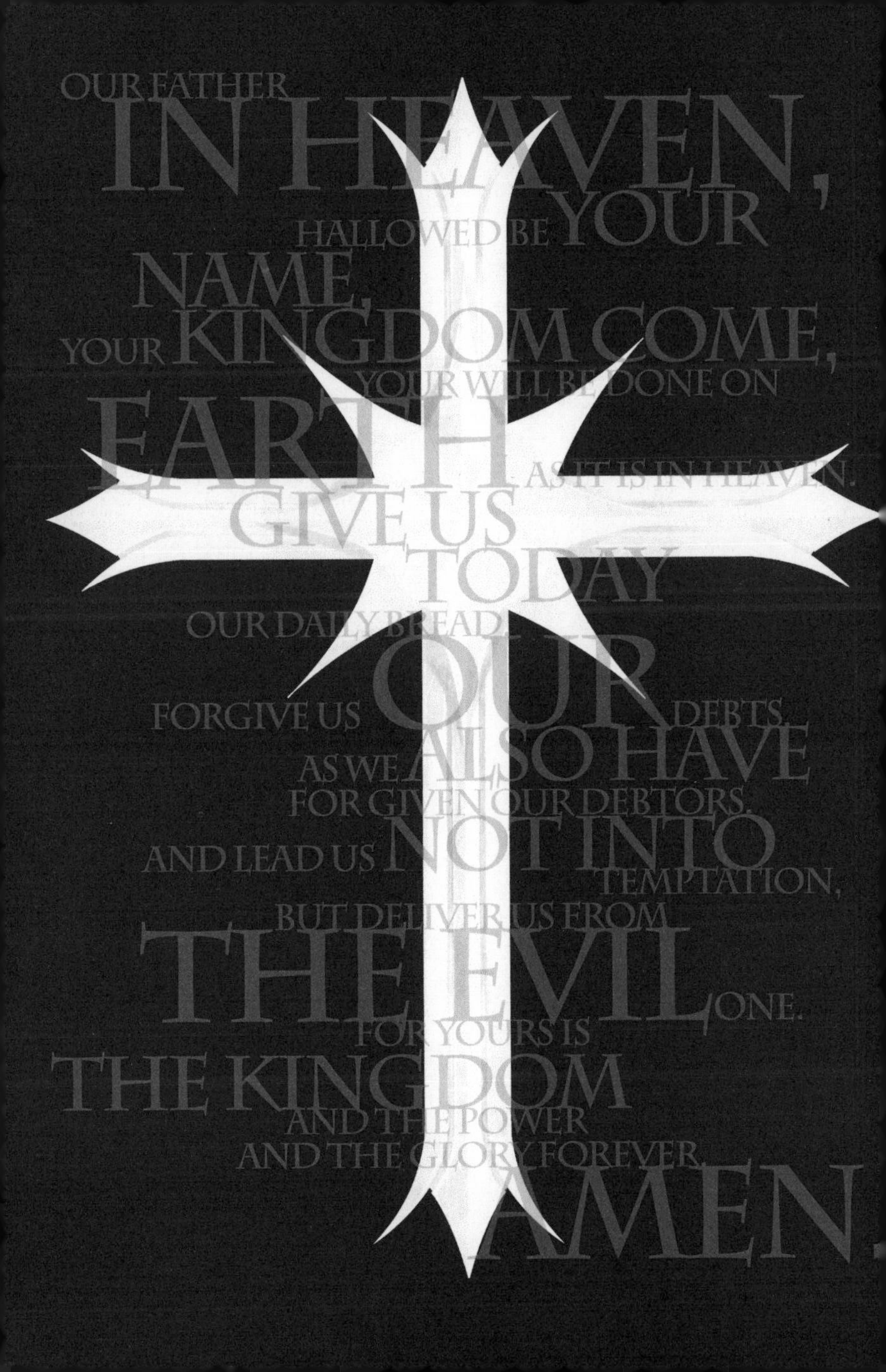
OUR FATHER
IN HEAVEN,
HALLOWED BE YOUR
NAME,
YOUR KINGDOM COME,
YOUR WILL BE DONE ON
EARTH AS IT IS IN HEAVEN.
GIVE US
TODAY
OUR DAILY BREAD.
FORGIVE US OUR DEBTS,
AS WE ALSO HAVE
FORGIVEN OUR DEBTORS.
AND LEAD US NOT INTO
TEMPTATION,
BUT DELIVER US FROM
THE EVIL ONE.
FOR YOURS IS
THE KINGDOM
AND THE POWER
AND THE GLORY FOREVER.
AMEN.

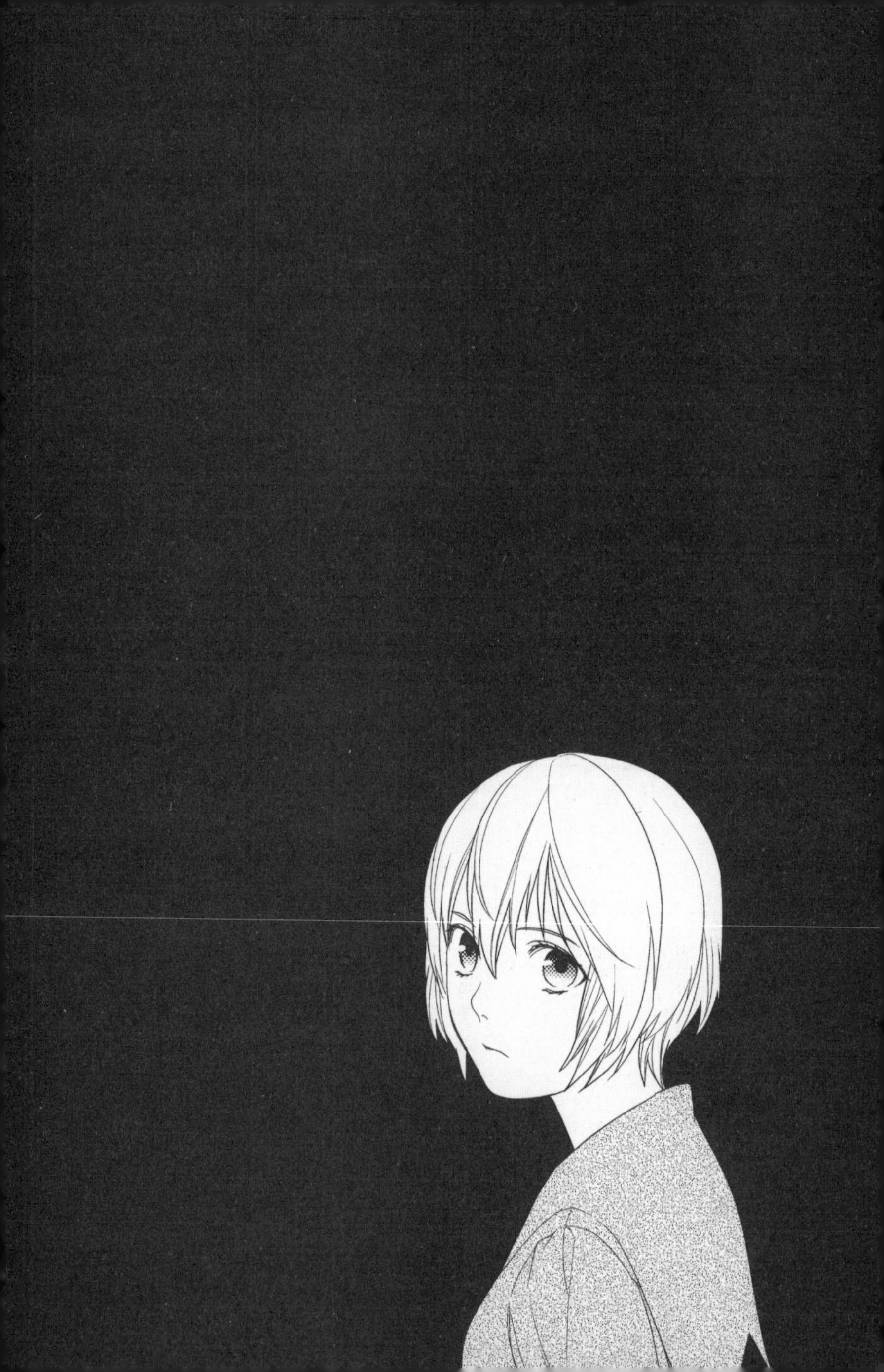

Pouu
EIGHTEENTH
EVENT
tink
tap
rattle

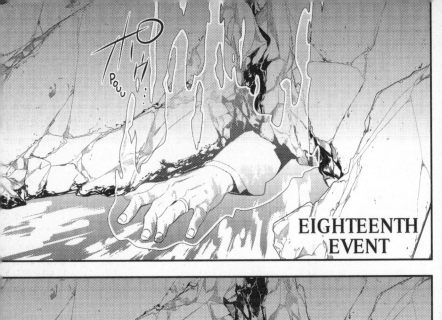

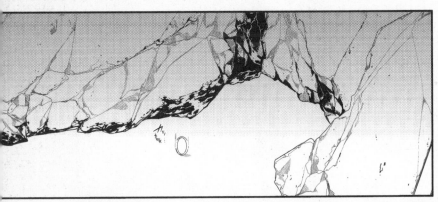

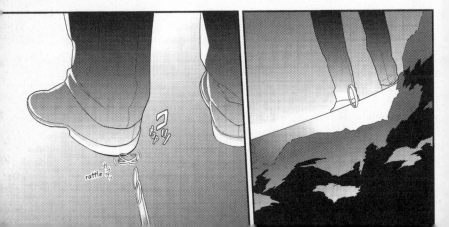

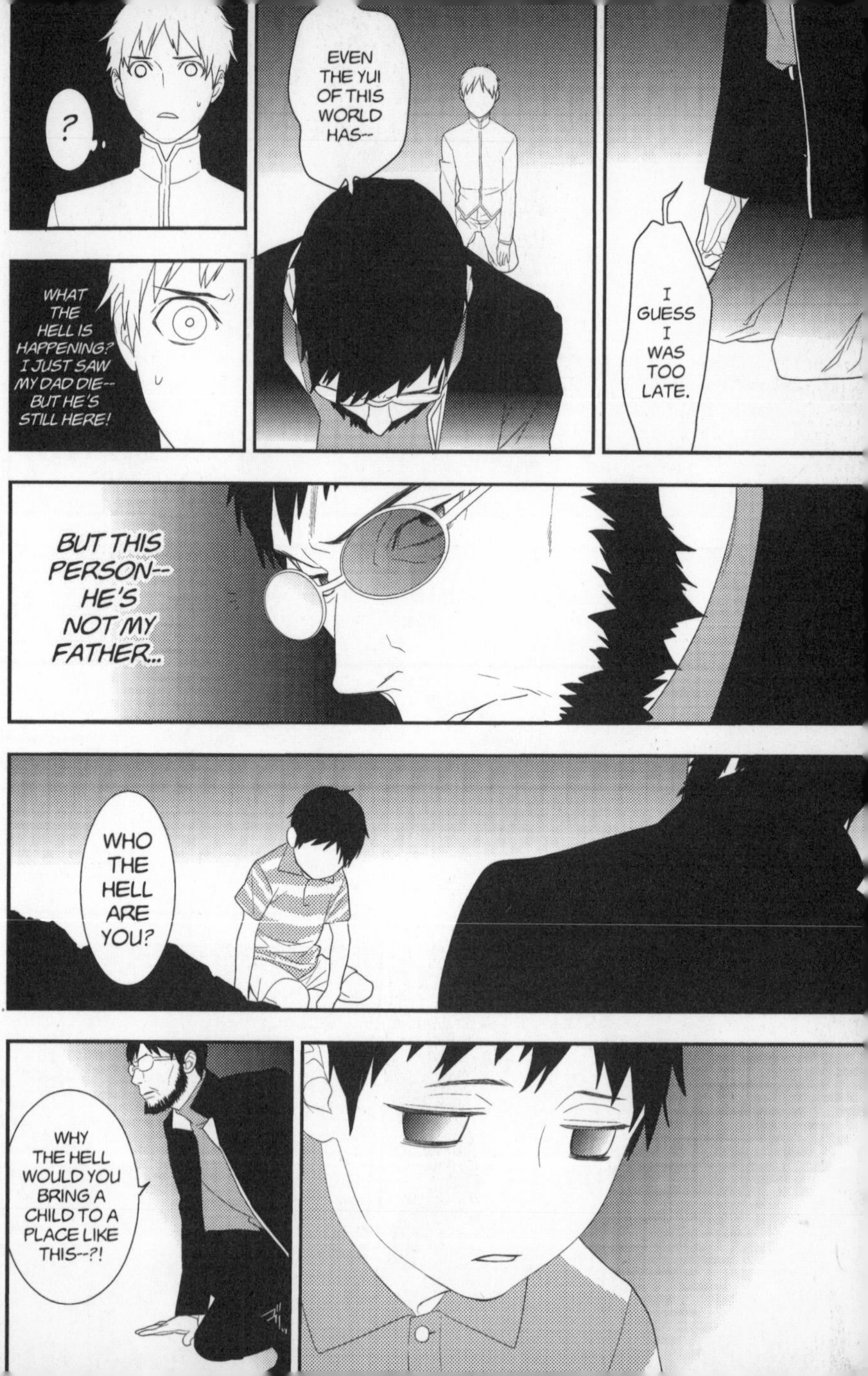
I GUESS I WAS TOO LATE.
EVEN THE YUI OF THIS WORLD HAS--
?
WHAT THE HELL IS HAPPENING? I JUST SAW MY DAD DIE-- BUT HE'S STILL HERE!
BUT THIS PERSON-- HE'S NOT MY FATHER...
WHO THE HELL ARE YOU?
WHY THE HELL WOULD YOU BRING A CHILD TO A PLACE LIKE THIS--?!

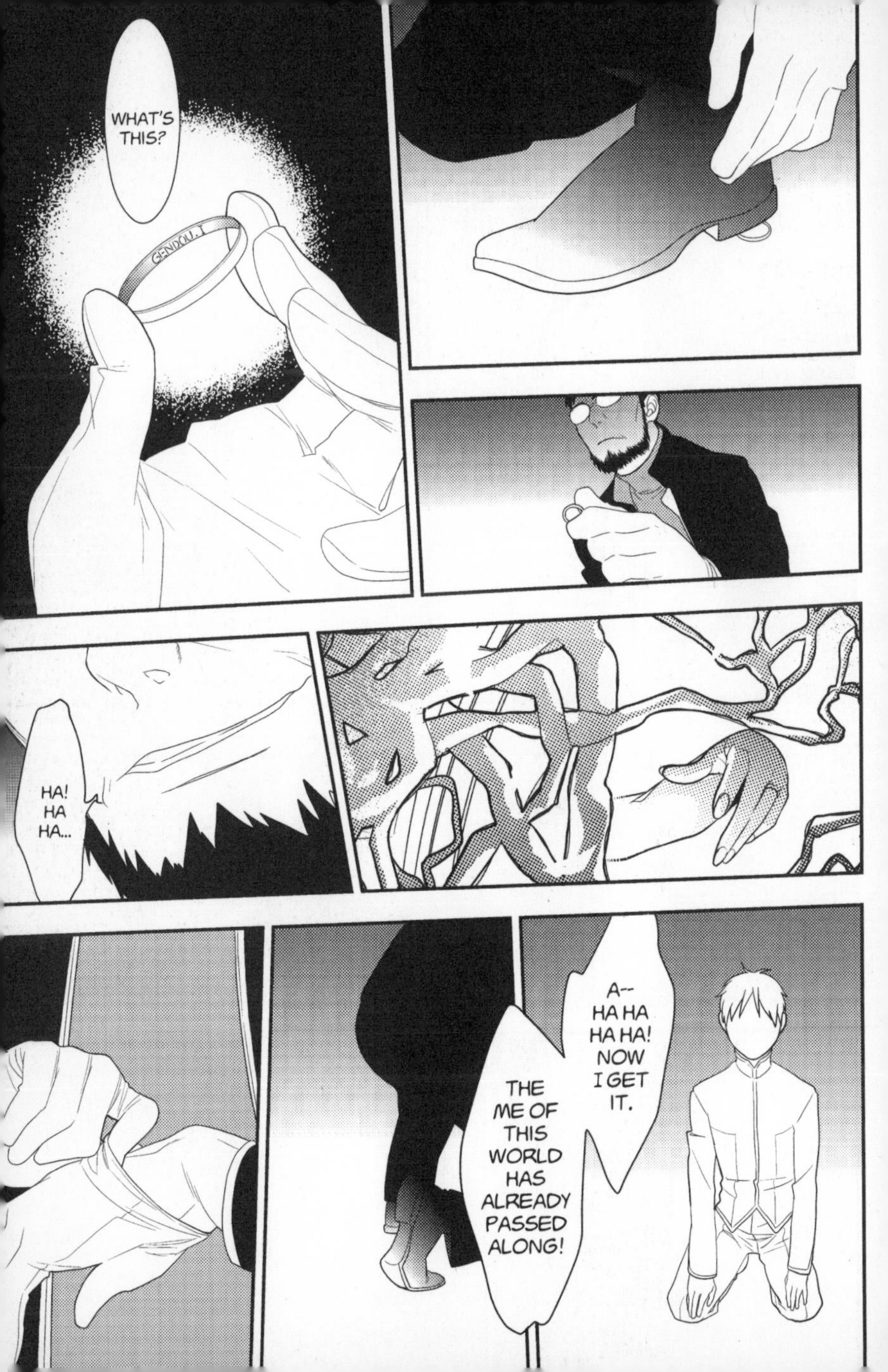
WHAT'S THIS?
GENDOU.I
HA! HA HA...
A-- HA HA HA HA! NOW I GET IT.
THE ME OF THIS WORLD HAS ALREADY PASSED ALONG!

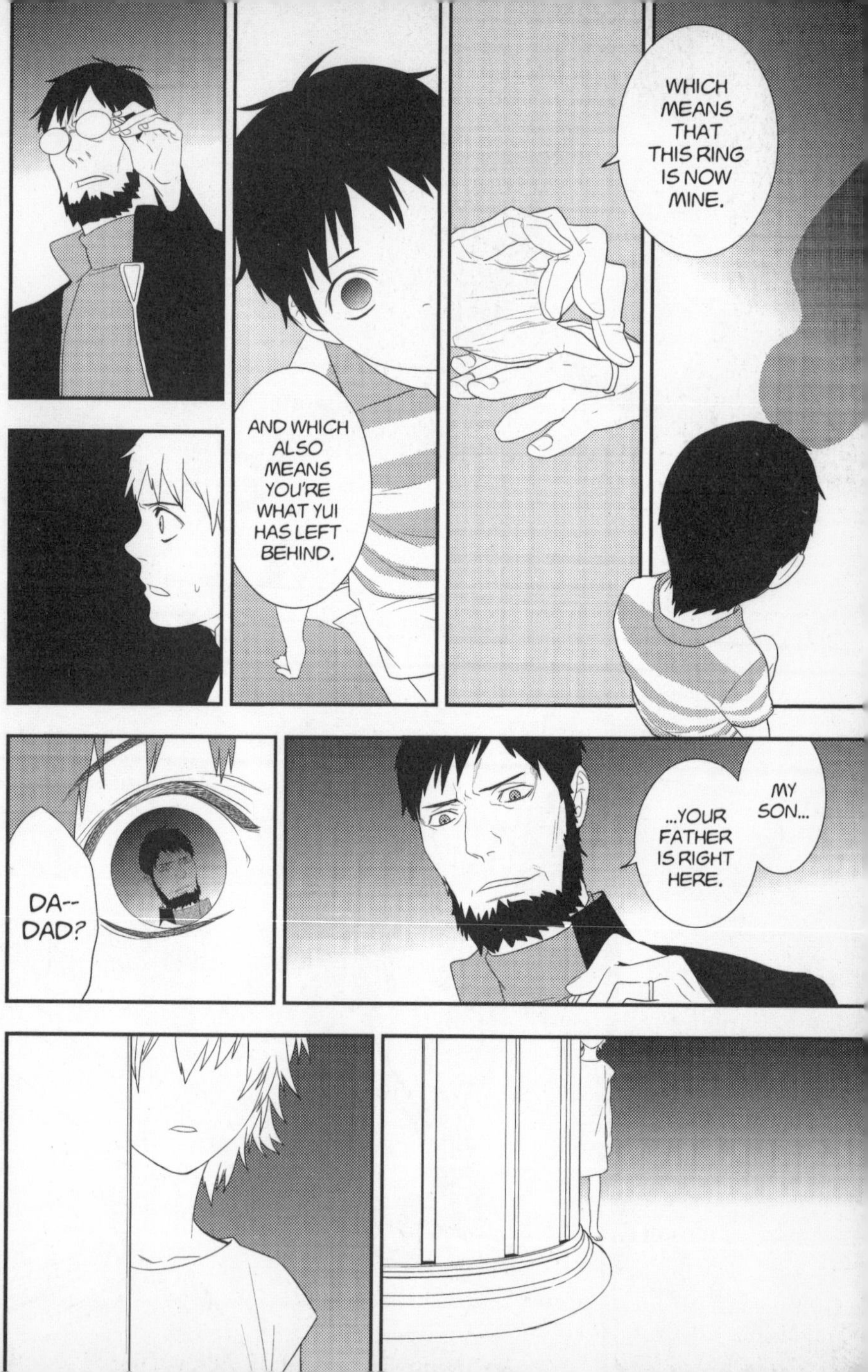
WHICH MEANS THAT THIS RING IS NOW MINE.
AND WHICH ALSO MEANS YOU'RE WHAT YUI HAS LEFT BEHIND.
MY SON...
...YOUR FATHER IS RIGHT HERE.
DA-- DAD?

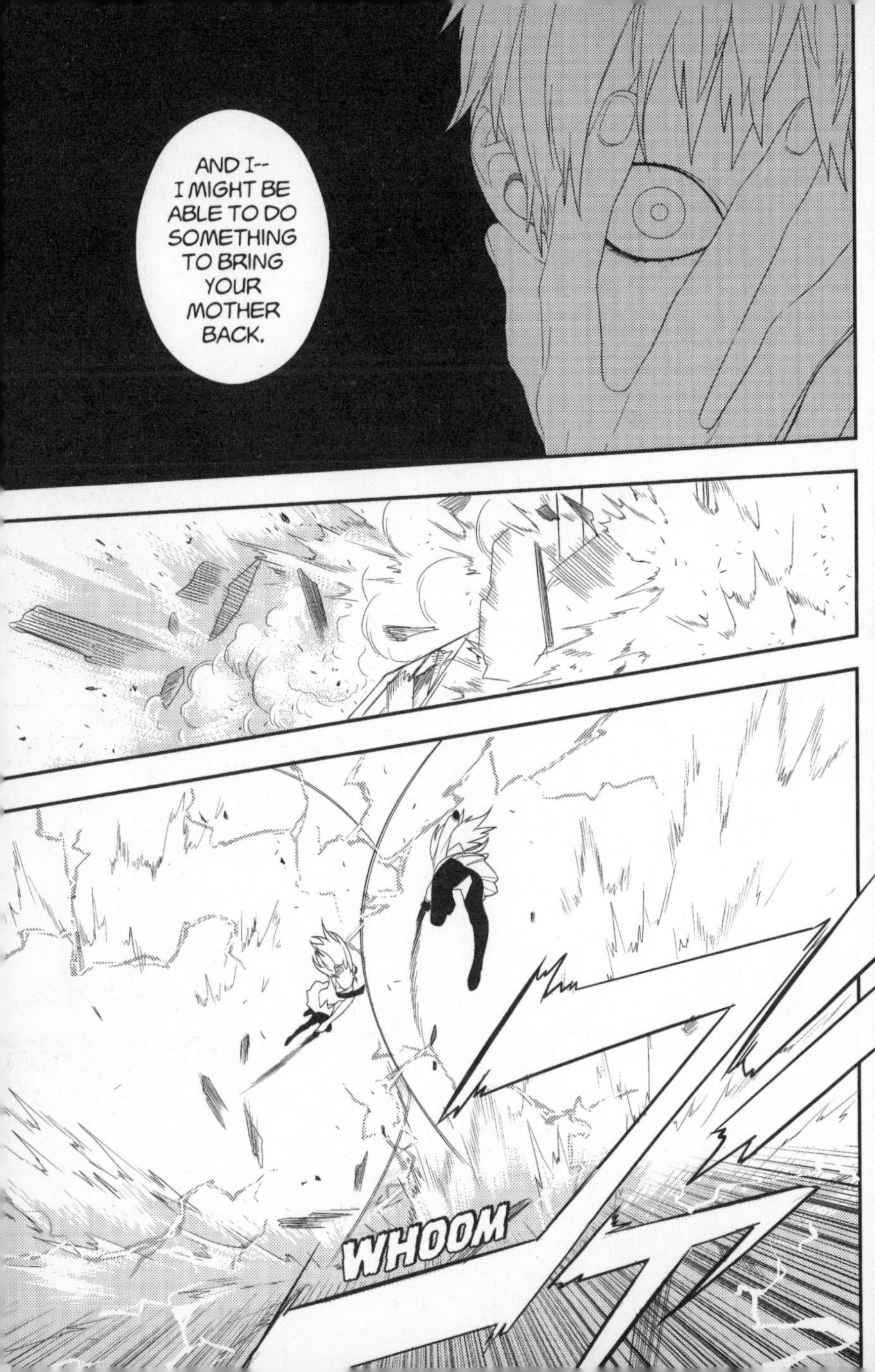
AND I-- I MIGHT BE ABLE TO DO SOMETHING TO BRING YOUR MOTHER BACK.
WHOOM

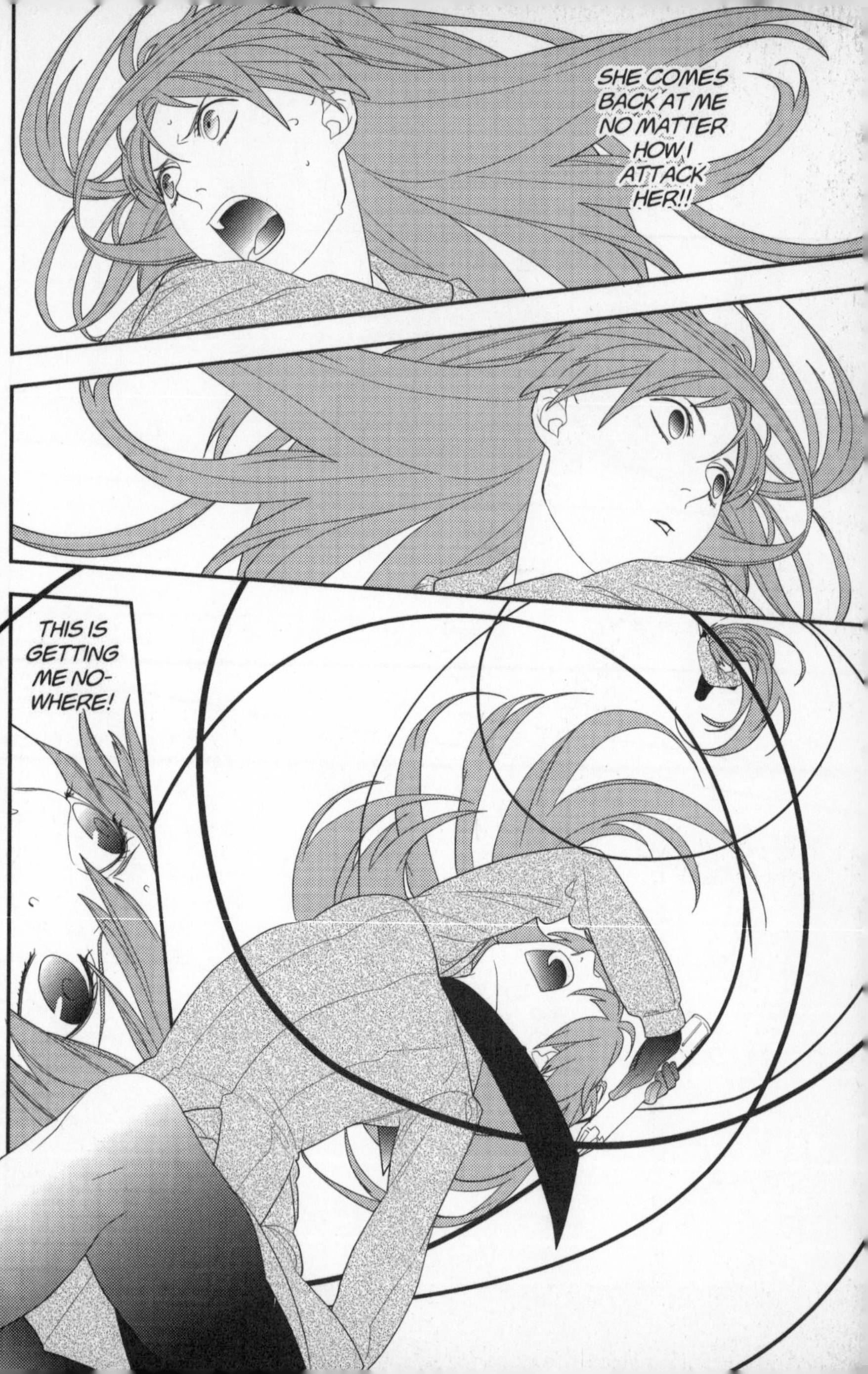
SHE COMES BACK AT ME NO MATTER HOW I ATTACK HER!!
THIS IS GETTING ME NO-WHERE!

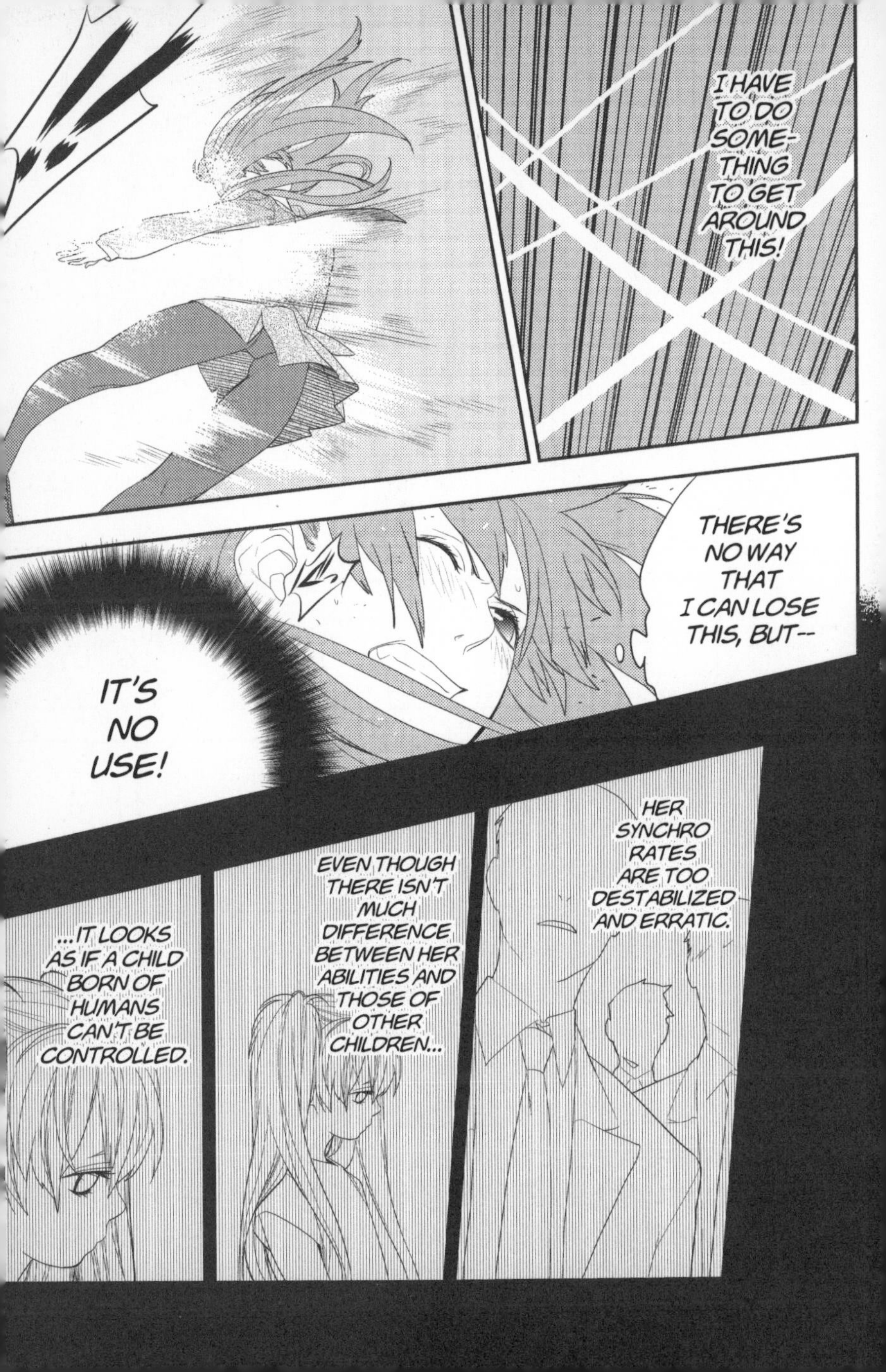
I HAVE TO DO SOME-THING TO GET AROUND THIS!
THERE'S NO WAY THAT I CAN LOSE THIS, BUT--
IT'S NO USE!
HER SYNCHRO RATES ARE TOO DESTABILIZED AND ERRATIC.
EVEN THOUGH THERE ISN'T MUCH DIFFERENCE BETWEEN HER ABILITIES AND THOSE OF OTHER CHILDREN...
...IT LOOKS AS IF A CHILD BORN OF HUMANS CAN'T BE CONTROLLED.

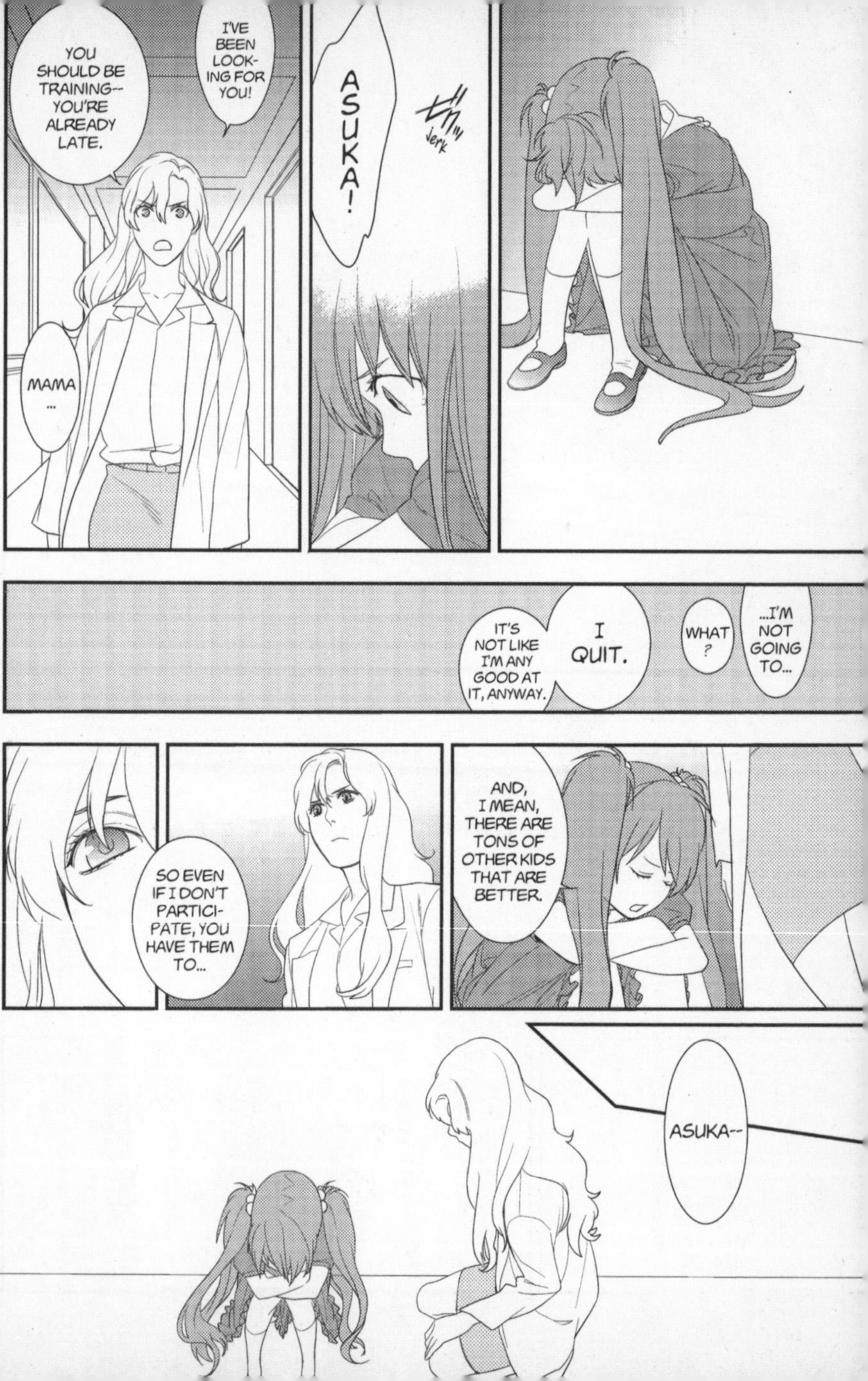
ASUKA!
jerk
I'VE BEEN LOOKING FOR YOU!
YOU SHOULD BE TRAINING-- YOU'RE ALREADY LATE.
MAMA ...
...I'M NOT GOING TO...
WHAT ?
I QUIT.
IT'S NOT LIKE I'M ANY GOOD AT IT, ANYWAY.
AND, I MEAN, THERE ARE TONS OF OTHER KIDS THAT ARE BETTER.
SO EVEN IF I DON'T PARTICIPATE, YOU HAVE THEM TO...
ASUKA--

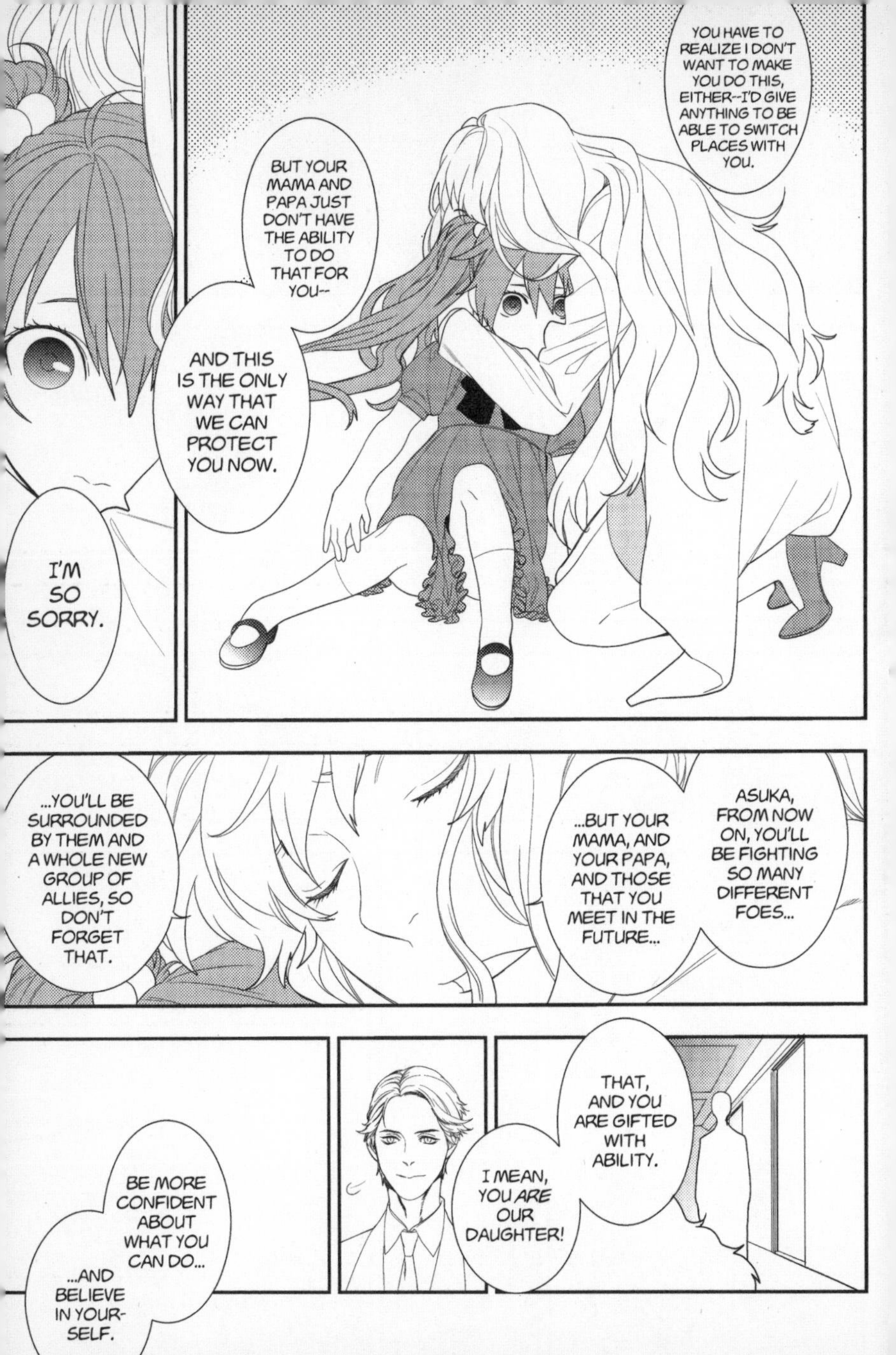
YOU HAVE TO REALIZE I DON'T WANT TO MAKE YOU DO THIS, EITHER--I'D GIVE ANYTHING TO BE ABLE TO SWITCH PLACES WITH YOU.
BUT YOUR MAMA AND PAPA JUST DON'T HAVE THE ABILITY TO DO THAT FOR YOU--
AND THIS IS THE ONLY WAY THAT WE CAN PROTECT YOU NOW.
I'M SO SORRY.
ASUKA, FROM NOW ON, YOU'LL BE FIGHTING SO MANY DIFFERENT FOES...
...BUT YOUR MAMA, AND YOUR PAPA, AND THOSE THAT YOU MEET IN THE FUTURE...
...YOU'LL BE SURROUNDED BY THEM AND A WHOLE NEW GROUP OF ALLIES, SO DON'T FORGET THAT.
THAT, AND YOU ARE GIFTED WITH ABILITY.
I MEAN, YOU *ARE* OUR DAUGHTER!
BE MORE CONFIDENT ABOUT WHAT YOU CAN DO...
...AND BELIEVE IN YOURSELF.

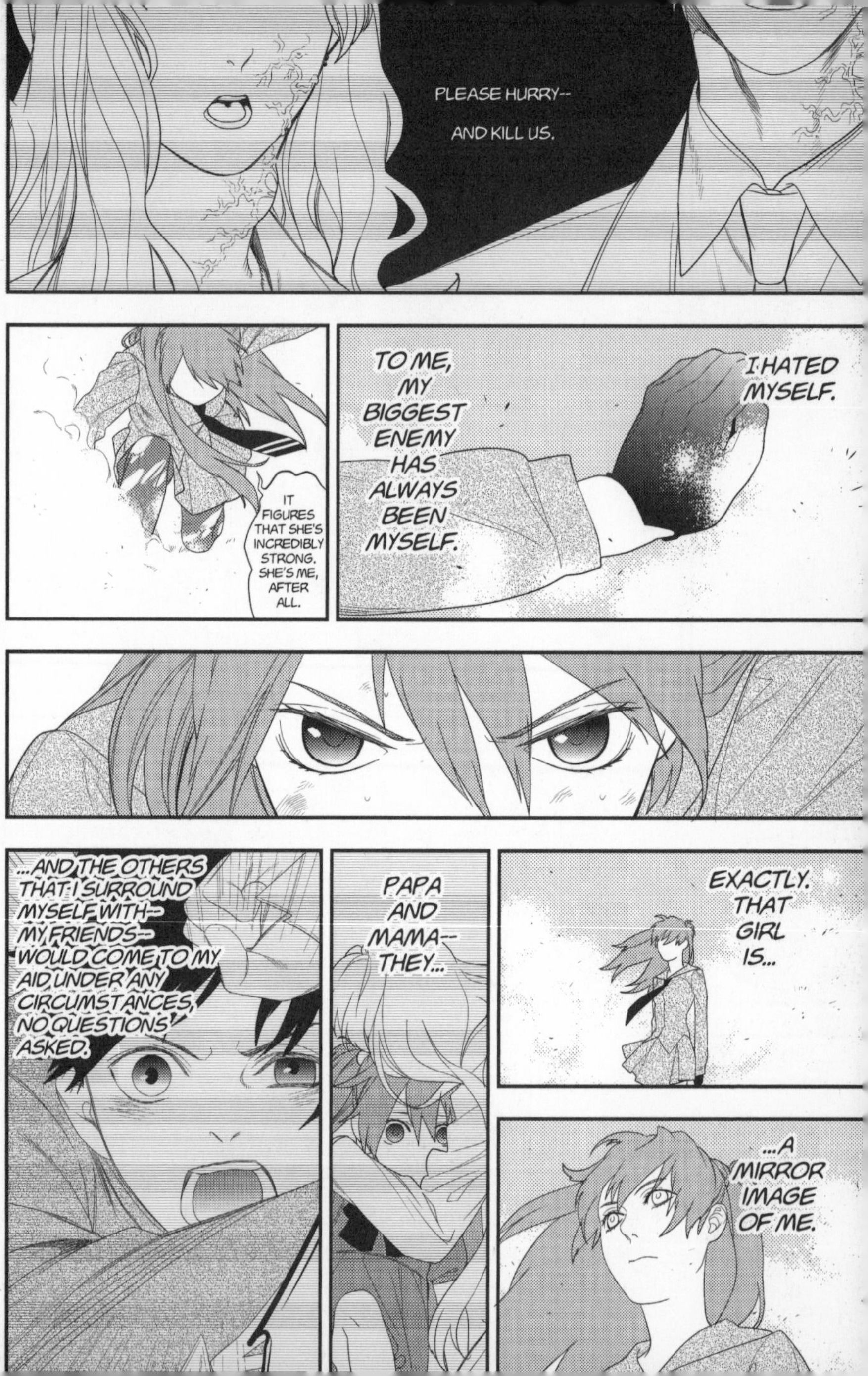
PLEASE HURRY--
AND KILL US.
I HATED MYSELF.
TO ME, MY BIGGEST ENEMY HAS ALWAYS BEEN MYSELF.
IT FIGURES THAT SHE'S INCREDIBLY STRONG. SHE'S ME, AFTER ALL.
EXACTLY. THAT GIRL IS...
...A MIRROR IMAGE OF ME.
PAPA AND MAMA-- THEY...
...AND THE OTHERS THAT I SURROUND MYSELF WITH-- MY FRIENDS-- WOULD COME TO MY AID UNDER ANY CIRCUMSTANCES, NO QUESTIONS ASKED.

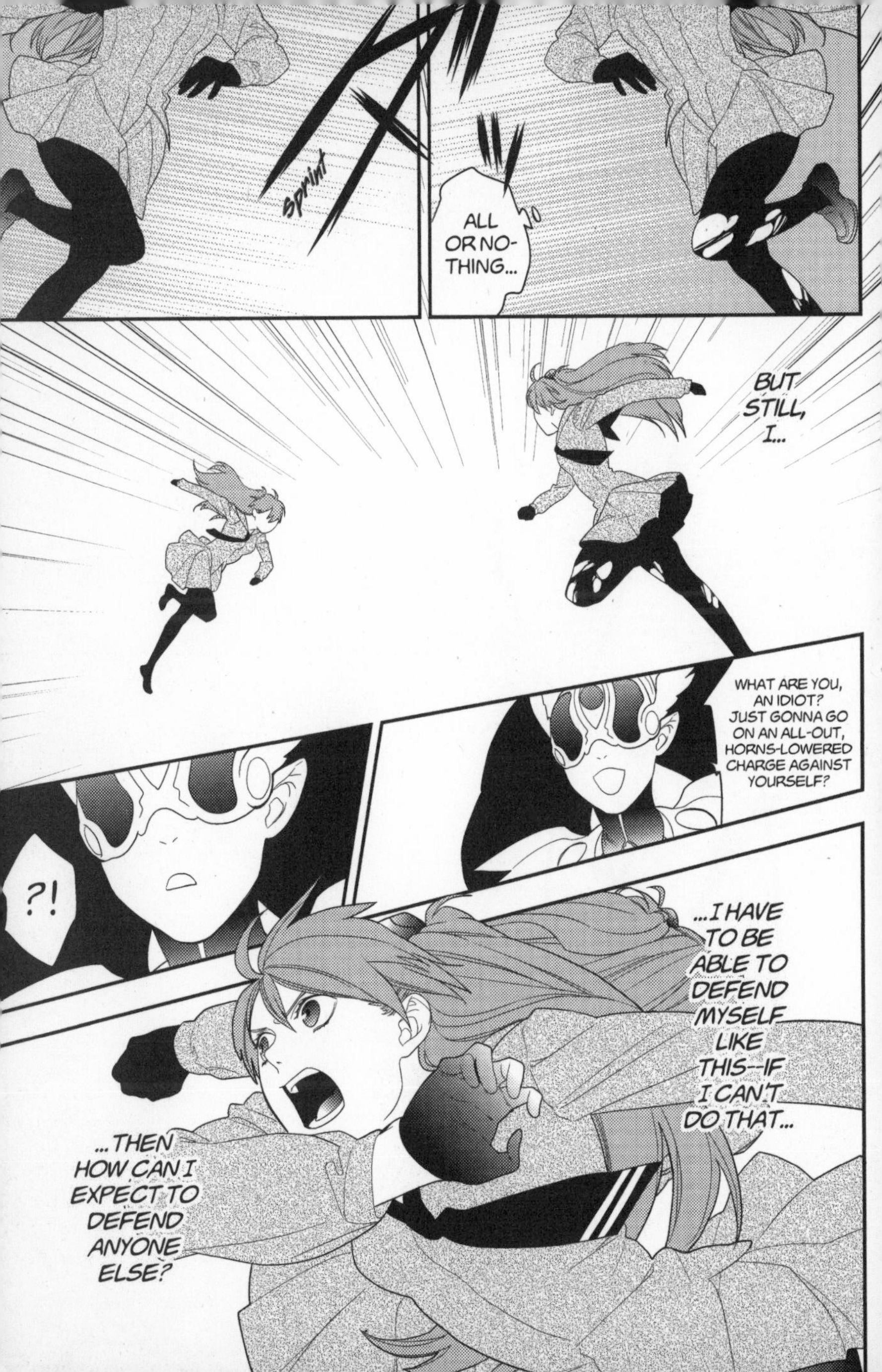
ALL OR NO-THING...
Sprint
BUT STILL, I...
WHAT ARE YOU, AN IDIOT? JUST GONNA GO ON AN ALL-OUT, HORNS-LOWERED CHARGE AGAINST YOURSELF?
?!
...I HAVE TO BE ABLE TO DEFEND MYSELF LIKE THIS--IF I CAN'T DO THAT...
...THEN HOW CAN I EXPECT TO DEFEND ANYONE ELSE?

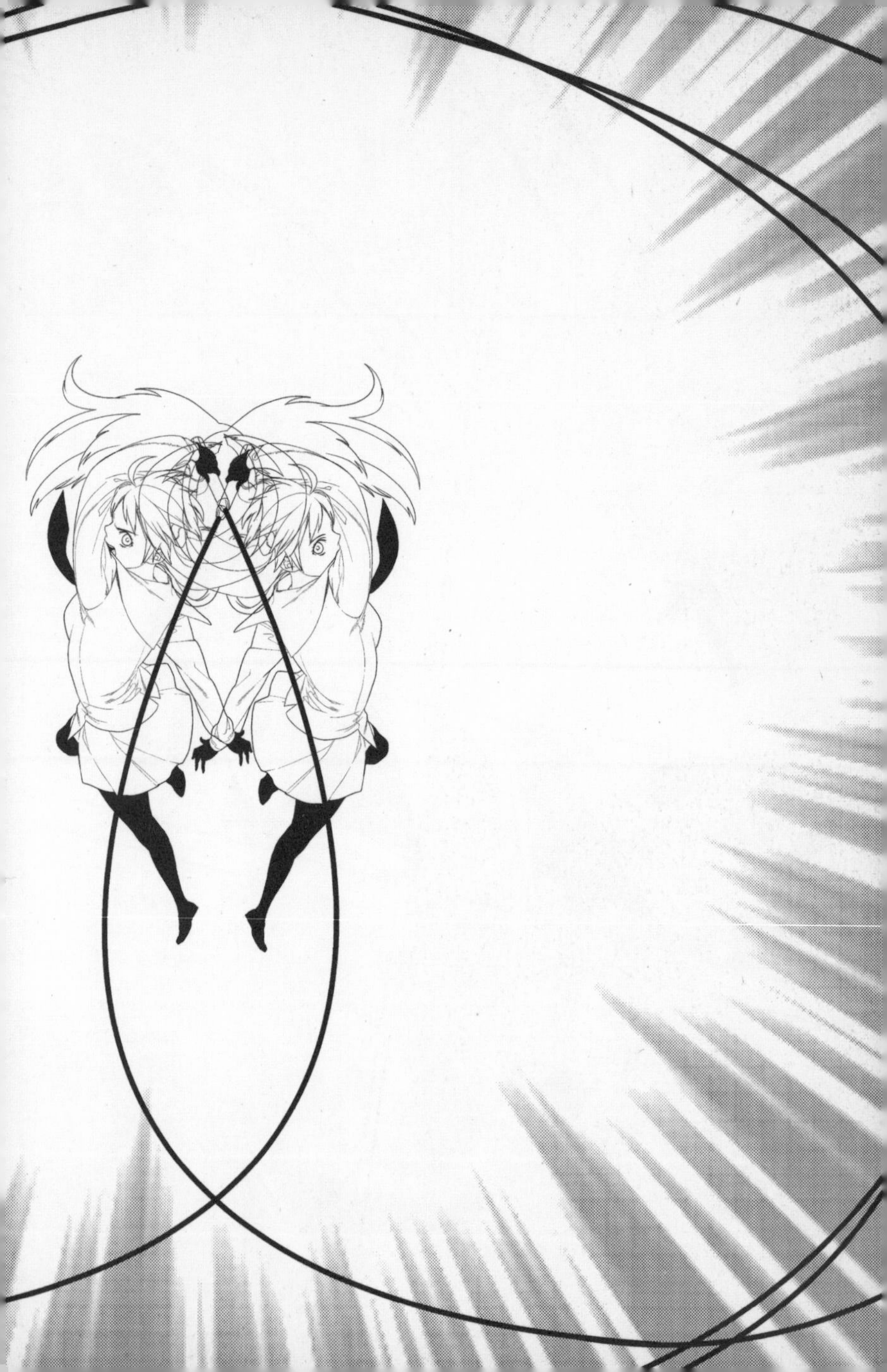

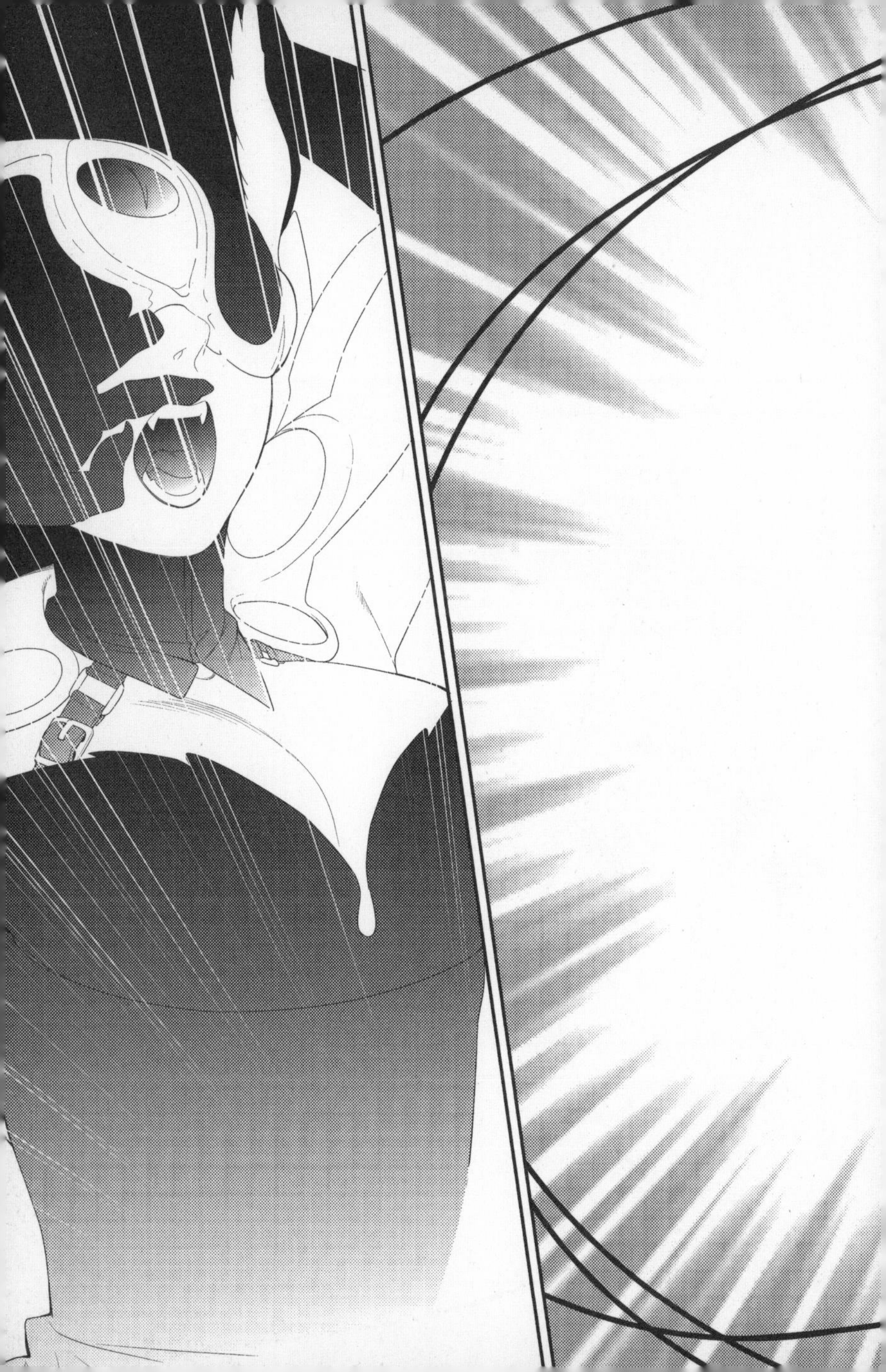

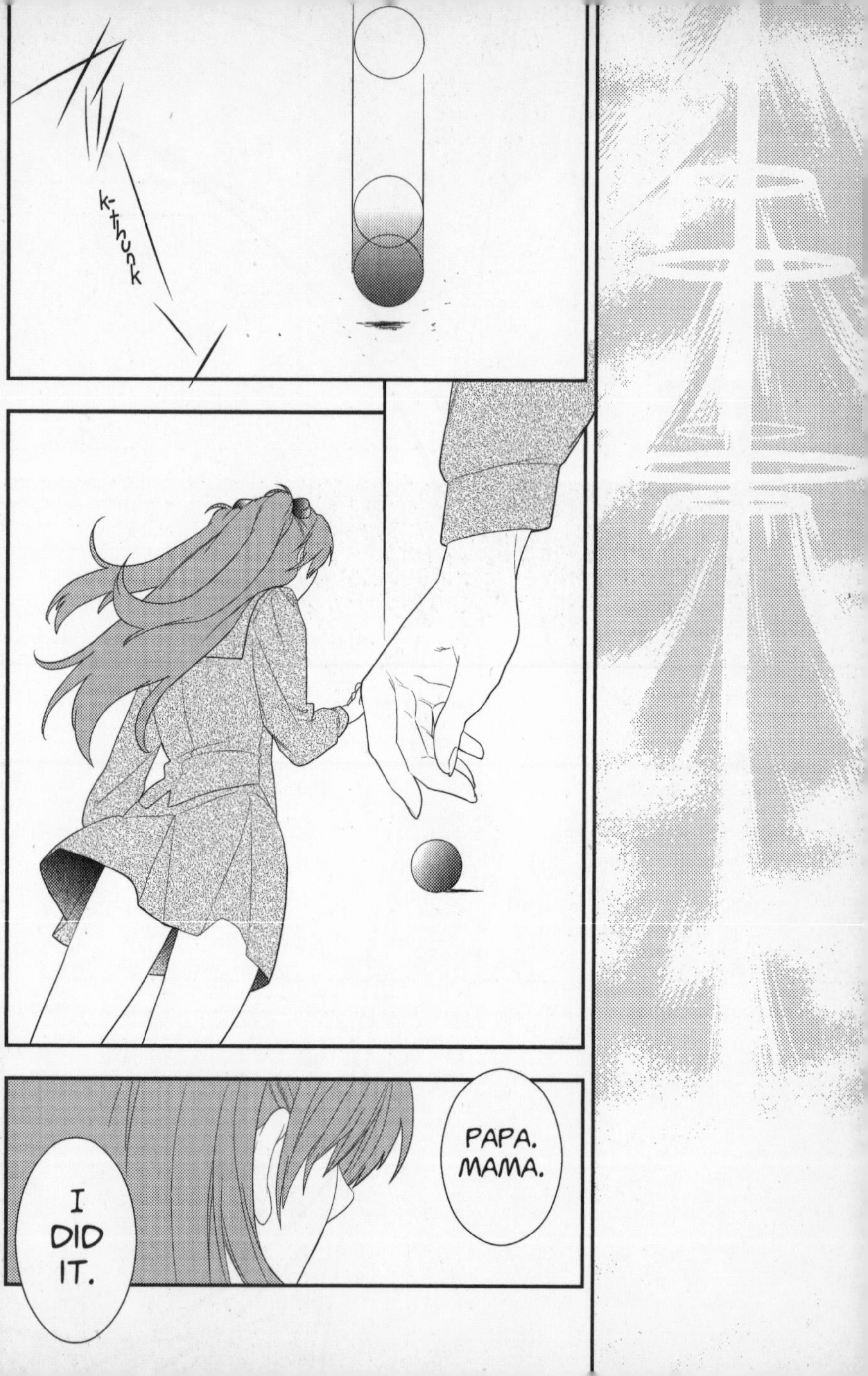
k-thunk
PAPA. MAMA.
I DID IT.

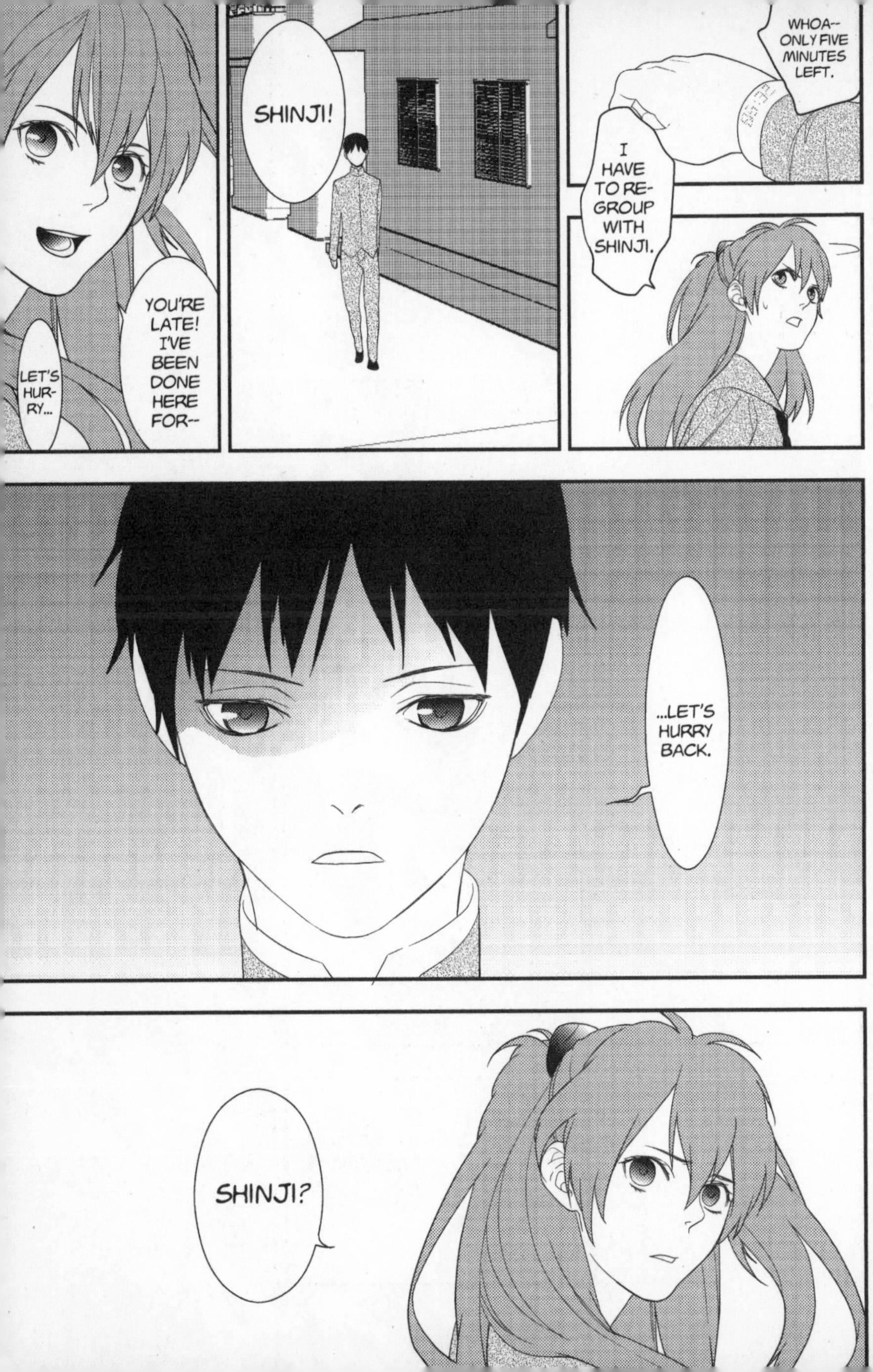
WHOA-- ONLY FIVE MINUTES LEFT.
I HAVE TO RE-GROUP WITH SHINJI.
SHINJI!
YOU'RE LATE! I'VE BEEN DONE HERE FOR--
LET'S HUR-RY...
...LET'S HURRY BACK.
SHINJI?

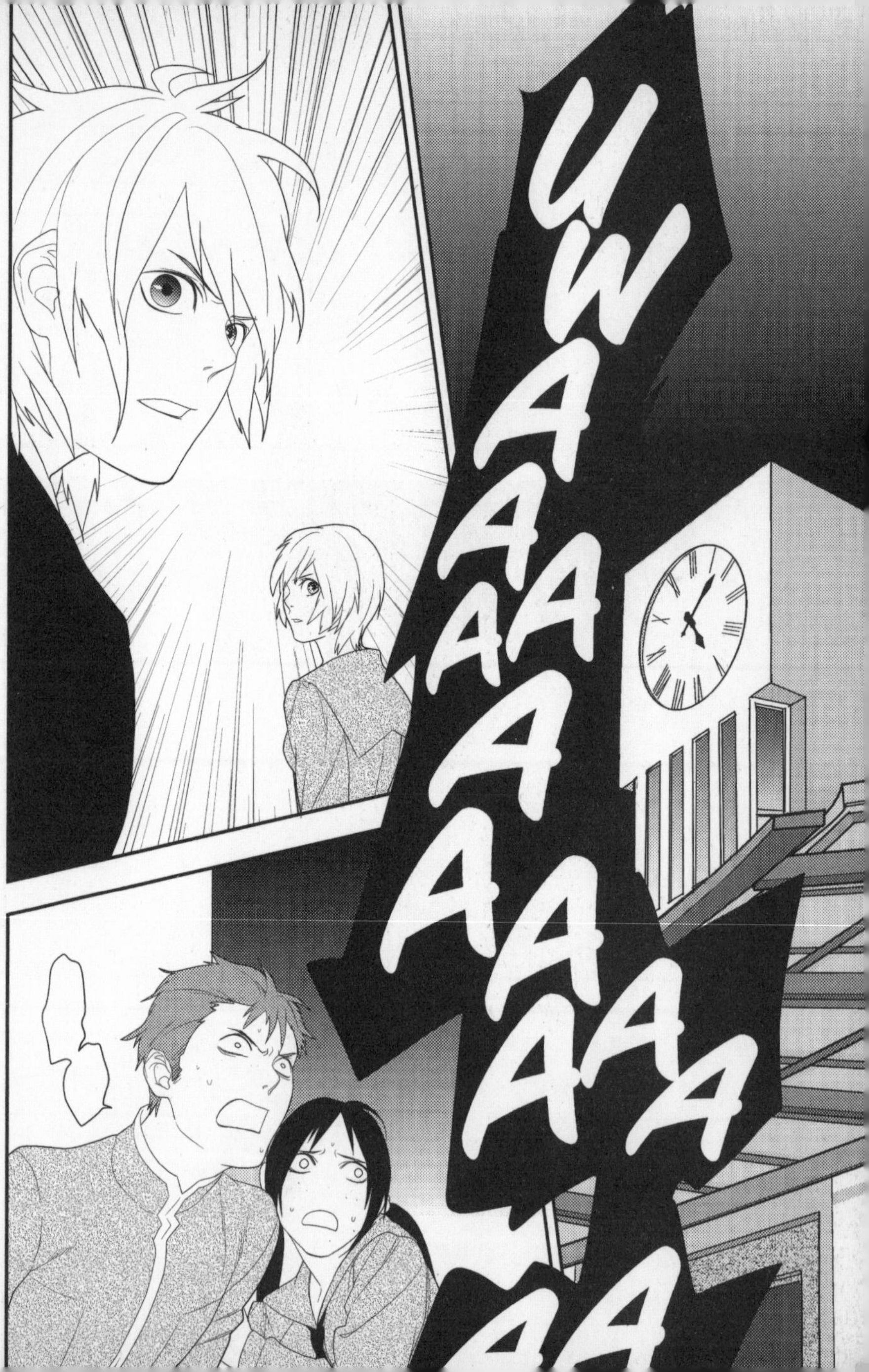
UWAAAAAAAAAAAAA

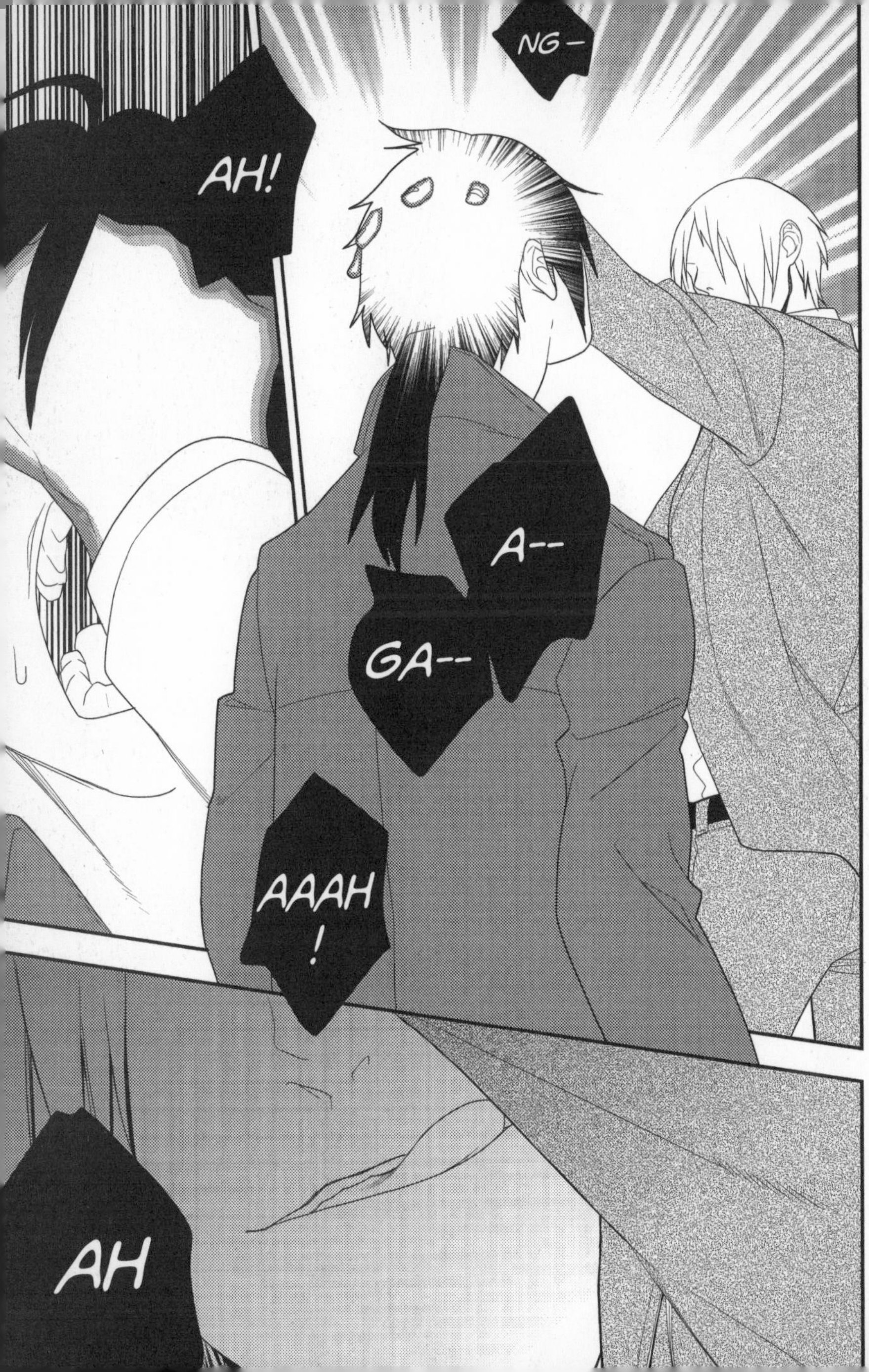
NG–
AH!
A--
GA--
AAAH !
AH

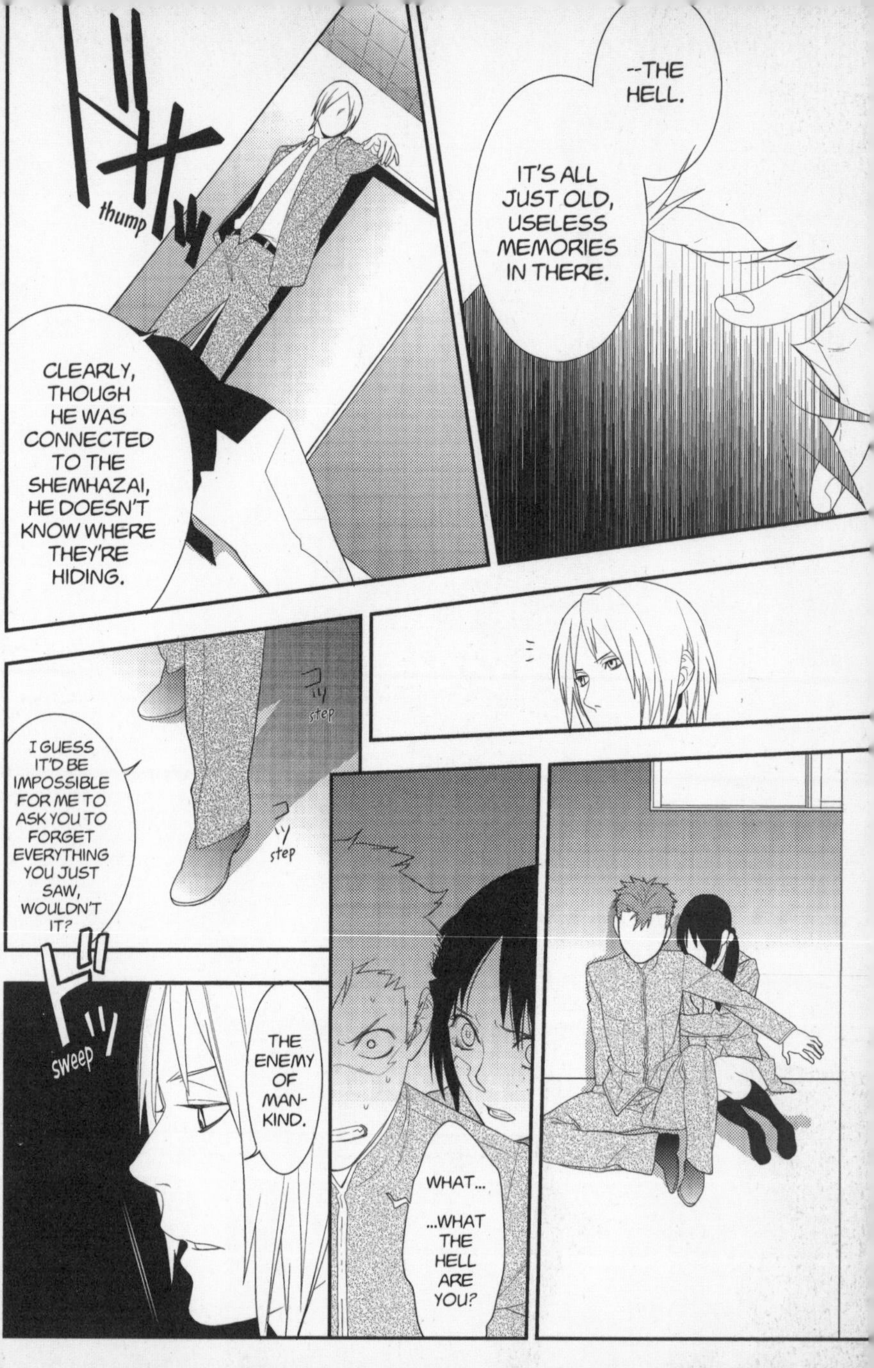
--THE HELL.
IT'S ALL JUST OLD, USELESS MEMORIES IN THERE.
thump
CLEARLY, THOUGH HE WAS CONNECTED TO THE SHEMHAZAI, HE DOESN'T KNOW WHERE THEY'RE HIDING.
step
step
I GUESS IT'D BE IMPOSSIBLE FOR ME TO ASK YOU TO FORGET EVERYTHING YOU JUST SAW, WOULDN'T IT?
WHAT...
...WHAT THE HELL ARE YOU?
sweep
THE ENEMY OF MAN-KIND.

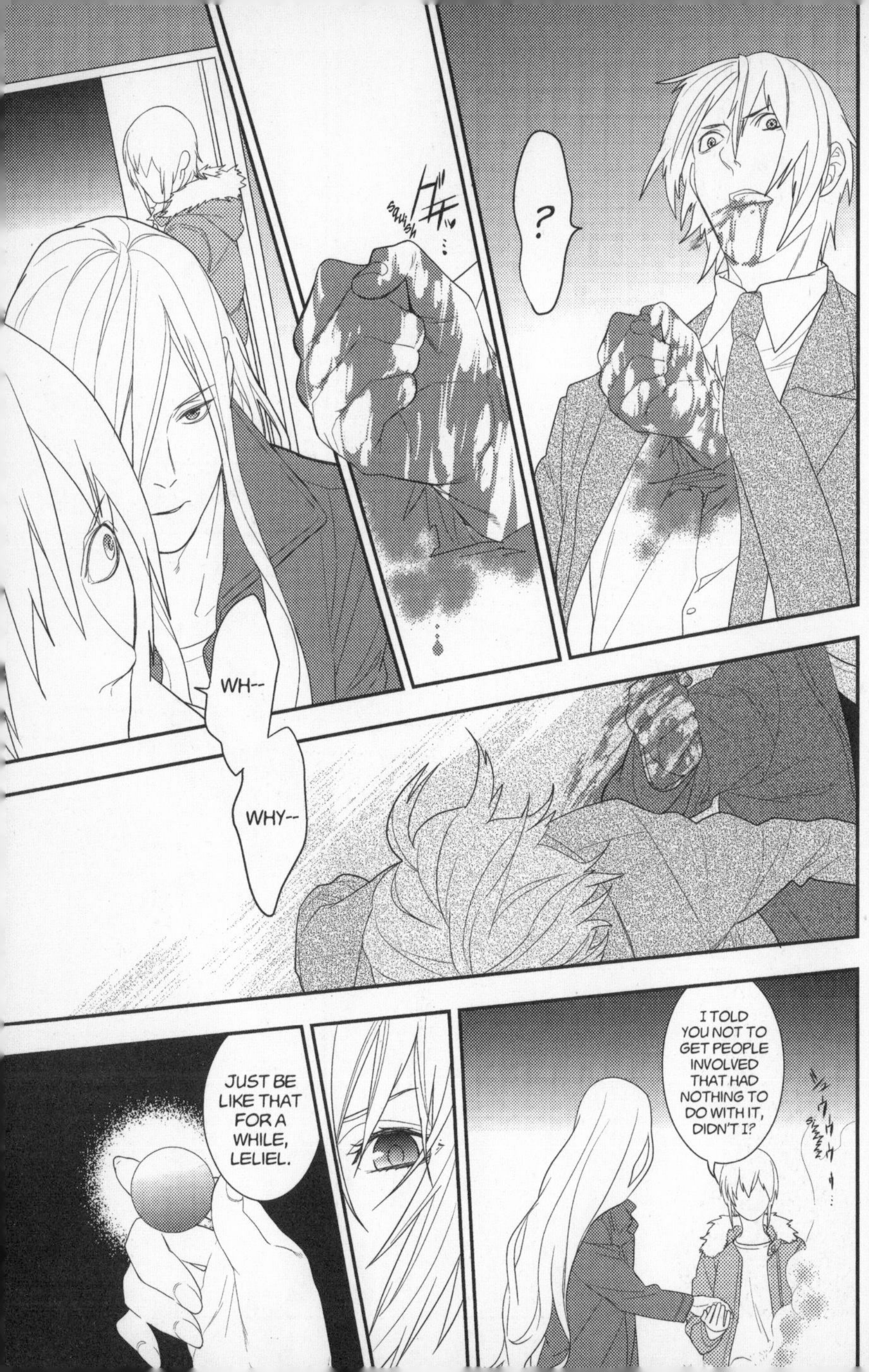
?
 グチッ…
squish
WH--
WHY--
I TOLD YOU NOT TO GET PEOPLE INVOLVED THAT HAD NOTHING TO DO WITH IT, DIDN'T I?
ジュウウウゥ…
SIZZZZZ
JUST BE LIKE THAT FOR A WHILE, LELIEL.

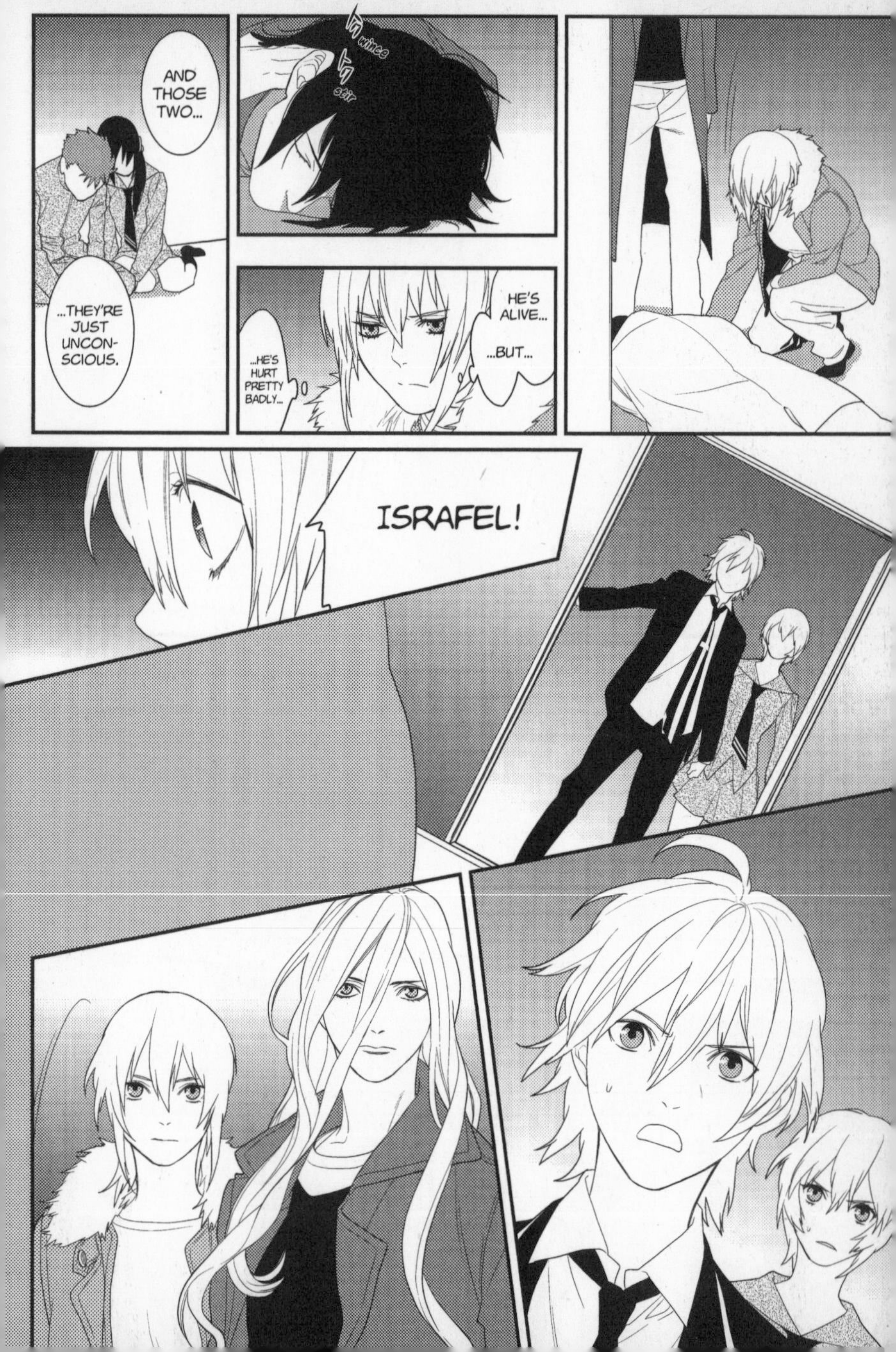
wince
stir
HE'S ALIVE...
...BUT...
...HE'S HURT PRETTY BADLY...
AND THOSE TWO...
...THEY'RE JUST UNCON-SCIOUS.
ISRAFEL!

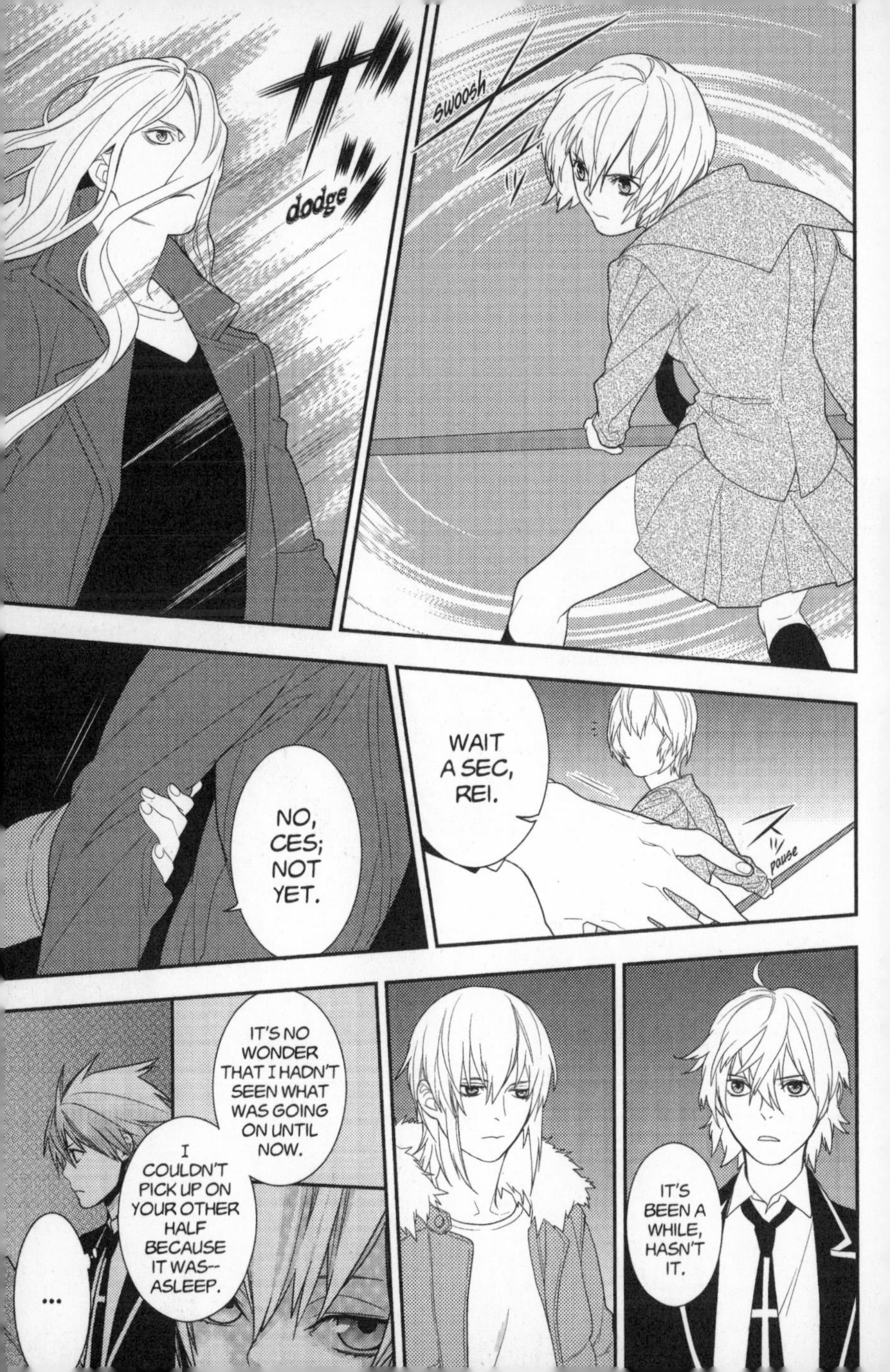
swoosh
dodge
WAIT A SEC, REI.
pause
NO, CES; NOT YET.
IT'S BEEN A WHILE, HASN'T IT.
IT'S NO WONDER THAT I HADN'T SEEN WHAT WAS GOING ON UNTIL NOW.
I COULDN'T PICK UP ON YOUR OTHER HALF BECAUSE IT WAS-- ASLEEP.
...

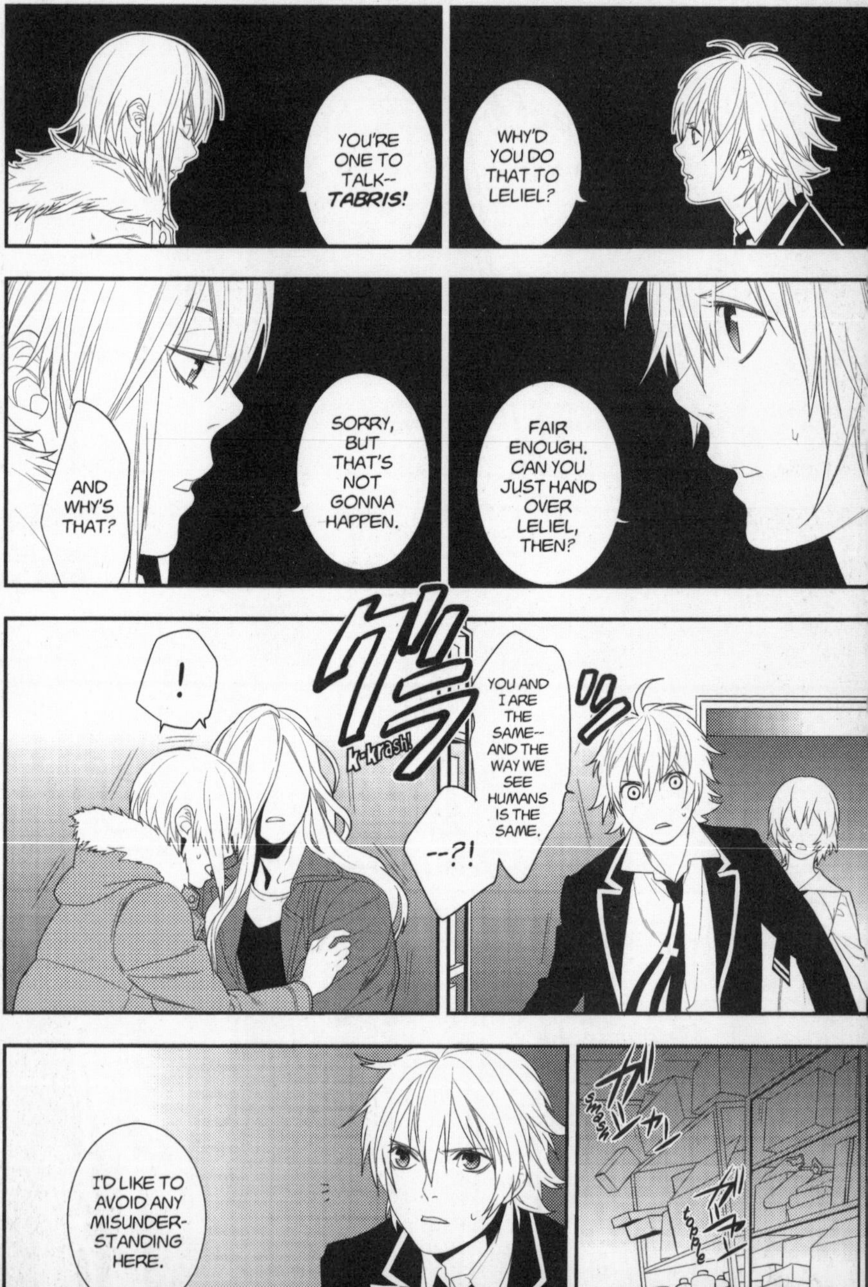
WHY'D YOU DO THAT TO LELIEL?
YOU'RE ONE TO TALK-- TABRIS!
FAIR ENOUGH. CAN YOU JUST HAND OVER LELIEL, THEN?
SORRY, BUT THAT'S NOT GONNA HAPPEN.
AND WHY'S THAT?
YOU AND I ARE THE SAME-- AND THE WAY WE SEE HUMANS IS THE SAME.
K-KRASH!
!
--?!
smash
topple
I'D LIKE TO AVOID ANY MISUNDER-STANDING HERE.

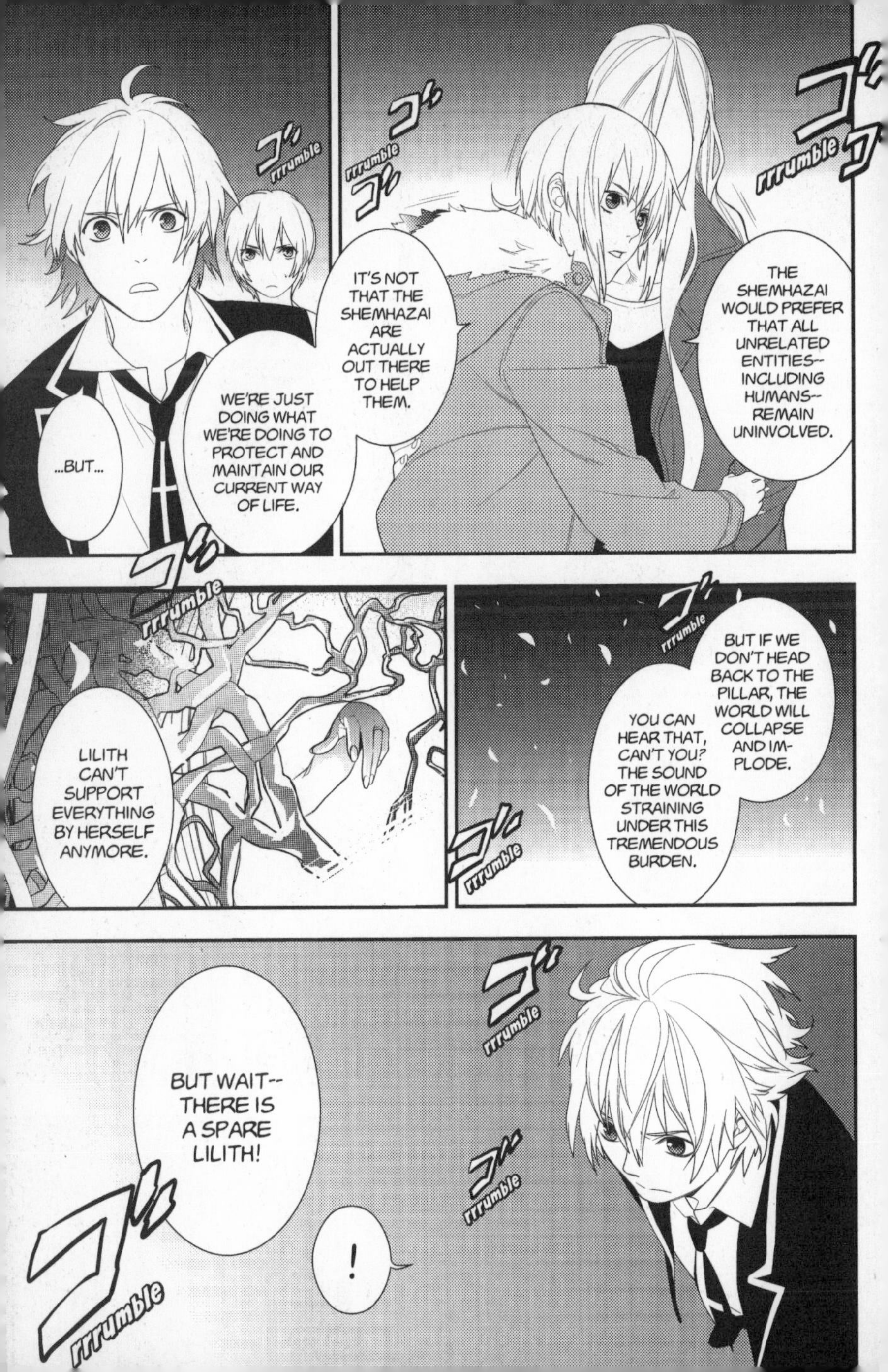
rrrumble
THE SHEMHAZAI WOULD PREFER THAT ALL UNRELATED ENTITIES--INCLUDING HUMANS--REMAIN UNINVOLVED.
rrrumble
IT'S NOT THAT THE SHEMHAZAI ARE ACTUALLY OUT THERE TO HELP THEM.
rrrumble
WE'RE JUST DOING WHAT WE'RE DOING TO PROTECT AND MAINTAIN OUR CURRENT WAY OF LIFE.
...BUT...
rrrumble
BUT IF WE DON'T HEAD BACK TO THE PILLAR, THE WORLD WILL COLLAPSE AND IM-PLODE.
YOU CAN HEAR THAT, CAN'T YOU? THE SOUND OF THE WORLD STRAINING UNDER THIS TREMENDOUS BURDEN.
rrrumble
rrrumble
LILITH CAN'T SUPPORT EVERYTHING BY HERSELF ANYMORE.
rrrumble
rrrumble
!
BUT WAIT--THERE IS A SPARE LILITH!
rrrumble

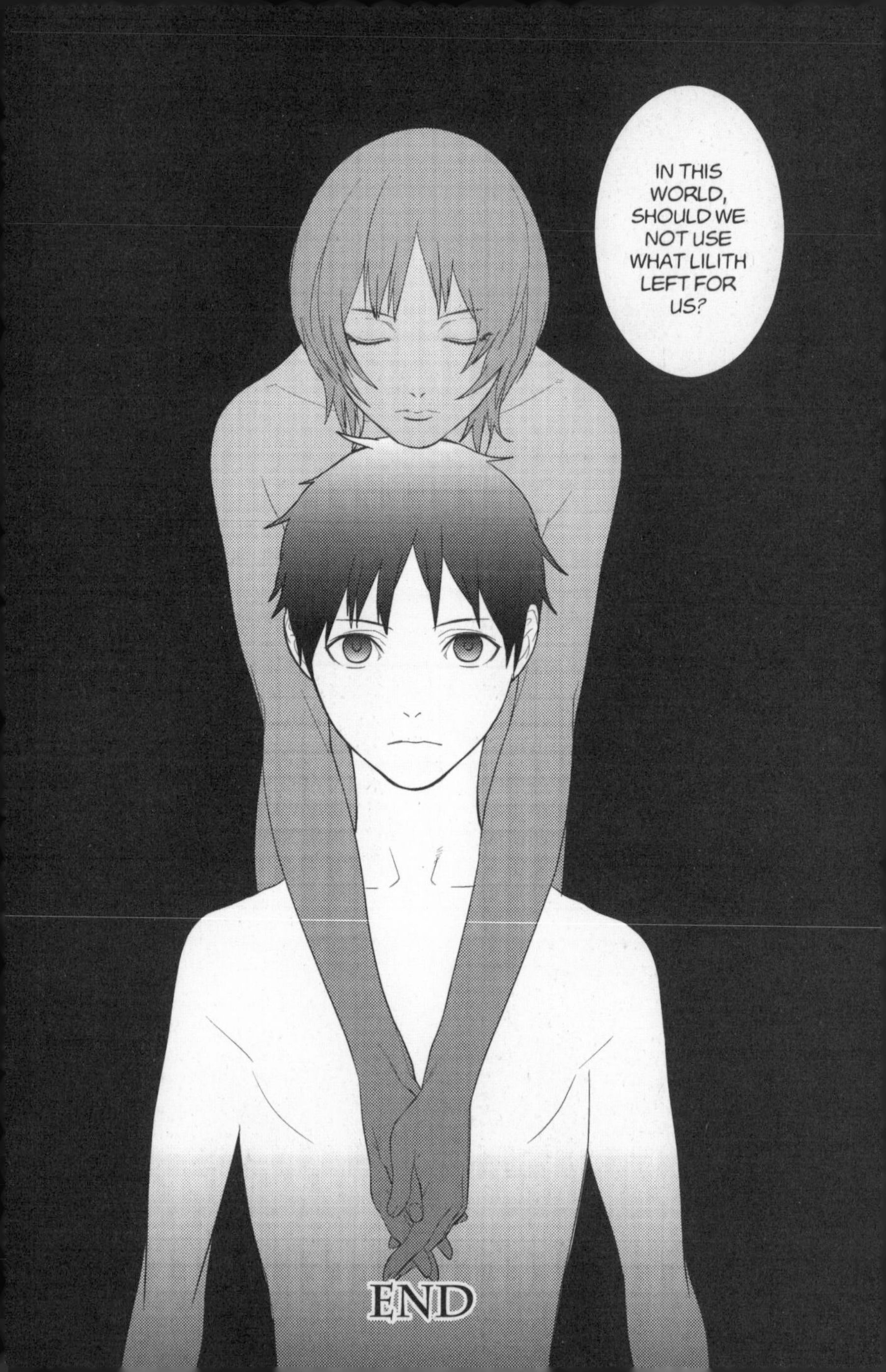
IN THIS WORLD, SHOULD WE NOT USE WHAT LILITH LEFT FOR US?
END

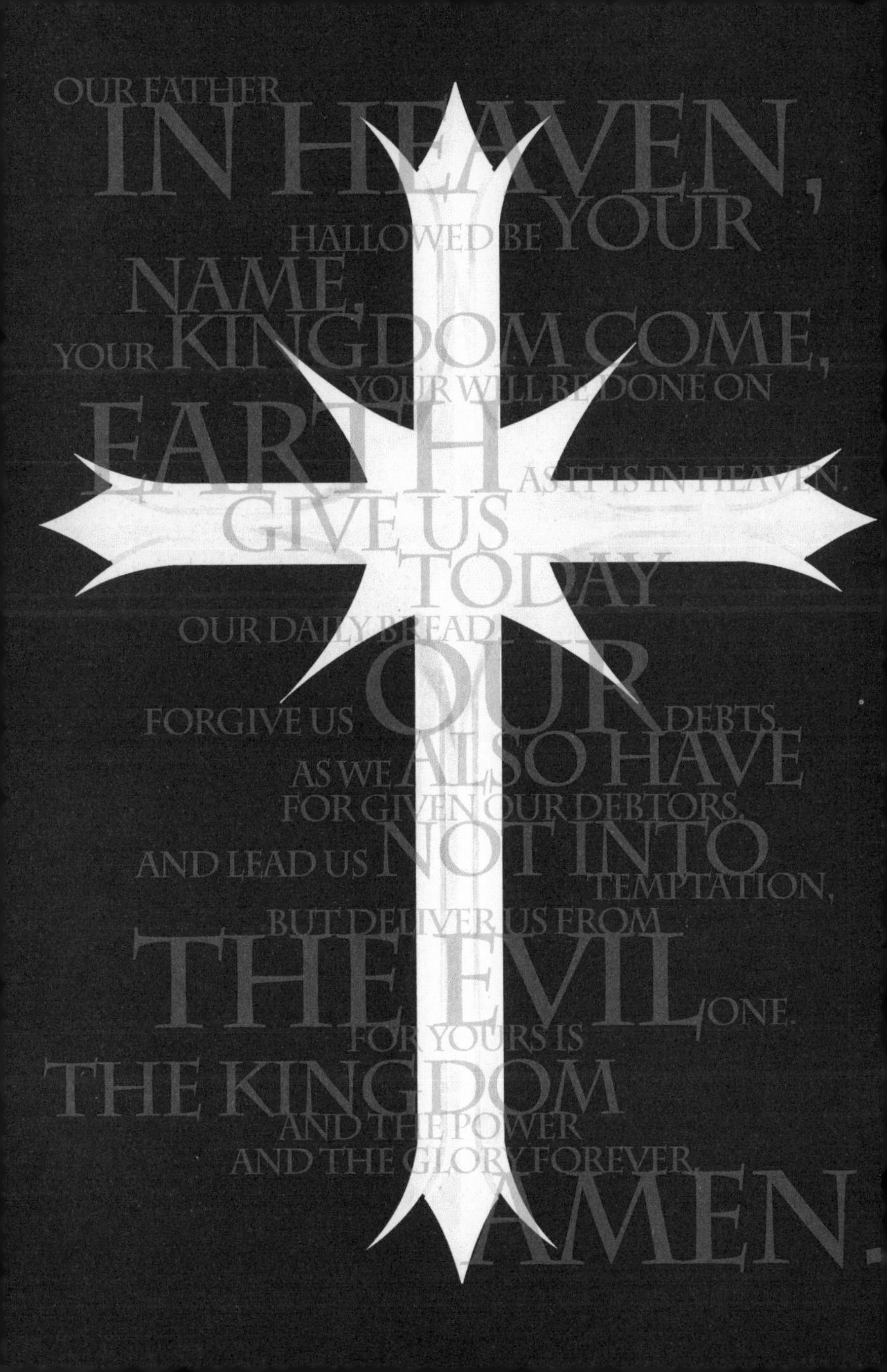
OUR FATHER
IN HEAVEN,
HALLOWED BE YOUR
NAME,
YOUR KINGDOM COME,
YOUR WILL BE DONE ON
EARTH AS IT IS IN HEAVEN.
GIVE US
TODAY
OUR DAILY BREAD.
FORGIVE US OUR DEBTS,
AS WE ALSO HAVE
FOR GIVEN OUR DEBTORS.
AND LEAD US NOT INTO
TEMPTATION,
BUT DELIVER US FROM
THE EVIL ONE.
FOR YOURS IS
THE KINGDOM
AND THE POWER
AND THE GLORY FOREVER.
AMEN.

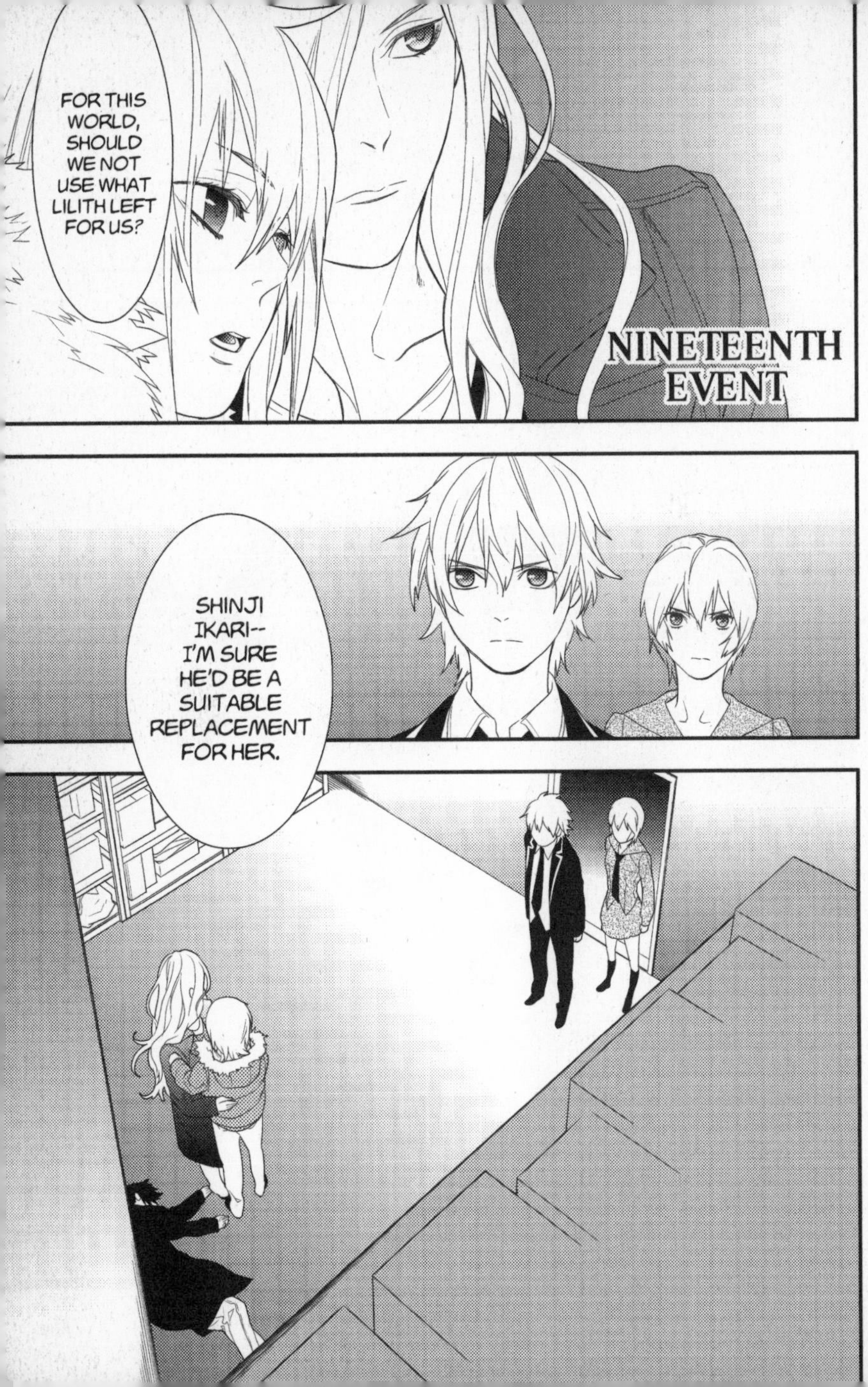
FOR THIS WORLD, SHOULD WE NOT USE WHAT LILITH LEFT FOR US?
NINETEENTH EVENT
SHINJI IKARI-- I'M SURE HE'D BE A SUITABLE REPLACEMENT FOR HER.

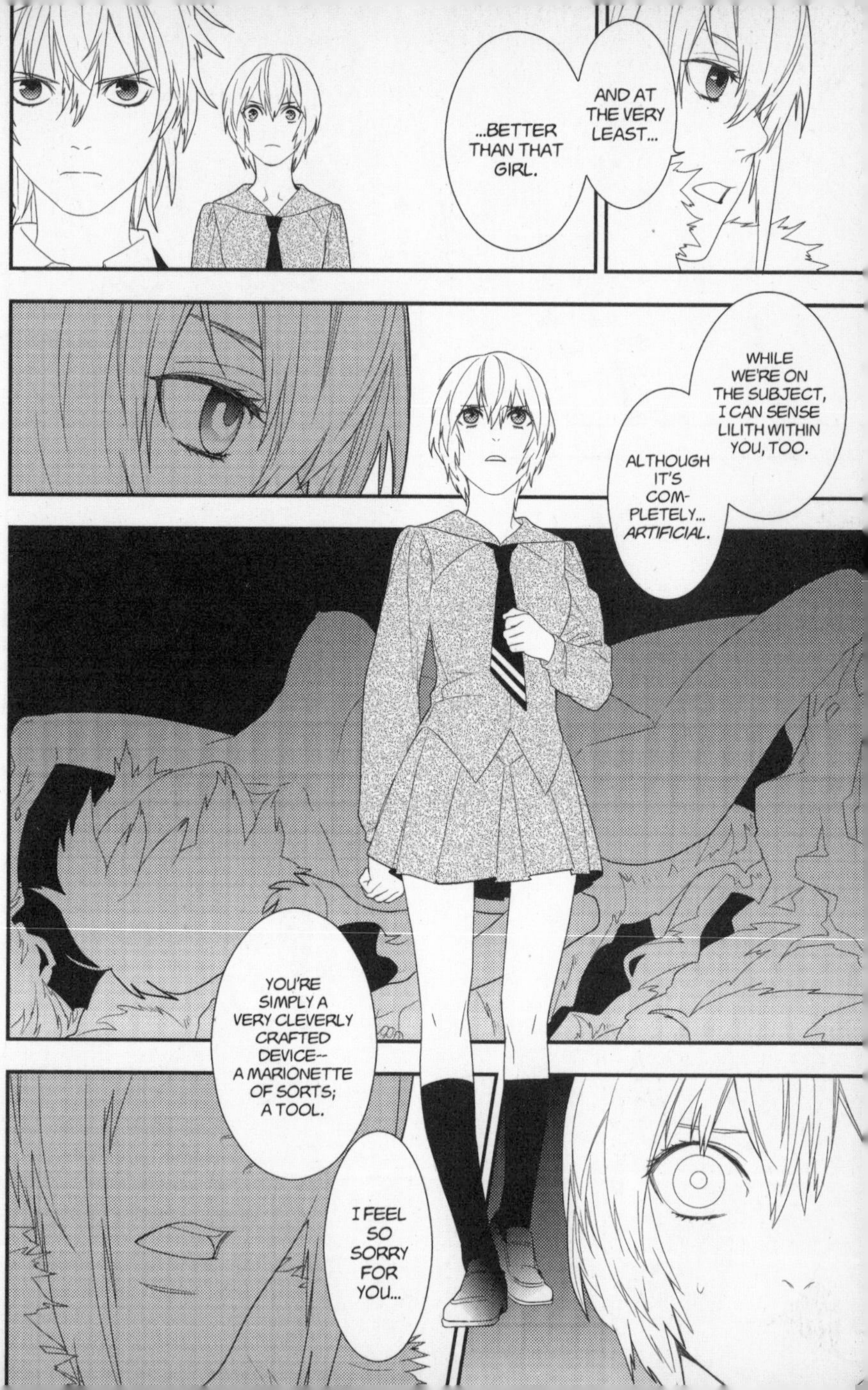
AND AT THE VERY LEAST...
...BETTER THAN THAT GIRL.
WHILE WE'RE ON THE SUBJECT, I CAN SENSE LILITH WITHIN YOU, TOO.
ALTHOUGH IT'S COM-PLETELY... *ARTIFICIAL*.
YOU'RE SIMPLY A VERY CLEVERLY CRAFTED DEVICE-- A MARIONETTE OF SORTS; A TOOL.
I FEEL SO SORRY FOR YOU...

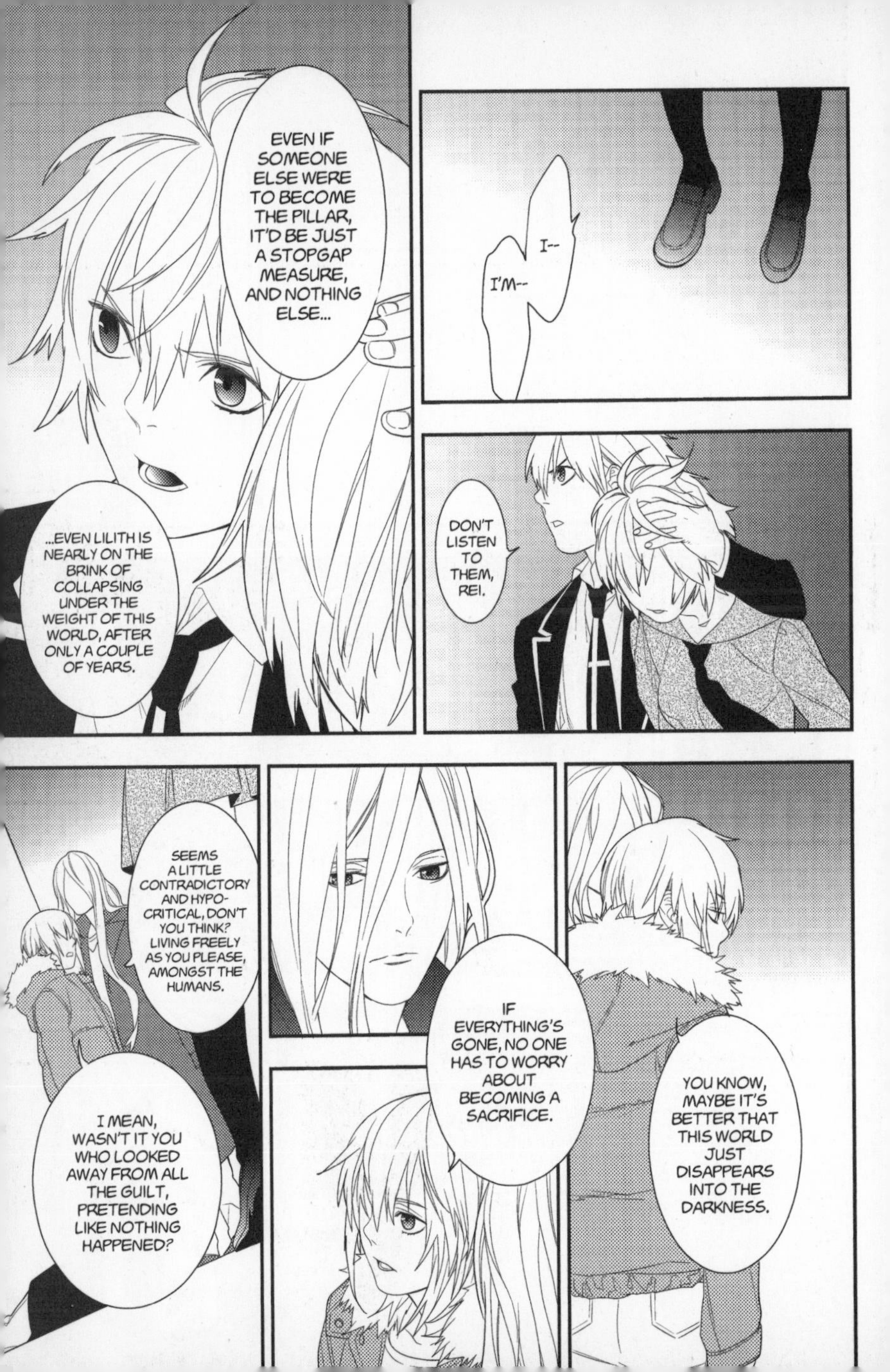
I--
I'M--
DON'T LISTEN TO THEM, REI.
EVEN IF SOMEONE ELSE WERE TO BECOME THE PILLAR, IT'D BE JUST A STOPGAP MEASURE, AND NOTHING ELSE...
...EVEN LILITH IS NEARLY ON THE BRINK OF COLLAPSING UNDER THE WEIGHT OF THIS WORLD, AFTER ONLY A COUPLE OF YEARS.
YOU KNOW, MAYBE IT'S BETTER THAT THIS WORLD JUST DISAPPEARS INTO THE DARKNESS.
IF EVERYTHING'S GONE, NO ONE HAS TO WORRY ABOUT BECOMING A SACRIFICE.
SEEMS A LITTLE CONTRADICTORY AND HYPO-CRITICAL, DON'T YOU THINK? LIVING FREELY AS YOU PLEASE, AMONGST THE HUMANS.
I MEAN, WASN'T IT YOU WHO LOOKED AWAY FROM ALL THE GUILT, PRETENDING LIKE NOTHING HAPPENED?

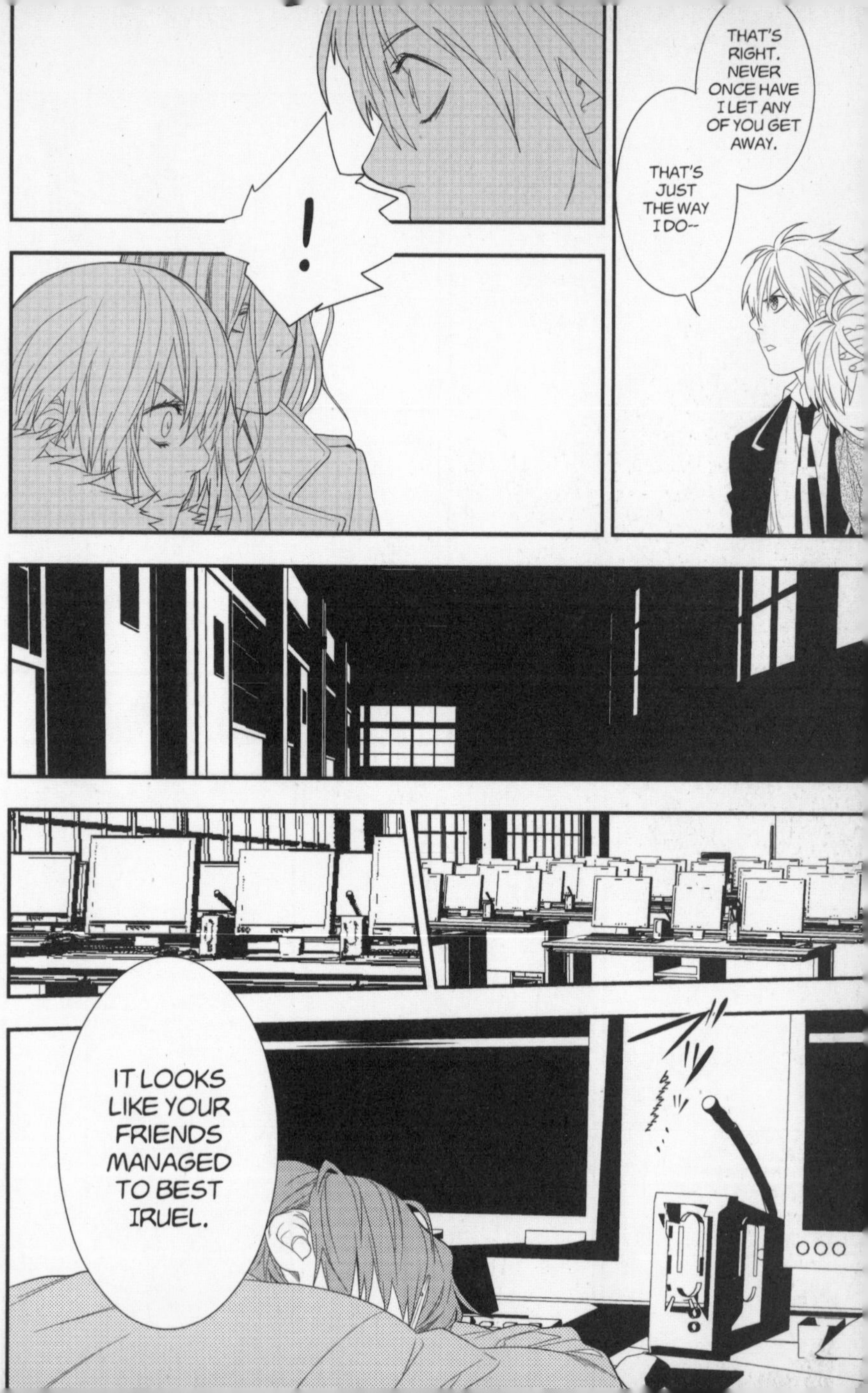
THAT'S RIGHT. NEVER ONCE HAVE I LET ANY OF YOU GET AWAY.
THAT'S JUST THE WAY I DO--
!
IT LOOKS LIKE YOUR FRIENDS MANAGED TO BEST IRUEL.

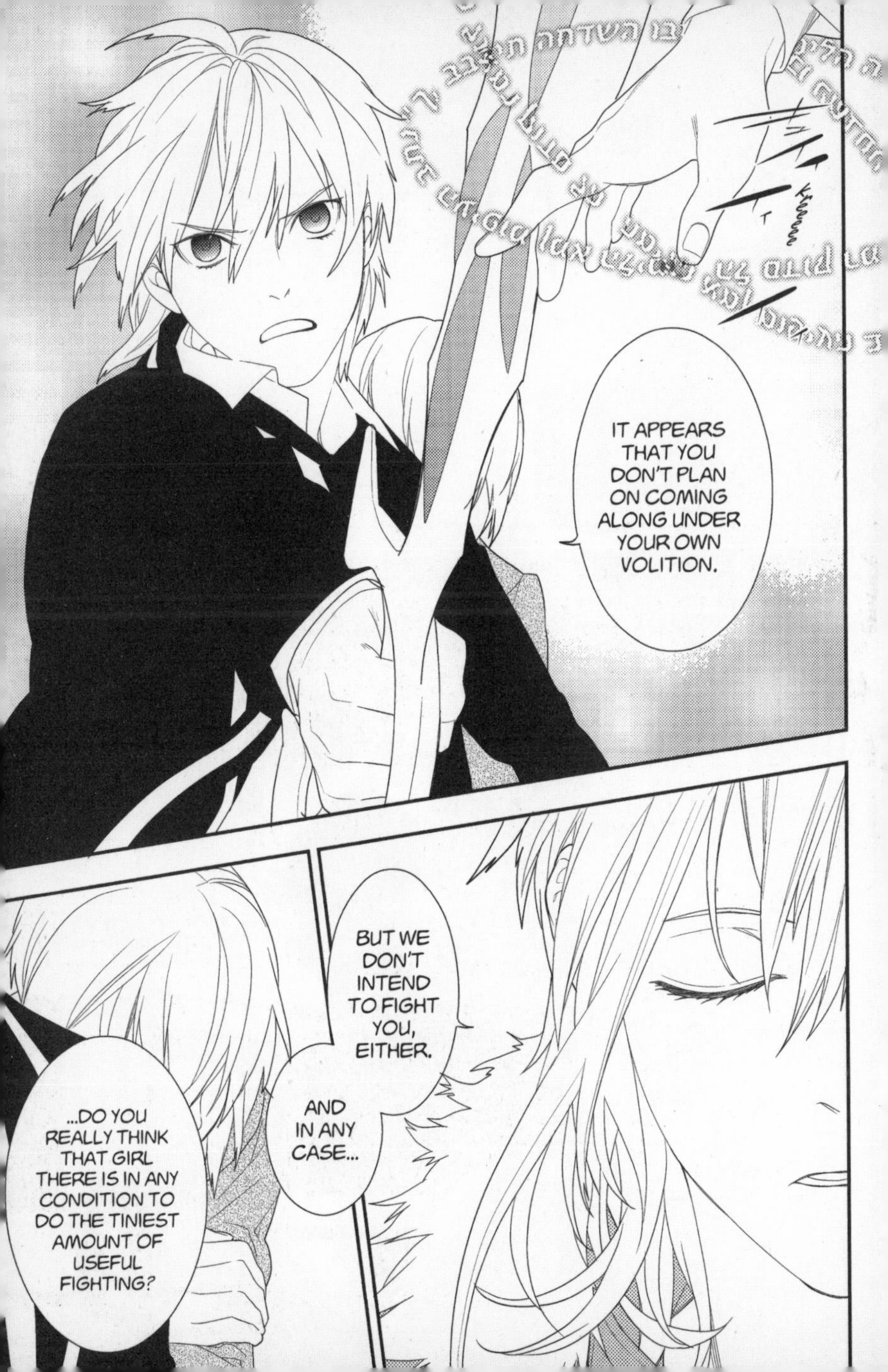
IT APPEARS THAT YOU DON'T PLAN ON COMING ALONG UNDER YOUR OWN VOLITION.
BUT WE DON'T INTEND TO FIGHT YOU, EITHER.
AND IN ANY CASE...
...DO YOU REALLY THINK THAT GIRL THERE IS IN ANY CONDITION TO DO THE TINIEST AMOUNT OF USEFUL FIGHTING?

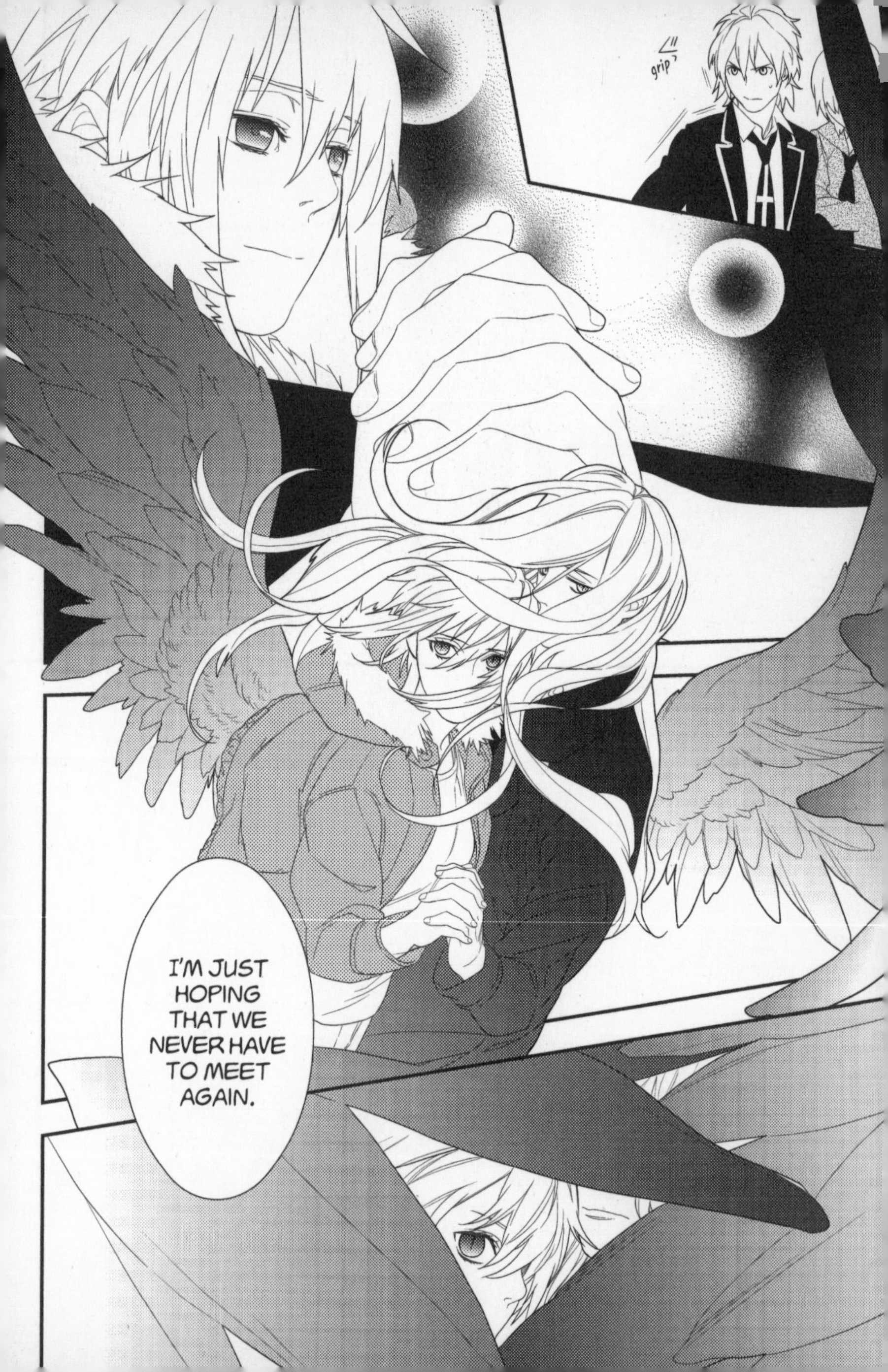
grip
I'M JUST HOPING THAT WE NEVER HAVE TO MEET AGAIN.

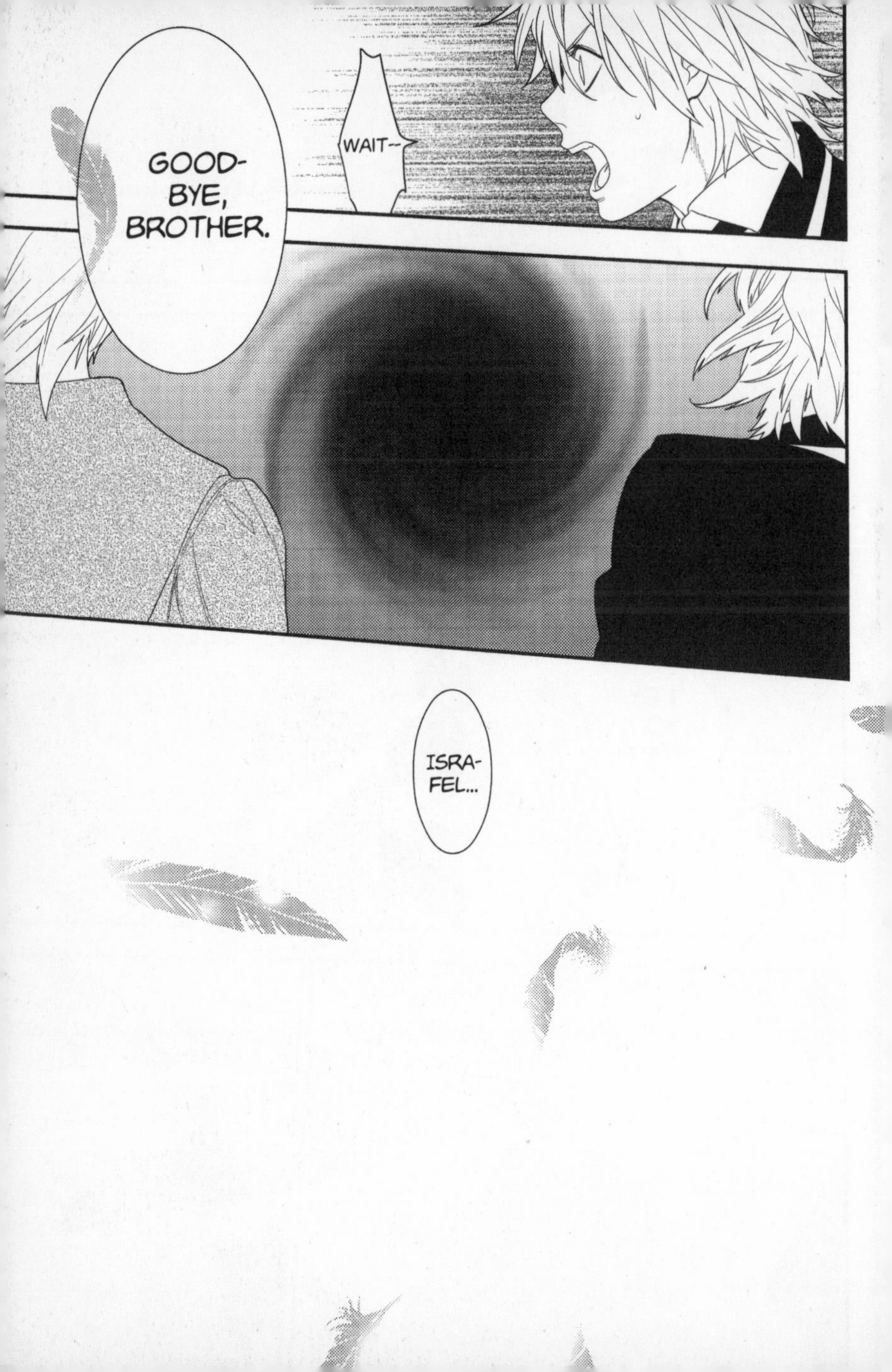
WAIT--
GOOD-BYE, BROTHER.
ISRA-FEL...

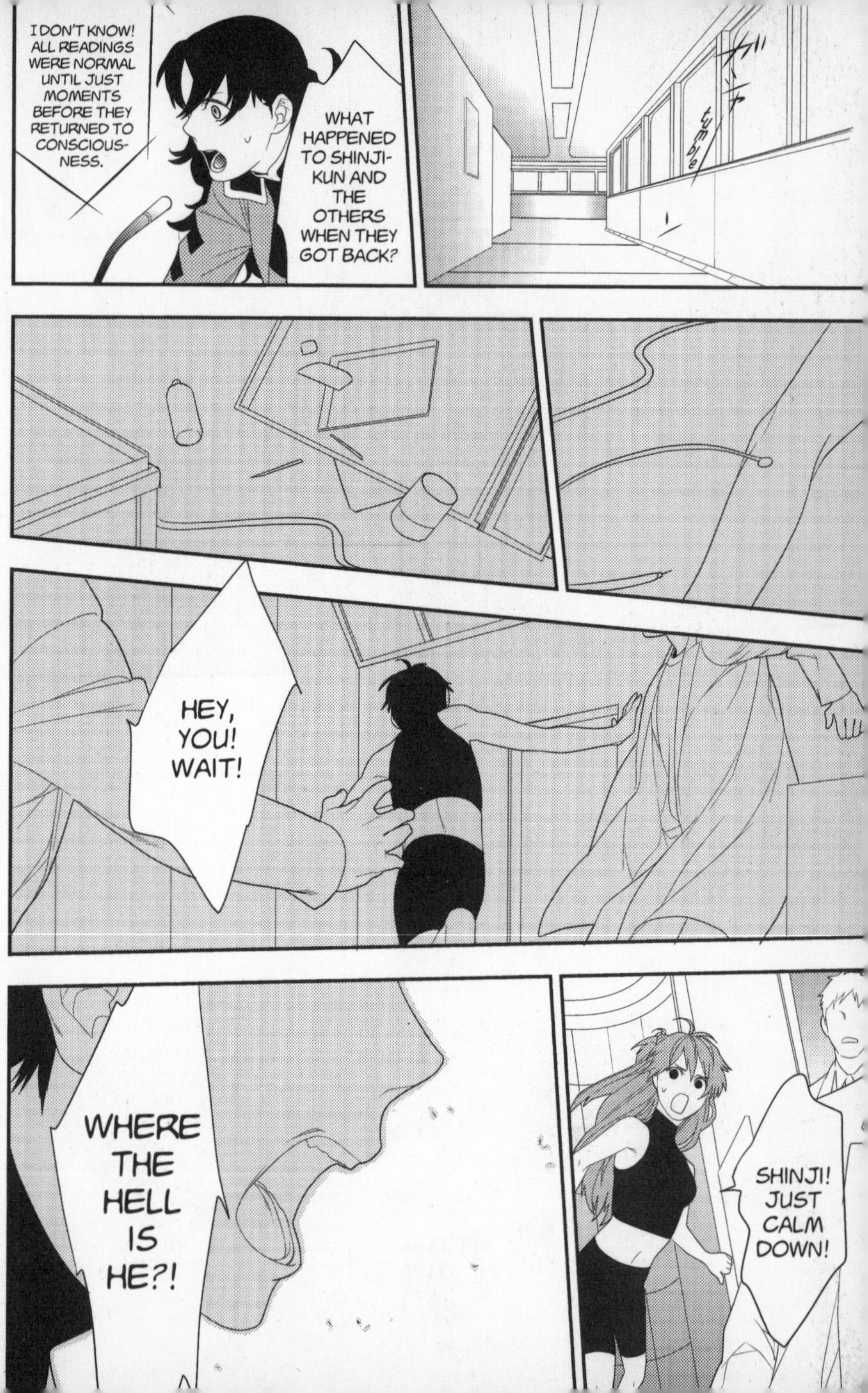
tumble
WHAT HAPPENED TO SHINJI-KUN AND THE OTHERS WHEN THEY GOT BACK?
I DON'T KNOW! ALL READINGS WERE NORMAL UNTIL JUST MOMENTS BEFORE THEY RETURNED TO CONSCIOUSNESS.
HEY, YOU! WAIT!
SHINJI! JUST CALM DOWN!
WHERE THE HELL IS HE?!

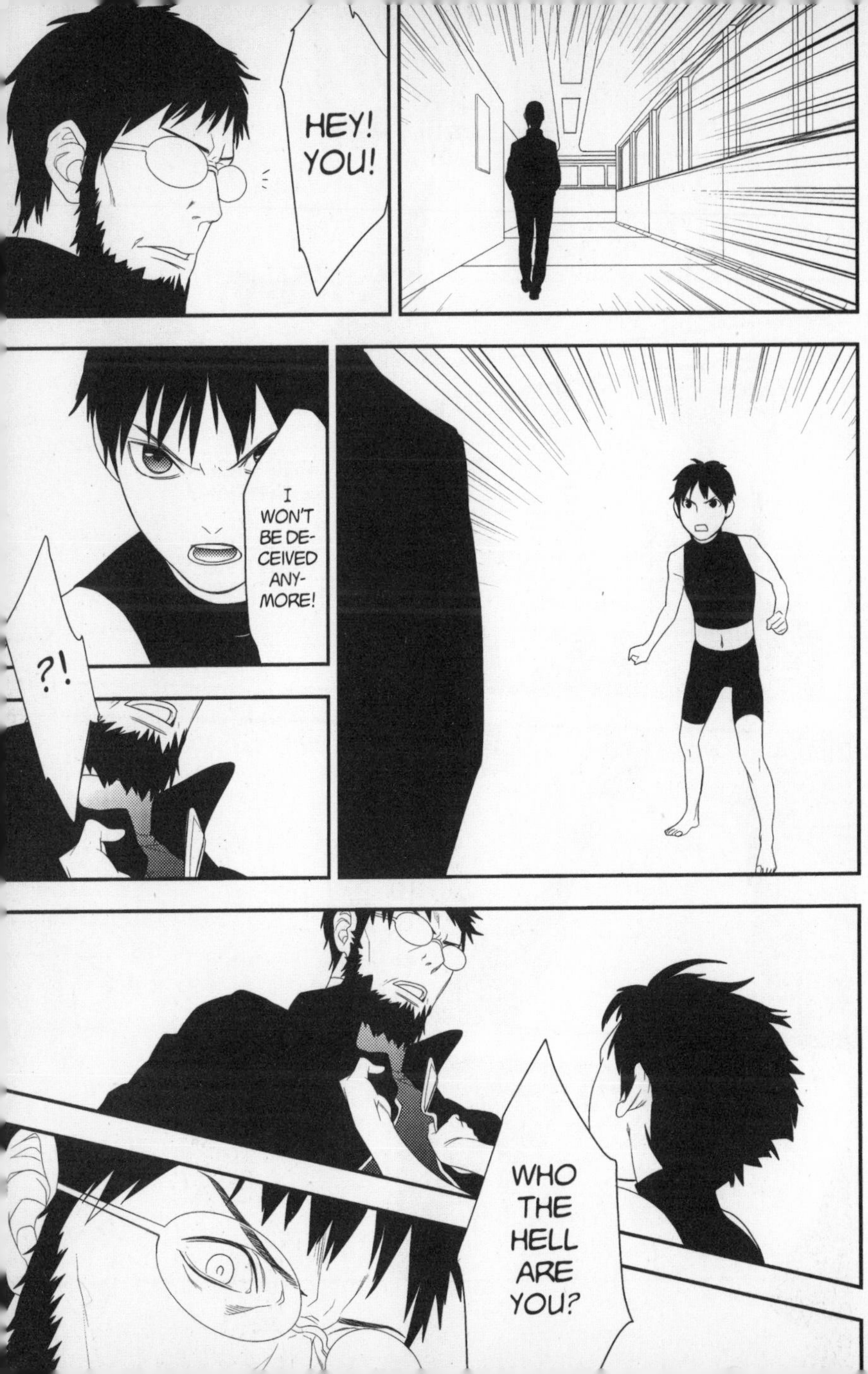
HEY! YOU!
I WON'T BE DECEIVED ANYMORE!
?!
WHO THE HELL ARE YOU?

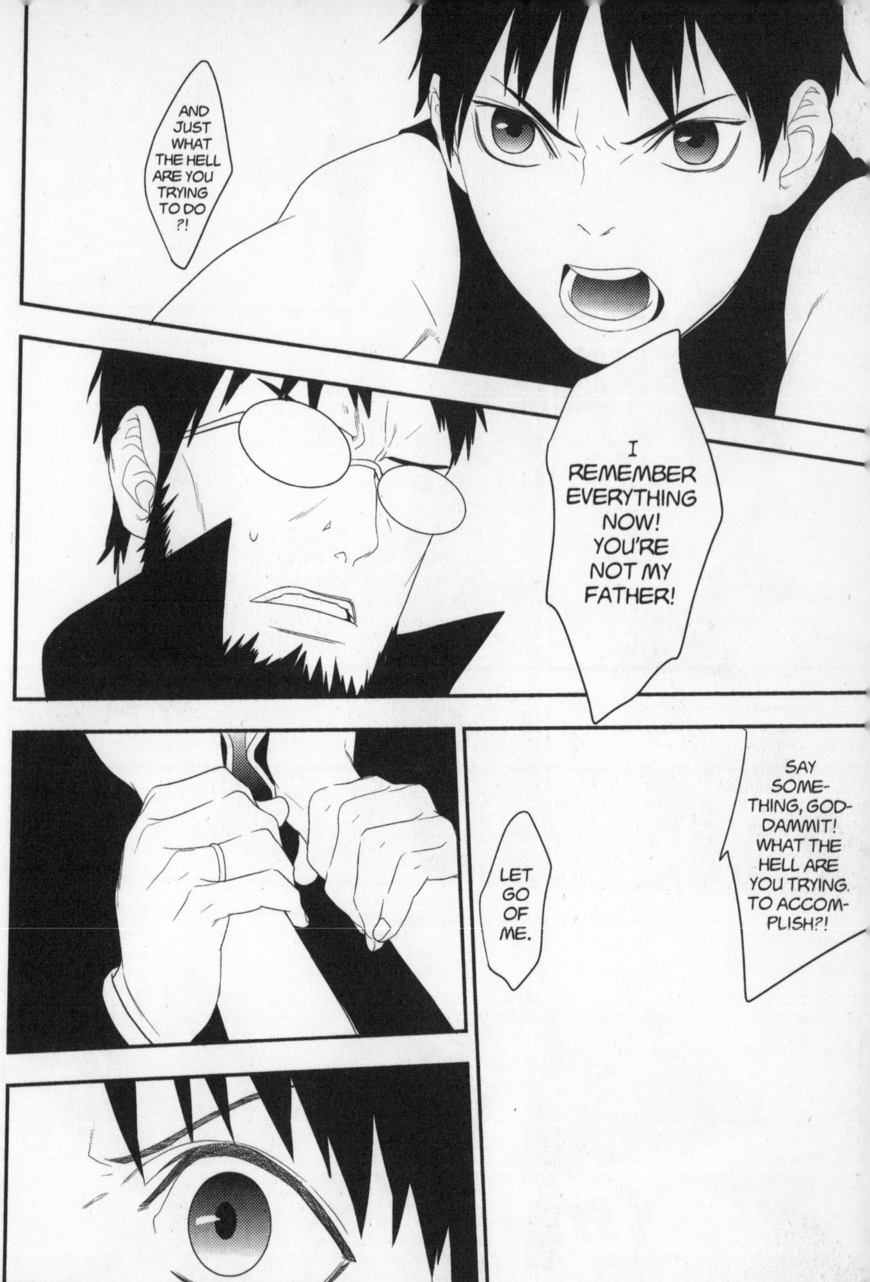
AND JUST WHAT THE HELL ARE YOU TRYING TO DO?!
I REMEMBER EVERYTHING NOW! YOU'RE NOT MY FATHER!
SAY SOMETHING, GODDAMMIT! WHAT THE HELL ARE YOU TRYING TO ACCOMPLISH?!
LET GO OF ME.

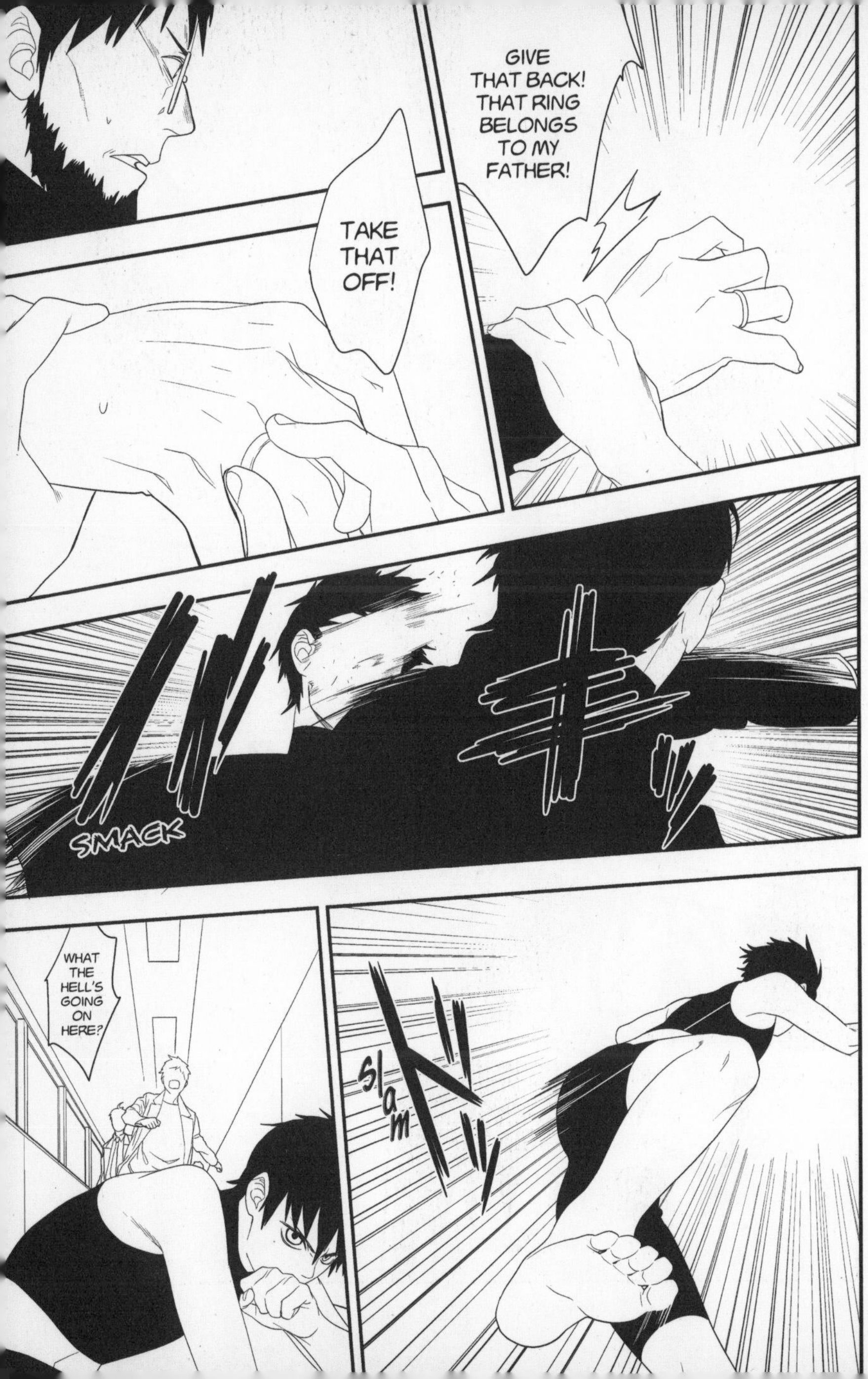

GIVE THAT BACK! THAT RING BELONGS TO MY FATHER!
TAKE THAT OFF!
SMACK
slam
WHAT THE HELL'S GOING ON HERE?

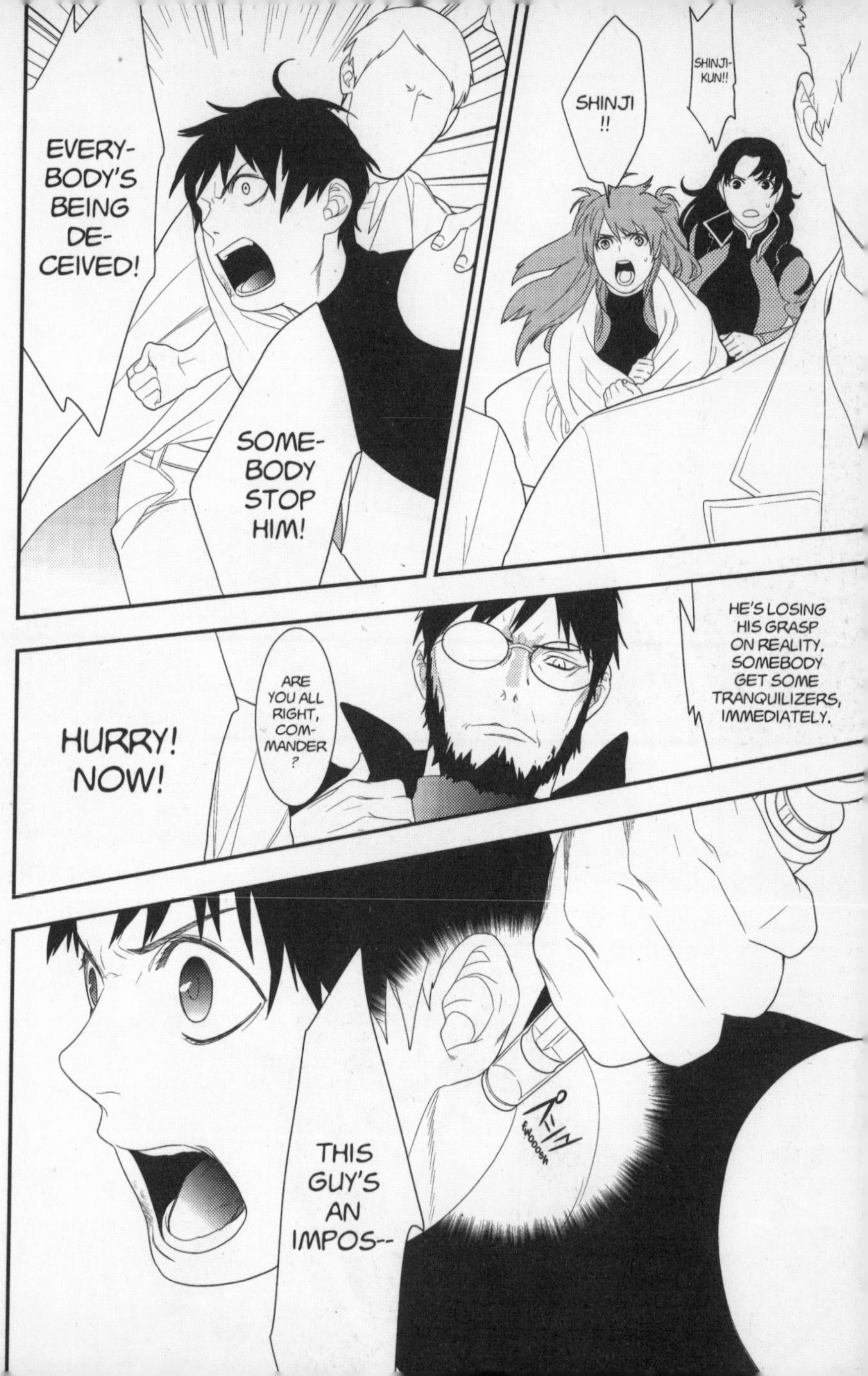
SHINJI-KUN!!
SHINJI !!
EVERY-BODY'S BEING DE-CEIVED!
SOME-BODY STOP HIM!
HE'S LOSING HIS GRASP ON REALITY. SOMEBODY GET SOME TRANQUILIZERS, IMMEDIATELY.
ARE YOU ALL RIGHT, COM-MANDER ?
HURRY! NOW!
FWOOOSH
THIS GUY'S AN IMPOS--

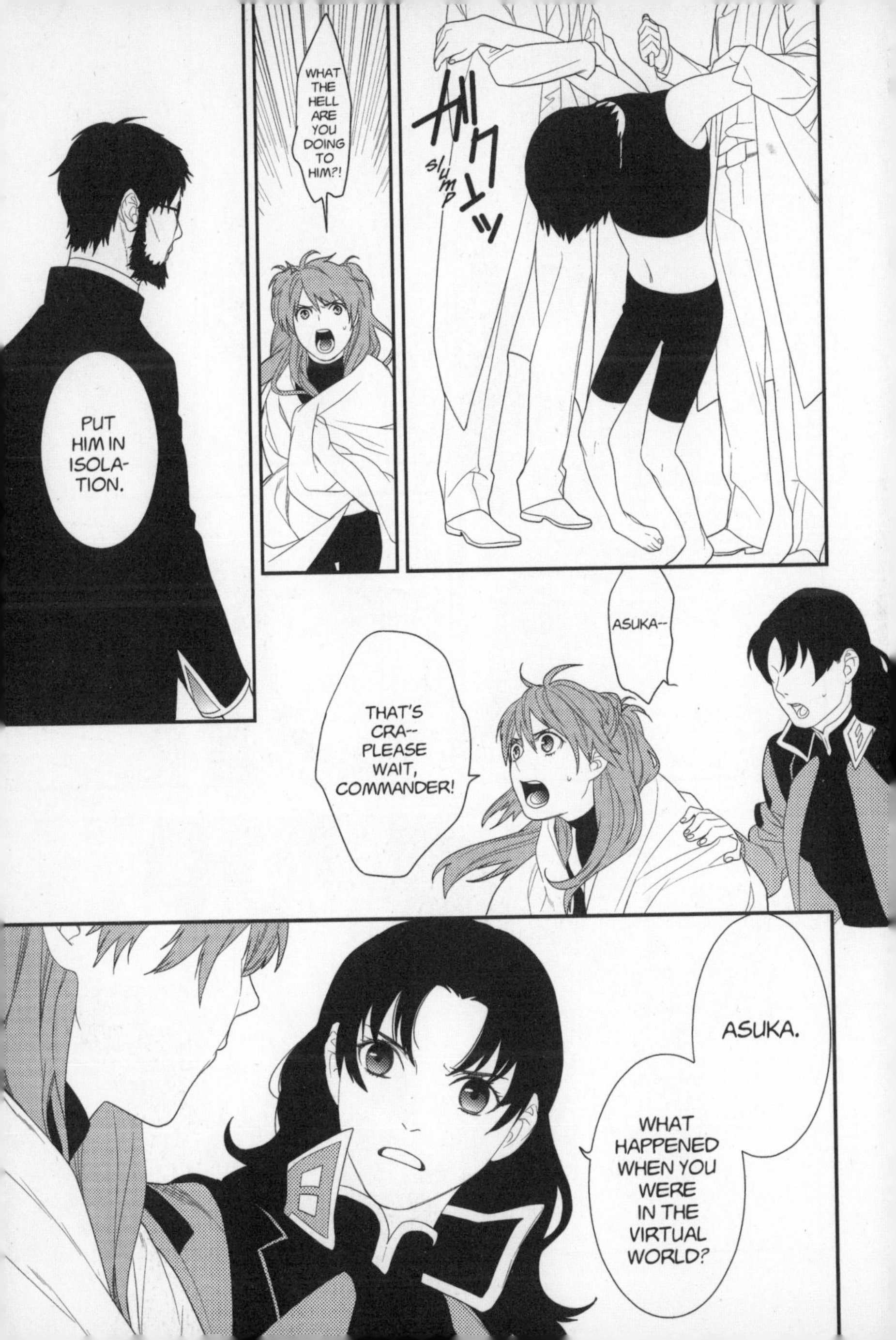
slump
WHAT THE HELL ARE YOU DOING TO HIM?!
PUT HIM IN ISOLATION.
ASUKA--
THAT'S CRA-- PLEASE WAIT, COMMANDER!
ASUKA.
WHAT HAPPENED WHEN YOU WERE IN THE VIRTUAL WORLD?

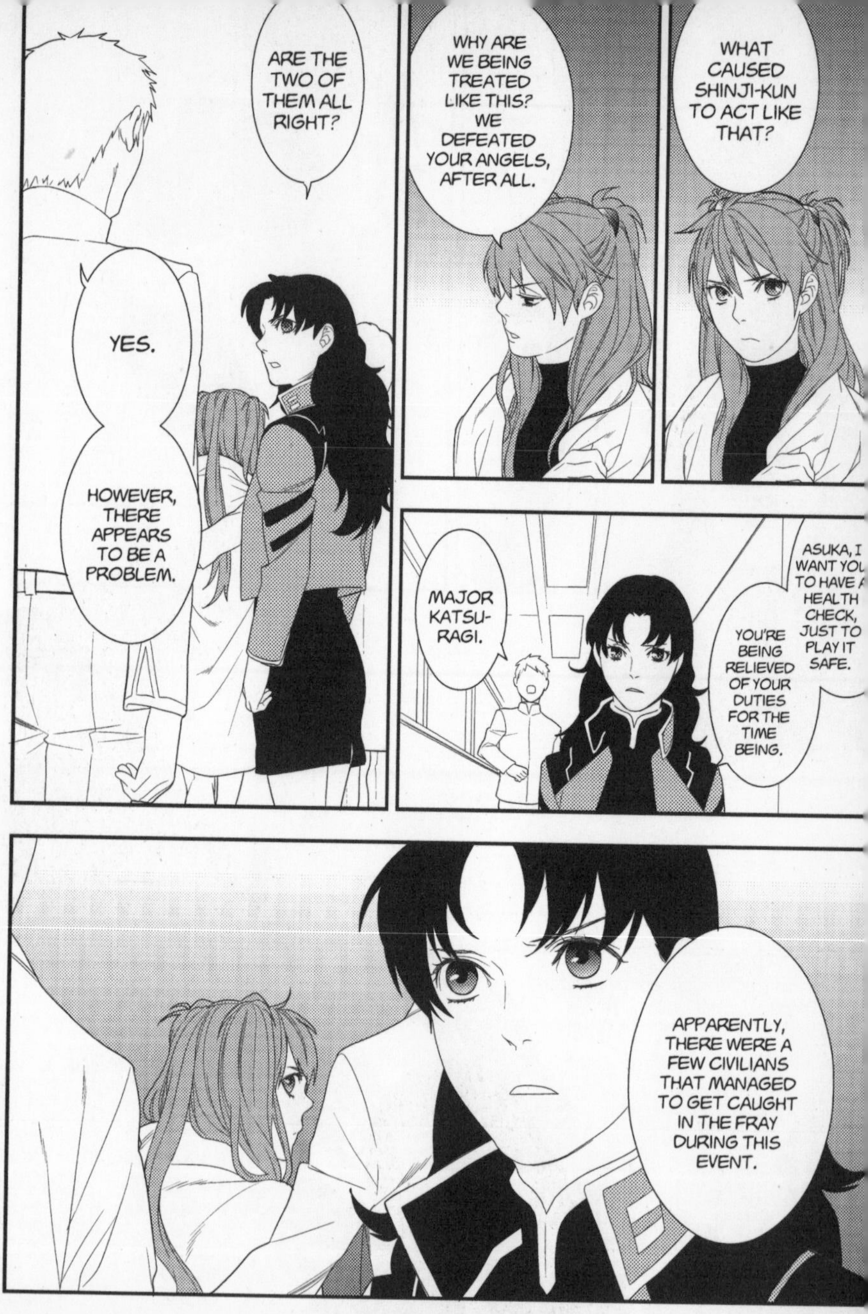
WHAT CAUSED SHINJI-KUN TO ACT LIKE THAT?
WHY ARE WE BEING TREATED LIKE THIS? WE DEFEATED YOUR ANGELS, AFTER ALL.
ASUKA, I WANT YOU TO HAVE A HEALTH CHECK, JUST TO PLAY IT SAFE.
YOU'RE BEING RELIEVED OF YOUR DUTIES FOR THE TIME BEING.
MAJOR KATSU-RAGI.
ARE THE TWO OF THEM ALL RIGHT?
YES.
HOWEVER, THERE APPEARS TO BE A PROBLEM.
APPARENTLY, THERE WERE A FEW CIVILIANS THAT MANAGED TO GET CAUGHT IN THE FRAY DURING THIS EVENT.

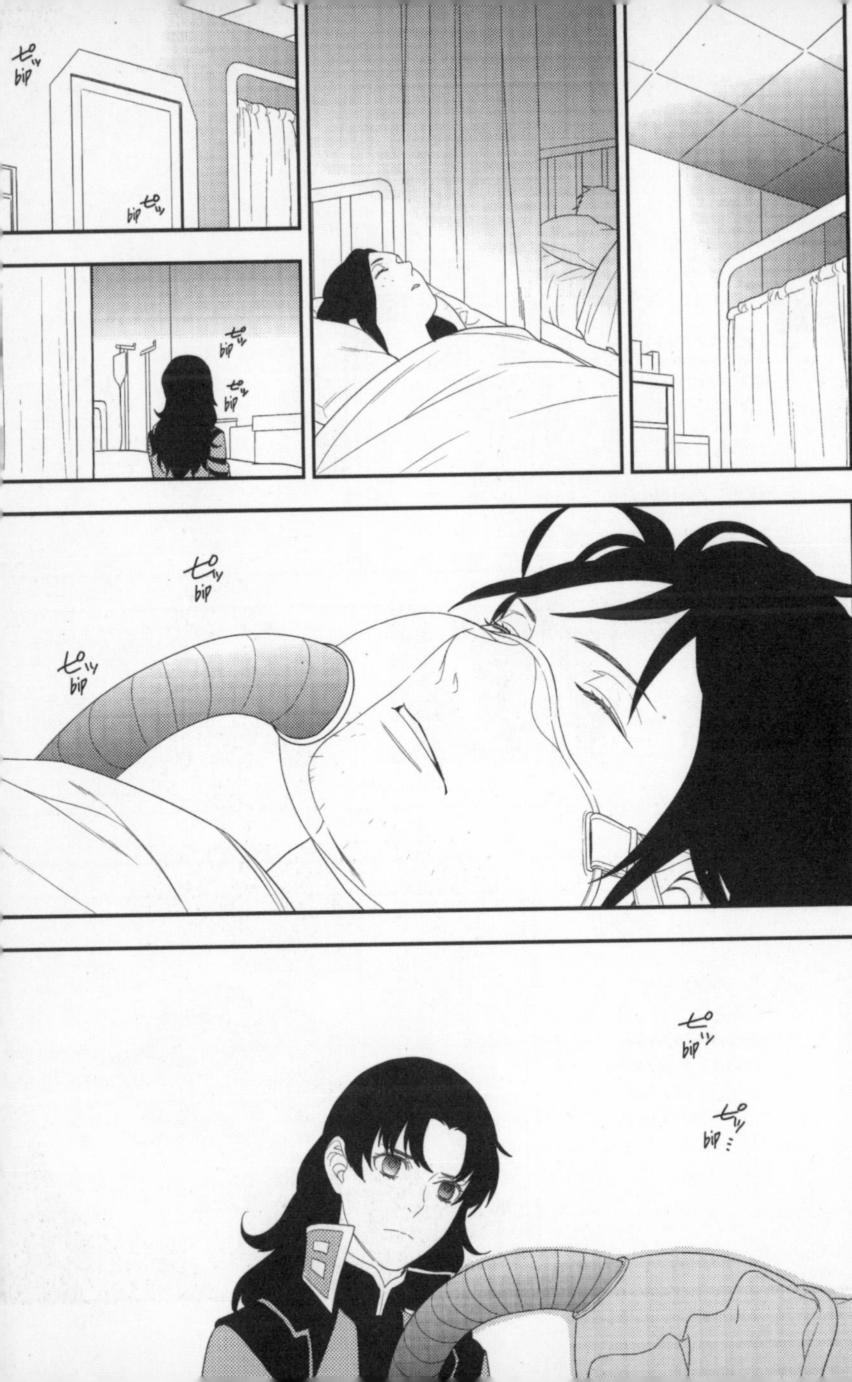
ピッ bip
bip ピッ
ピッ bip
ピッ bip
ピッ bip
ピッ bip
ピッ bip
ピッ bip…

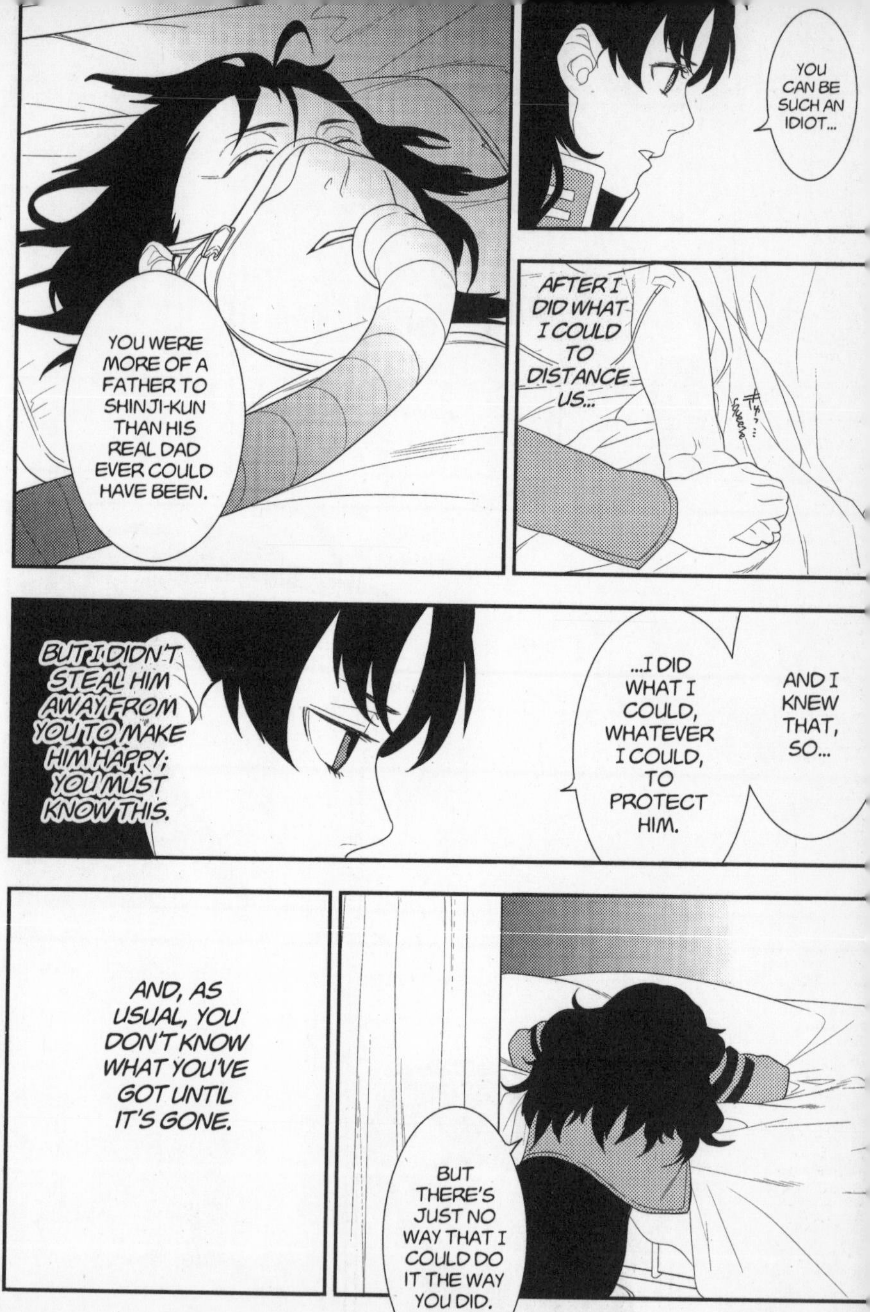

YOU CAN BE SUCH AN IDIOT...
AFTER I DID WHAT I COULD TO DISTANCE US...
YOU WERE MORE OF A FATHER TO SHINJI-KUN THAN HIS REAL DAD EVER COULD HAVE BEEN.
AND I KNEW THAT, SO...
...I DID WHAT I COULD, WHATEVER I COULD, TO PROTECT HIM.
BUT I DIDN'T STEAL HIM AWAY FROM YOU TO MAKE HIM HAPPY; YOU MUST KNOW THIS.
BUT THERE'S JUST NO WAY THAT I COULD DO IT THE WAY YOU DID.
AND, AS USUAL, YOU DON'T KNOW WHAT YOU'VE GOT UNTIL IT'S GONE.

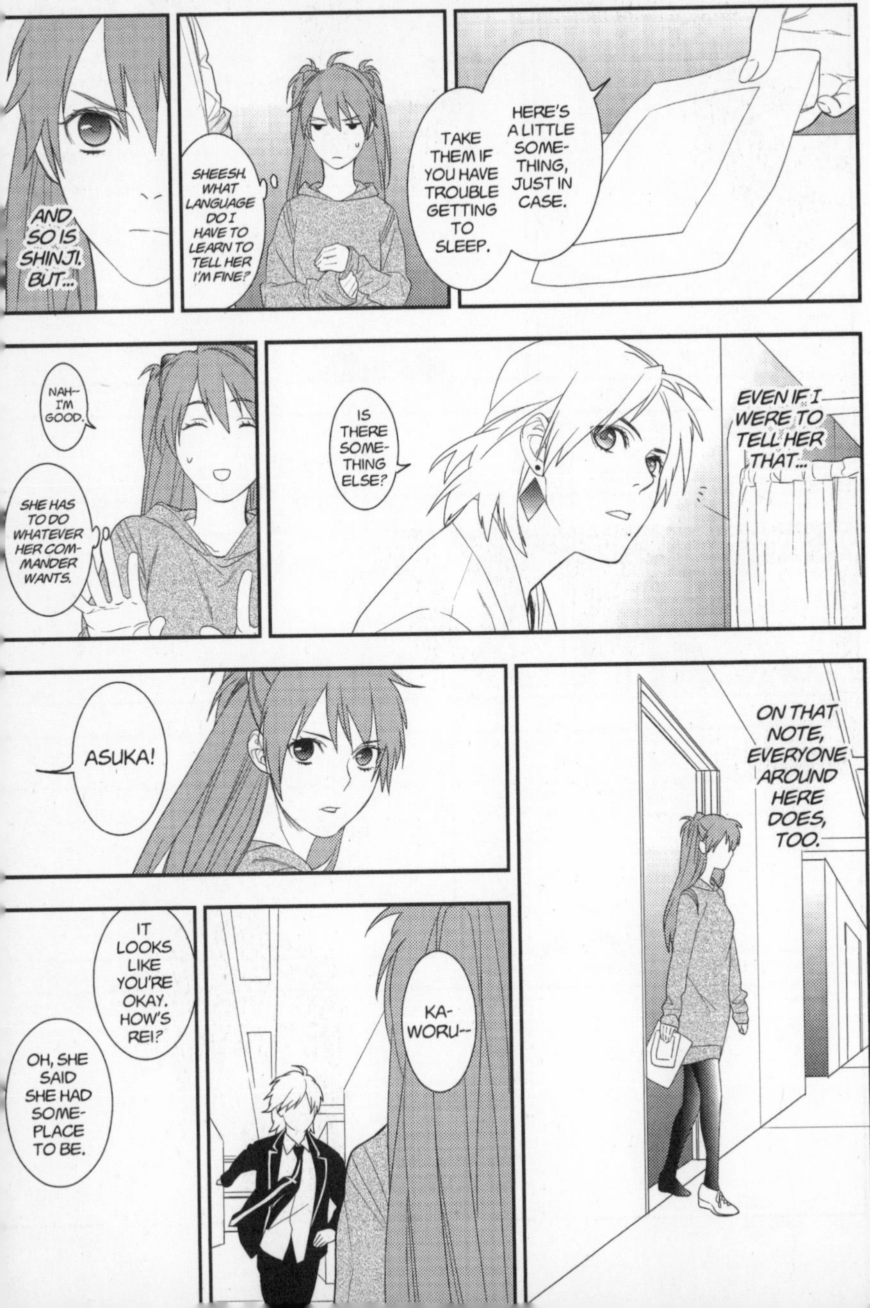
HERE'S A LITTLE SOMETHING, JUST IN CASE.
TAKE THEM IF YOU HAVE TROUBLE GETTING TO SLEEP.
SHEESH. WHAT LANGUAGE DO I HAVE TO LEARN TO TELL HER I'M FINE?
AND SO IS SHINJI. BUT...
EVEN IF I WERE TO TELL HER THAT...
IS THERE SOMETHING ELSE?
NAH-- I'M GOOD.
SHE HAS TO DO WHATEVER HER COMMANDER WANTS.
ON THAT NOTE, EVERYONE AROUND HERE DOES, TOO.
ASUKA!
KA-WORU--
IT LOOKS LIKE YOU'RE OKAY. HOW'S REI?
OH, SHE SAID SHE HAD SOMEPLACE TO BE.

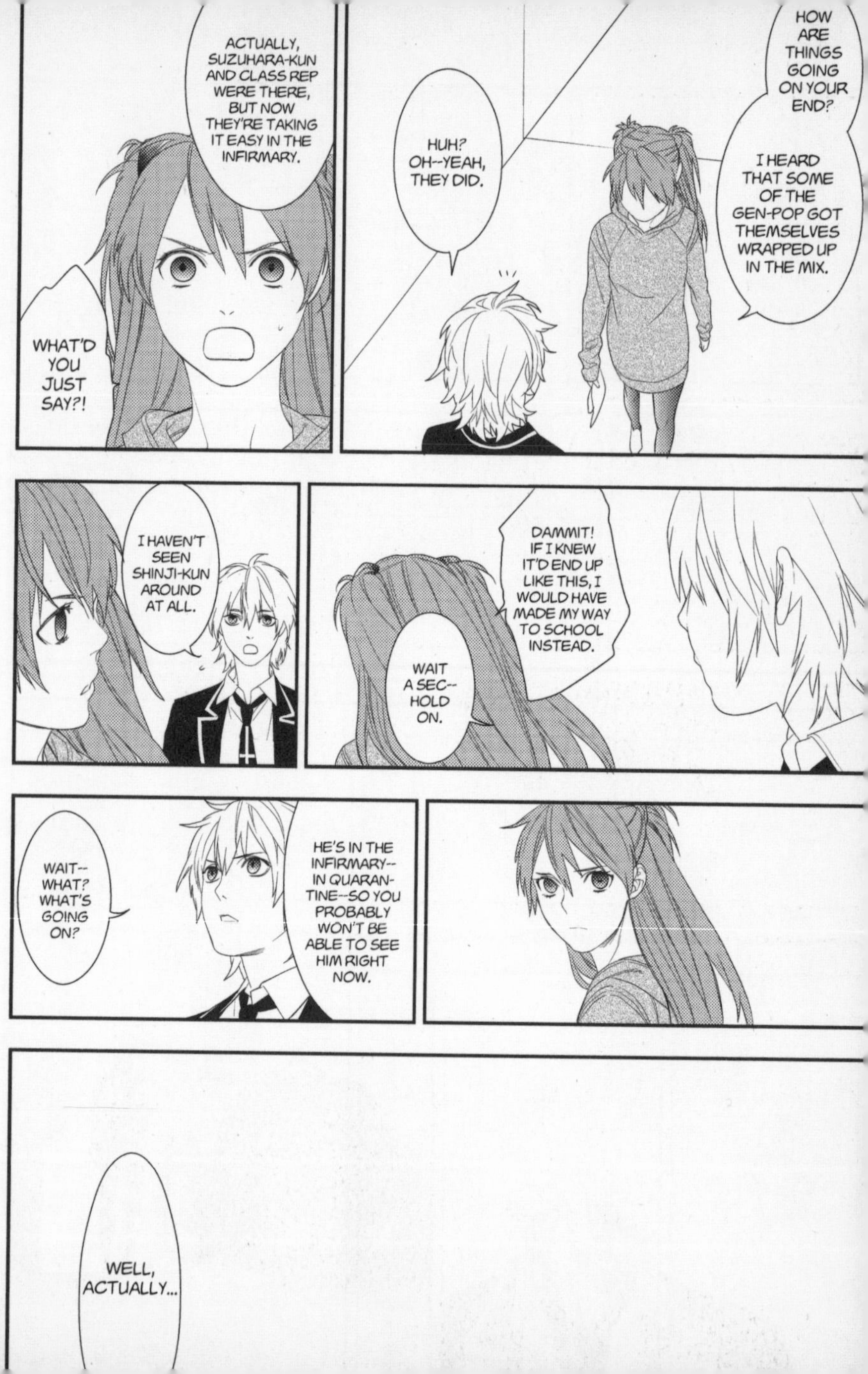
HOW ARE THINGS GOING ON YOUR END?
I HEARD THAT SOME OF THE GEN-POP GOT THEMSELVES WRAPPED UP IN THE MIX.
HUH? OH--YEAH, THEY DID.
ACTUALLY, SUZUHARA-KUN AND CLASS REP WERE THERE, BUT NOW THEY'RE TAKING IT EASY IN THE INFIRMARY.
WHAT'D YOU JUST SAY?!
DAMMIT! IF I KNEW IT'D END UP LIKE THIS, I WOULD HAVE MADE MY WAY TO SCHOOL INSTEAD.
WAIT A SEC-- HOLD ON.
I HAVEN'T SEEN SHINJI-KUN AROUND AT ALL.
HE'S IN THE INFIRMARY-- IN QUARAN-TINE--SO YOU PROBABLY WON'T BE ABLE TO SEE HIM RIGHT NOW.
WAIT-- WHAT? WHAT'S GOING ON?
WELL, ACTUALLY...

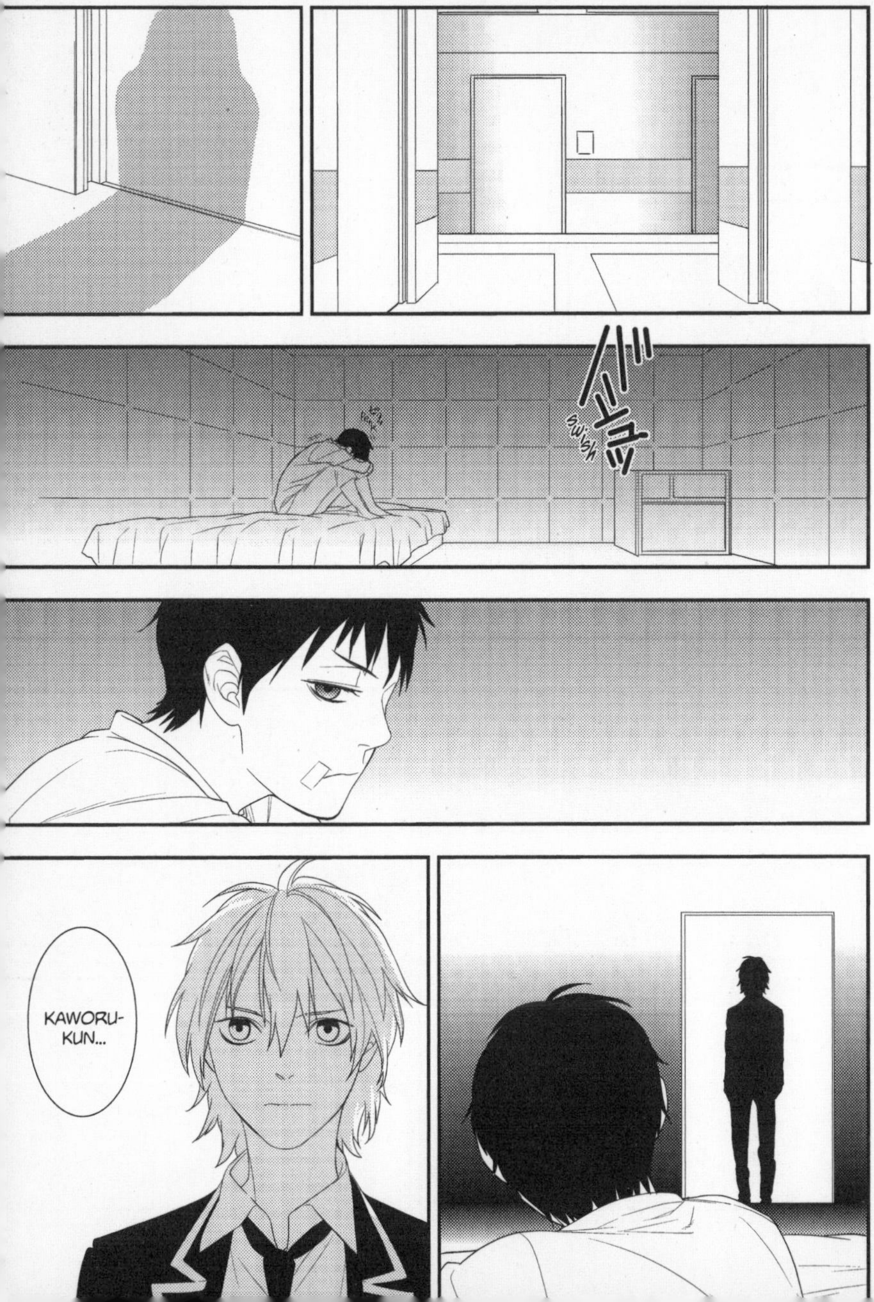
swish
KAWORU-KUN...

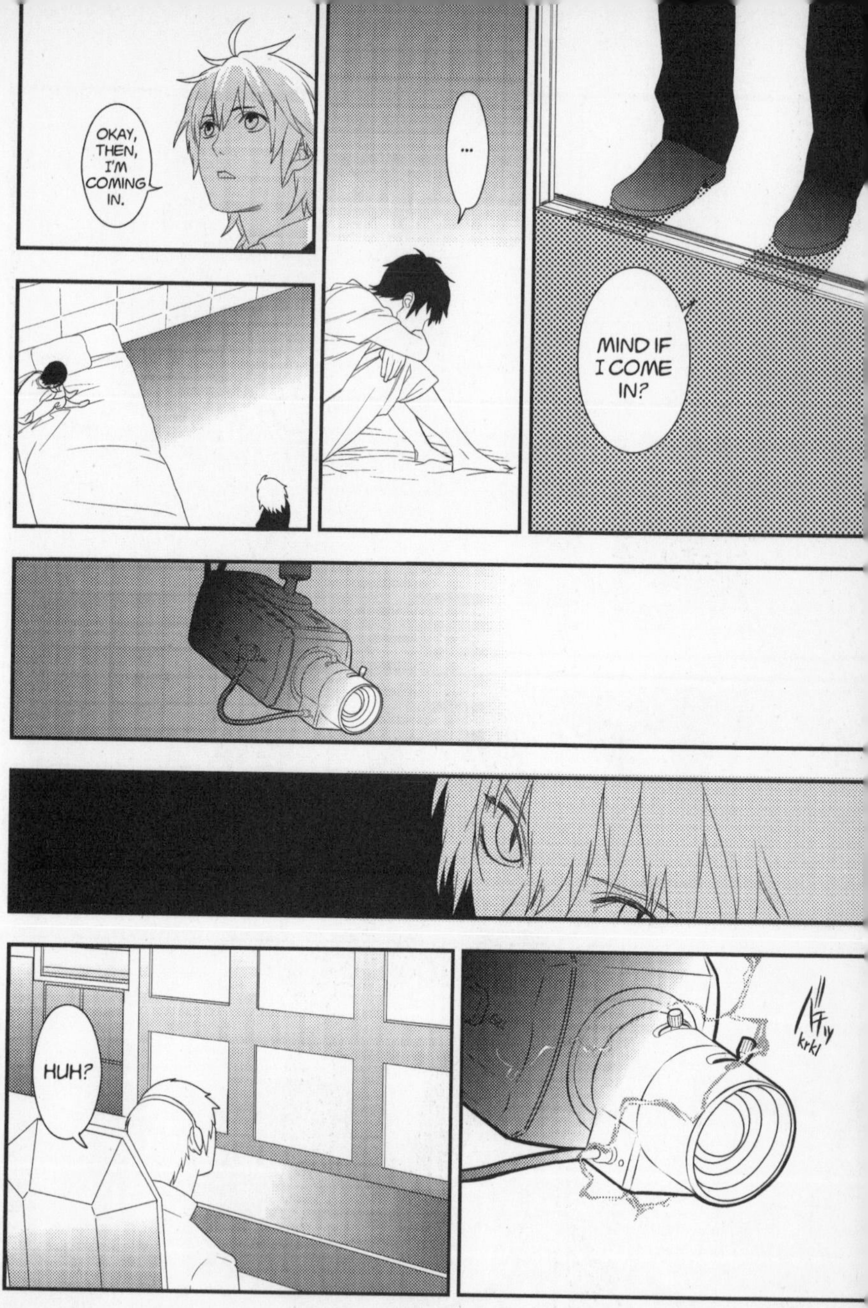
MIND IF I COME IN?
...
OKAY, THEN, I'M COMING IN.
krkl
HUH?

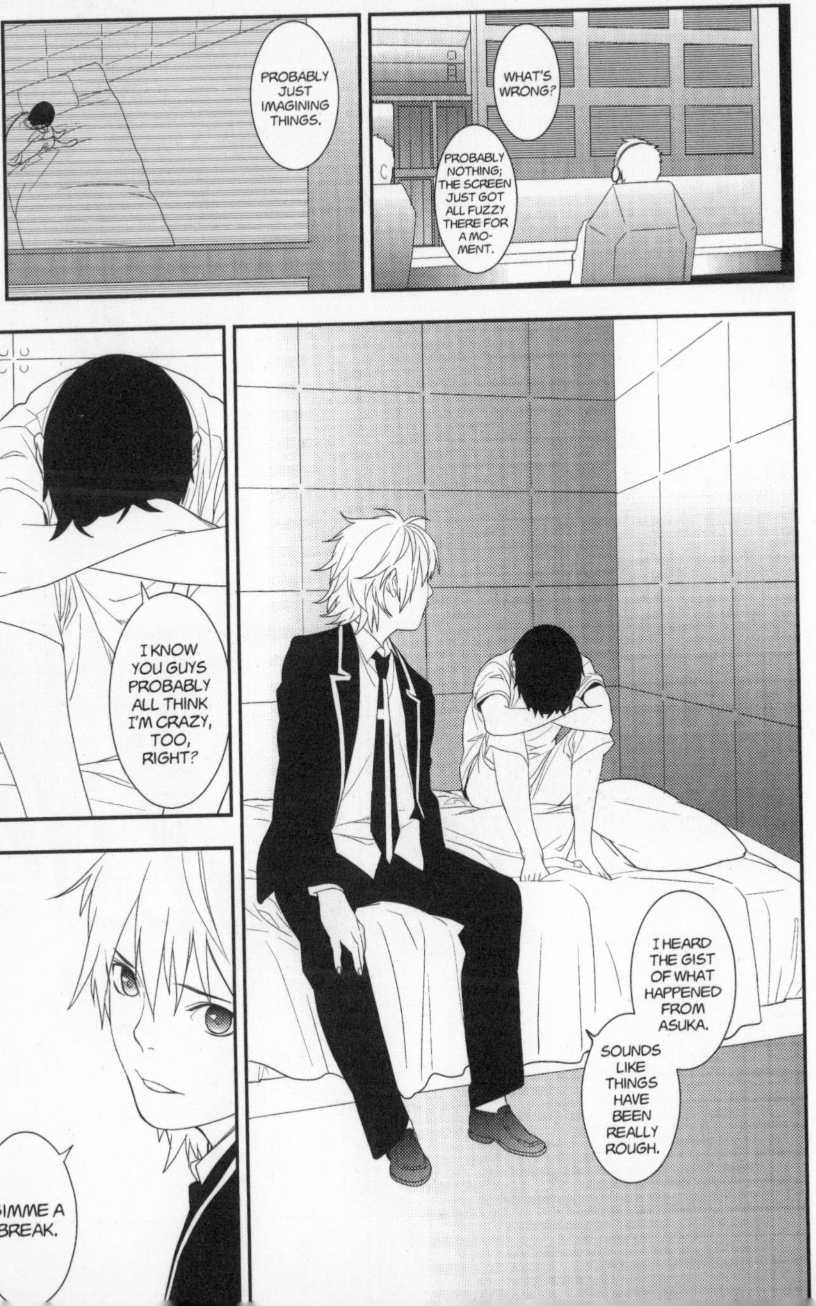
WHAT'S WRONG?
PROBABLY NOTHING; THE SCREEN JUST GOT ALL FUZZY THERE FOR A MO-MENT.
PROBABLY JUST IMAGINING THINGS.
I HEARD THE GIST OF WHAT HAPPENED FROM ASUKA.
SOUNDS LIKE THINGS HAVE BEEN REALLY ROUGH.
I KNOW YOU GUYS PROBABLY ALL THINK I'M CRAZY, TOO, RIGHT?
GIMME A BREAK.

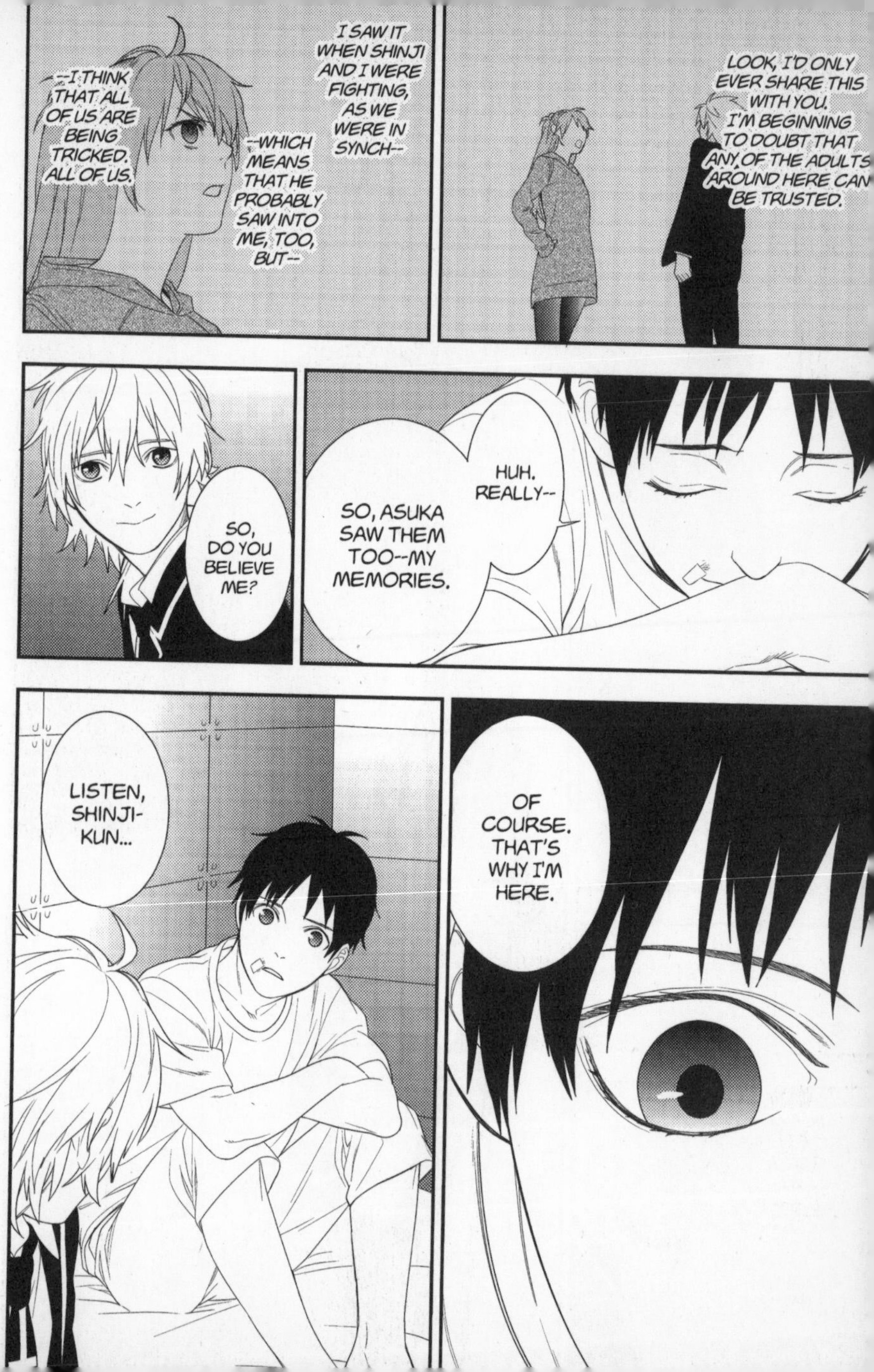
LOOK, I'D ONLY EVER SHARE THIS WITH YOU. I'M BEGINNING TO DOUBT THAT ANY OF THE ADULTS AROUND HERE CAN BE TRUSTED.
I SAW IT WHEN SHINJI AND I WERE FIGHTING, AS WE WERE IN SYNCH--
--WHICH MEANS THAT HE PROBABLY SAW INTO ME, TOO, BUT--
--I THINK THAT ALL OF US ARE BEING TRICKED. ALL OF US.
HUH. REALLY--
SO, ASUKA SAW THEM TOO--MY MEMORIES.
SO, DO YOU BELIEVE ME?
OF COURSE. THAT'S WHY I'M HERE.
LISTEN, SHINJI-KUN...

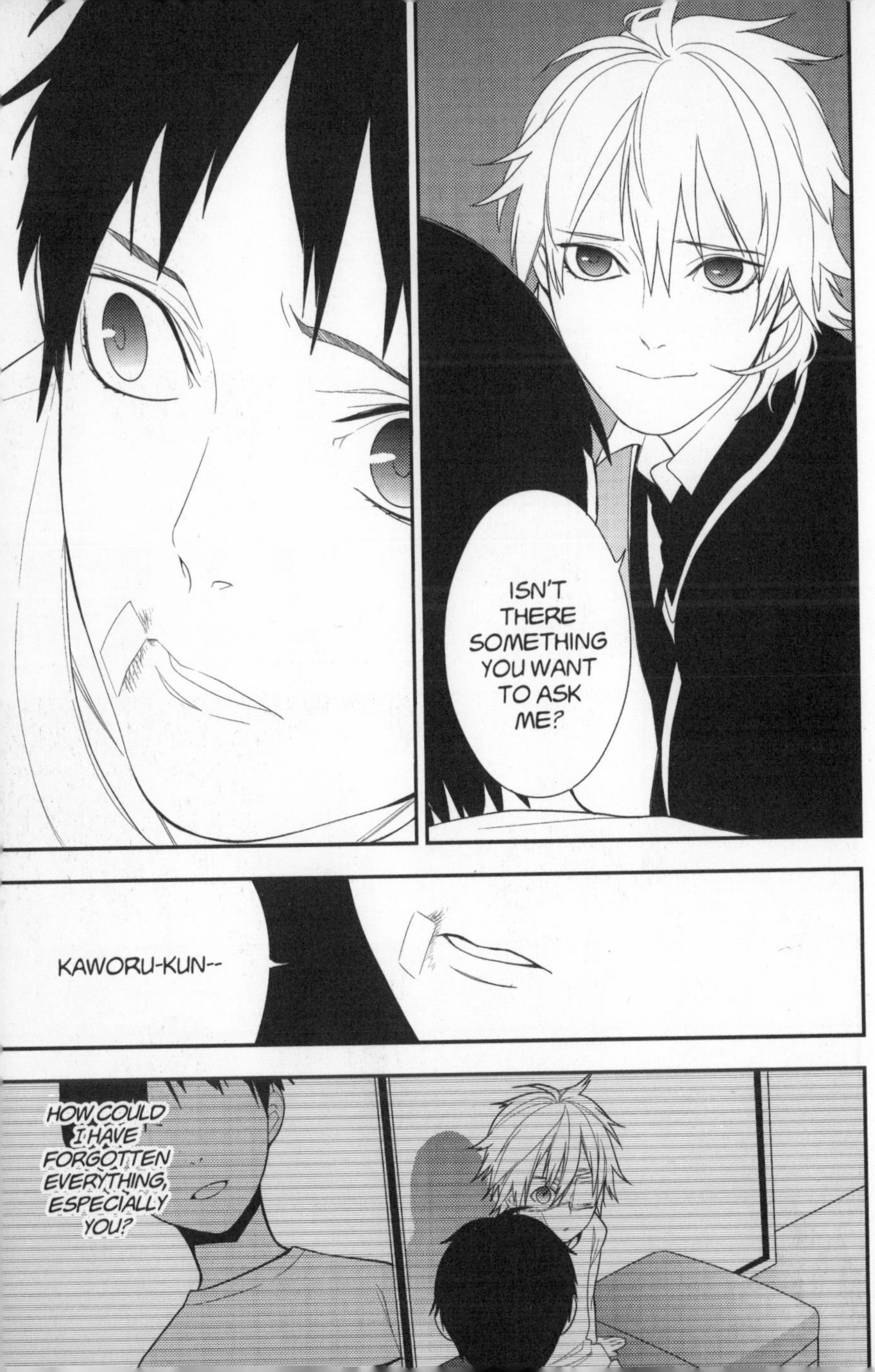
ISN'T THERE SOMETHING YOU WANT TO ASK ME?
KAWORU-KUN--
HOW COULD I HAVE FORGOTTEN EVERYTHING, ESPECIALLY YOU?

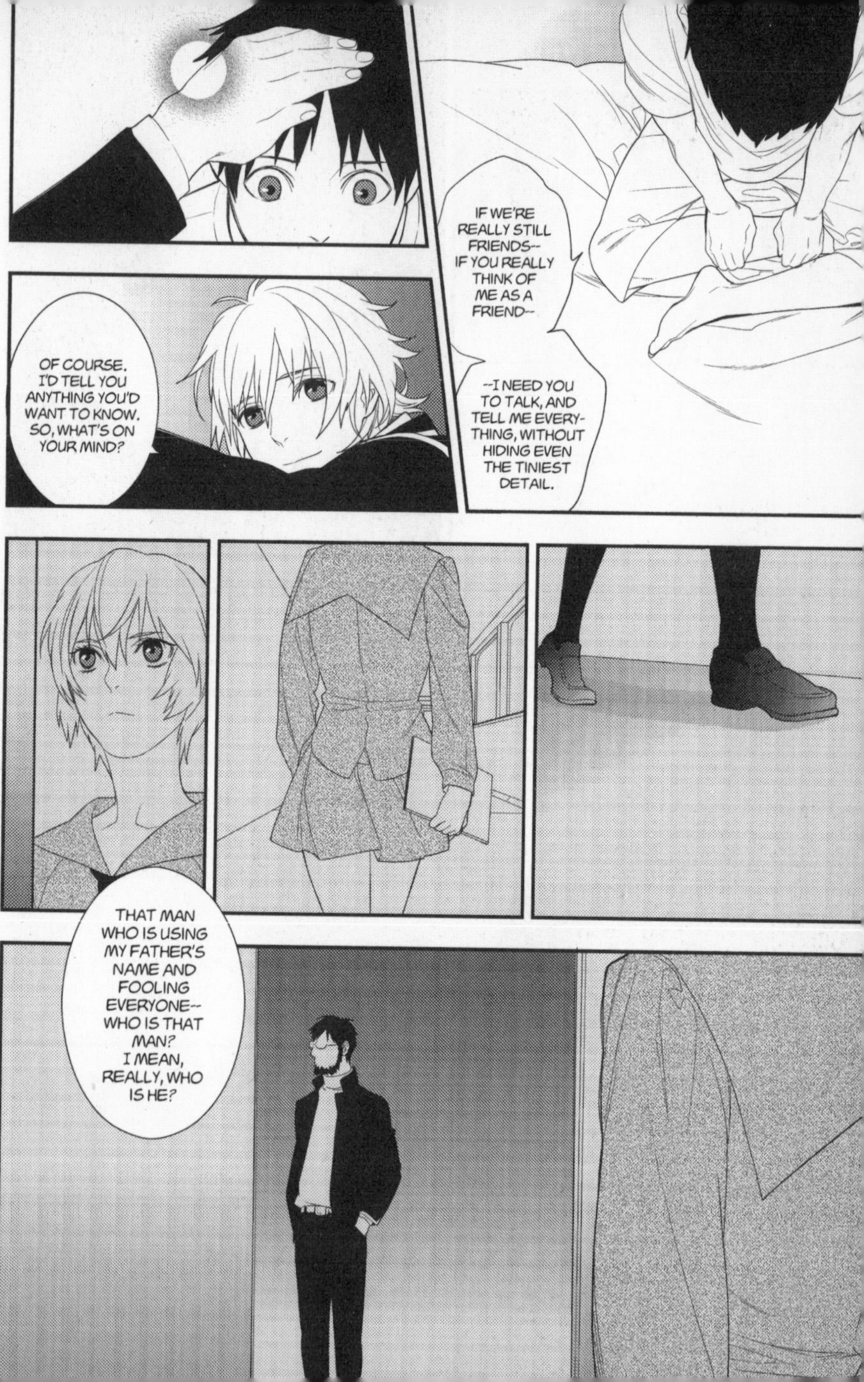
IF WE'RE REALLY STILL FRIENDS-- IF YOU REALLY THINK OF ME AS A FRIEND--
--I NEED YOU TO TALK, AND TELL ME EVERYTHING, WITHOUT HIDING EVEN THE TINIEST DETAIL.
OF COURSE. I'D TELL YOU ANYTHING YOU'D WANT TO KNOW. SO, WHAT'S ON YOUR MIND?
THAT MAN WHO IS USING MY FATHER'S NAME AND FOOLING EVERYONE-- WHO IS THAT MAN? I MEAN, REALLY, WHO IS HE?

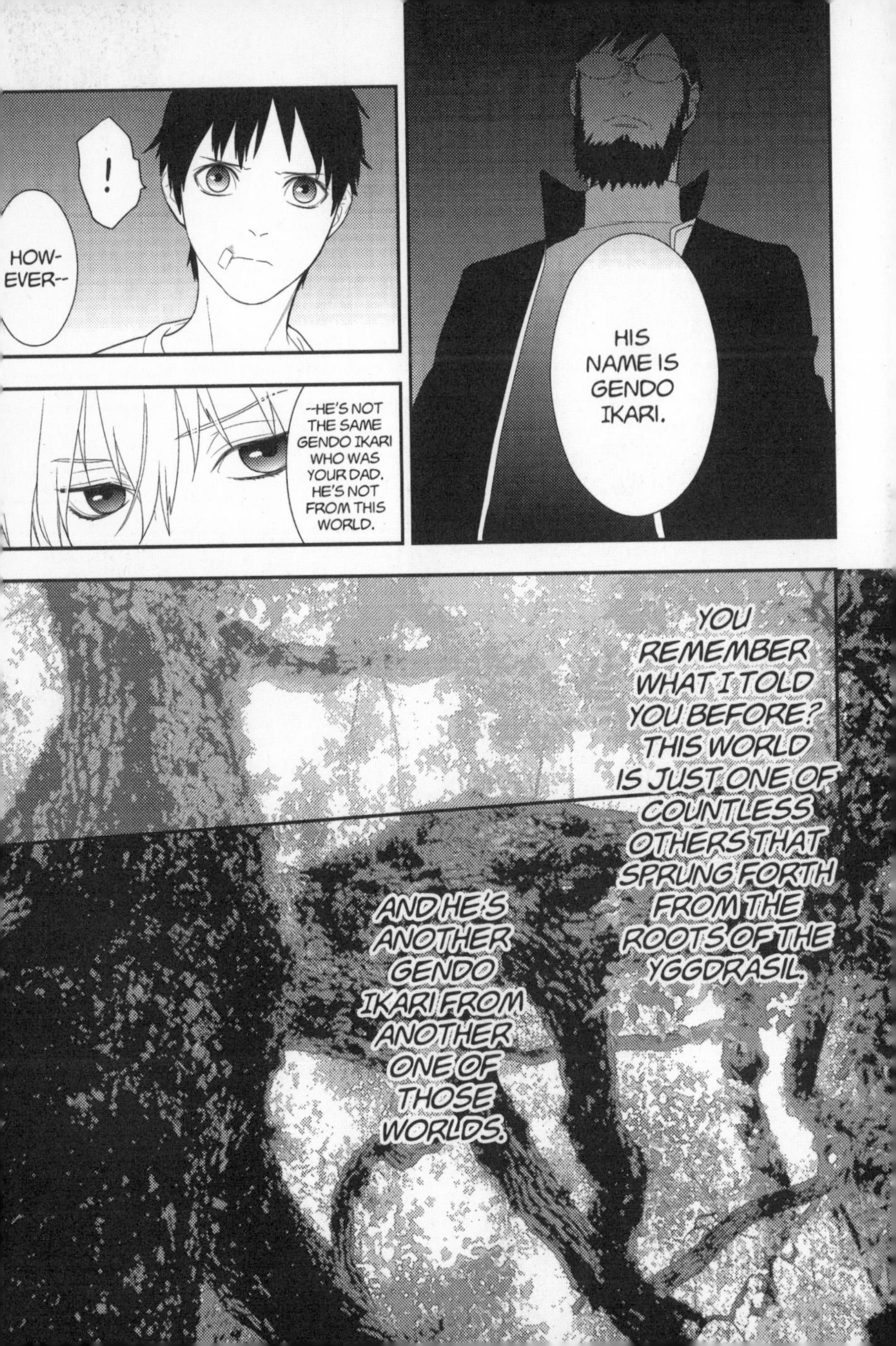
HIS NAME IS GENDO IKARI.
!
HOW-EVER--
--HE'S NOT THE SAME GENDO IKARI WHO WAS YOUR DAD. HE'S NOT FROM THIS WORLD.
YOU REMEMBER WHAT I TOLD YOU BEFORE? THIS WORLD IS JUST ONE OF COUNTLESS OTHERS THAT SPRUNG FORTH FROM THE ROOTS OF THE YGGDRASIL.
AND HE'S ANOTHER GENDO IKARI FROM ANOTHER ONE OF THOSE WORLDS.

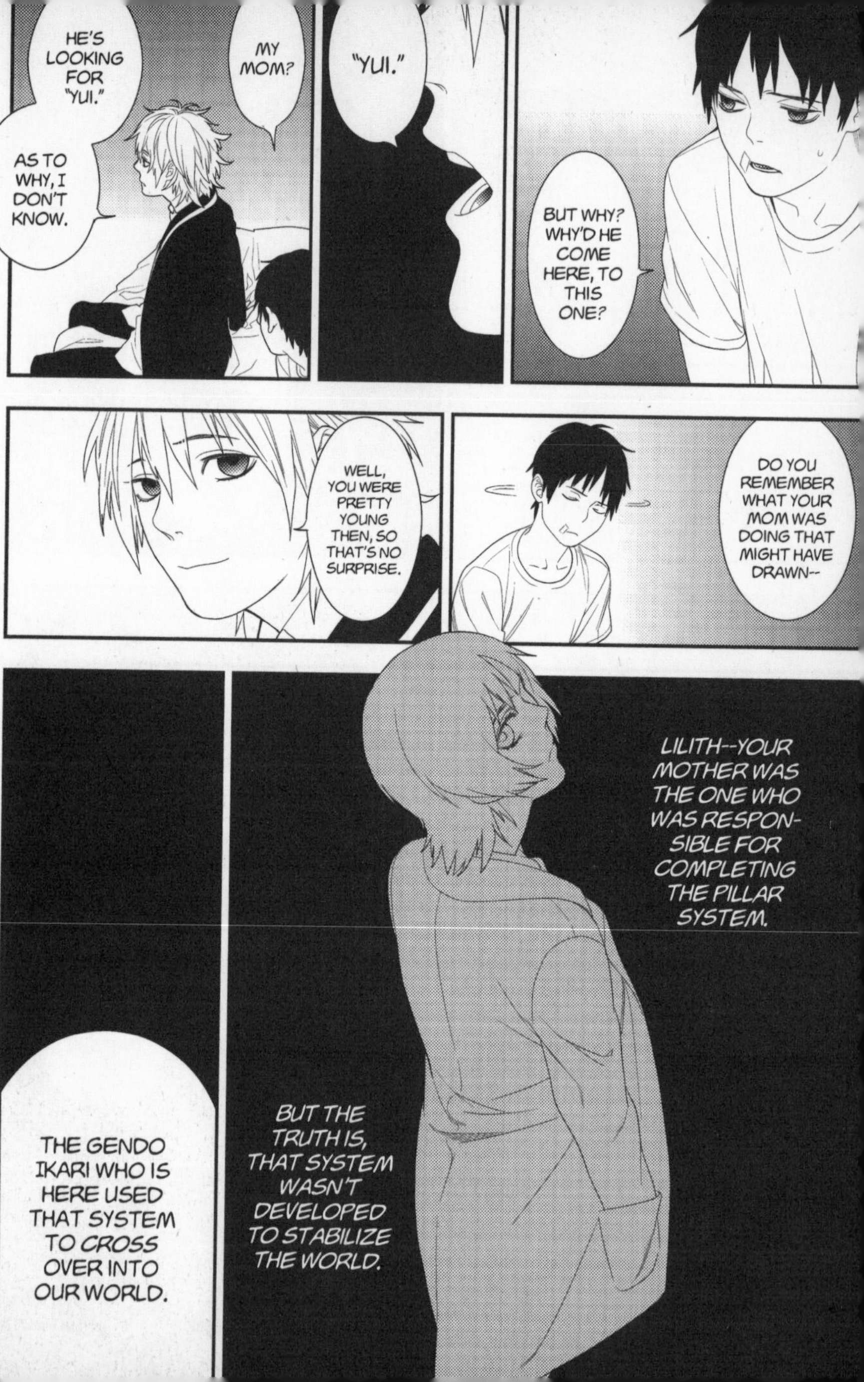
BUT WHY? WHY'D HE COME HERE, TO THIS ONE?
"YUI."
MY MOM?
HE'S LOOKING FOR "YUI."
AS TO WHY, I DON'T KNOW.
DO YOU REMEMBER WHAT YOUR MOM WAS DOING THAT MIGHT HAVE DRAWN--
WELL, YOU WERE PRETTY YOUNG THEN, SO THAT'S NO SURPRISE.
LILITH--YOUR MOTHER WAS THE ONE WHO WAS RESPON-SIBLE FOR COMPLETING THE PILLAR SYSTEM.
BUT THE TRUTH IS, THAT SYSTEM WASN'T DEVELOPED TO STABILIZE THE WORLD.
THE GENDO IKARI WHO IS HERE USED THAT SYSTEM TO *CROSS OVER* INTO OUR WORLD.

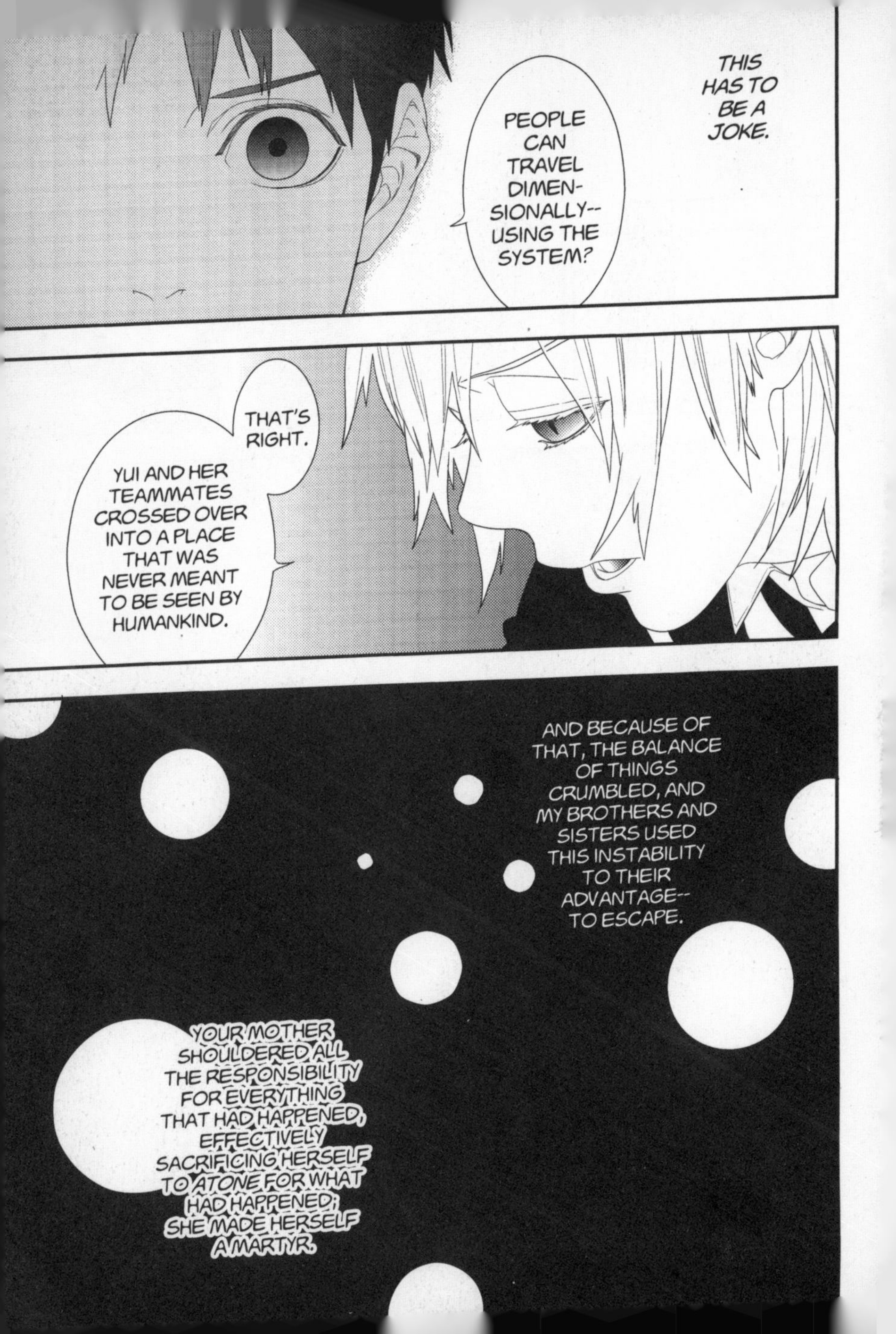
THIS HAS TO BE A JOKE.
PEOPLE CAN TRAVEL DIMEN-SIONALLY-- USING THE SYSTEM?
THAT'S RIGHT.
YUI AND HER TEAMMATES CROSSED OVER INTO A PLACE THAT WAS NEVER MEANT TO BE SEEN BY HUMANKIND.
AND BECAUSE OF THAT, THE BALANCE OF THINGS CRUMBLED, AND MY BROTHERS AND SISTERS USED THIS INSTABILITY TO THEIR ADVANTAGE-- TO ESCAPE.
YOUR MOTHER SHOULDERED ALL THE RESPONSIBILITY FOR EVERYTHING THAT HAD HAPPENED, EFFECTIVELY SACRIFICING HERSELF TO ATONE FOR WHAT HAD HAPPENED; SHE MADE HERSELF A MARTYR.

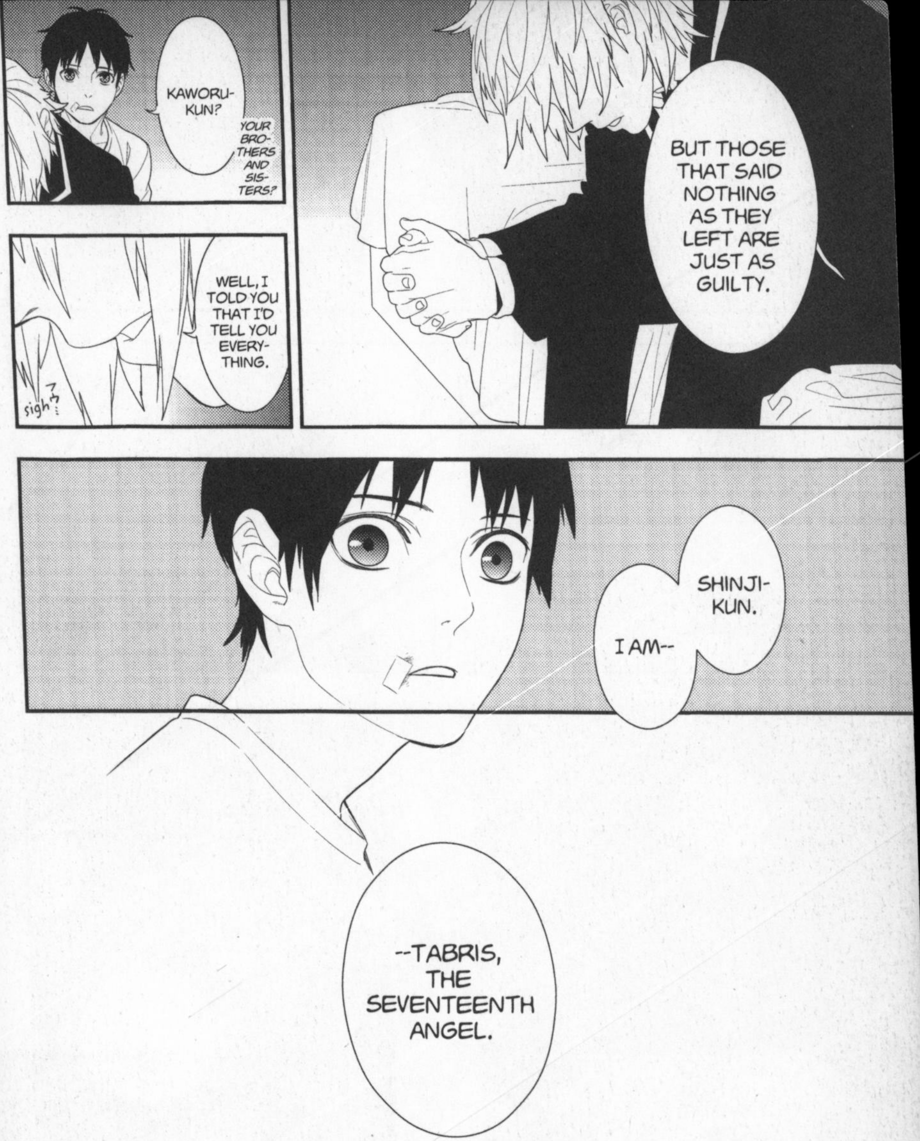
BUT THOSE THAT SAID NOTHING AS THEY LEFT ARE JUST AS GUILTY.
KAWORU-KUN?
YOUR BROTHERS AND SISTERS?
WELL, I TOLD YOU THAT I'D TELL YOU EVERYTHING.
sigh
SHINJI-KUN.
I AM--
--TABRIS, THE SEVENTEENTH ANGEL.

END

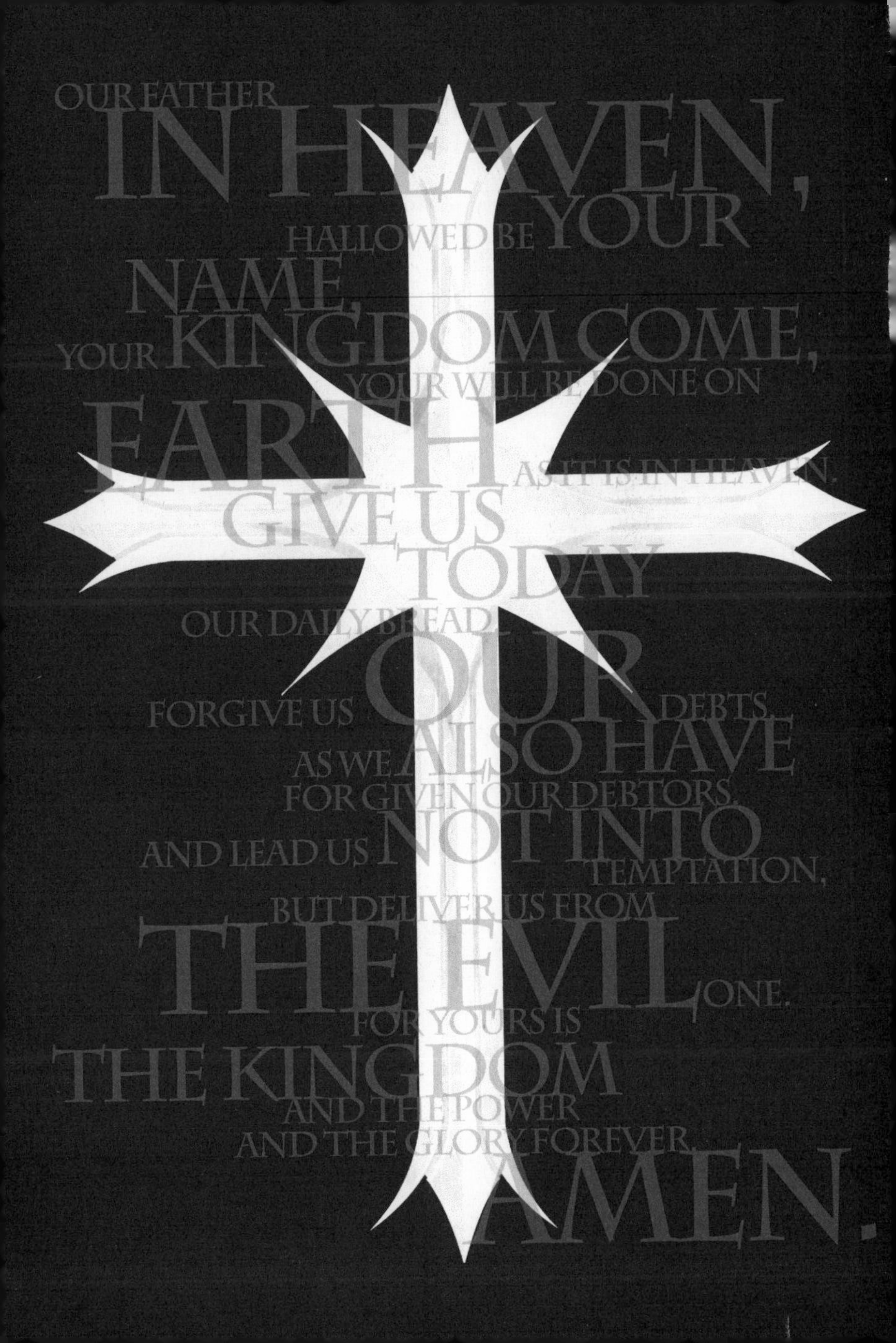
OUR FATHER
IN HEAVEN,
HALLOWED BE YOUR
NAME,
YOUR KINGDOM COME,
YOUR WILL BE DONE ON
EARTH AS IT IS IN HEAVEN.
GIVE US
TODAY
OUR DAILY BREAD.
FORGIVE US OUR DEBTS,
AS WE ALSO HAVE
FORGIVEN OUR DEBTORS.
AND LEAD US NOT INTO
TEMPTATION,
BUT DELIVER US FROM
THE EVIL ONE.
FOR YOURS IS
THE KINGDOM
AND THE POWER
AND THE GLORY FOREVER.
AMEN.

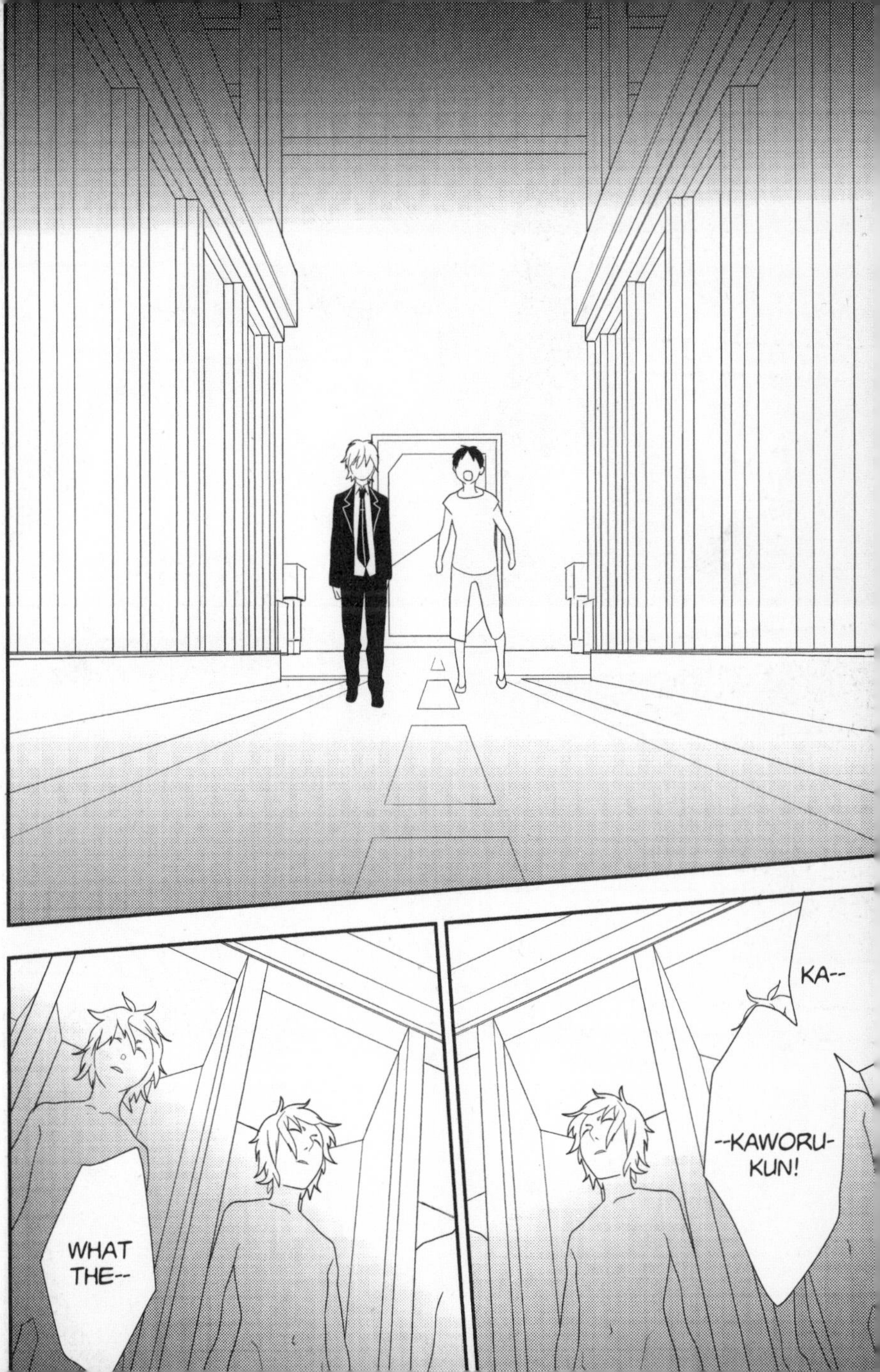
KA--
--KAWORU-KUN!
WHAT THE--

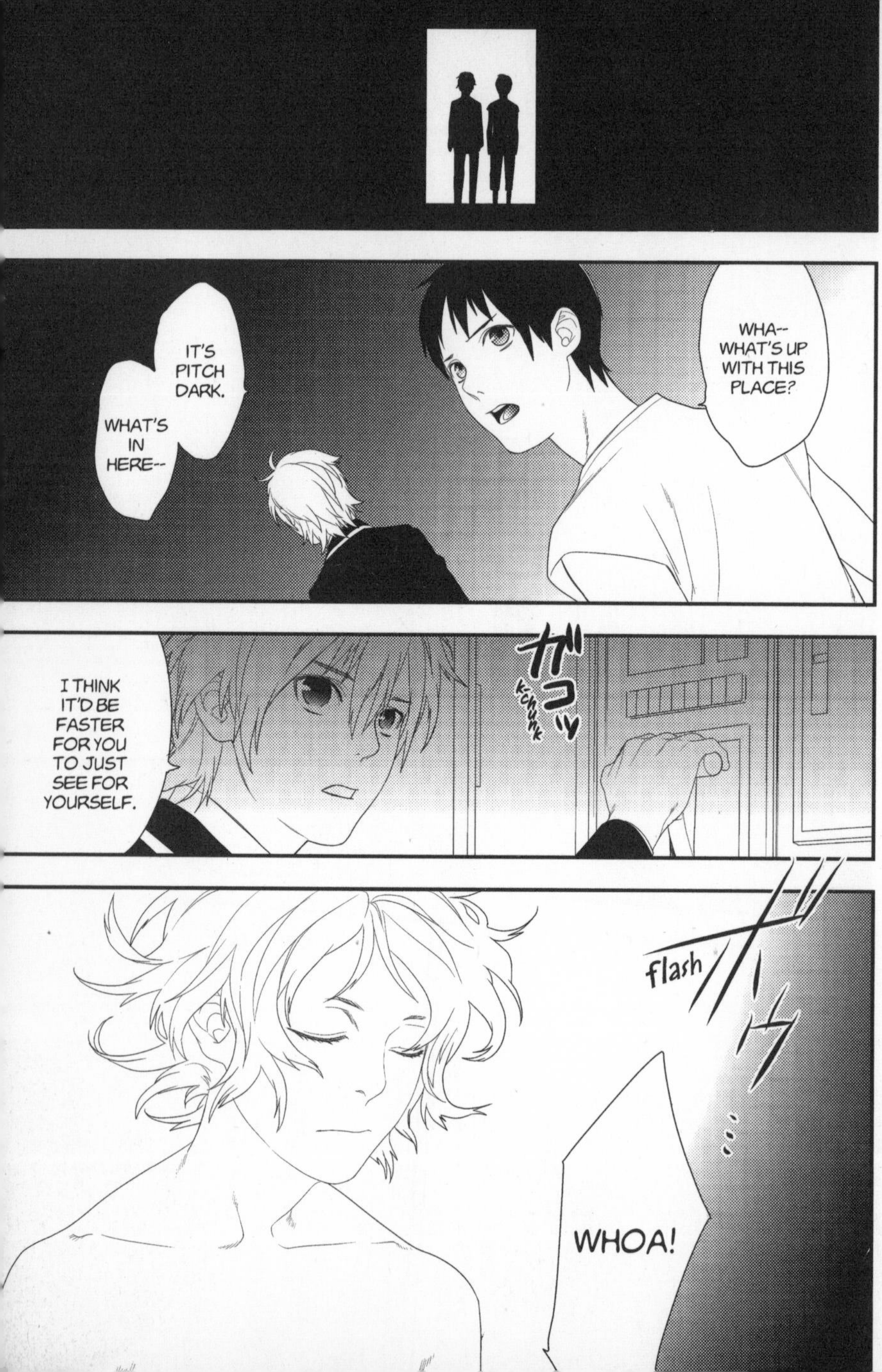
WHA-- WHAT'S UP WITH THIS PLACE?
IT'S PITCH DARK.
WHAT'S IN HERE--
ガコッ
k-chunk
I THINK IT'D BE FASTER FOR YOU TO JUST SEE FOR YOURSELF.
flash
WHOA!

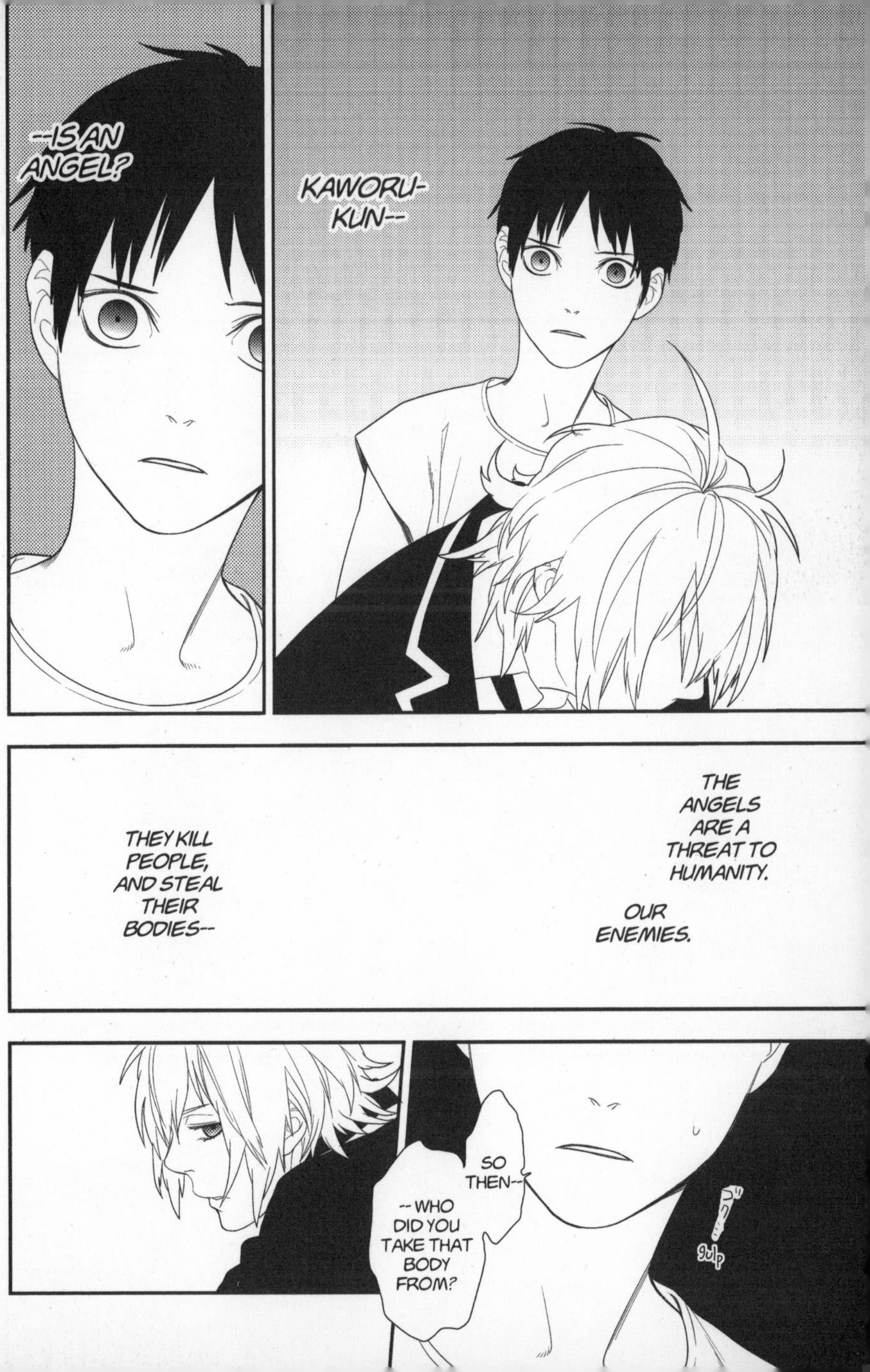
KAWORU-KUN--
--IS AN ANGEL?
THE ANGELS ARE A THREAT TO HUMANITY.
OUR ENEMIES.
THEY KILL PEOPLE, AND STEAL THEIR BODIES--
SO THEN--
--WHO DID YOU TAKE THAT BODY FROM?
gulp

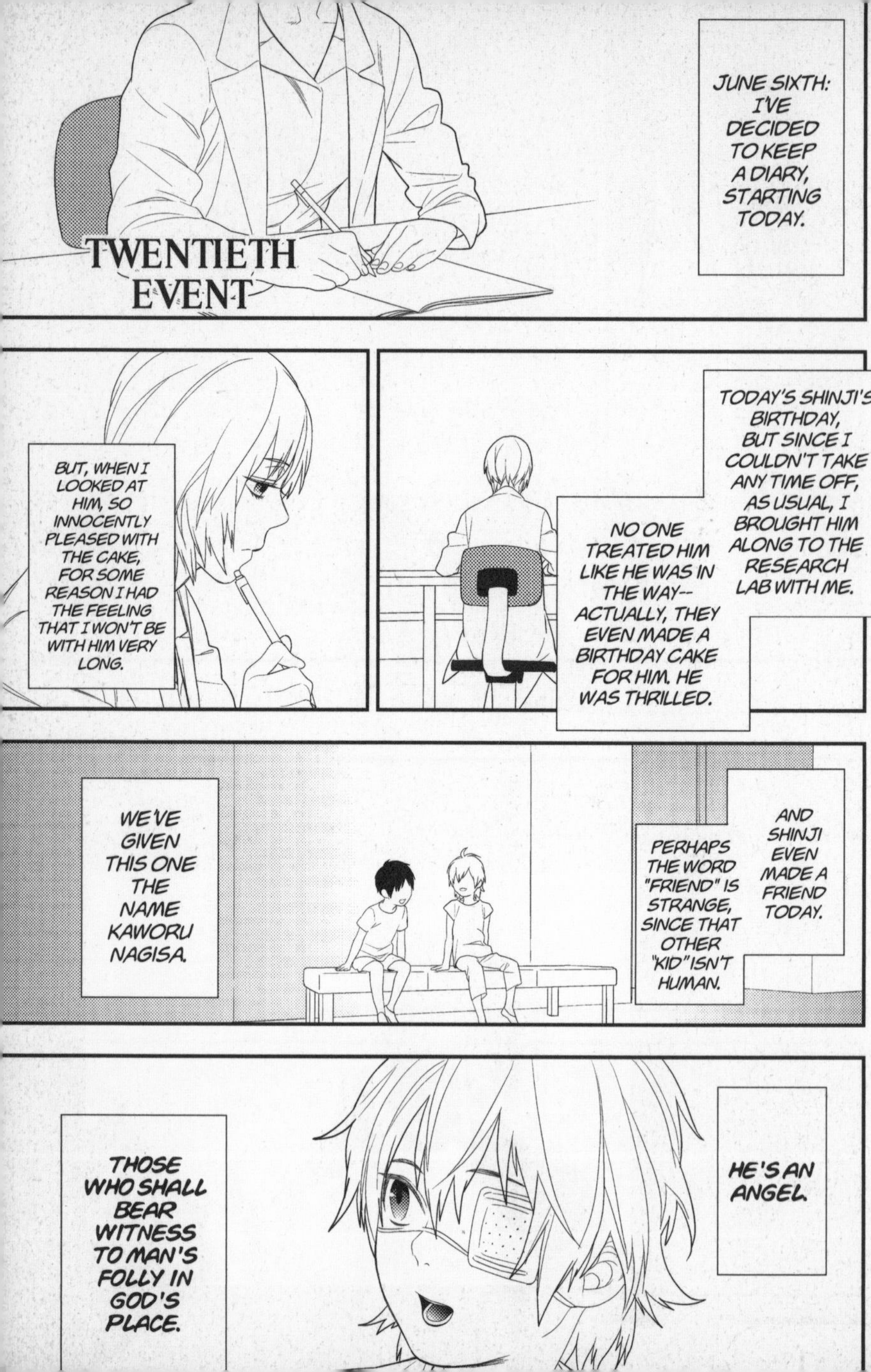
JUNE SIXTH: I'VE DECIDED TO KEEP A DIARY, STARTING TODAY.
TWENTIETH EVENT
TODAY'S SHINJI'S BIRTHDAY, BUT SINCE I COULDN'T TAKE ANY TIME OFF, AS USUAL, I BROUGHT HIM ALONG TO THE RESEARCH LAB WITH ME.
NO ONE TREATED HIM LIKE HE WAS IN THE WAY-- ACTUALLY, THEY EVEN MADE A BIRTHDAY CAKE FOR HIM. HE WAS THRILLED.
BUT, WHEN I LOOKED AT HIM, SO INNOCENTLY PLEASED WITH THE CAKE, FOR SOME REASON I HAD THE FEELING THAT I WON'T BE WITH HIM VERY LONG.
AND SHINJI EVEN MADE A FRIEND TODAY.
PERHAPS THE WORD "FRIEND" IS STRANGE, SINCE THAT OTHER "KID" ISN'T HUMAN.
WE'VE GIVEN THIS ONE THE NAME KAWORU NAGISA.
HE'S AN ANGEL.
THOSE WHO SHALL BEAR WITNESS TO MAN'S FOLLY IN GOD'S PLACE.

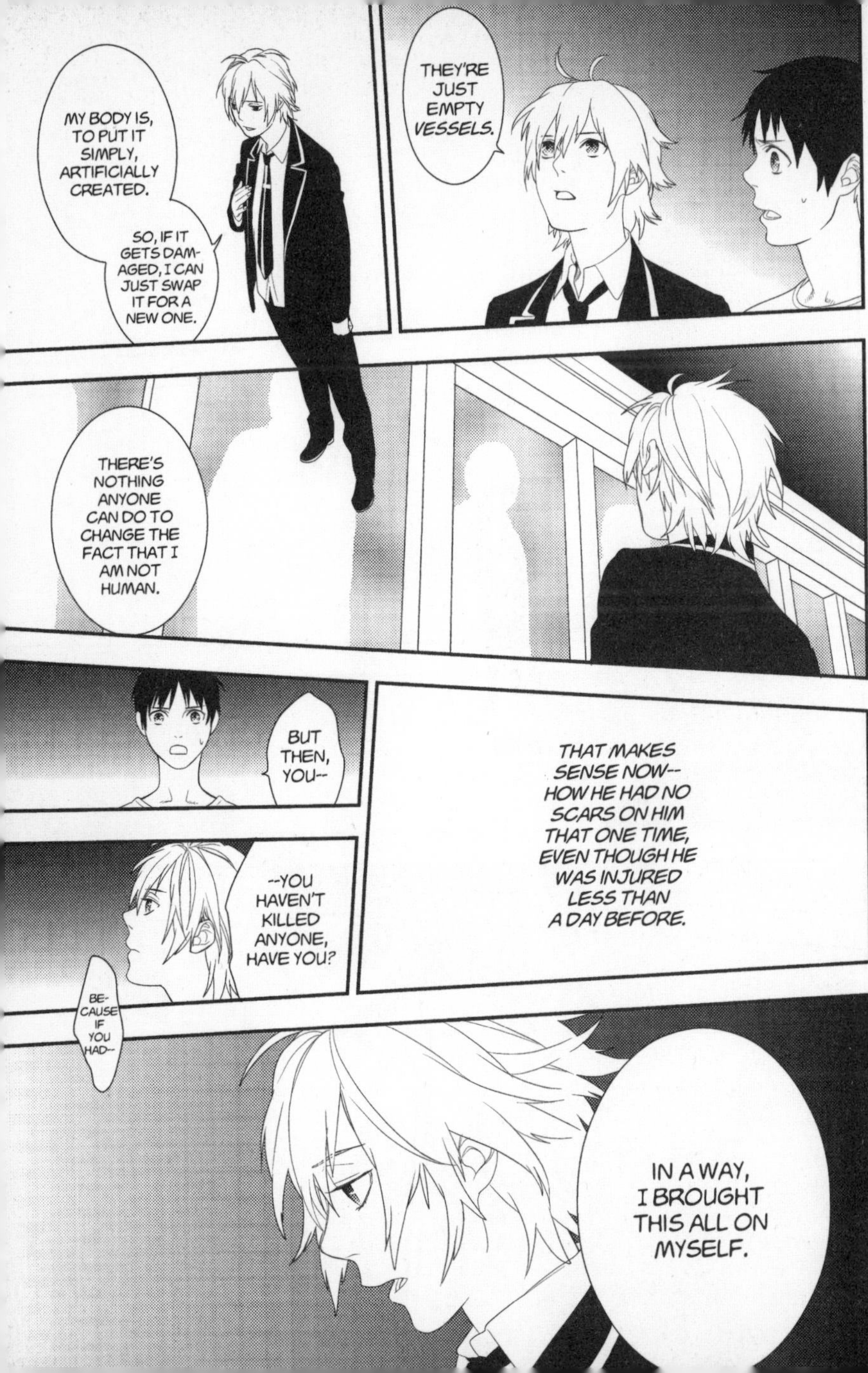
THEY'RE JUST EMPTY VESSELS.
MY BODY IS, TO PUT IT SIMPLY, ARTIFICIALLY CREATED.
SO, IF IT GETS DAM-AGED, I CAN JUST SWAP IT FOR A NEW ONE.
THERE'S NOTHING ANYONE CAN DO TO CHANGE THE FACT THAT I AM NOT HUMAN.
THAT MAKES SENSE NOW-- HOW HE HAD NO SCARS ON HIM THAT ONE TIME, EVEN THOUGH HE WAS INJURED LESS THAN A DAY BEFORE.
BUT THEN, YOU--
--YOU HAVEN'T KILLED ANYONE, HAVE YOU?
BE-CAUSE IF YOU HAD--
IN A WAY, I BROUGHT THIS ALL ON MYSELF.

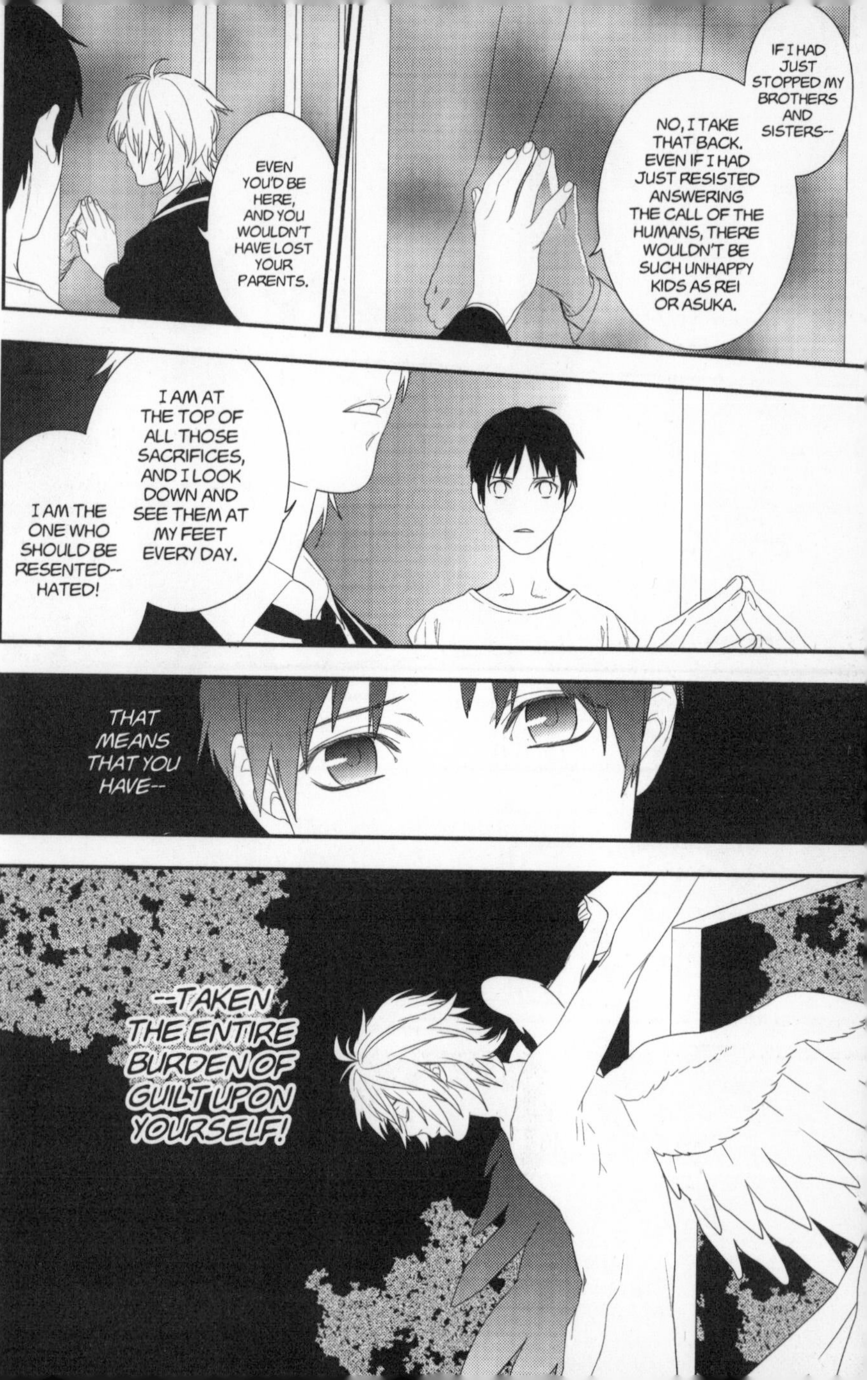
IF I HAD JUST STOPPED MY BROTHERS AND SISTERS--
NO, I TAKE THAT BACK. EVEN IF I HAD JUST RESISTED ANSWERING THE CALL OF THE HUMANS, THERE WOULDN'T BE SUCH UNHAPPY KIDS AS REI OR ASUKA.
EVEN YOU'D BE HERE, AND YOU WOULDN'T HAVE LOST YOUR PARENTS.
I AM AT THE TOP OF ALL THOSE SACRIFICES, AND I LOOK DOWN AND SEE THEM AT MY FEET EVERY DAY.
I AM THE ONE WHO SHOULD BE RESENTED--HATED!
THAT MEANS THAT YOU HAVE--
--TAKEN THE ENTIRE BURDEN OF GUILT UPON YOURSELF!

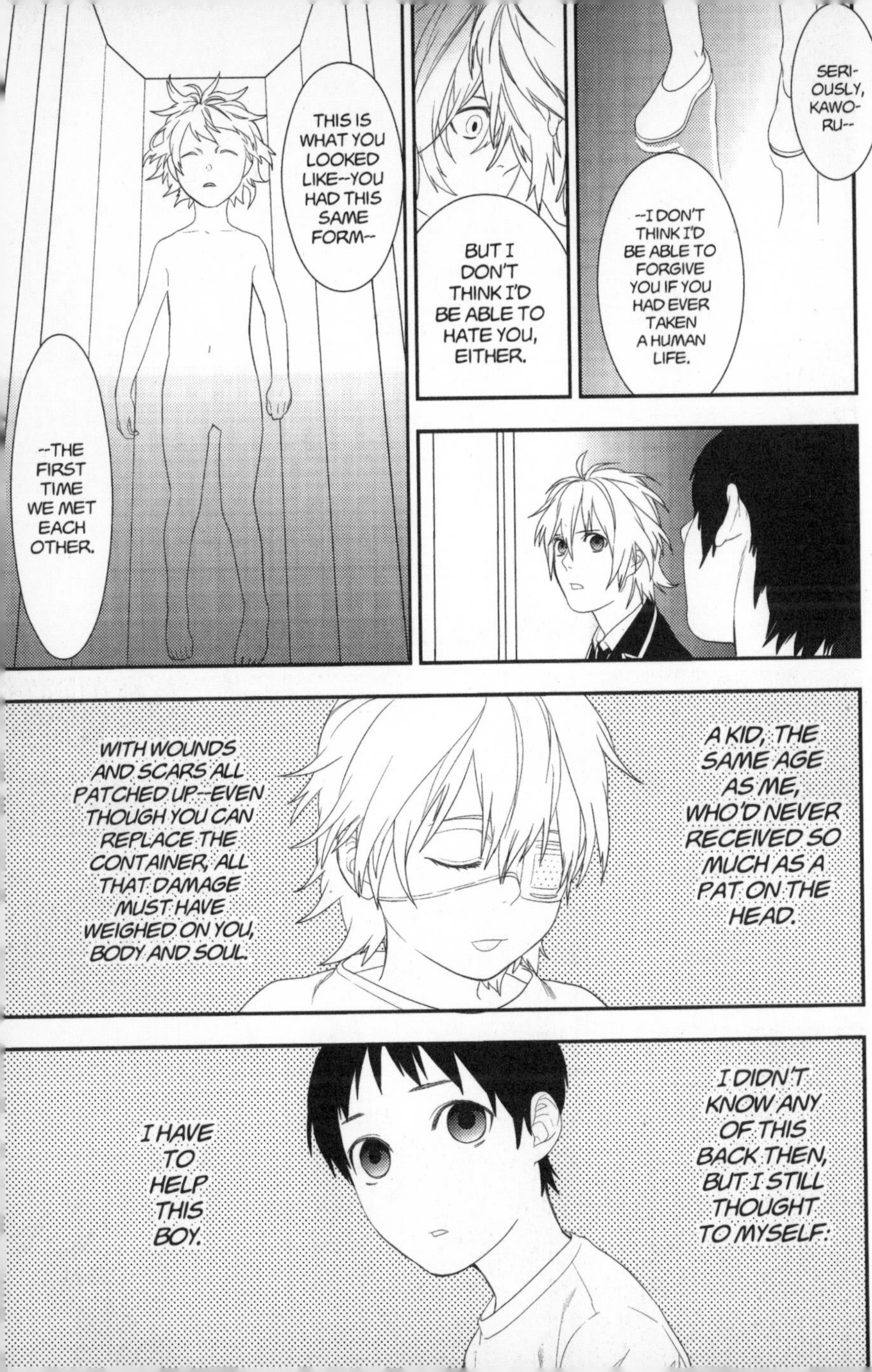
SERI-OUSLY, KAWO-RU--
--I DON'T THINK I'D BE ABLE TO FORGIVE YOU IF YOU HAD EVER TAKEN A HUMAN LIFE.
BUT I DON'T THINK I'D BE ABLE TO HATE YOU, EITHER.
THIS IS WHAT YOU LOOKED LIKE--YOU HAD THIS SAME FORM--
--THE FIRST TIME WE MET EACH OTHER.
A KID, THE SAME AGE AS ME, WHO'D NEVER RECEIVED SO MUCH AS A PAT ON THE HEAD.
WITH WOUNDS AND SCARS ALL PATCHED UP--EVEN THOUGH YOU CAN REPLACE THE CONTAINER, ALL THAT DAMAGE MUST HAVE WEIGHED ON YOU, BODY AND SOUL.
I DIDN'T KNOW ANY OF THIS BACK THEN, BUT I STILL THOUGHT TO MYSELF:
I HAVE TO HELP THIS BOY.

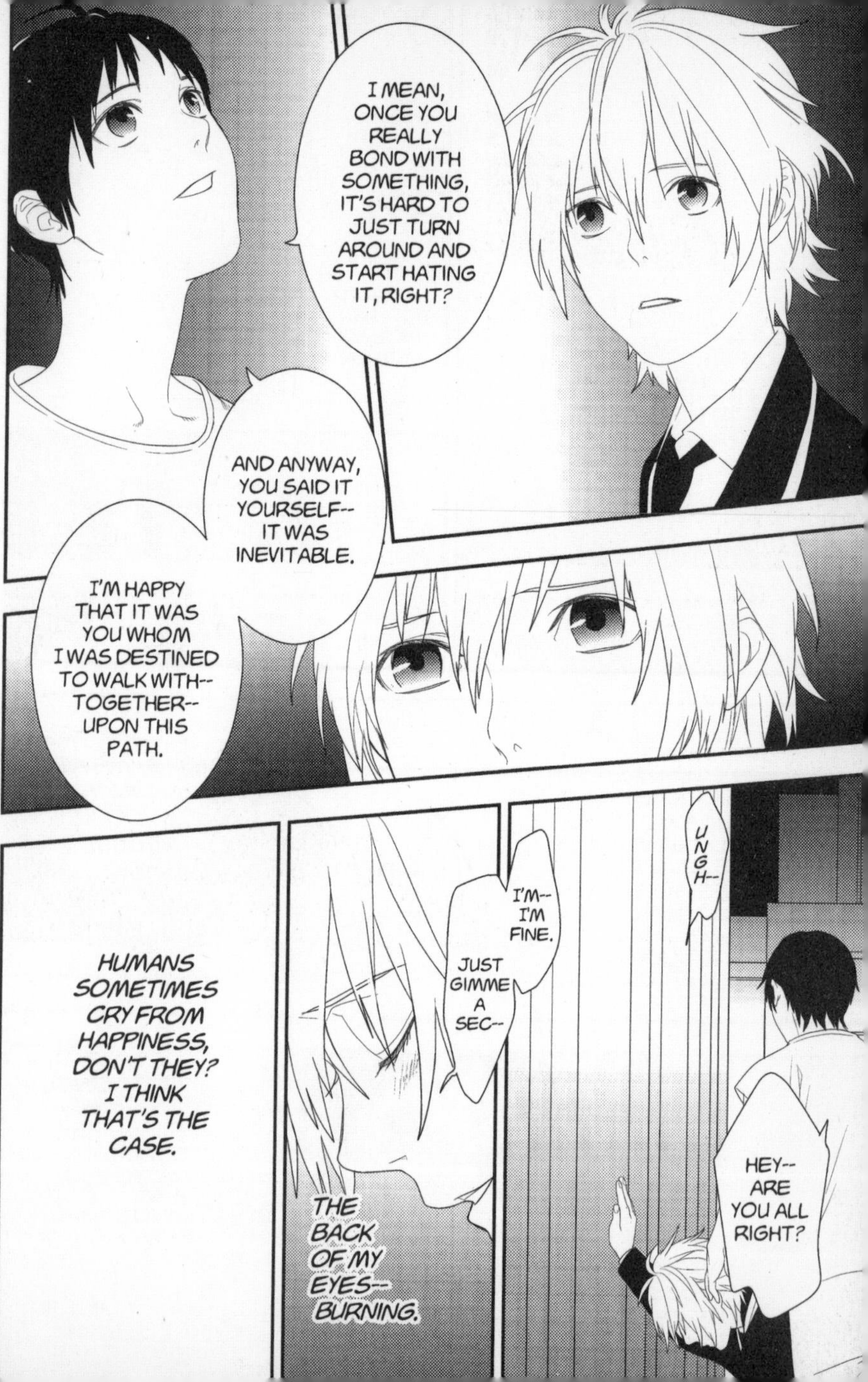
I MEAN, ONCE YOU REALLY BOND WITH SOMETHING, IT'S HARD TO JUST TURN AROUND AND START HATING IT, RIGHT?
AND ANYWAY, YOU SAID IT YOURSELF-- IT WAS INEVITABLE.
I'M HAPPY THAT IT WAS YOU WHOM I WAS DESTINED TO WALK WITH-- TOGETHER-- UPON THIS PATH.
UNGH--
HEY-- ARE YOU ALL RIGHT?
I'M-- I'M FINE.
JUST GIMME A SEC--
THE BACK OF MY EYES-- BURNING.
HUMANS SOMETIMES CRY FROM HAPPINESS, DON'T THEY? I THINK THAT'S THE CASE.

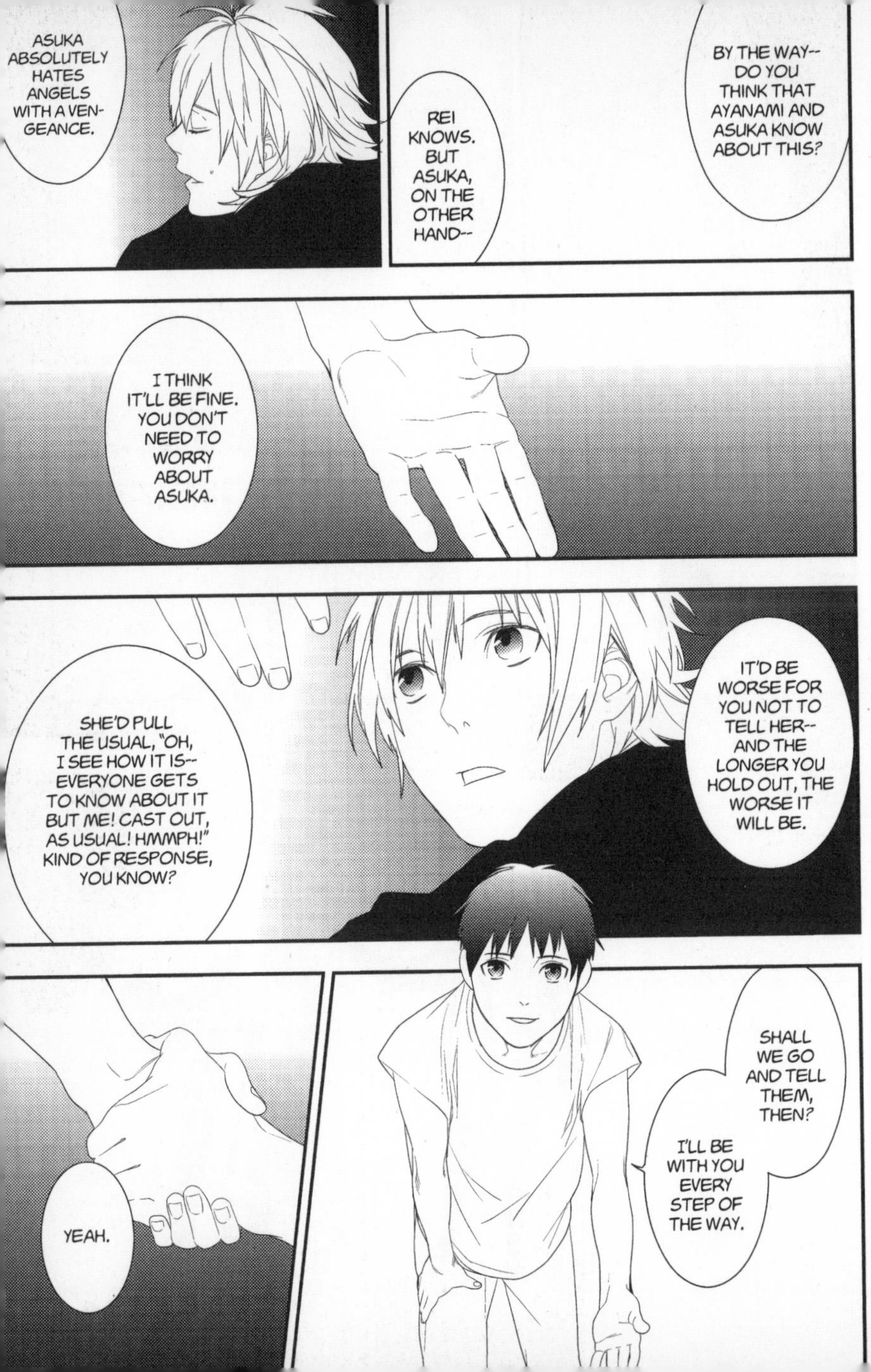
BY THE WAY-- DO YOU THINK THAT AYANAMI AND ASUKA KNOW ABOUT THIS?
REI KNOWS. BUT ASUKA, ON THE OTHER HAND--
ASUKA ABSOLUTELY HATES ANGELS WITH A VEN-GEANCE.
I THINK IT'LL BE FINE. YOU DON'T NEED TO WORRY ABOUT ASUKA.
IT'D BE WORSE FOR YOU NOT TO TELL HER-- AND THE LONGER YOU HOLD OUT, THE WORSE IT WILL BE.
SHE'D PULL THE USUAL, "OH, I SEE HOW IT IS-- EVERYONE GETS TO KNOW ABOUT IT BUT ME! CAST OUT, AS USUAL! HMMPH!" KIND OF RESPONSE, YOU KNOW?
SHALL WE GO AND TELL THEM, THEN?
I'LL BE WITH YOU EVERY STEP OF THE WAY.
YEAH.

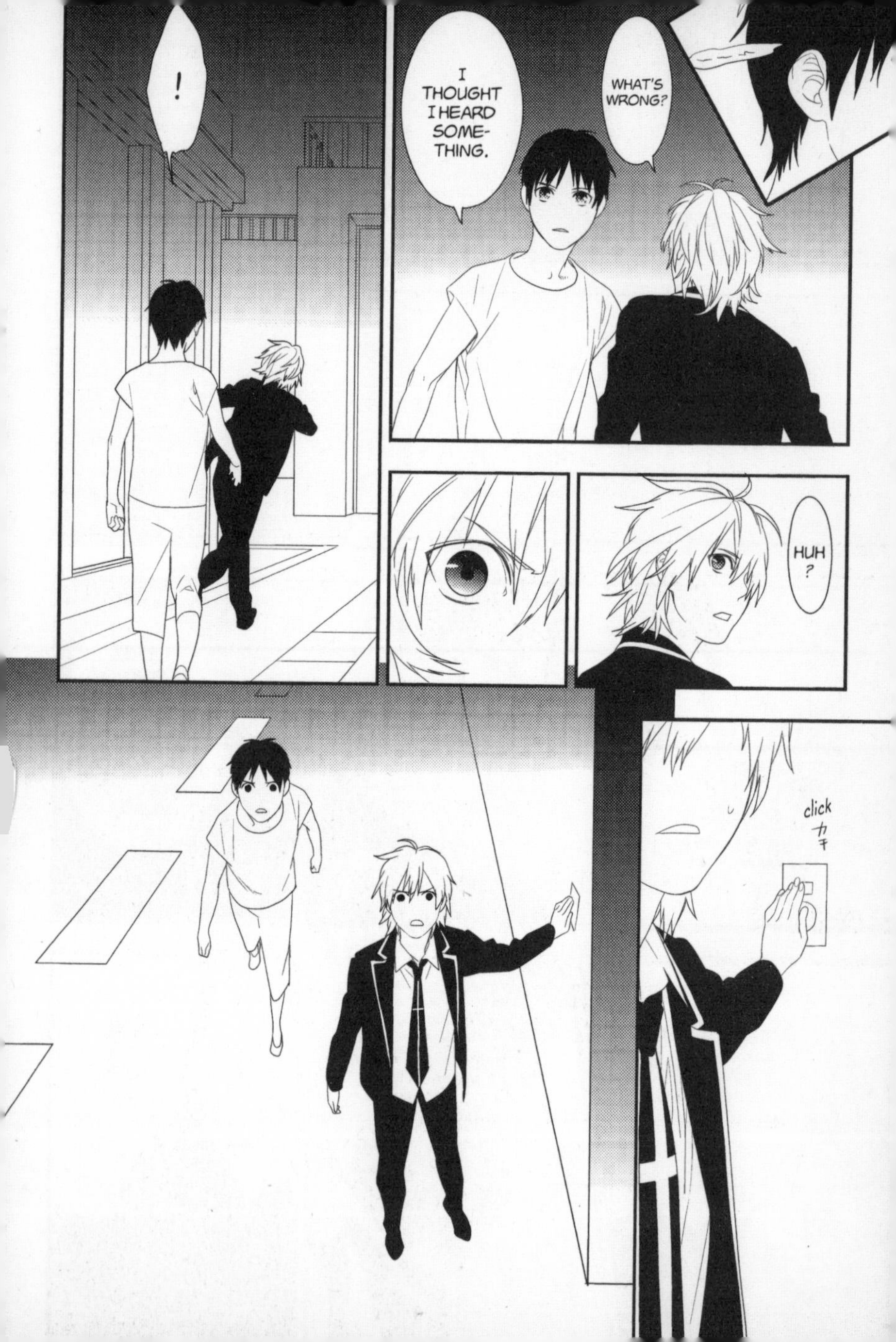
WHAT'S WRONG?
I THOUGHT I HEARD SOME-THING.
HUH ?
!
click
カチ

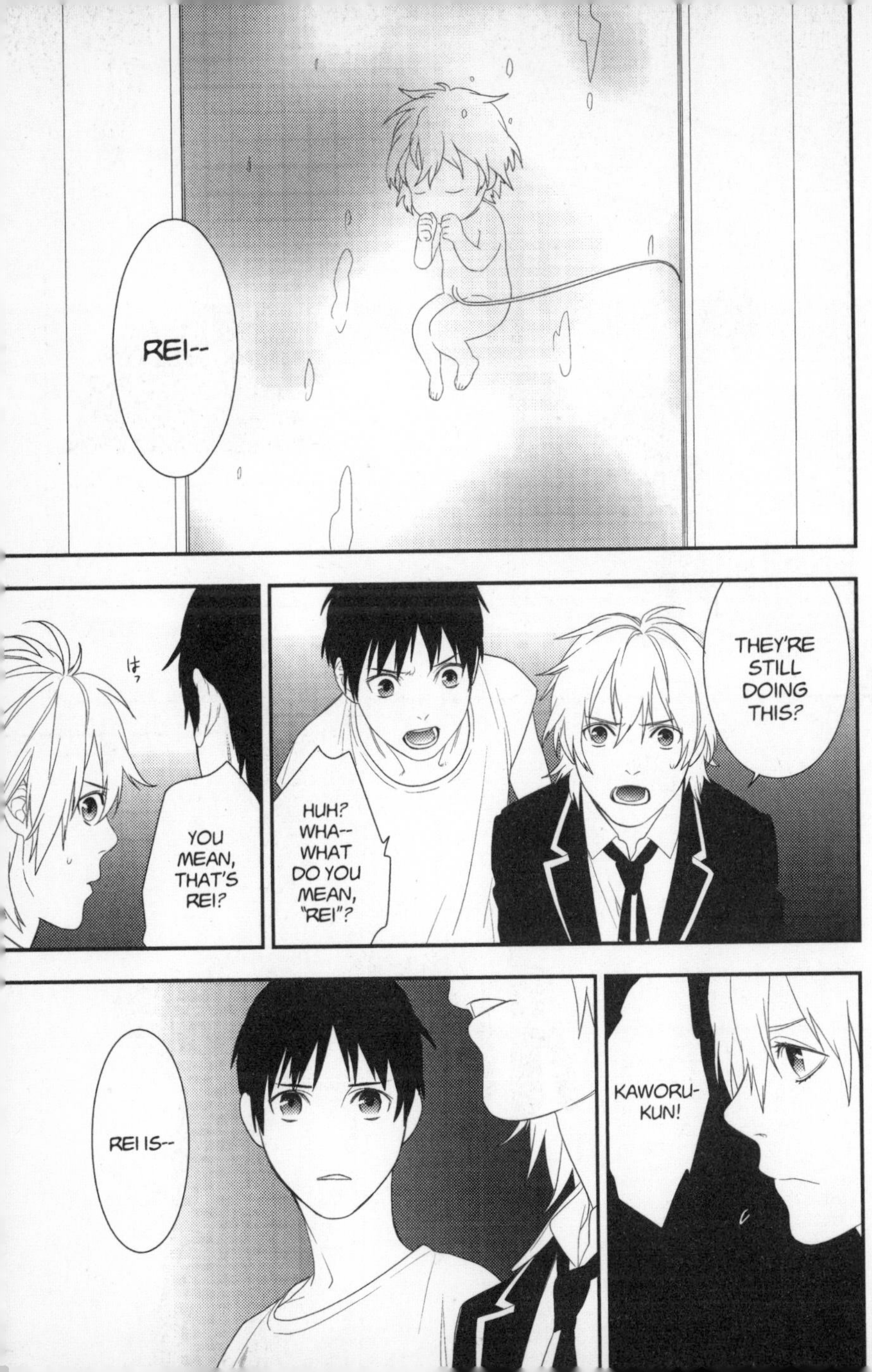
REI--
THEY'RE STILL DOING THIS?
HUH? WHA-- WHAT DO YOU MEAN, "REI"?
はっ
YOU MEAN, THAT'S REI?
KAWORU-KUN!
REI IS--

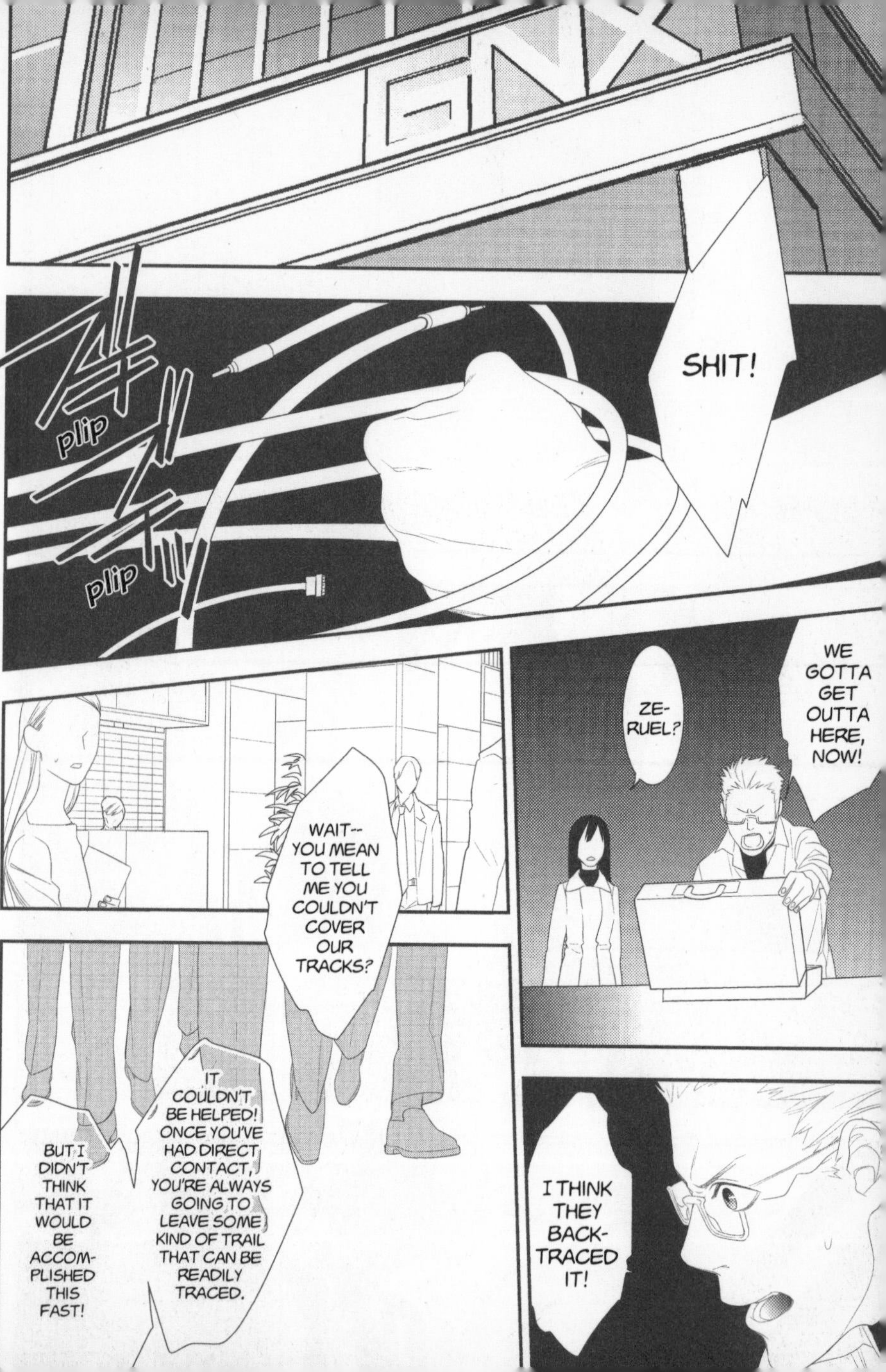
GNX
SHIT!
plip
plip
WE GOTTA GET OUTTA HERE, NOW!
ZE-RUEL?
WAIT-- YOU MEAN TO TELL ME YOU COULDN'T COVER OUR TRACKS?
I THINK THEY BACK-TRACED IT!
IT COULDN'T BE HELPED! ONCE YOU'VE HAD DIRECT CONTACT, YOU'RE ALWAYS GOING TO LEAVE SOME KIND OF TRAIL THAT CAN BE READILY TRACED.
BUT I DIDN'T THINK THAT IT WOULD BE ACCOM-PLISHED THIS FAST!

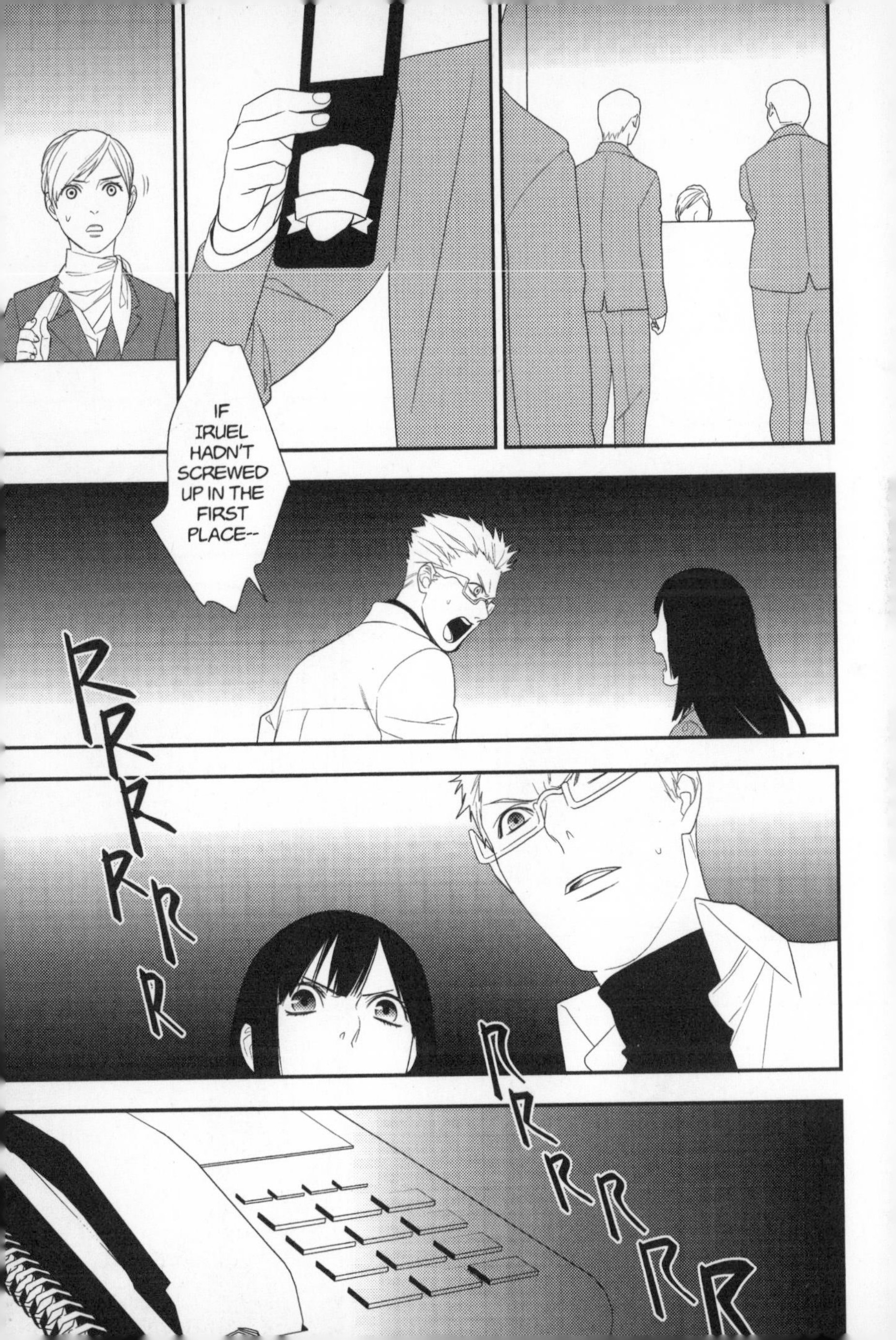
IF IRUEL HADN'T SCREWED UP IN THE FIRST PLACE--
RRRRRR
RRRRRRR

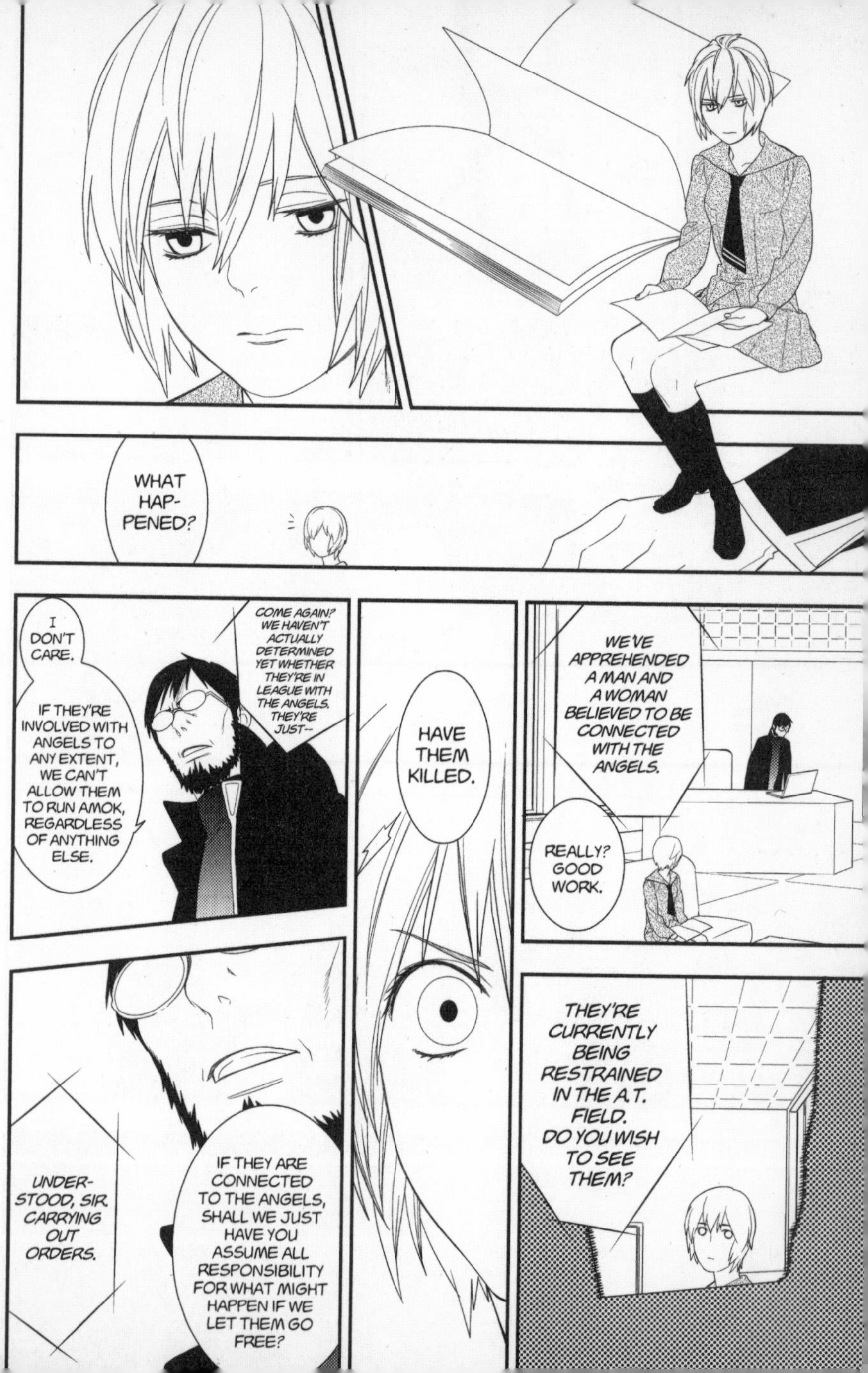
WHAT HAP-PENED?
WE'VE APPREHENDED A MAN AND A WOMAN BELIEVED TO BE CONNECTED WITH THE ANGELS.
REALLY? GOOD WORK.
THEY'RE CURRENTLY BEING RESTRAINED IN THE A.T. FIELD. DO YOU WISH TO SEE THEM?
HAVE THEM KILLED.
COME AGAIN? WE HAVEN'T ACTUALLY DETERMINED YET WHETHER THEY'RE IN LEAGUE WITH THE ANGELS. THEY'RE JUST--
I DON'T CARE.
IF THEY'RE INVOLVED WITH ANGELS TO ANY EXTENT, WE CAN'T ALLOW THEM TO RUN AMOK, REGARDLESS OF ANYTHING ELSE.
IF THEY ARE CONNECTED TO THE ANGELS, SHALL WE JUST HAVE YOU ASSUME ALL RESPONSIBILITY FOR WHAT MIGHT HAPPEN IF WE LET THEM GO FREE?
UNDER-STOOD, SIR. CARRYING OUT ORDERS.

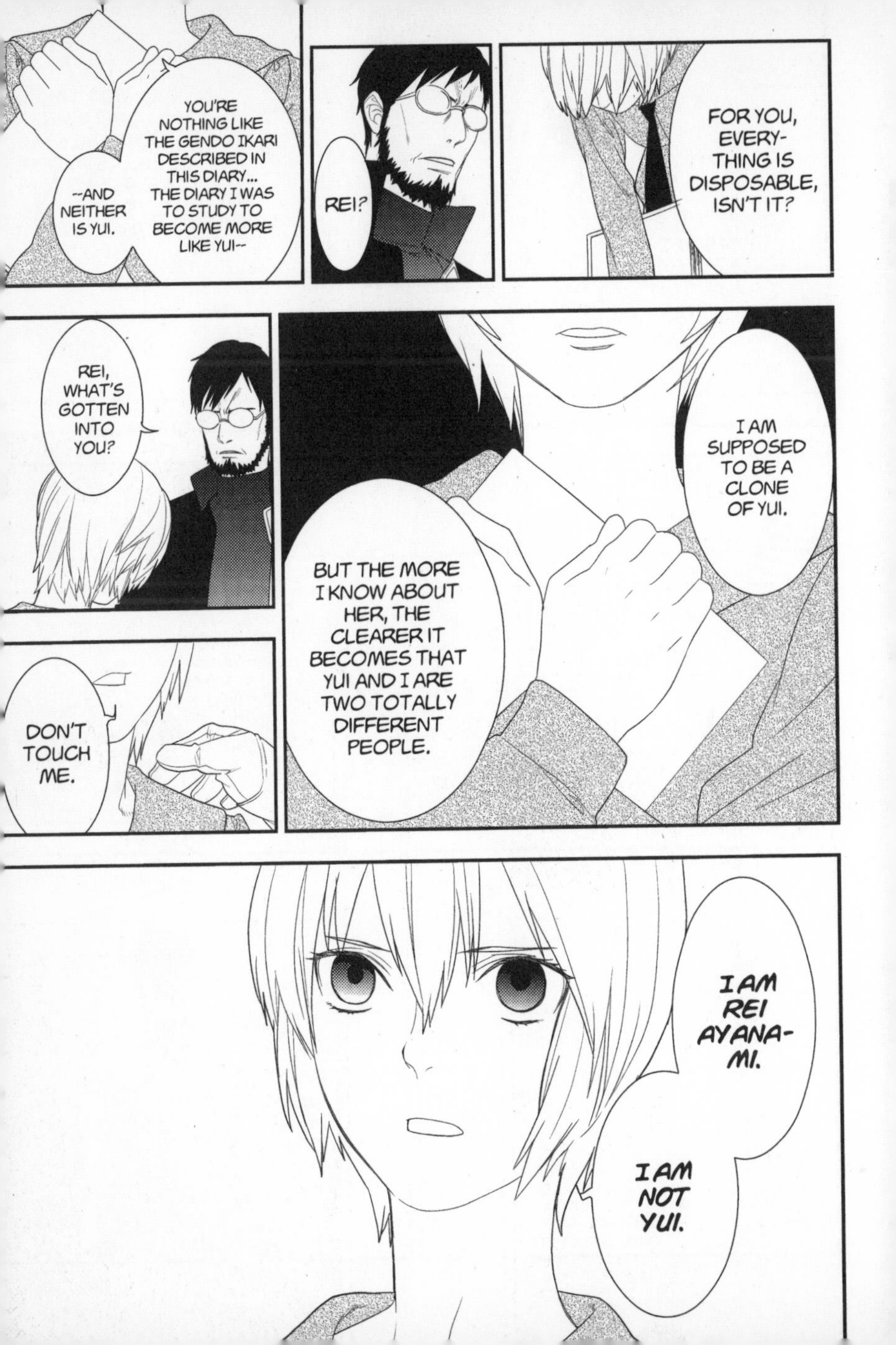
FOR YOU, EVERY-THING IS DISPOSABLE, ISN'T IT?
REI?
YOU'RE NOTHING LIKE THE GENDO IKARI DESCRIBED IN THIS DIARY... THE DIARY I WAS TO STUDY TO BECOME MORE LIKE YUI--
--AND NEITHER IS YUI.
I AM SUPPOSED TO BE A CLONE OF YUI.
BUT THE MORE I KNOW ABOUT HER, THE CLEARER IT BECOMES THAT YUI AND I ARE TWO TOTALLY DIFFERENT PEOPLE.
REI, WHAT'S GOTTEN INTO YOU?
DON'T TOUCH ME.
I AM REI AYANA-MI.
I AM NOT YUI.

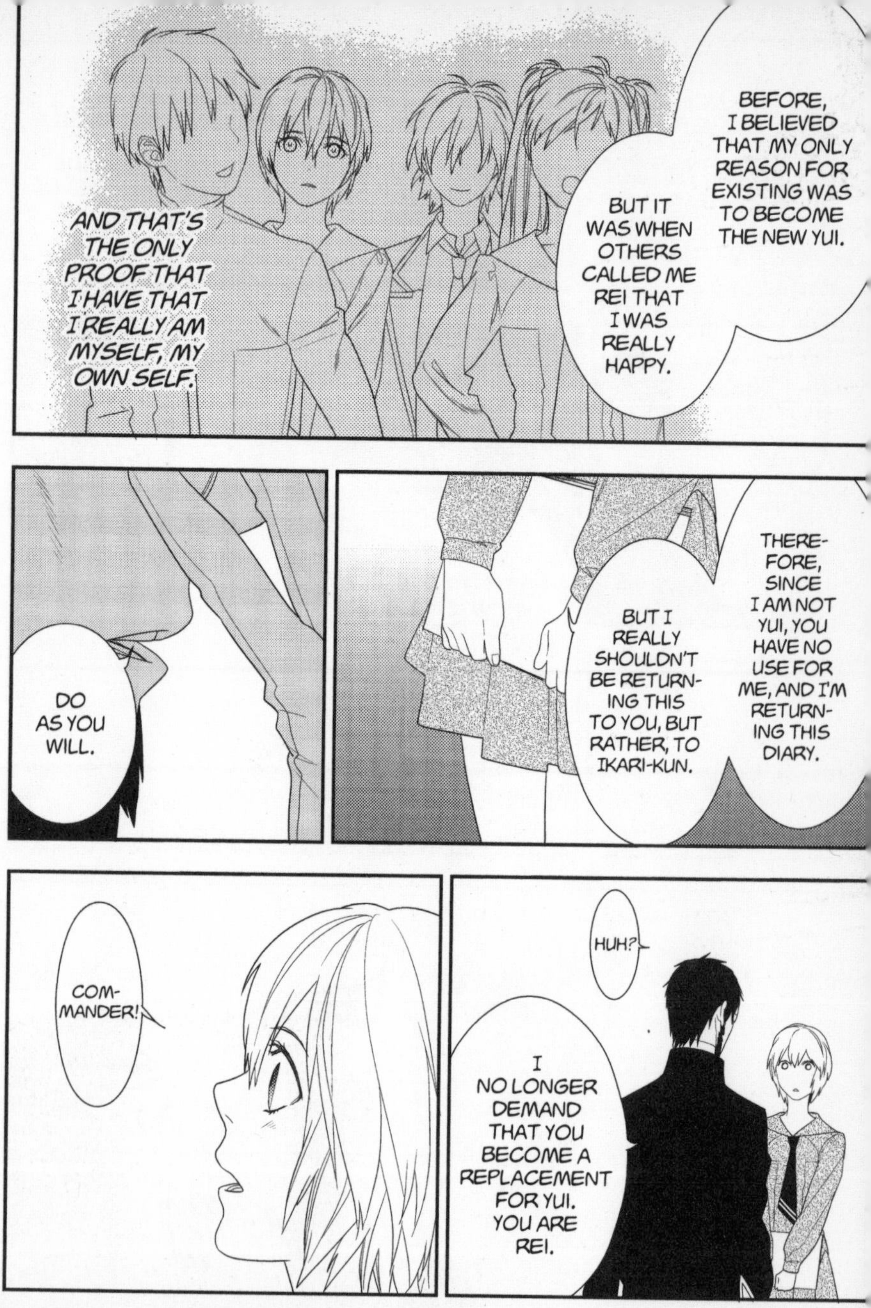
BEFORE, I BELIEVED THAT MY ONLY REASON FOR EXISTING WAS TO BECOME THE NEW YUI.
BUT IT WAS WHEN OTHERS CALLED ME REI THAT I WAS REALLY HAPPY.
AND THAT'S THE ONLY PROOF THAT I HAVE THAT I REALLY AM MYSELF, MY OWN SELF.
THEREFORE, SINCE I AM NOT YUI, YOU HAVE NO USE FOR ME, AND I'M RETURNING THIS DIARY.
BUT I REALLY SHOULDN'T BE RETURNING THIS TO YOU, BUT RATHER, TO IKARI-KUN.
DO AS YOU WILL.
HUH?
I NO LONGER DEMAND THAT YOU BECOME A REPLACEMENT FOR YUI. YOU ARE REI.
COMMANDER!

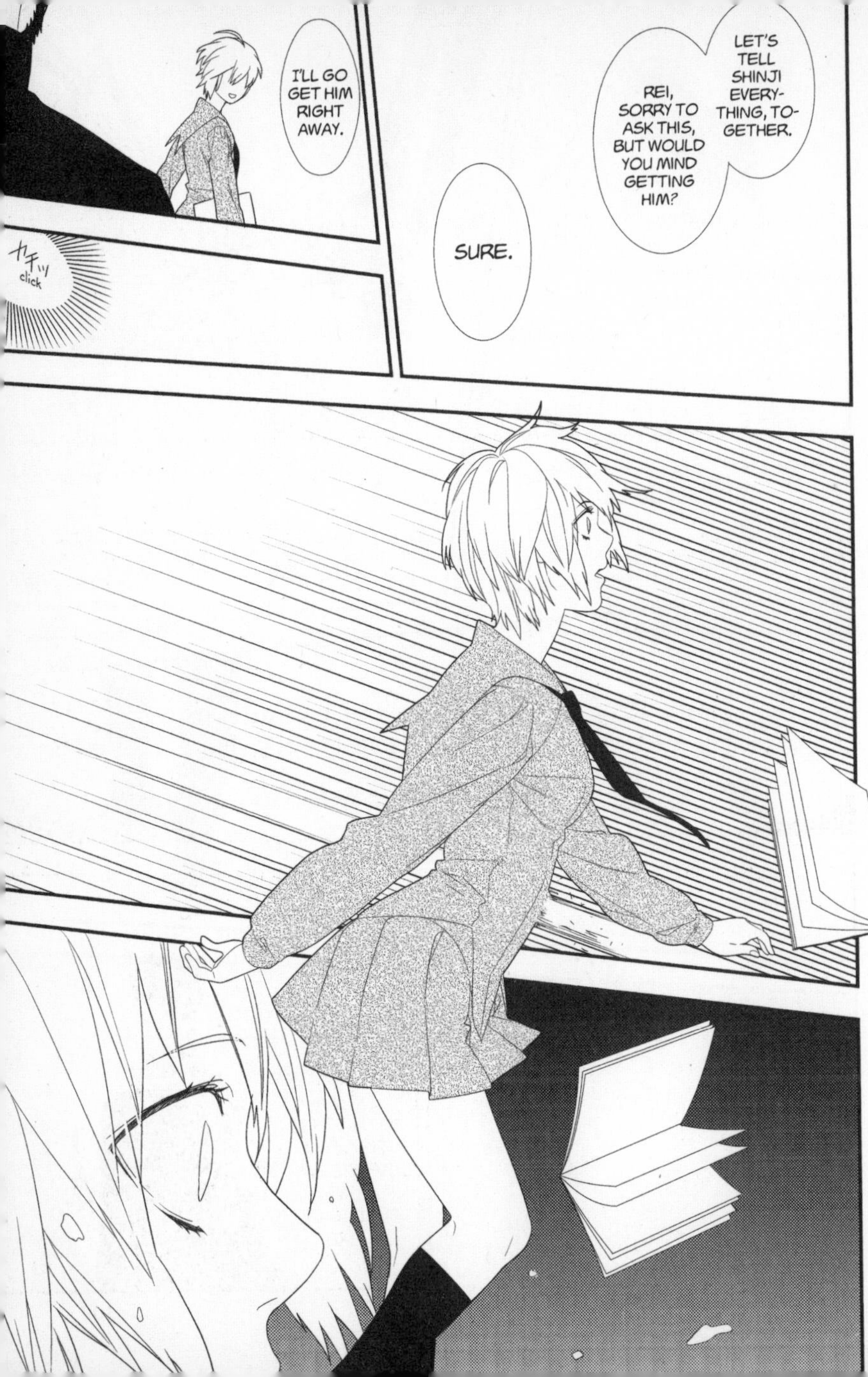
LET'S TELL SHINJI EVERY-THING, TO-GETHER.
REI, SORRY TO ASK THIS, BUT WOULD YOU MIND GETTING HIM?
SURE.
I'LL GO GET HIM RIGHT AWAY.
カチッ
click

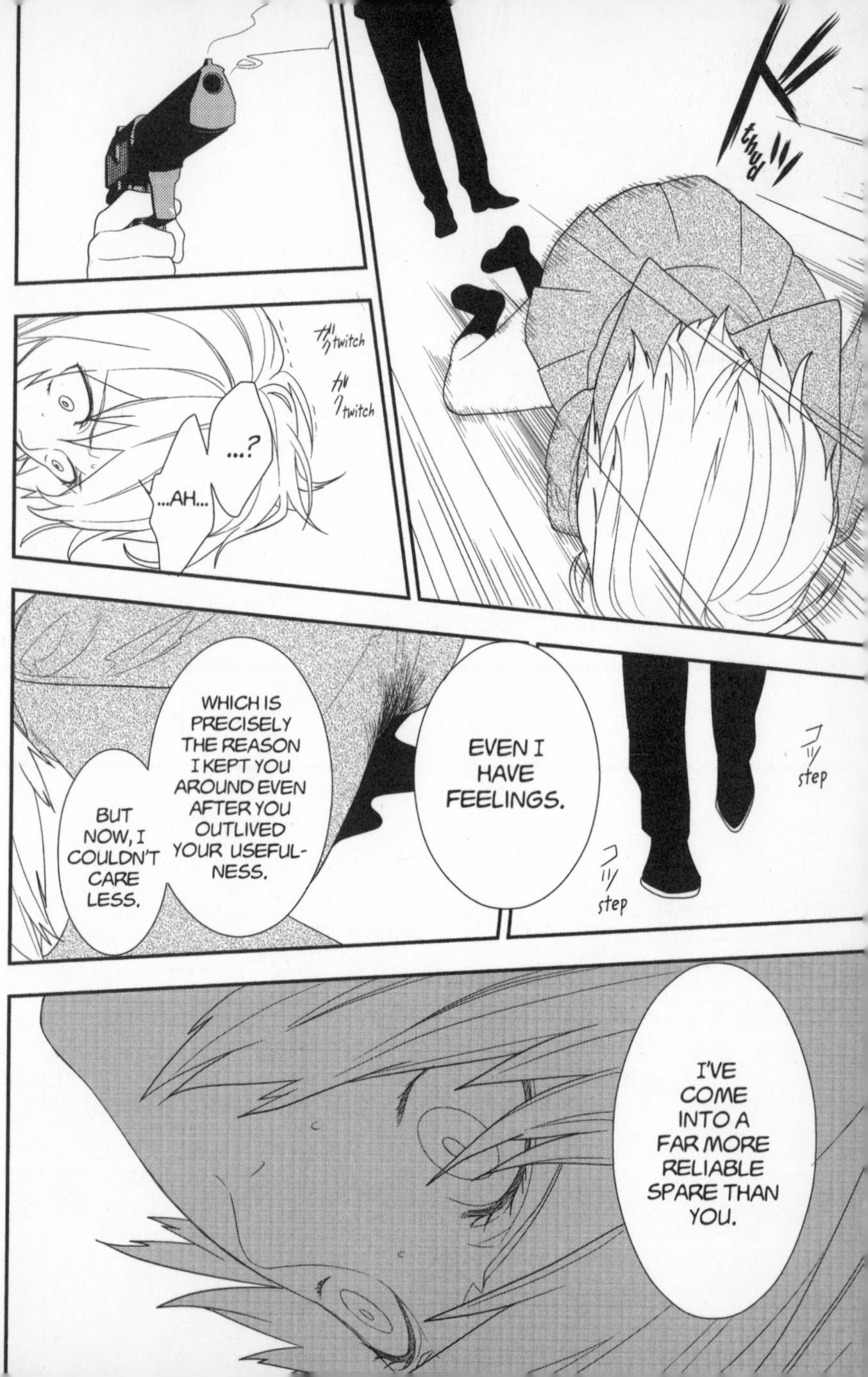
thud
twitch
twitch
...?
...AH...
EVEN I HAVE FEELINGS.
step
step
WHICH IS PRECISELY THE REASON I KEPT YOU AROUND EVEN AFTER YOU OUTLIVED YOUR USEFUL-NESS.
BUT NOW, I COULDN'T CARE LESS.
I'VE COME INTO A FAR MORE RELIABLE SPARE THAN YOU.

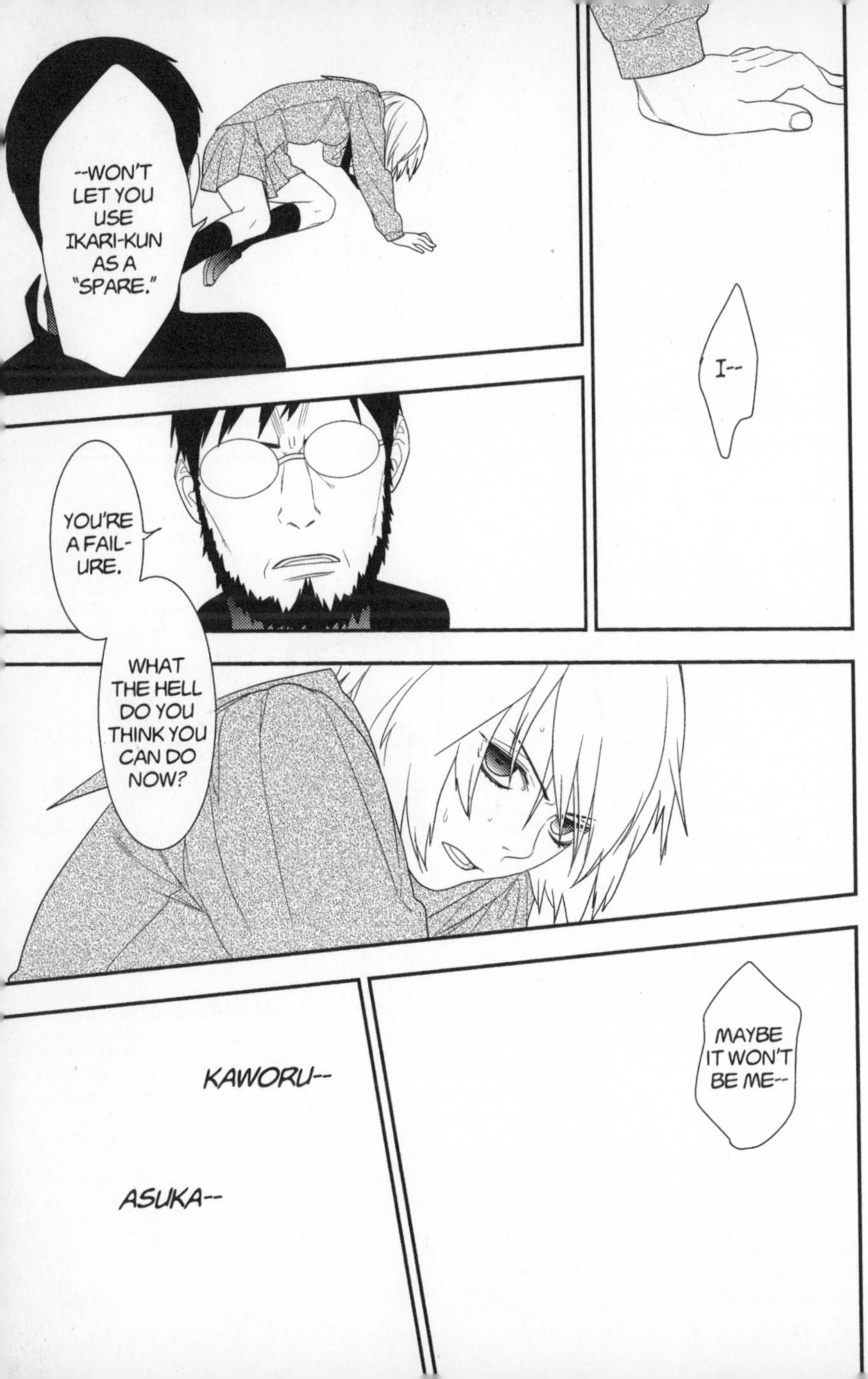
I--
--WON'T LET YOU USE IKARI-KUN AS A "SPARE."
YOU'RE A FAIL-URE.
WHAT THE HELL DO YOU THINK YOU CAN DO NOW?
MAYBE IT WON'T BE ME--
KAWORU--
ASUKA--

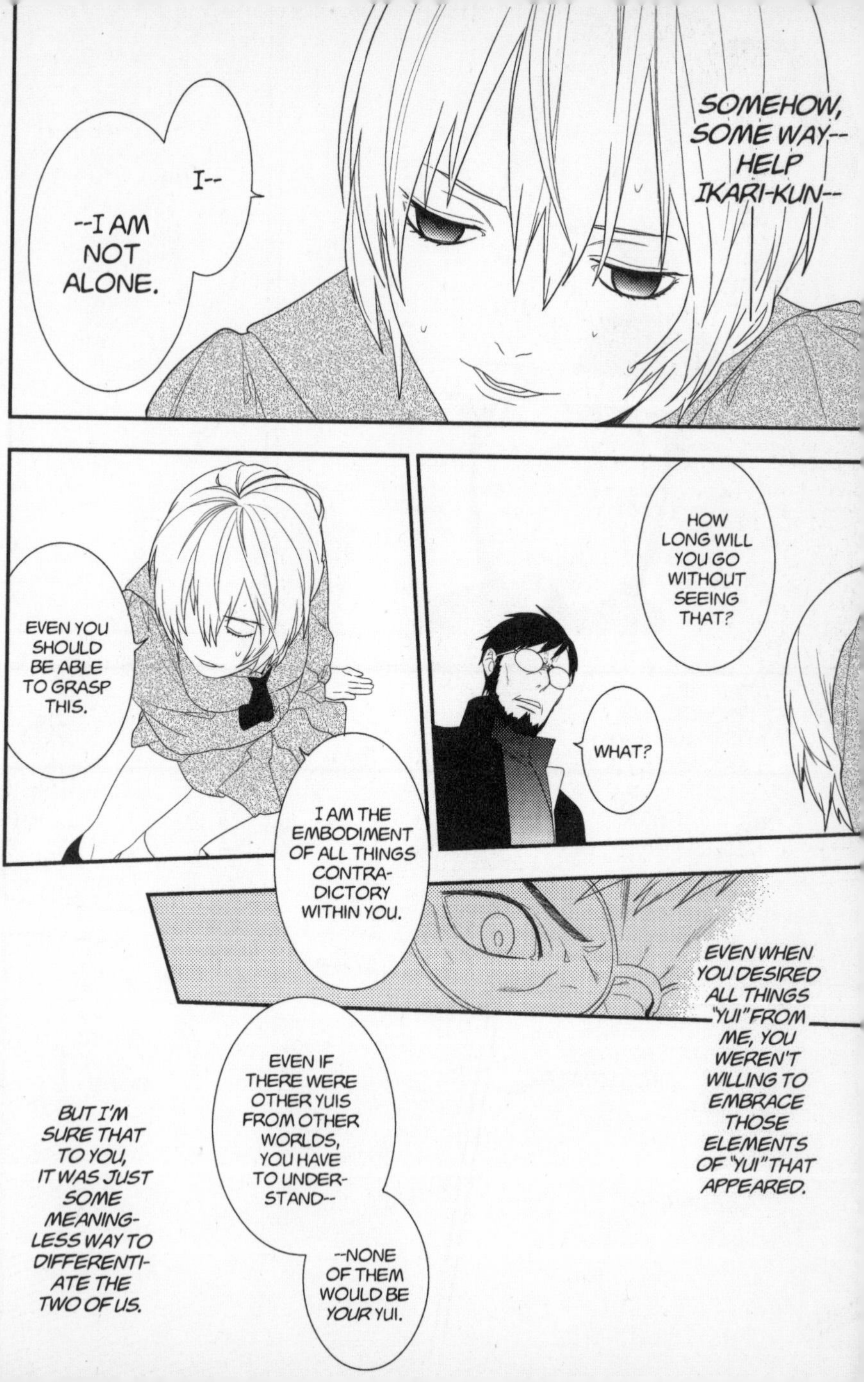
SOMEHOW, SOME WAY-- HELP IKARI-KUN--
I--
--I AM NOT ALONE.
HOW LONG WILL YOU GO WITHOUT SEEING THAT?
WHAT?
EVEN YOU SHOULD BE ABLE TO GRASP THIS.
I AM THE EMBODIMENT OF ALL THINGS CONTRA-DICTORY WITHIN YOU.
EVEN WHEN YOU DESIRED ALL THINGS "YUI" FROM ME, YOU WEREN'T WILLING TO EMBRACE THOSE ELEMENTS OF "YUI" THAT APPEARED.
EVEN IF THERE WERE OTHER YUIS FROM OTHER WORLDS, YOU HAVE TO UNDER-STAND--
--NONE OF THEM WOULD BE YOUR YUI.
BUT I'M SURE THAT TO YOU, IT WAS JUST SOME MEANING-LESS WAY TO DIFFERENTI-ATE THE TWO OF US.

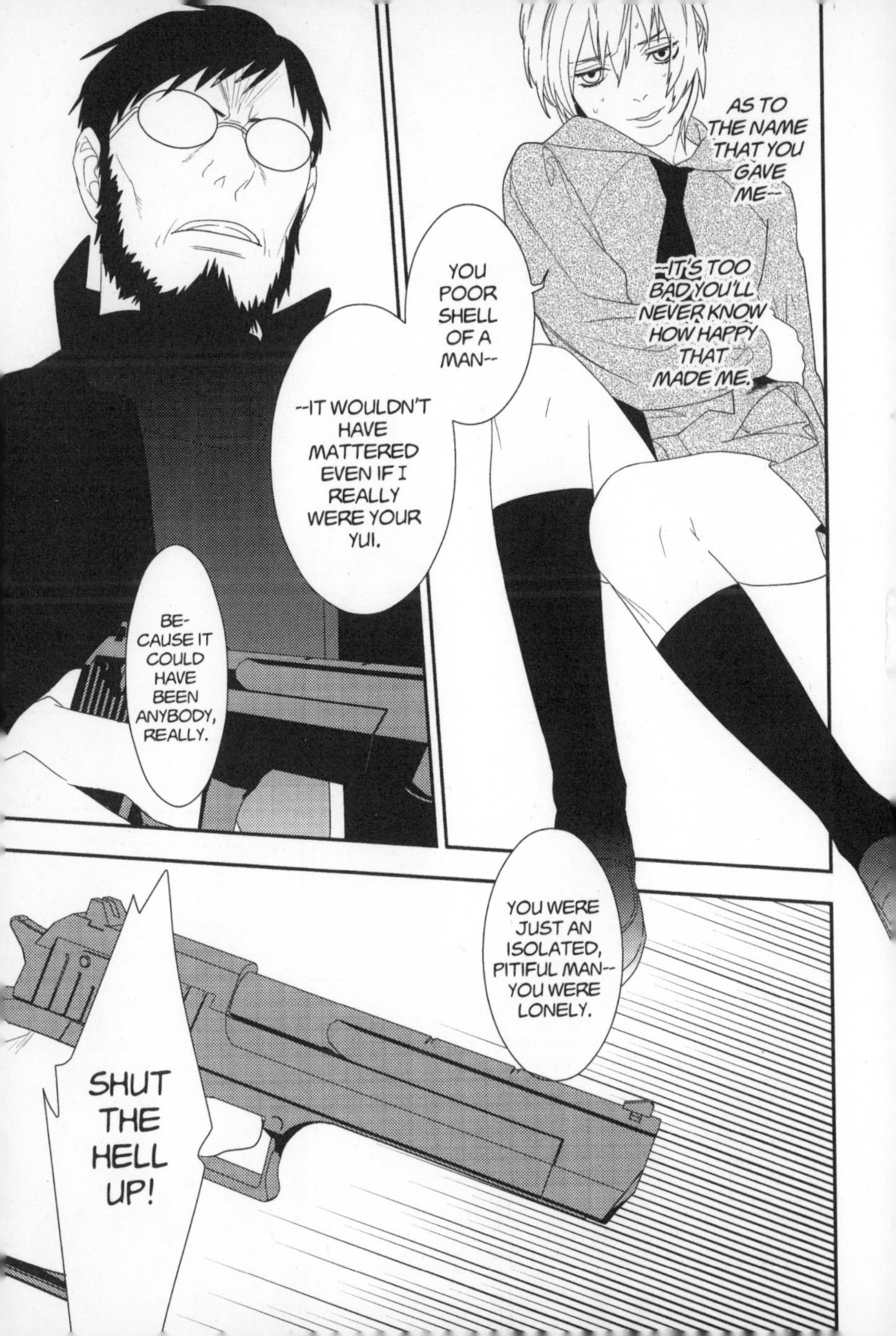
AS TO THE NAME THAT YOU GAVE ME--
--IT'S TOO BAD YOU'LL NEVER KNOW HOW HAPPY THAT MADE ME.
YOU POOR SHELL OF A MAN--
--IT WOULDN'T HAVE MATTERED EVEN IF I REALLY WERE YOUR YUI.
BE-CAUSE IT COULD HAVE BEEN ANYBODY, REALLY.
YOU WERE JUST AN ISOLATED, PITIFUL MAN-- YOU WERE LONELY.
SHUT THE HELL UP!

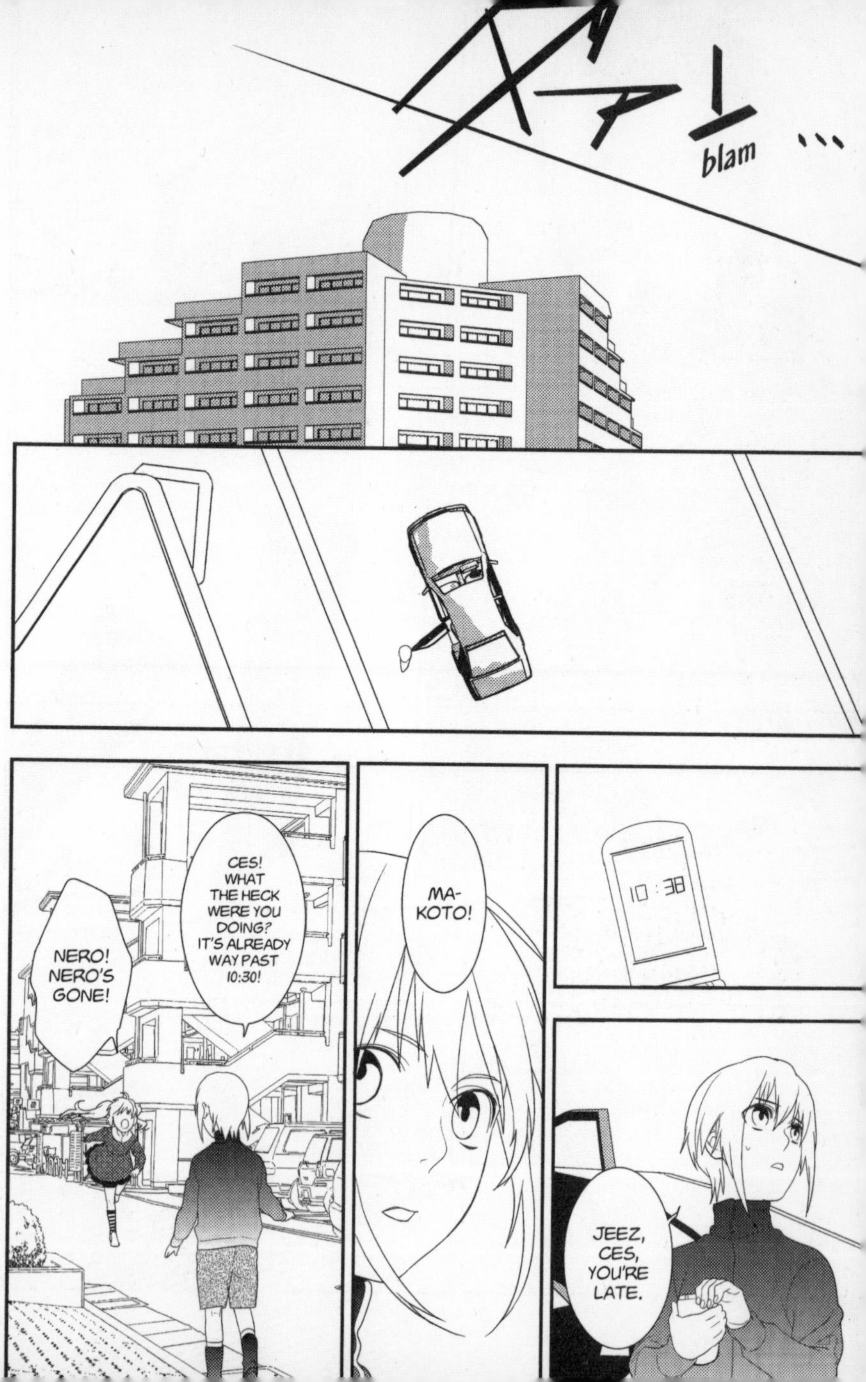
blam
...
10:38
JEEZ, CES, YOU'RE LATE.
MA-KOTO!
CES! WHAT THE HECK WERE YOU DOING? IT'S ALREADY WAY PAST 10:30!
NERO! NERO'S GONE!

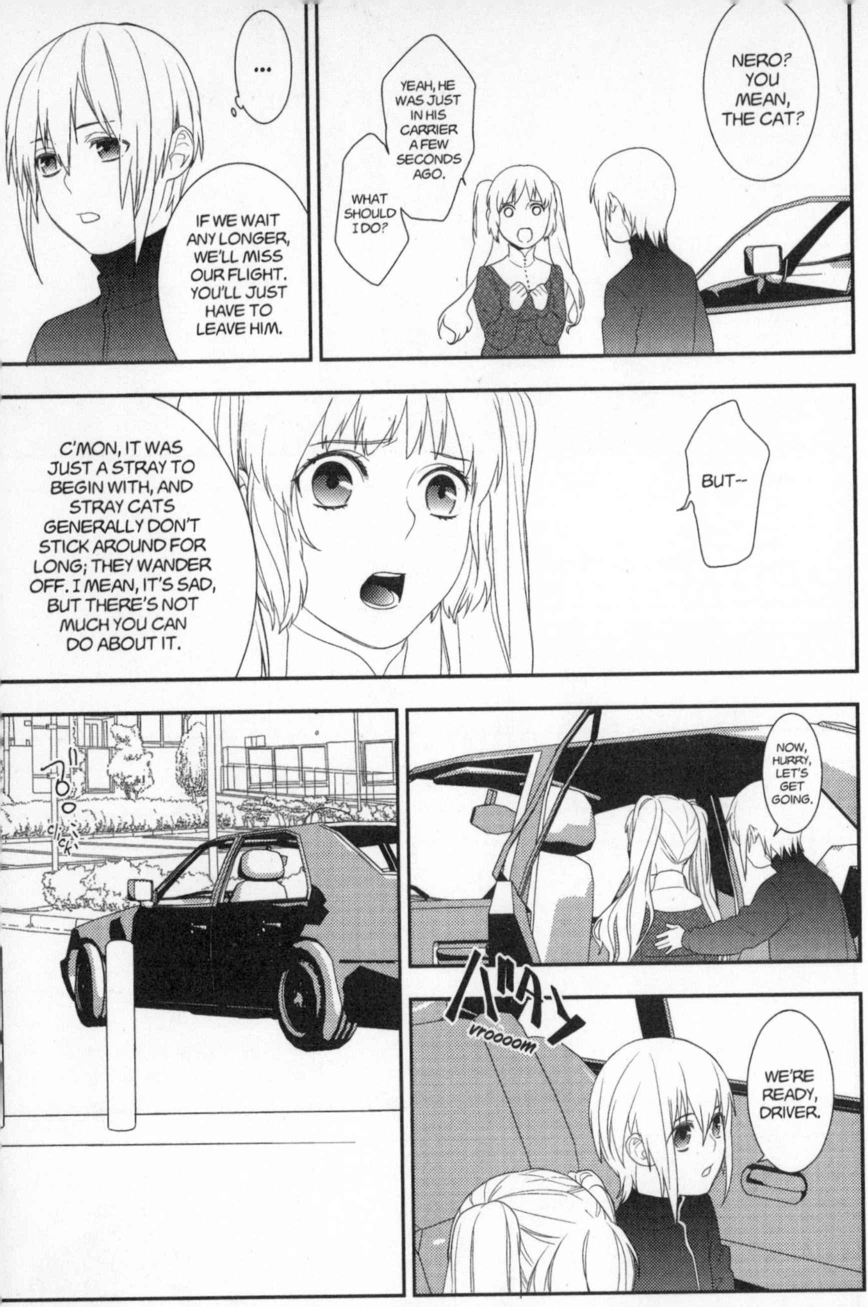
NERO? YOU MEAN, THE CAT?
YEAH, HE WAS JUST IN HIS CARRIER A FEW SECONDS AGO.
WHAT SHOULD I DO?
...
IF WE WAIT ANY LONGER, WE'LL MISS OUR FLIGHT. YOU'LL JUST HAVE TO LEAVE HIM.
BUT--
C'MON, IT WAS JUST A STRAY TO BEGIN WITH, AND STRAY CATS GENERALLY DON'T STICK AROUND FOR LONG; THEY WANDER OFF. I MEAN, IT'S SAD, BUT THERE'S NOT MUCH YOU CAN DO ABOUT IT.
NOW, HURRY, LET'S GET GOING.
vroooom
WE'RE READY, DRIVER.
click

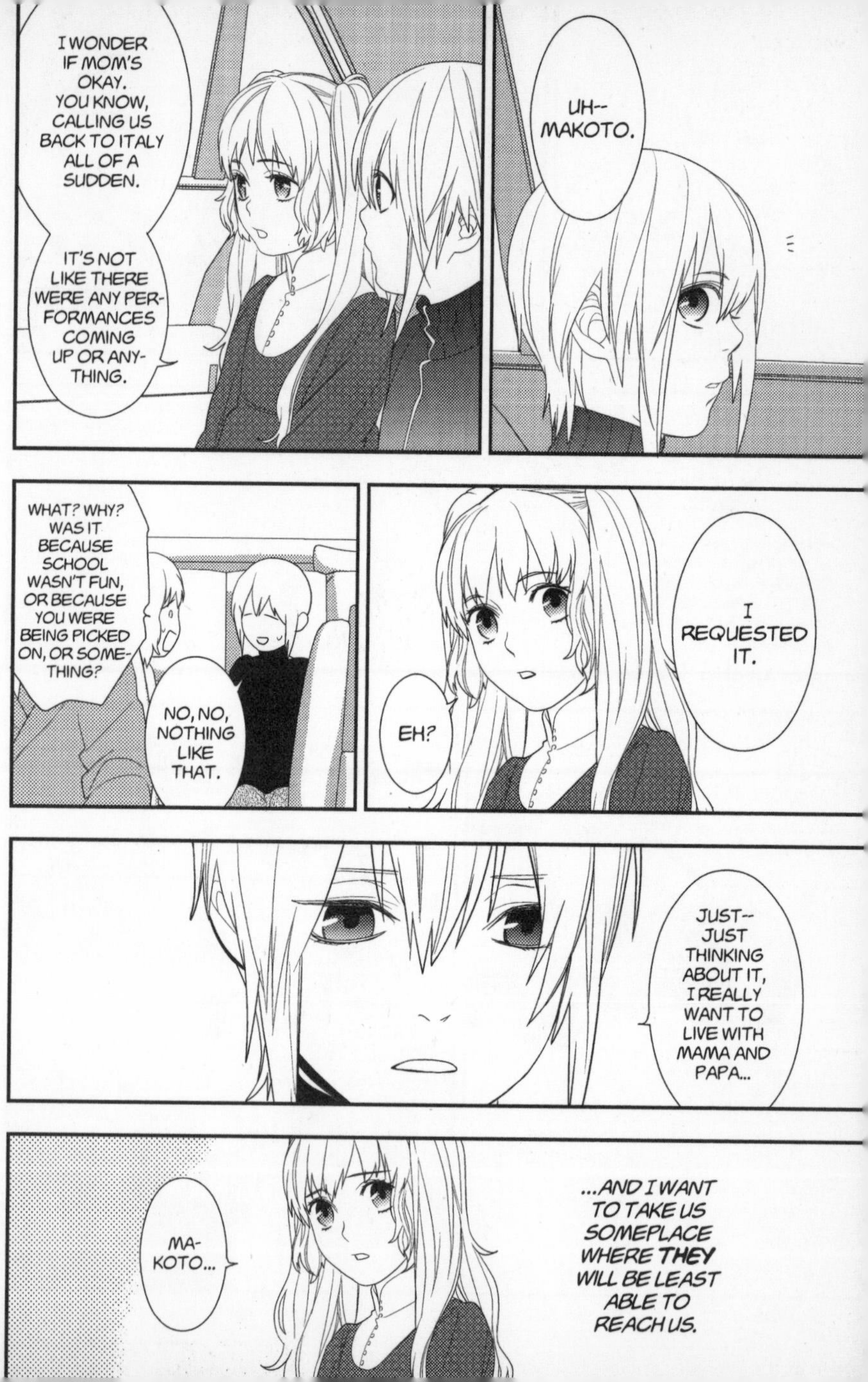
UH-- MAKOTO.
I WONDER IF MOM'S OKAY. YOU KNOW, CALLING US BACK TO ITALY ALL OF A SUDDEN.
IT'S NOT LIKE THERE WERE ANY PER-FORMANCES COMING UP OR ANY-THING.
I REQUESTED IT.
EH?
WHAT? WHY? WAS IT BECAUSE SCHOOL WASN'T FUN, OR BECAUSE YOU WERE BEING PICKED ON, OR SOME-THING?
NO, NO, NOTHING LIKE THAT.
JUST-- JUST THINKING ABOUT IT, I REALLY WANT TO LIVE WITH MAMA AND PAPA...
...AND I WANT TO TAKE US SOMEPLACE WHERE **THEY** WILL BE LEAST ABLE TO REACH US.
MA-KOTO...

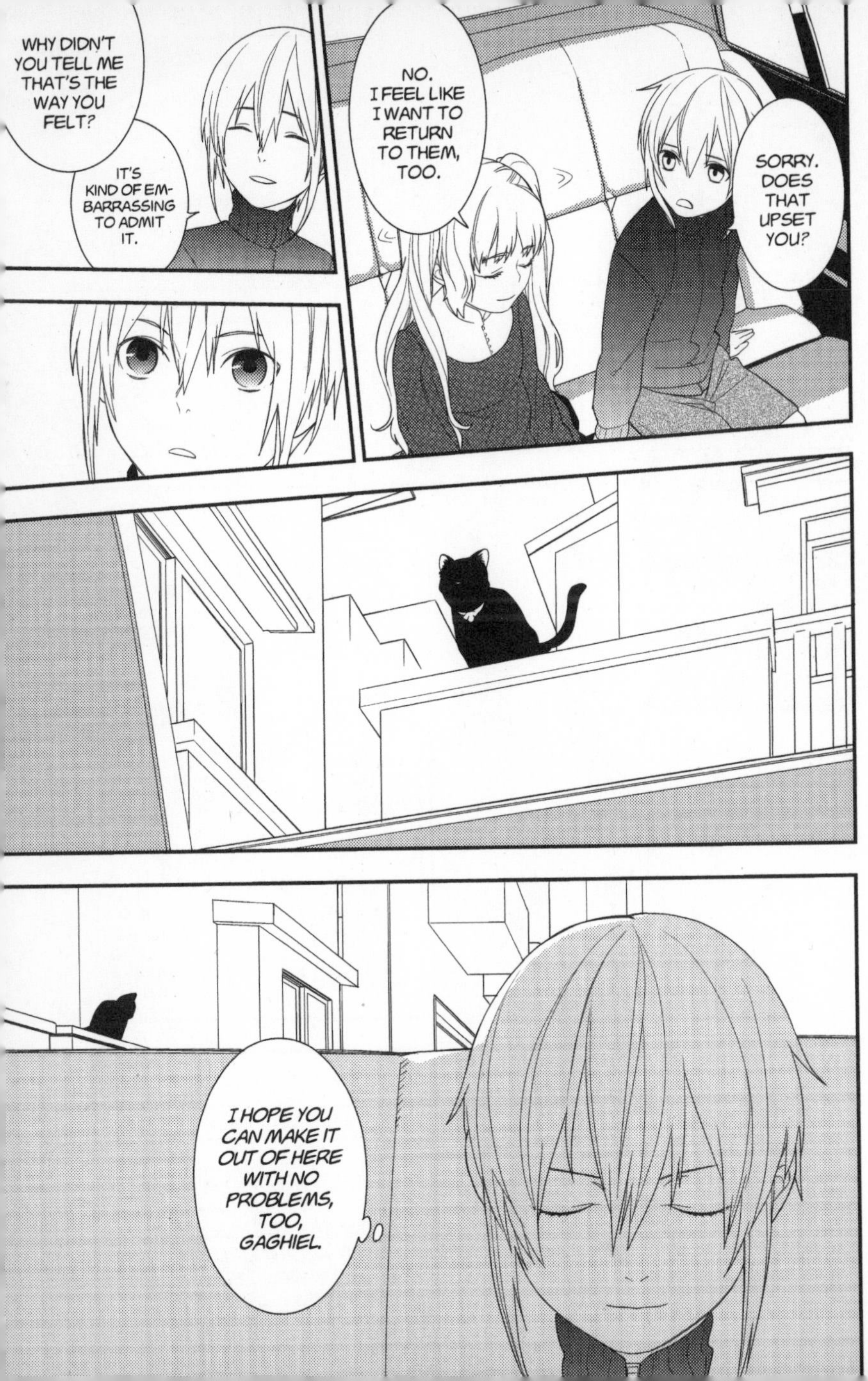
SORRY. DOES THAT UPSET YOU?
NO. I FEEL LIKE I WANT TO RETURN TO THEM, TOO.
WHY DIDN'T YOU TELL ME THAT'S THE WAY YOU FELT?
IT'S KIND OF EM-BARRASSING TO ADMIT IT.
I HOPE YOU CAN MAKE IT OUT OF HERE WITH NO PROBLEMS, TOO, GAGHIEL.

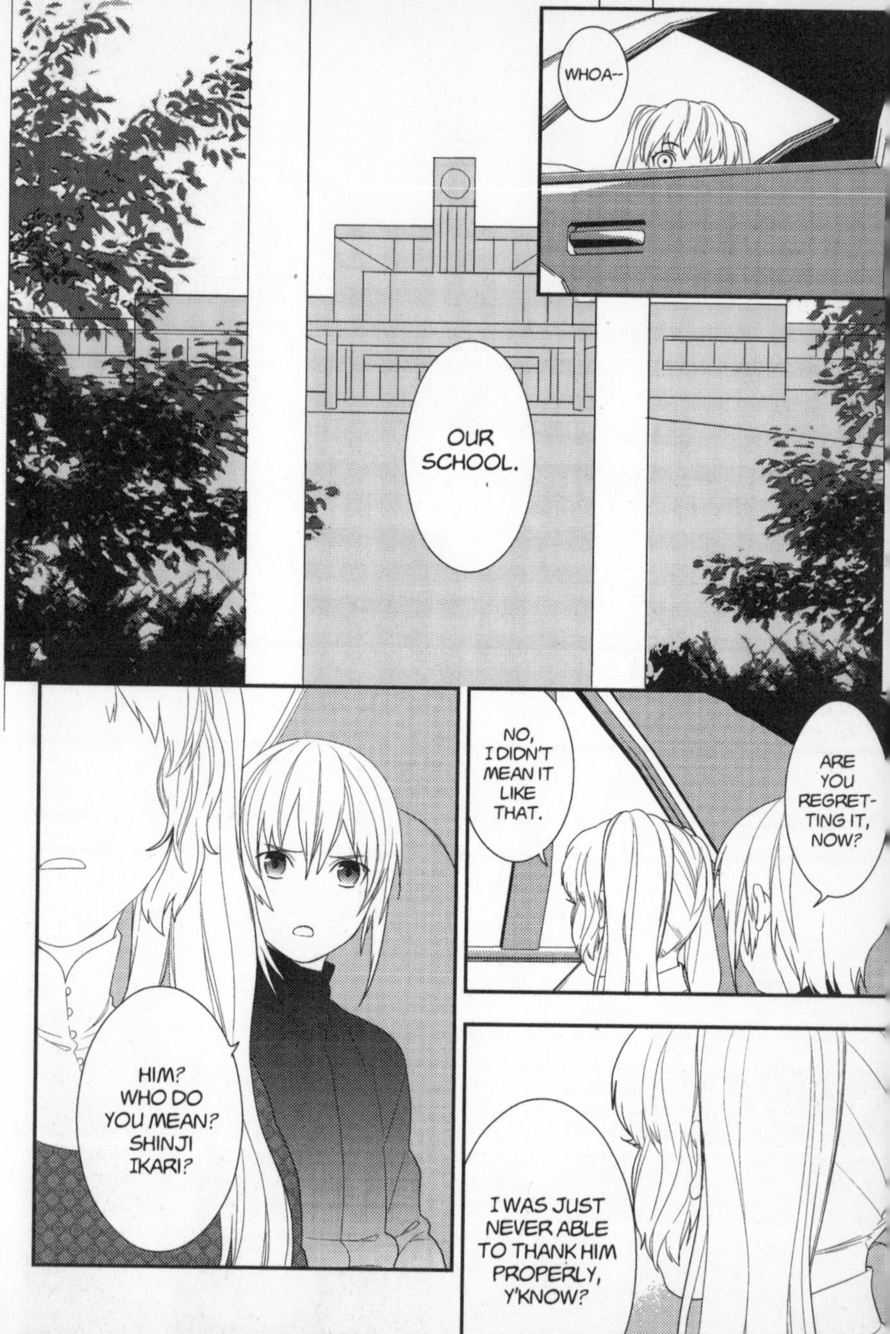
WHOA--
OUR SCHOOL.
ARE YOU REGRETTING IT, NOW?
NO, I DIDN'T MEAN IT LIKE THAT.
I WAS JUST NEVER ABLE TO THANK HIM PROPERLY, Y'KNOW?
HIM? WHO DO YOU MEAN? SHINJI IKARI?

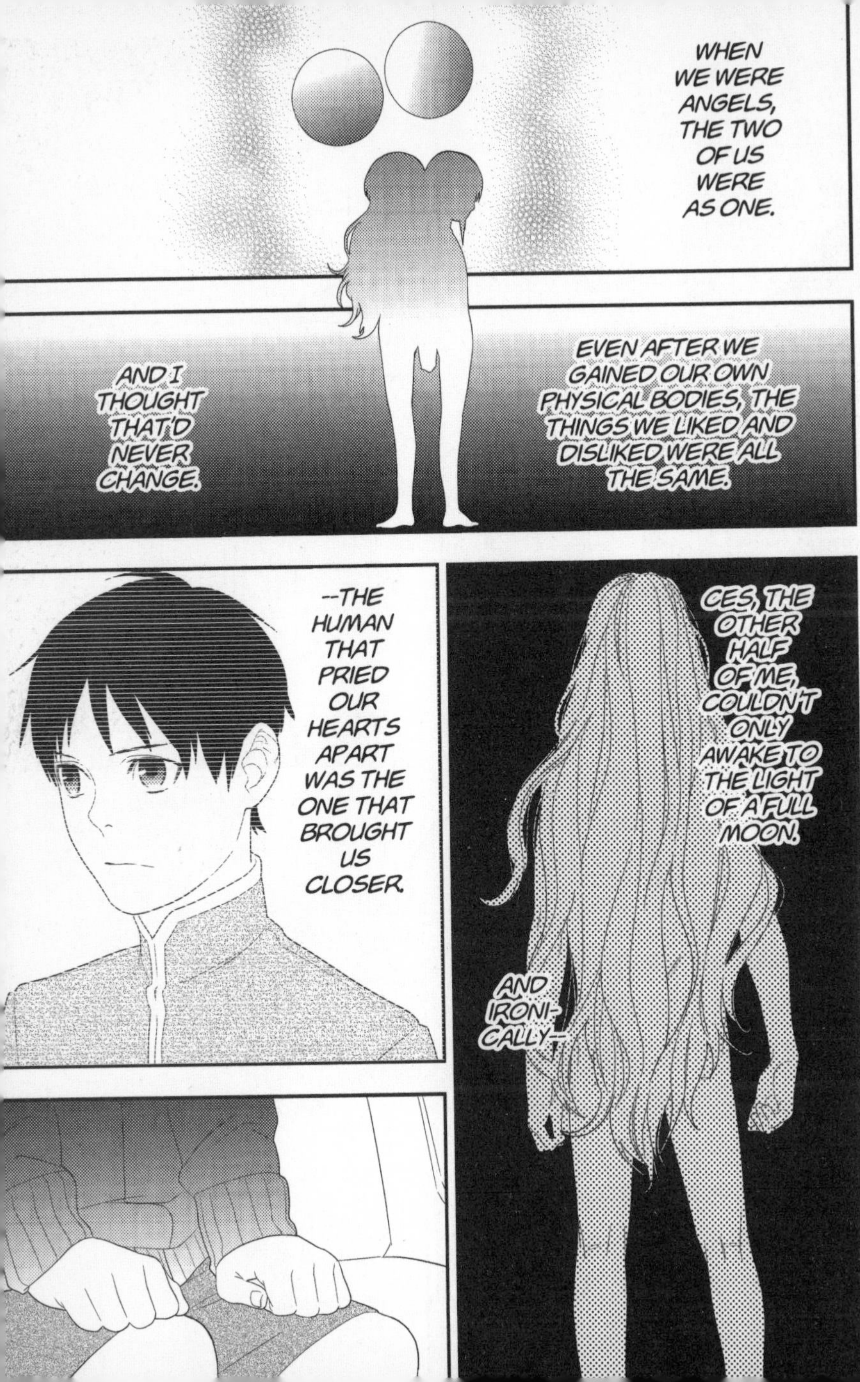
WHEN WE WERE ANGELS, THE TWO OF US WERE AS ONE.
EVEN AFTER WE GAINED OUR OWN PHYSICAL BODIES, THE THINGS WE LIKED AND DISLIKED WERE ALL THE SAME.
AND I THOUGHT THAT'D NEVER CHANGE.
CES, THE OTHER HALF OF ME, COULDN'T ONLY AWAKE TO THE LIGHT OF A FULL MOON.
AND IRONI-CALLY--
--THE HUMAN THAT PRIED OUR HEARTS APART WAS THE ONE THAT BROUGHT US CLOSER.

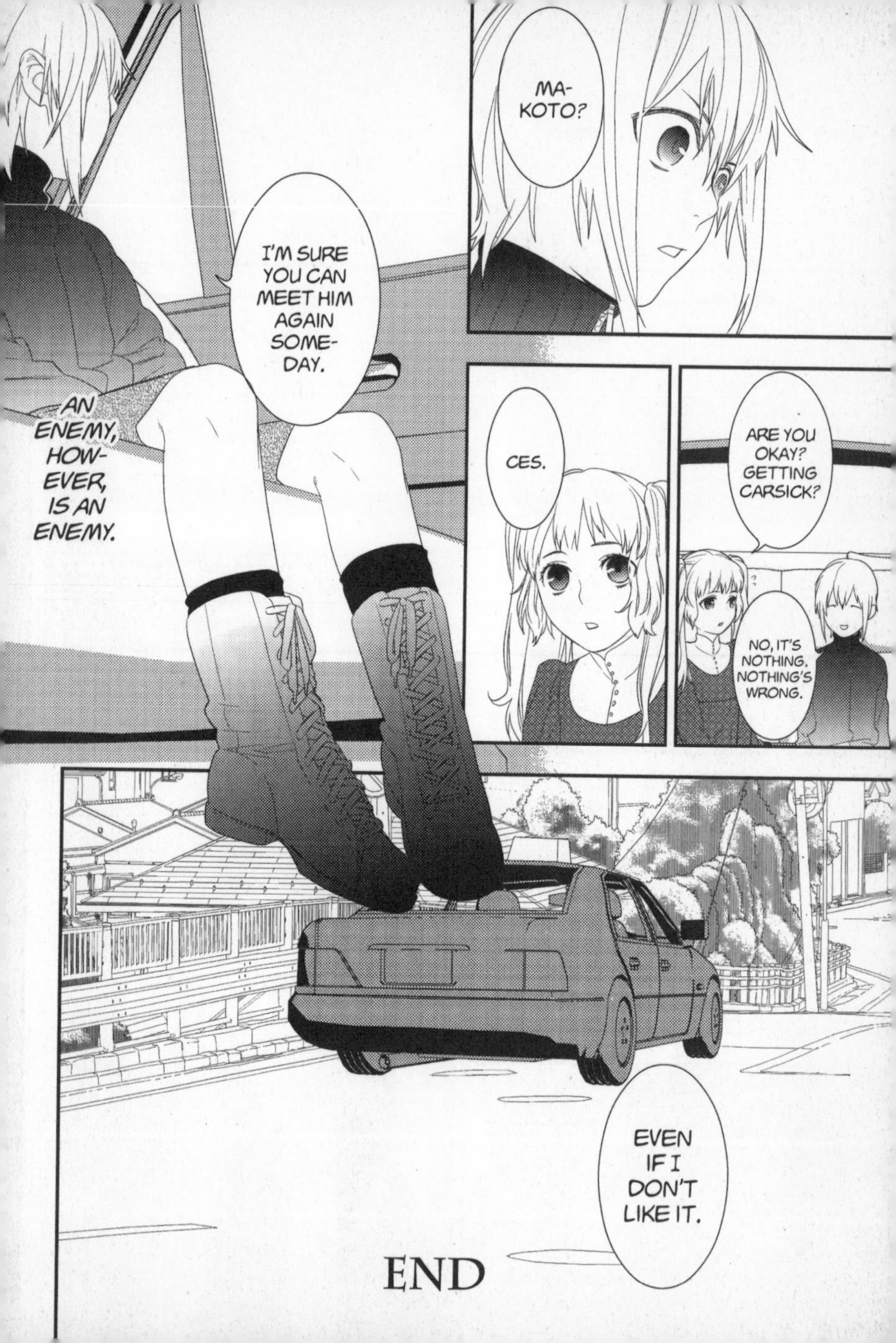
MA-KOTO?
ARE YOU OKAY? GETTING CARSICK?
NO, IT'S NOTHING. NOTHING'S WRONG.
CES.
I'M SURE YOU CAN MEET HIM AGAIN SOME-DAY.
AN ENEMY, HOW-EVER, IS AN ENEMY.
EVEN IF I DON'T LIKE IT.
END

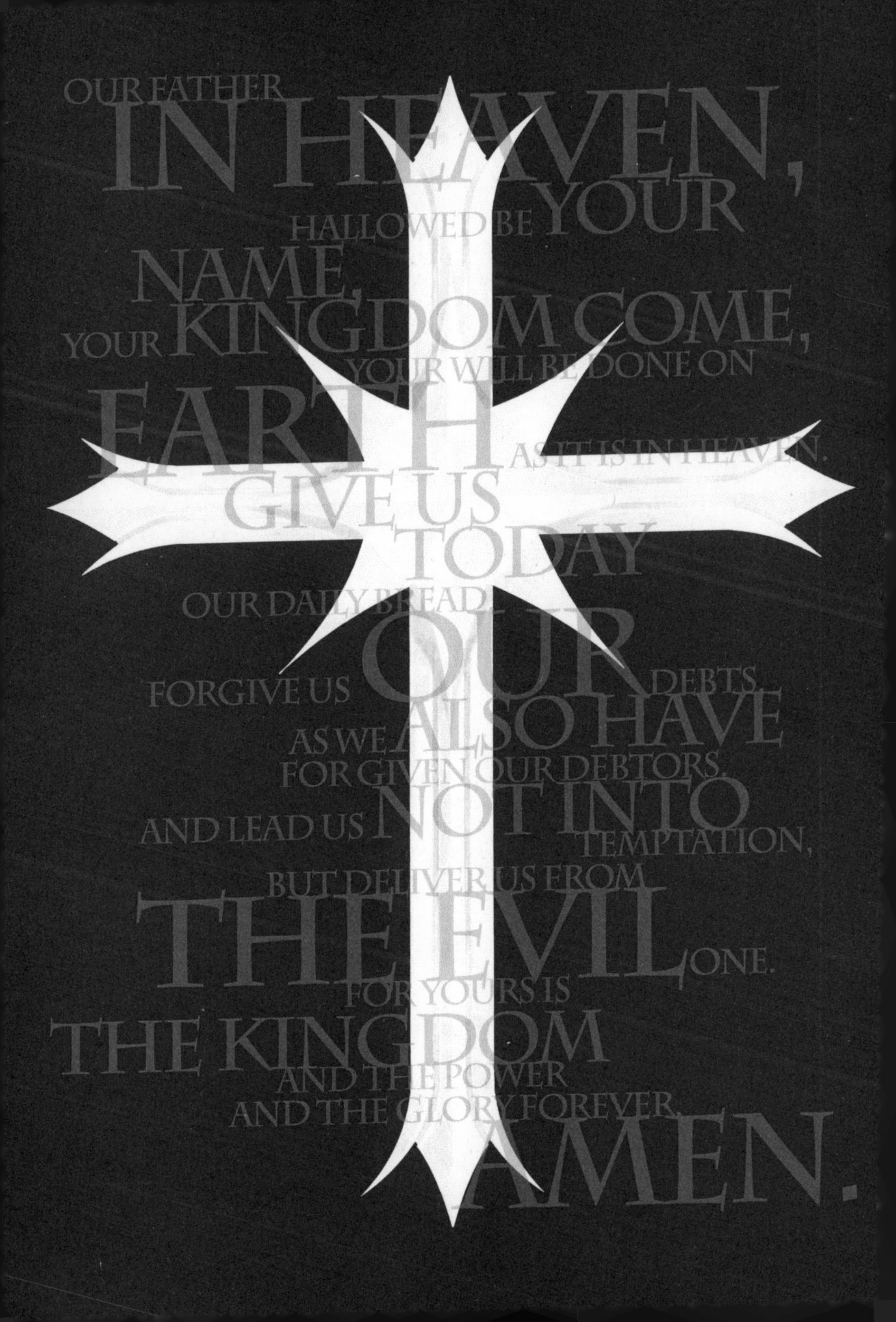
OUR FATHER
IN HEAVEN,
HALLOWED BE YOUR
NAME,
YOUR KINGDOM COME,
YOUR WILL BE DONE ON
EARTH AS IT IS IN HEAVEN.
GIVE US
TODAY
OUR DAILY BREAD.
FORGIVE US OUR DEBTS,
AS WE ALSO HAVE
FOR GIVEN OUR DEBTORS.
AND LEAD US NOT INTO
TEMPTATION,
BUT DELIVER US FROM
THE EVIL ONE.
FOR YOURS IS
THE KINGDOM
AND THE POWER
AND THE GLORY FOREVER.
AMEN.

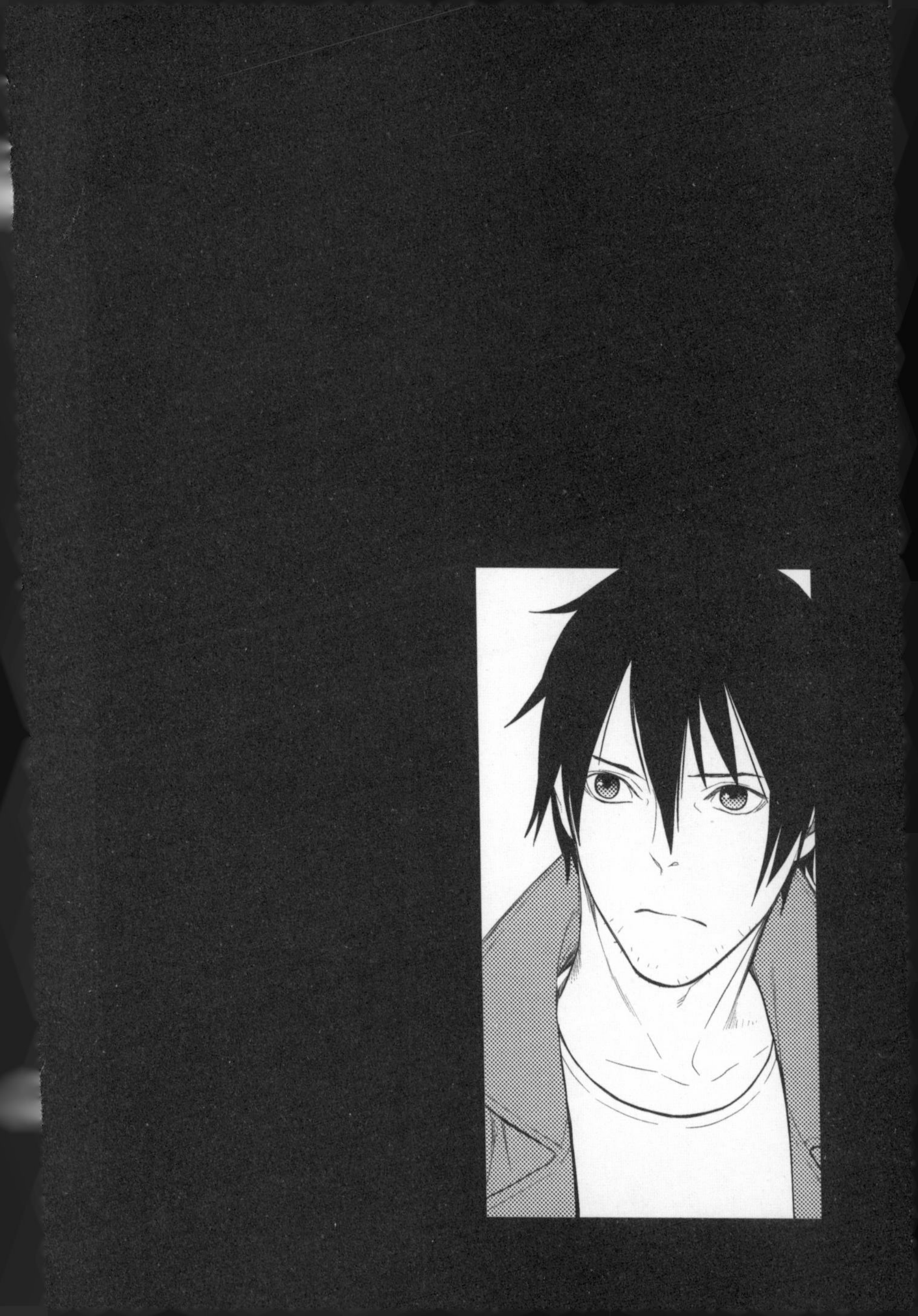

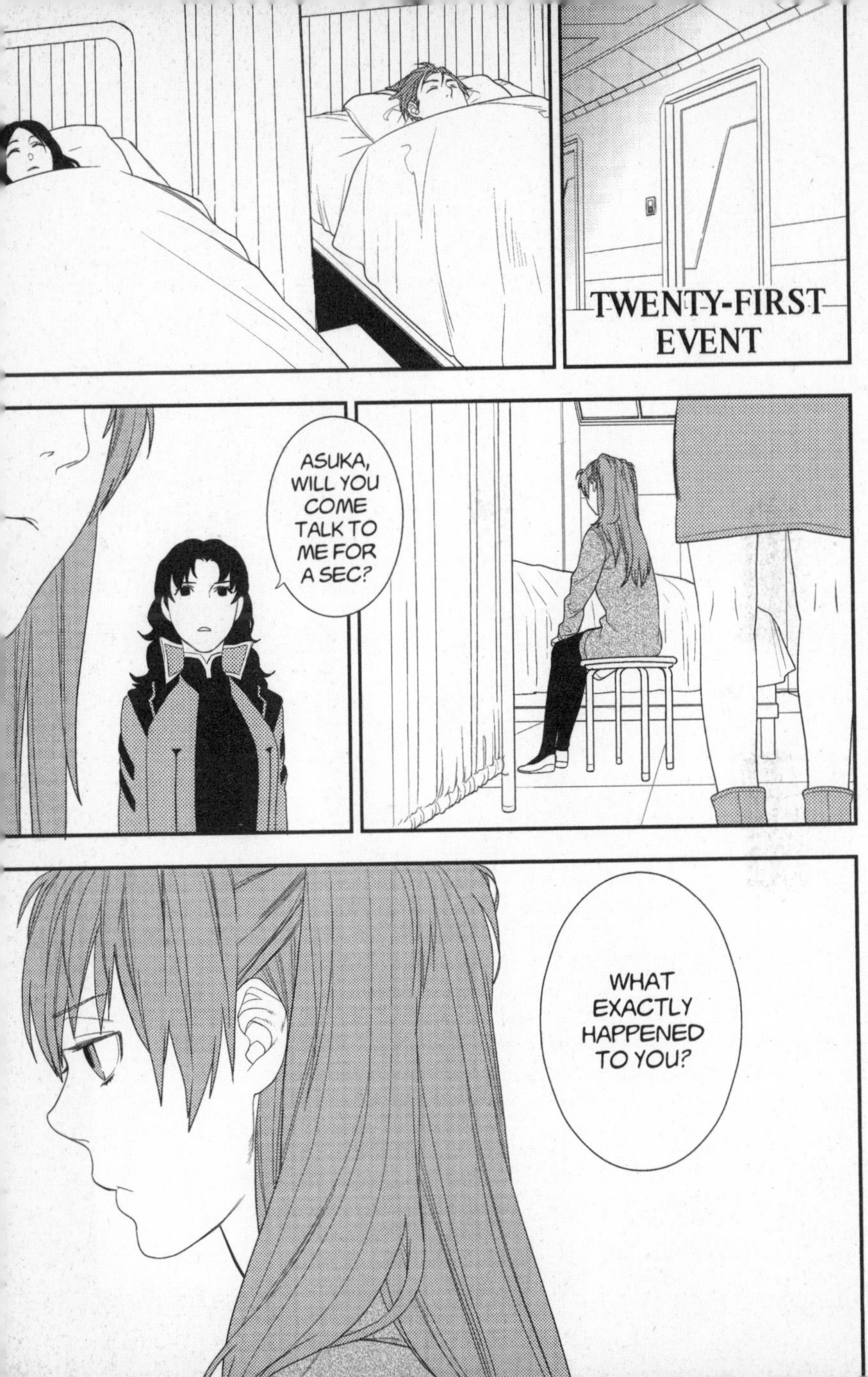
TWENTY-FIRST EVENT
ASUKA, WILL YOU COME TALK TO ME FOR A SEC?
WHAT EXACTLY HAPPENED TO YOU?

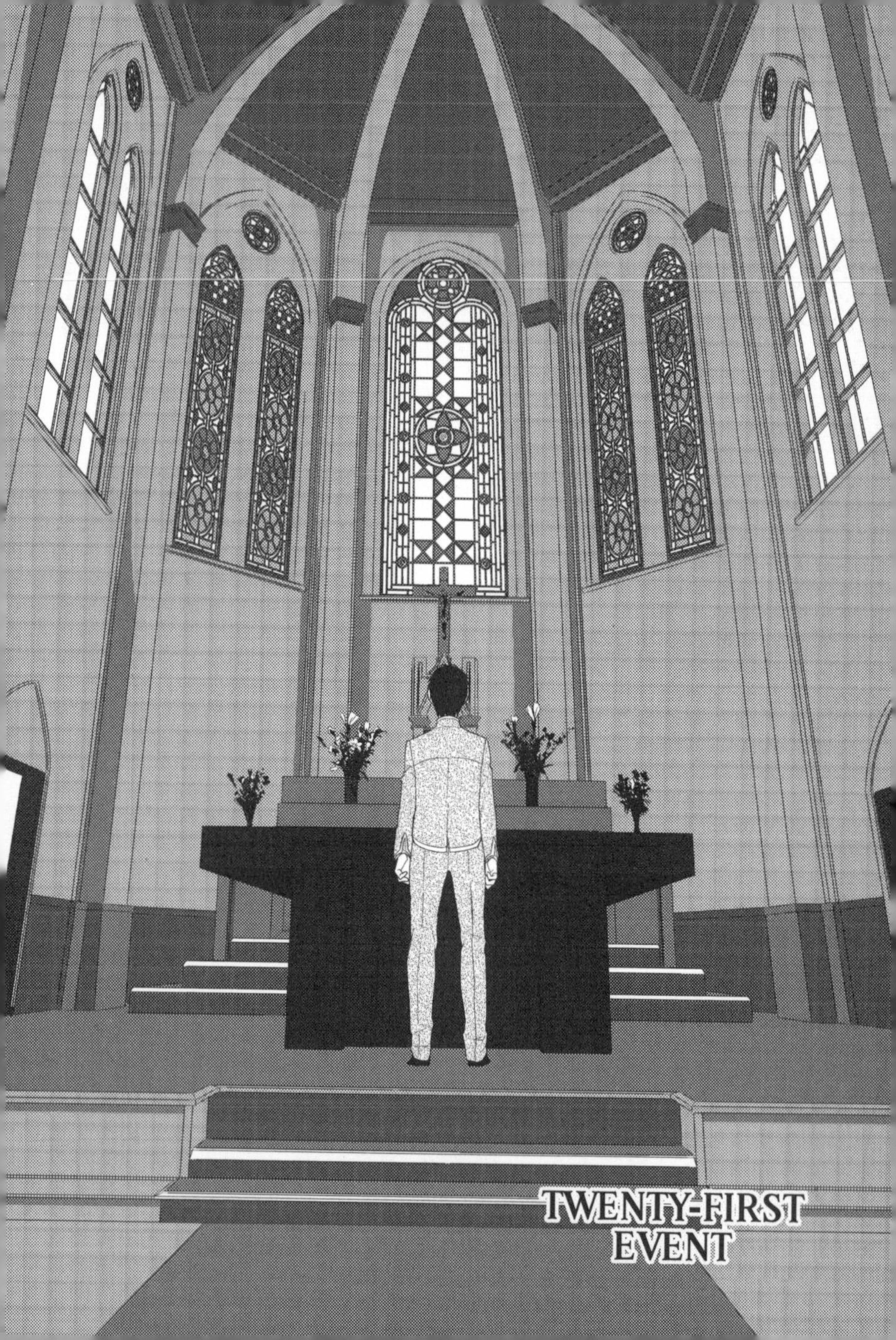
TWENTY-FIRST EVENT

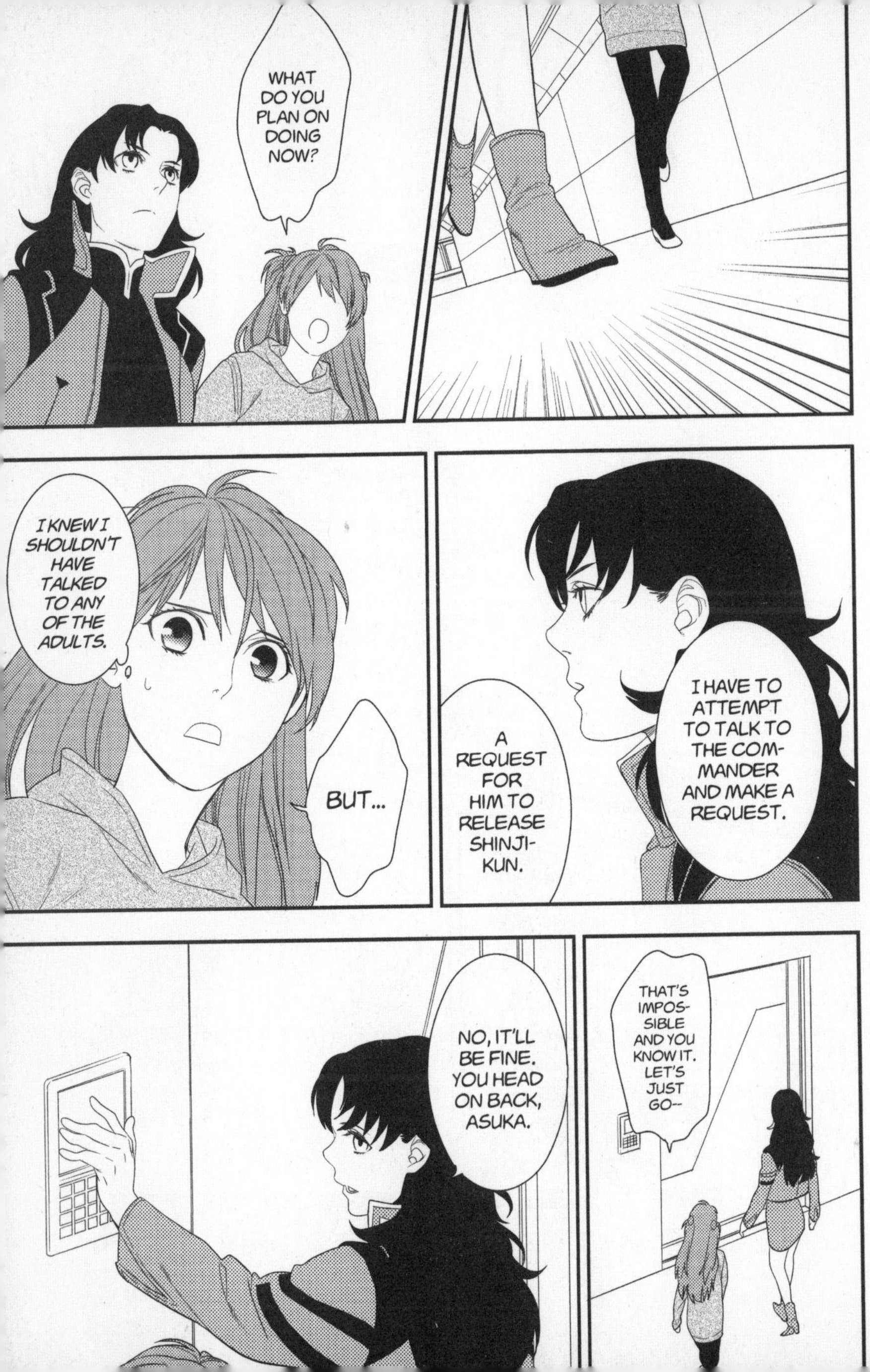
WHAT DO YOU PLAN ON DOING NOW?
I HAVE TO ATTEMPT TO TALK TO THE COM-MANDER AND MAKE A REQUEST.
A REQUEST FOR HIM TO RELEASE SHINJI-KUN.
I KNEW I SHOULDN'T HAVE TALKED TO ANY OF THE ADULTS.
BUT...
THAT'S IMPOS-SIBLE AND YOU KNOW IT. LET'S JUST GO--
NO, IT'LL BE FINE. YOU HEAD ON BACK, ASUKA.

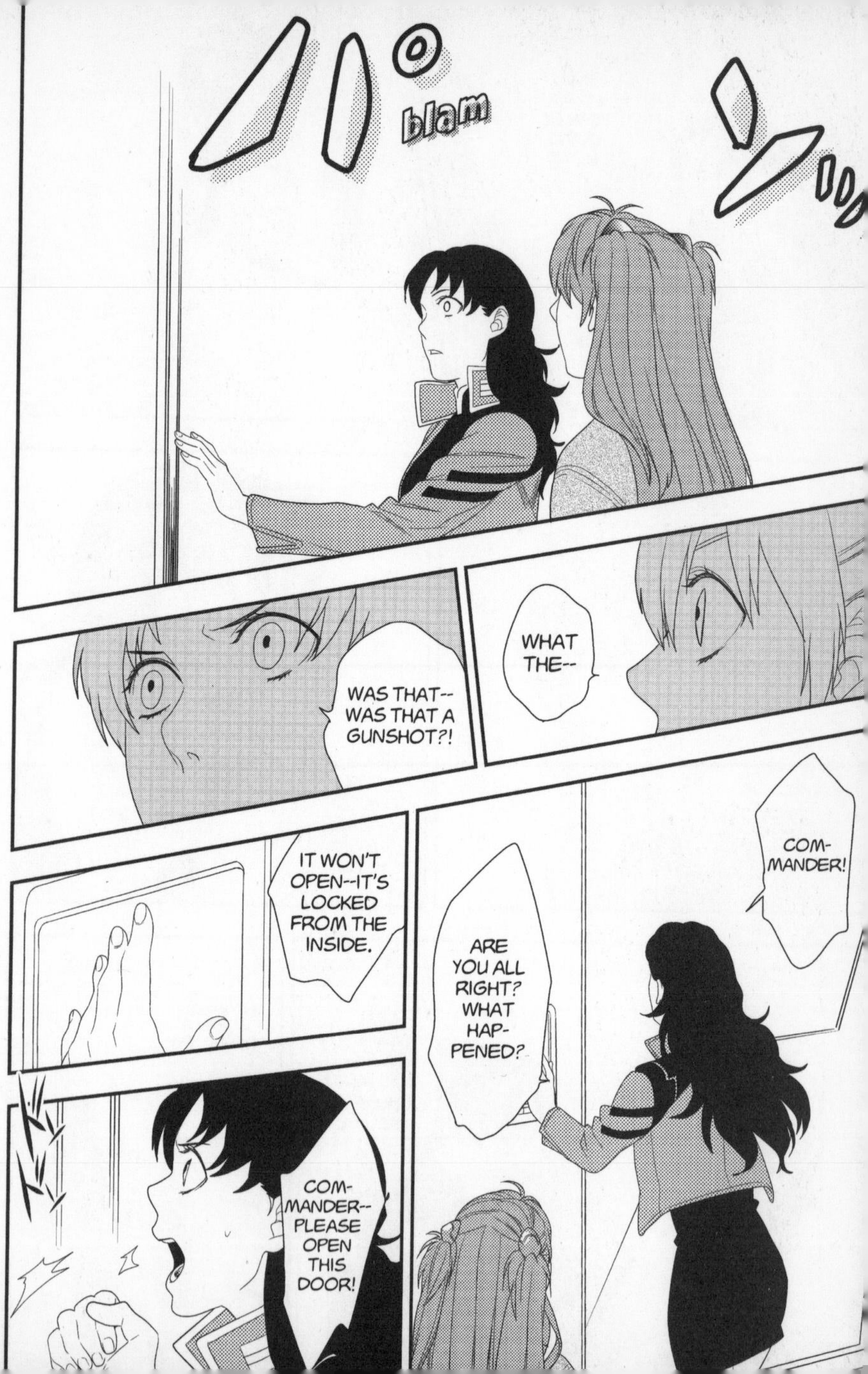
blam
WHAT THE--
WAS THAT-- WAS THAT A GUNSHOT?!
COM-MANDER!
ARE YOU ALL RIGHT? WHAT HAP-PENED?
IT WON'T OPEN--IT'S LOCKED FROM THE INSIDE.
COM-MANDER-- PLEASE OPEN THIS DOOR!

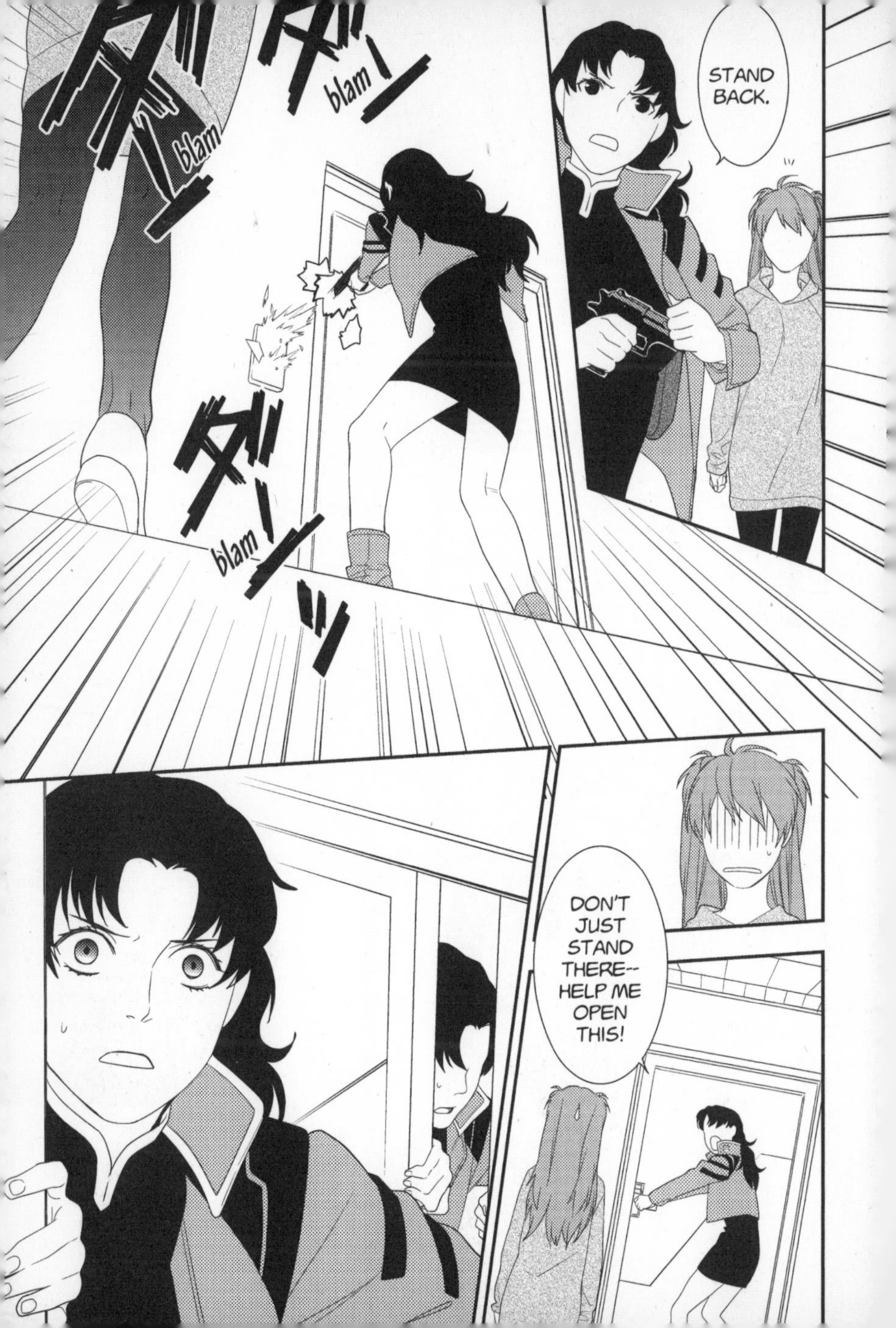
STAND BACK.
blam
blam
blam
DON'T JUST STAND THERE-- HELP ME OPEN THIS!

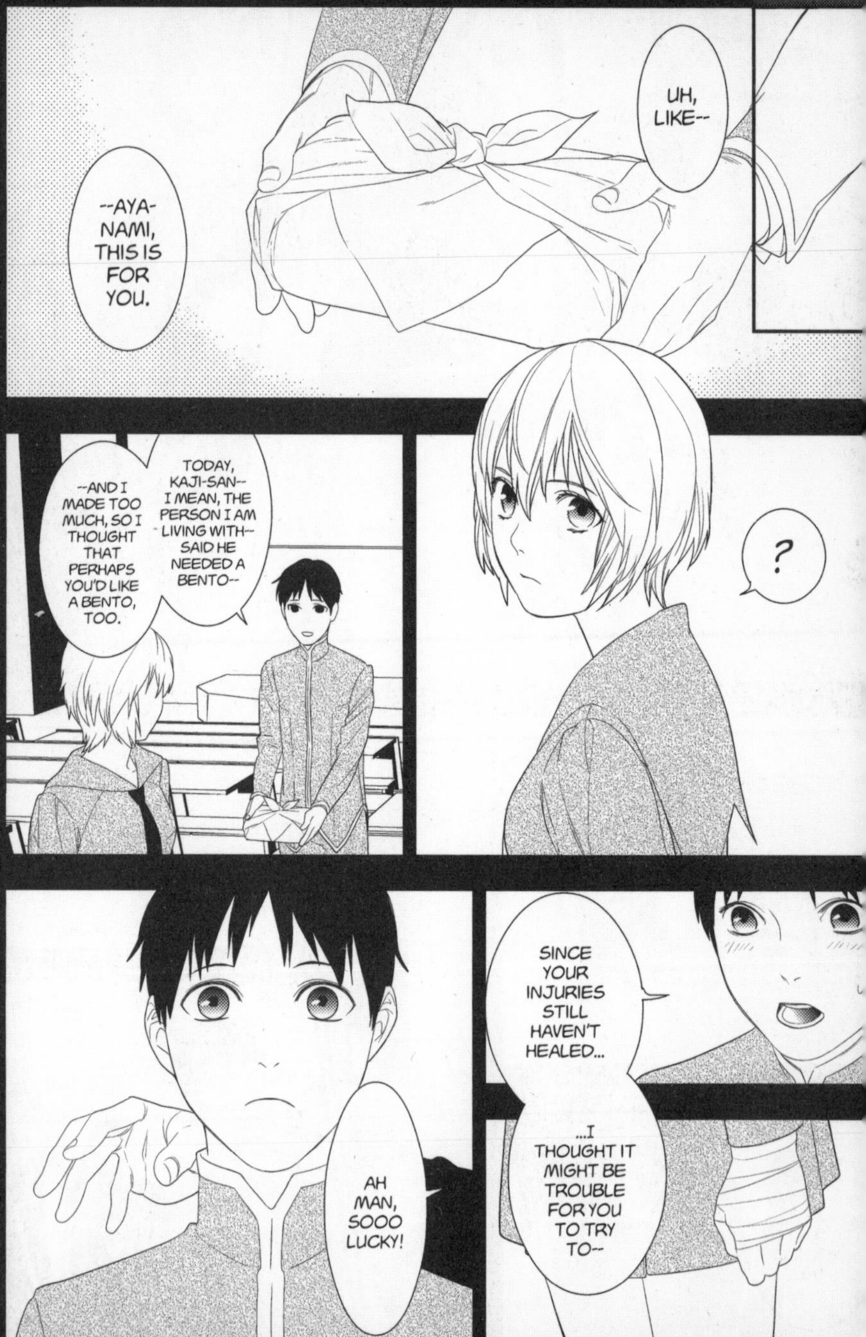
UH, LIKE--
--AYA-NAMI, THIS IS FOR YOU.
?
TODAY, KAJI-SAN-- I MEAN, THE PERSON I AM LIVING WITH-- SAID HE NEEDED A BENTO--
--AND I MADE TOO MUCH, SO I THOUGHT THAT PERHAPS YOU'D LIKE A BENTO, TOO.
SINCE YOUR INJURIES STILL HAVEN'T HEALED...
...I THOUGHT IT MIGHT BE TROUBLE FOR YOU TO TRY TO--
AH MAN, SOOO LUCKY!

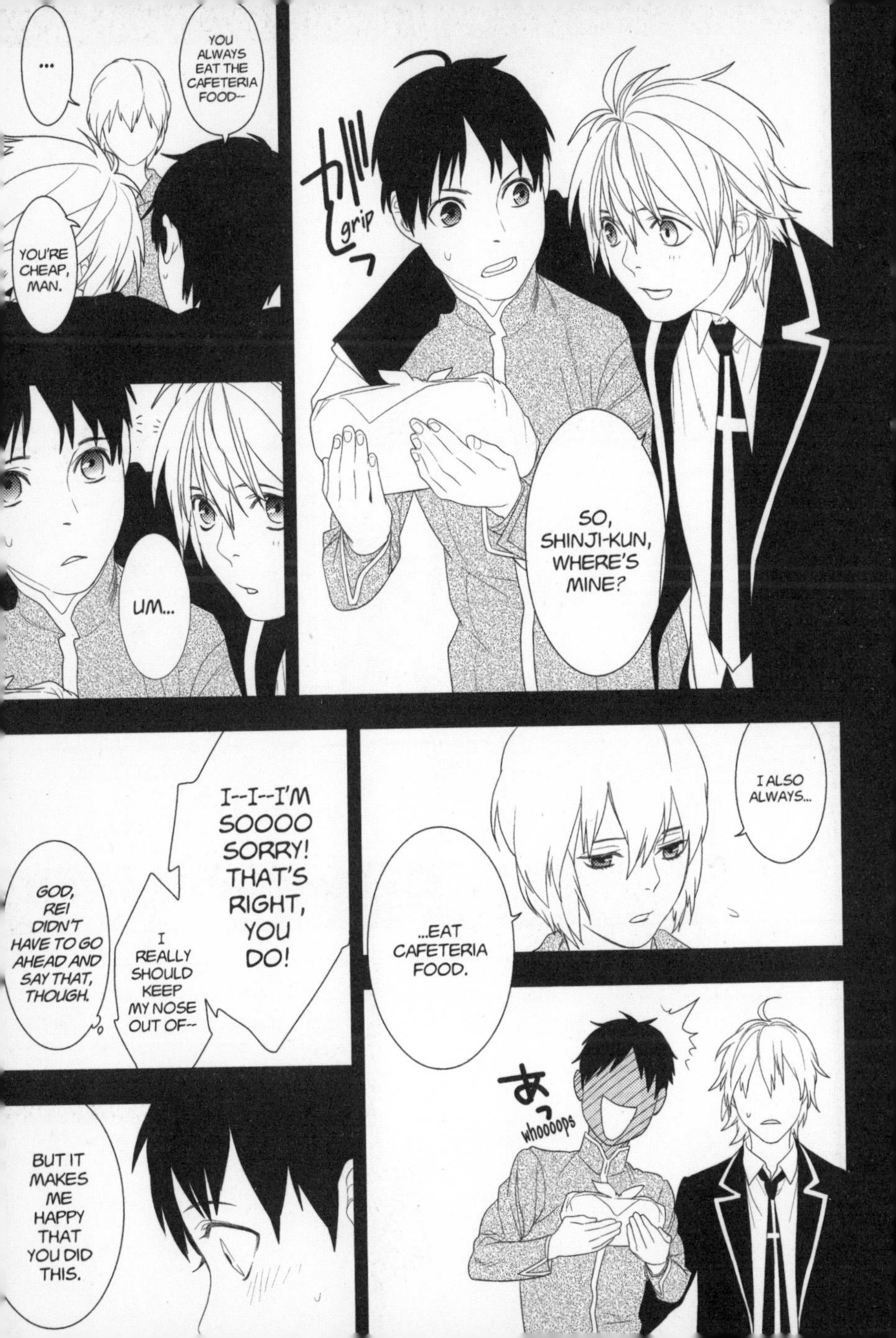
grip
SO, SHINJI-KUN, WHERE'S MINE?
YOU ALWAYS EAT THE CAFETERIA FOOD--
...
YOU'RE CHEAP, MAN.
UM...
I ALSO ALWAYS...
...EAT CAFETERIA FOOD.
あっ
whoooops
I--I--I'M SOOOO SORRY! THAT'S RIGHT, YOU DO!
I REALLY SHOULD KEEP MY NOSE OUT OF--
GOD, REI DIDN'T HAVE TO GO AHEAD AND SAY THAT, THOUGH.
BUT IT MAKES ME HAPPY THAT YOU DID THIS.

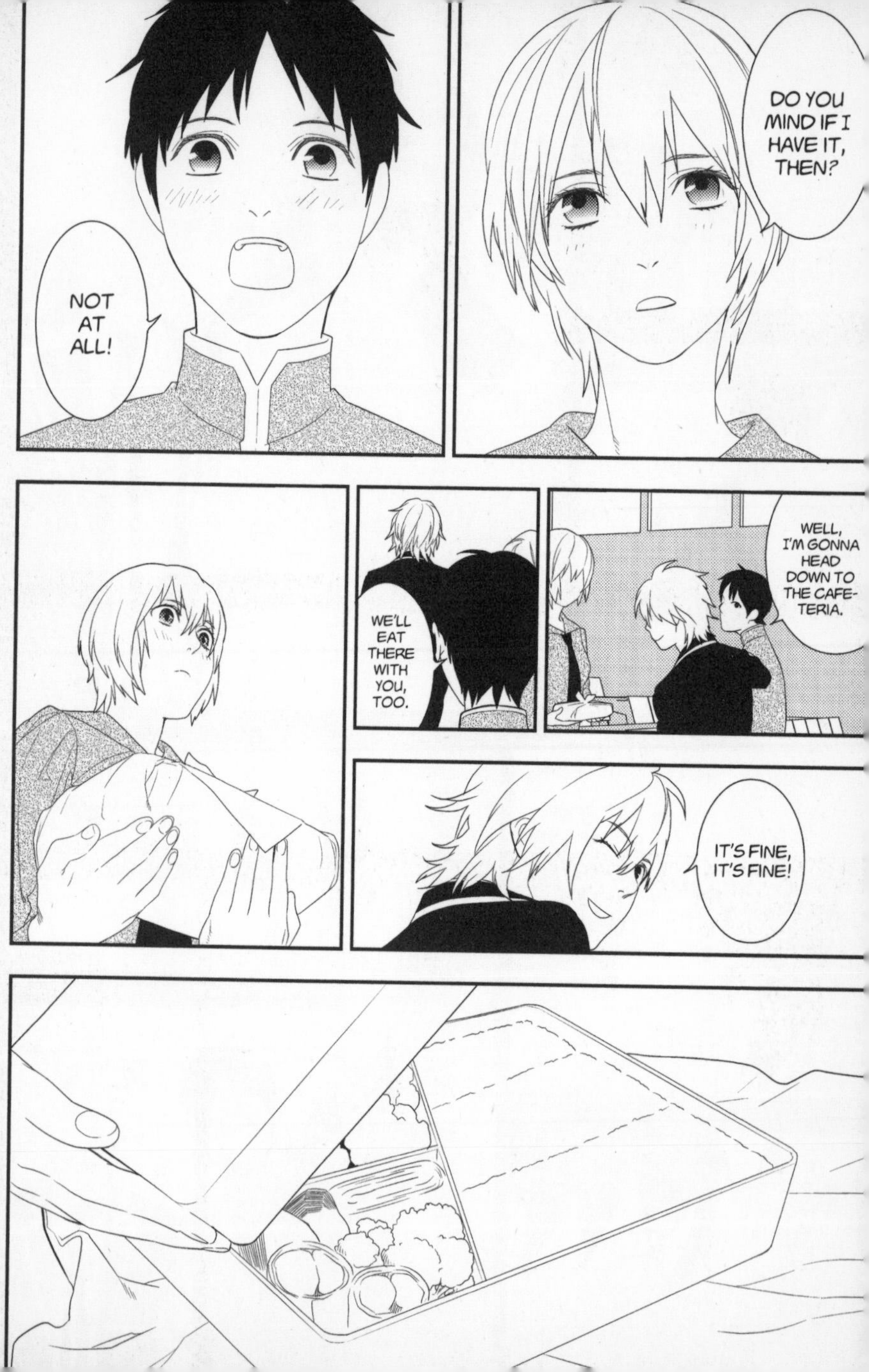
DO YOU MIND IF I HAVE IT, THEN?
NOT AT ALL!
WELL, I'M GONNA HEAD DOWN TO THE CAFE-TERIA.
WE'LL EAT THERE WITH YOU, TOO.
IT'S FINE, IT'S FINE!

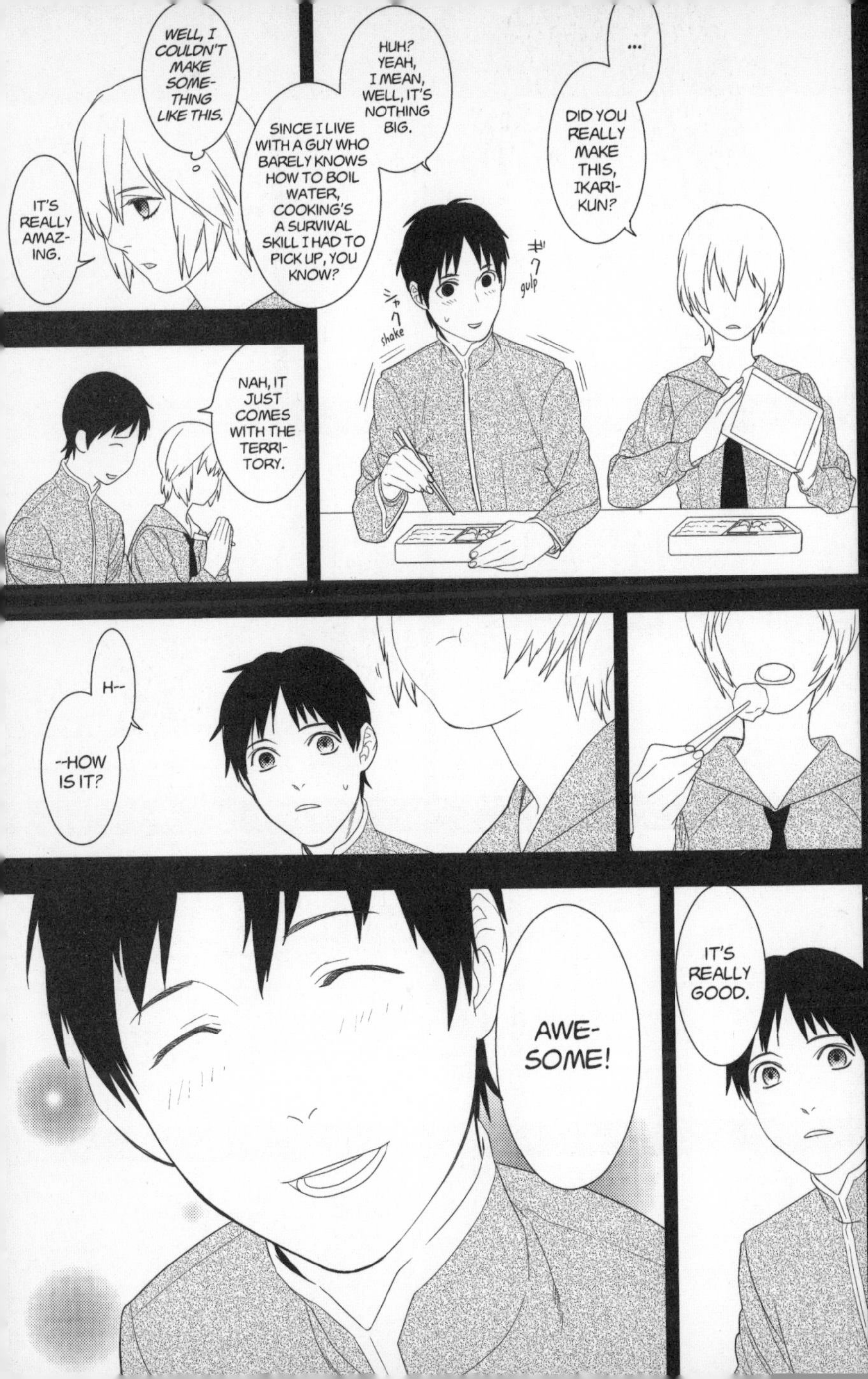
...
DID YOU REALLY MAKE THIS, IKARI-KUN?
HUH? YEAH, I MEAN, WELL, IT'S NOTHING BIG.
SINCE I LIVE WITH A GUY WHO BARELY KNOWS HOW TO BOIL WATER, COOKING'S A SURVIVAL SKILL I HAD TO PICK UP, YOU KNOW?
gulp
shake
WELL, I COULDN'T MAKE SOME-THING LIKE THIS.
IT'S REALLY AMAZ-ING.
NAH, IT JUST COMES WITH THE TERRI-TORY.
H--
--HOW IS IT?
IT'S REALLY GOOD.
AWE-SOME!

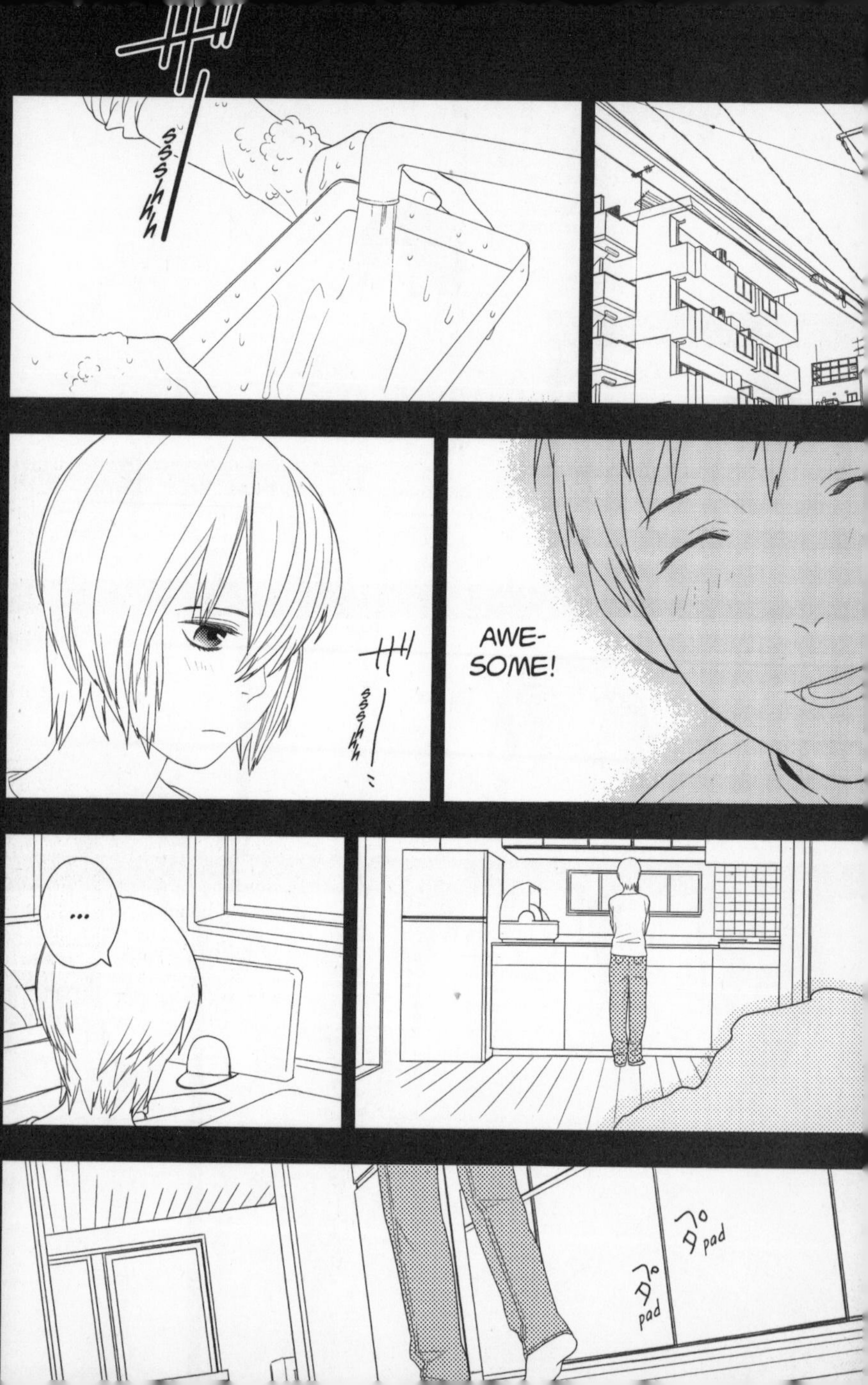
s-s-shhh
AWE-SOME!
ssshhh...
...
pad
pad

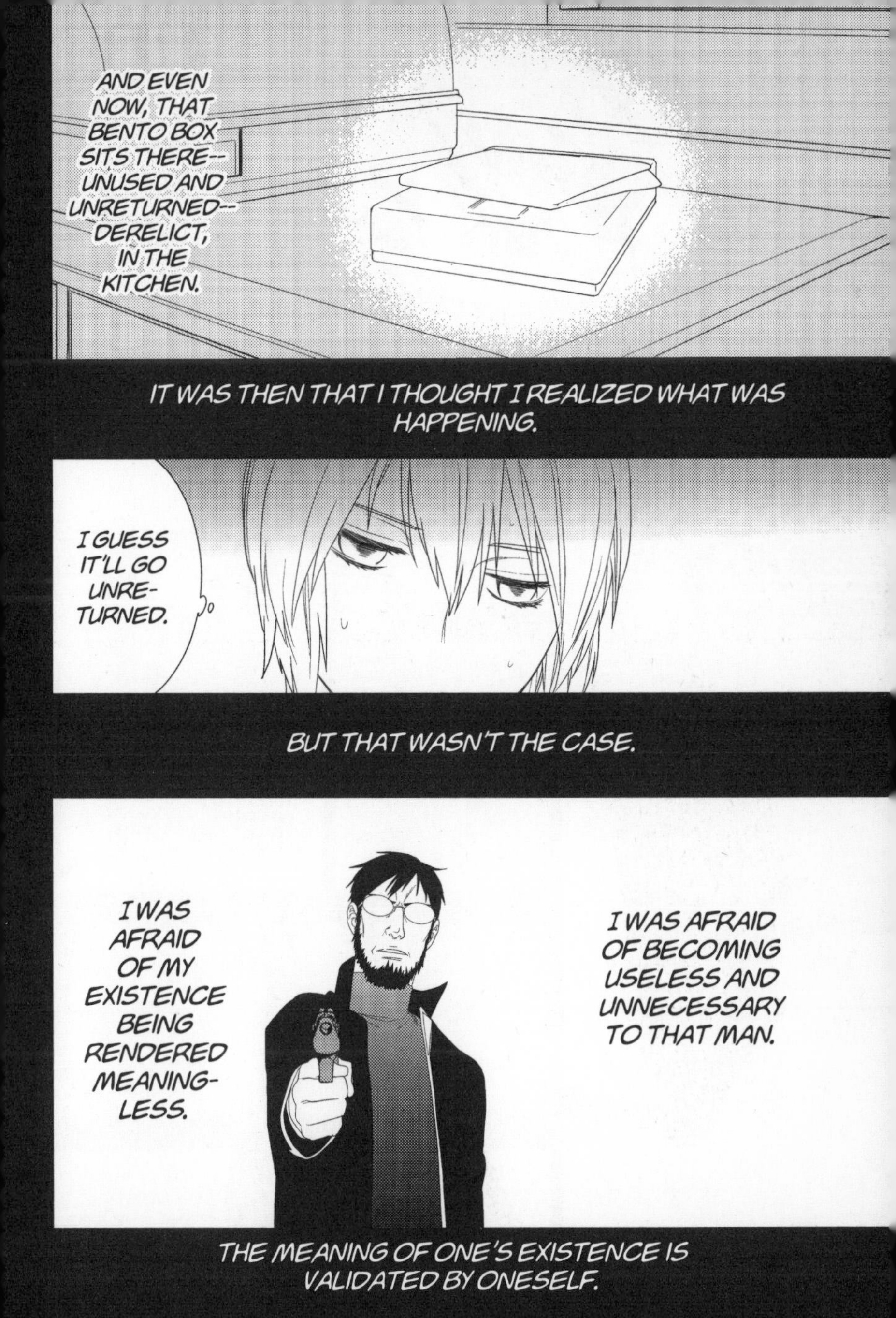
AND EVEN NOW, THAT BENTO BOX SITS THERE-- UNUSED AND UNRETURNED-- DERELICT, IN THE KITCHEN.
IT WAS THEN THAT I THOUGHT I REALIZED WHAT WAS HAPPENING.
I GUESS IT'LL GO UNRE-TURNED.
BUT THAT WASN'T THE CASE.
I WAS AFRAID OF BECOMING USELESS AND UNNECESSARY TO THAT MAN.
I WAS AFRAID OF MY EXISTENCE BEING RENDERED MEANING-LESS.
THE MEANING OF ONE'S EXISTENCE IS VALIDATED BY ONESELF.

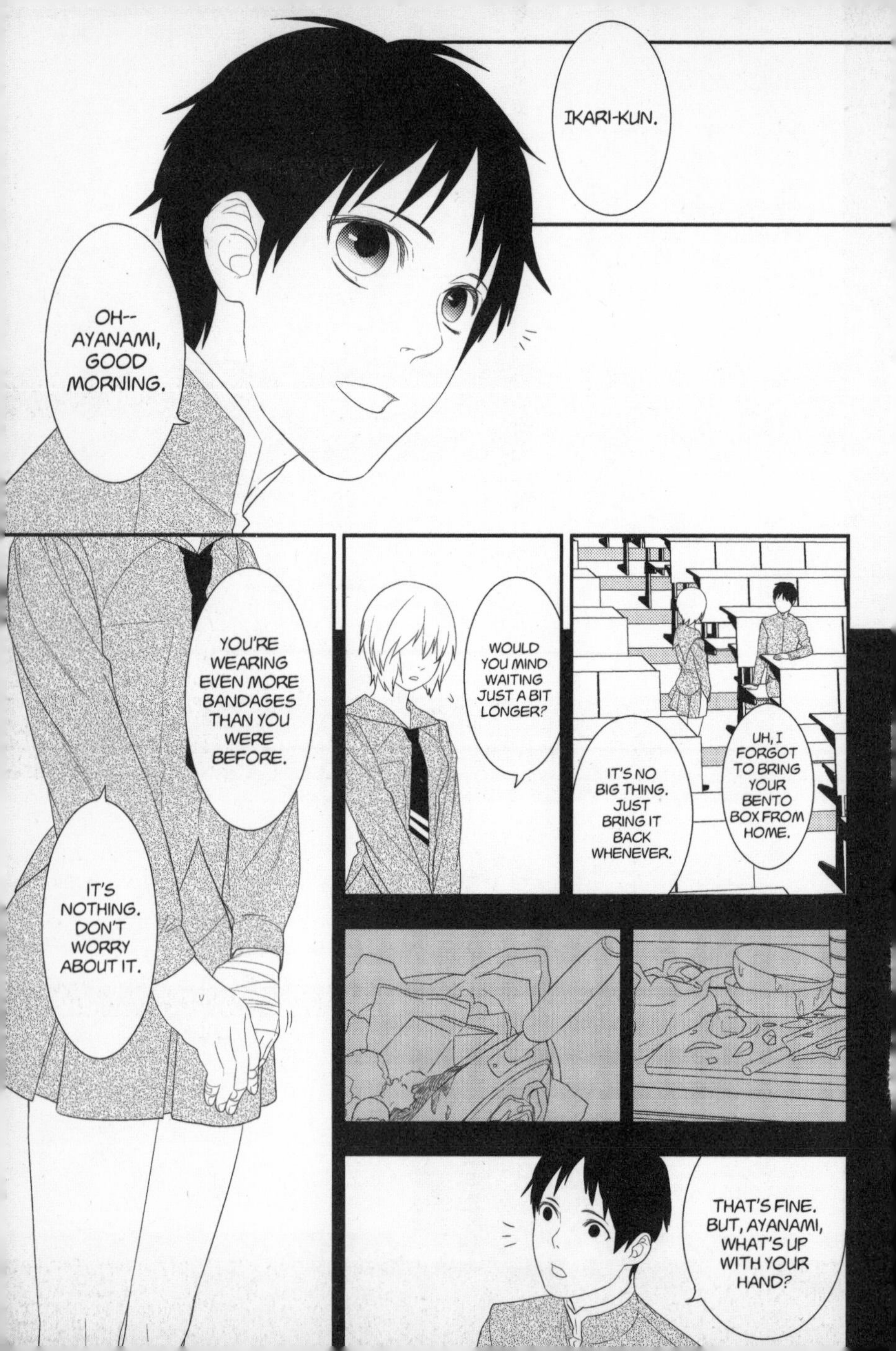
IKARI-KUN.
OH-- AYANAMI, GOOD MORNING.
UH, I FORGOT TO BRING YOUR BENTO BOX FROM HOME.
IT'S NO BIG THING. JUST BRING IT BACK WHENEVER.
WOULD YOU MIND WAITING JUST A BIT LONGER?
THAT'S FINE. BUT, AYANAMI, WHAT'S UP WITH YOUR HAND?
YOU'RE WEARING EVEN MORE BANDAGES THAN YOU WERE BEFORE.
IT'S NOTHING. DON'T WORRY ABOUT IT.

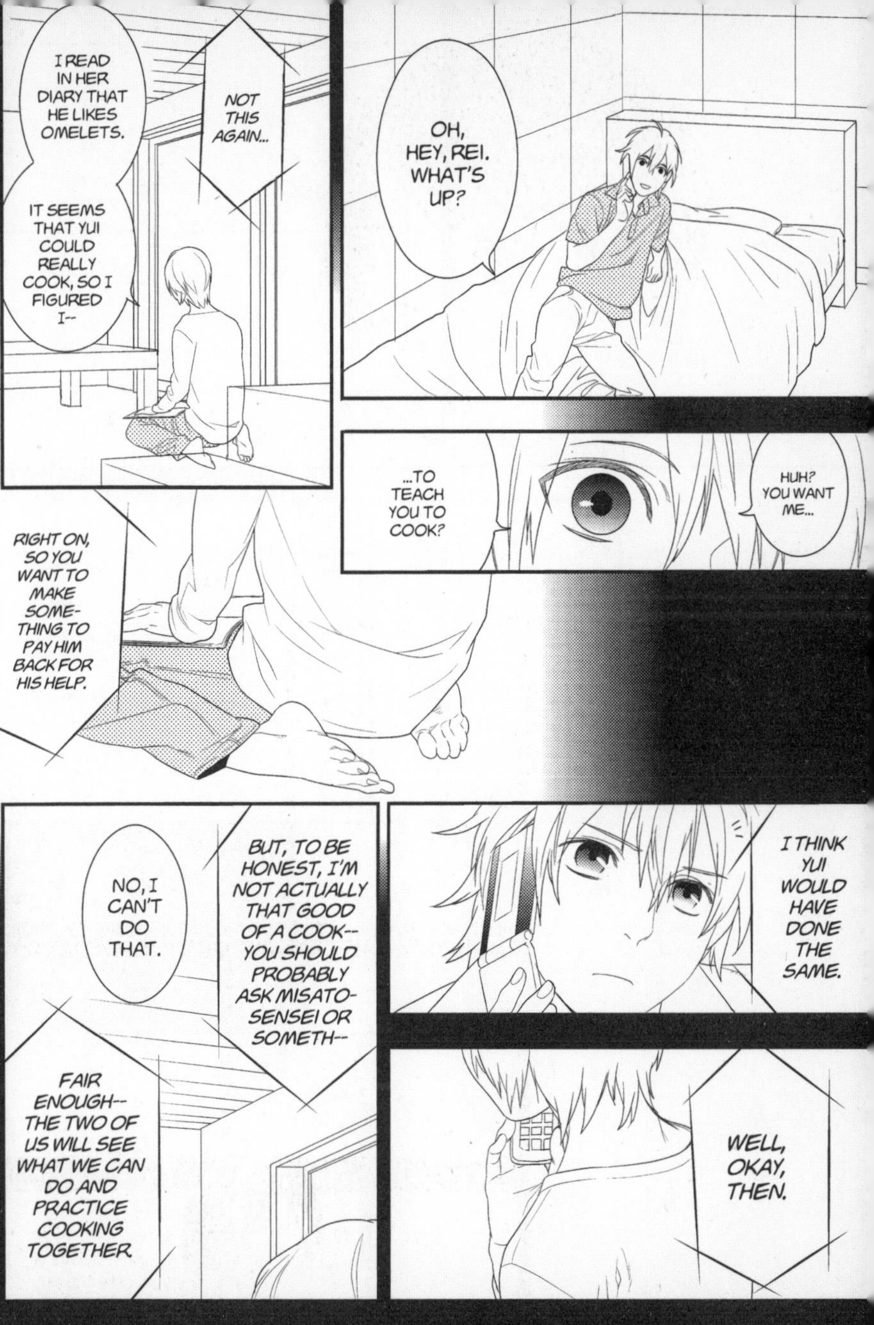
OH, HEY, REI. WHAT'S UP?
I READ IN HER DIARY THAT HE LIKES OMELETS.
NOT THIS AGAIN...
IT SEEMS THAT YUI COULD REALLY COOK, SO I FIGURED I--
HUH? YOU WANT ME...
...TO TEACH YOU TO COOK?
RIGHT ON, SO YOU WANT TO MAKE SOME-THING TO PAY HIM BACK FOR HIS HELP.
I THINK YUI WOULD HAVE DONE THE SAME.
WELL, OKAY, THEN.
BUT, TO BE HONEST, I'M NOT ACTUALLY THAT GOOD OF A COOK-- YOU SHOULD PROBABLY ASK MISATO-SENSEI OR SOMETH--
NO, I CAN'T DO THAT.
FAIR ENOUGH-- THE TWO OF US WILL SEE WHAT WE CAN DO AND PRACTICE COOKING TOGETHER.

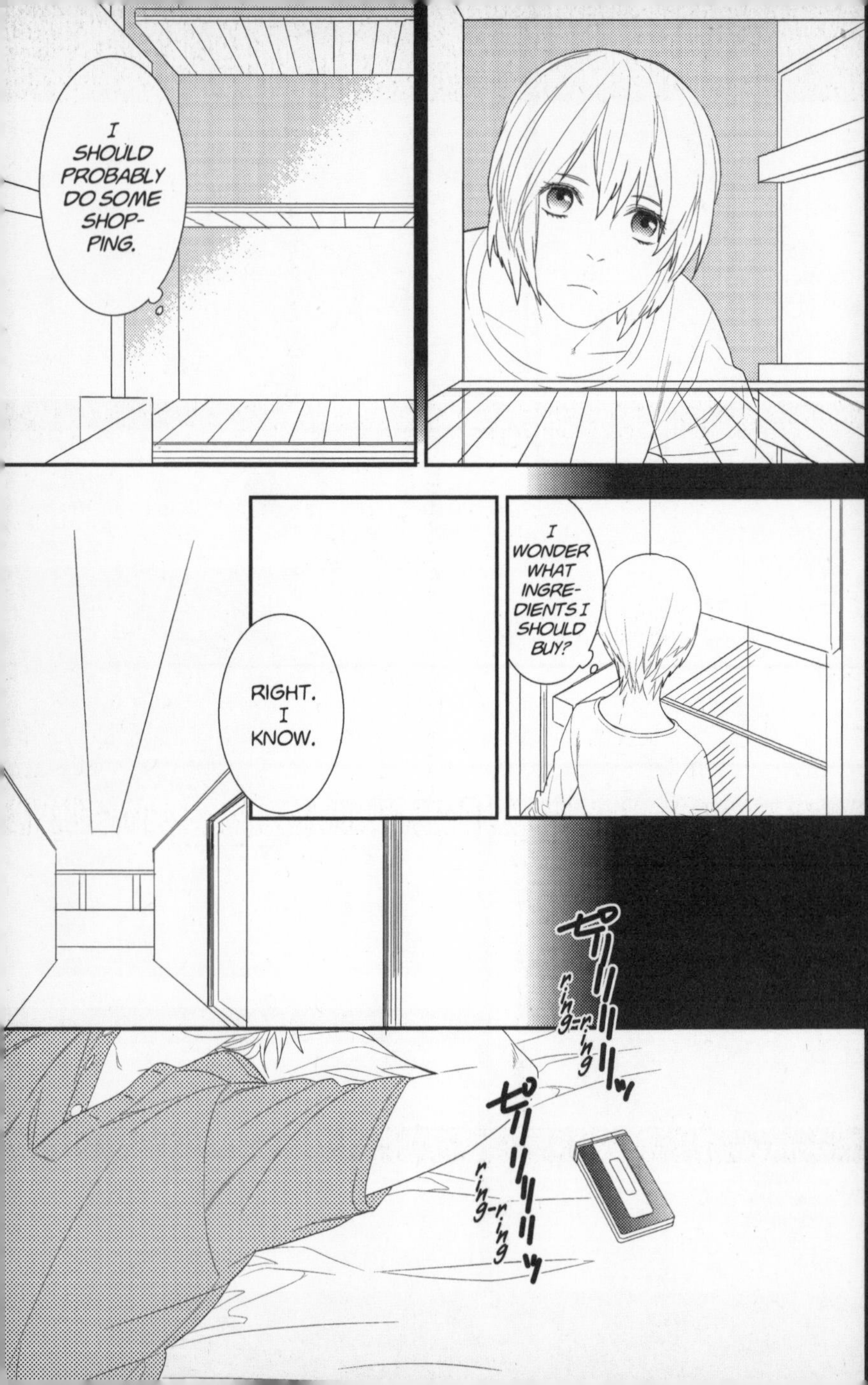
I SHOULD PROBABLY DO SOME SHOP-PING.
I WONDER WHAT INGRE-DIENTS I SHOULD BUY?
RIGHT. I KNOW.
ring-ring
ring-ring

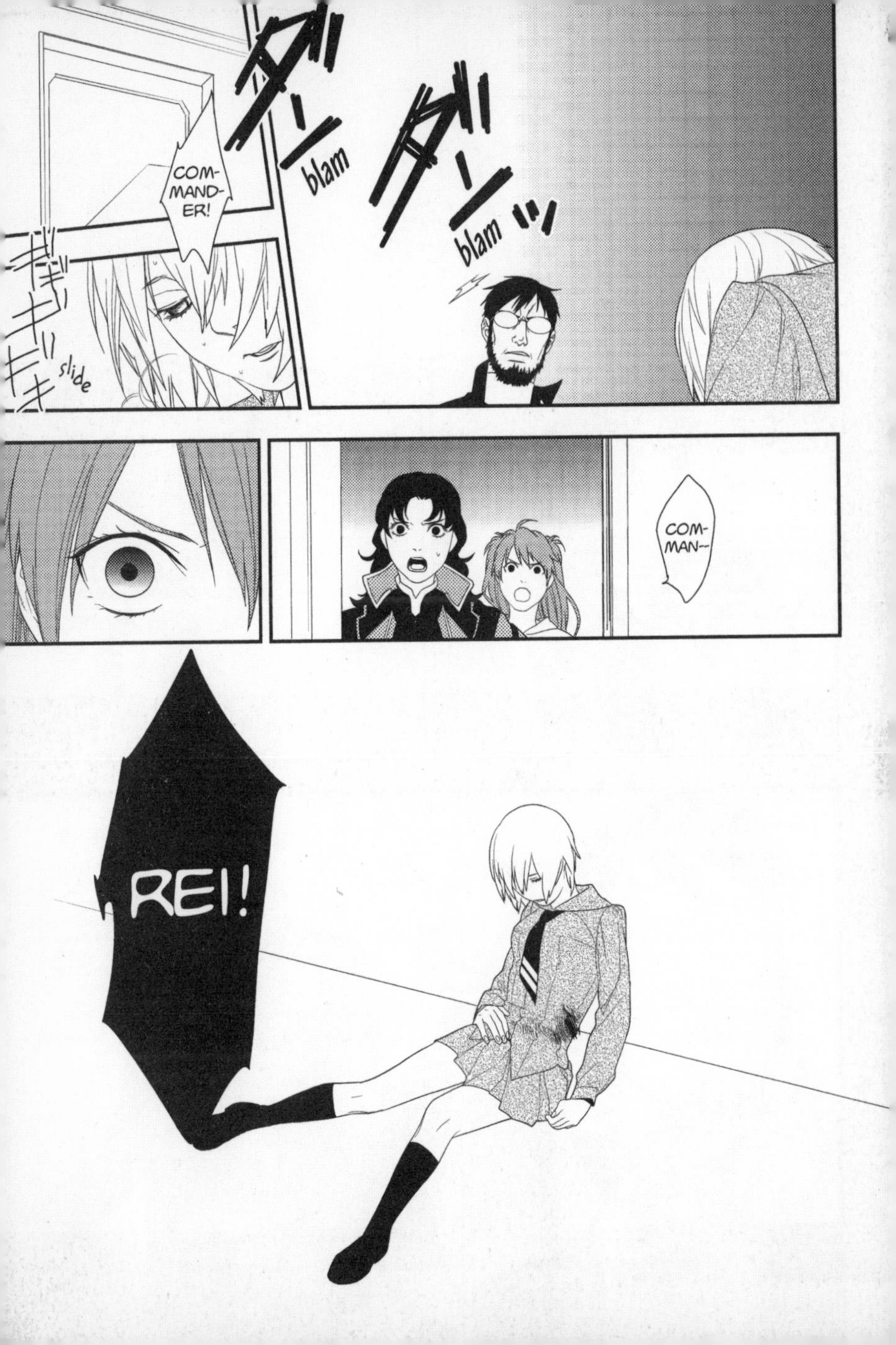
blam
blam
COM-MAND-ER!
slide
COM-MAN--
REI!

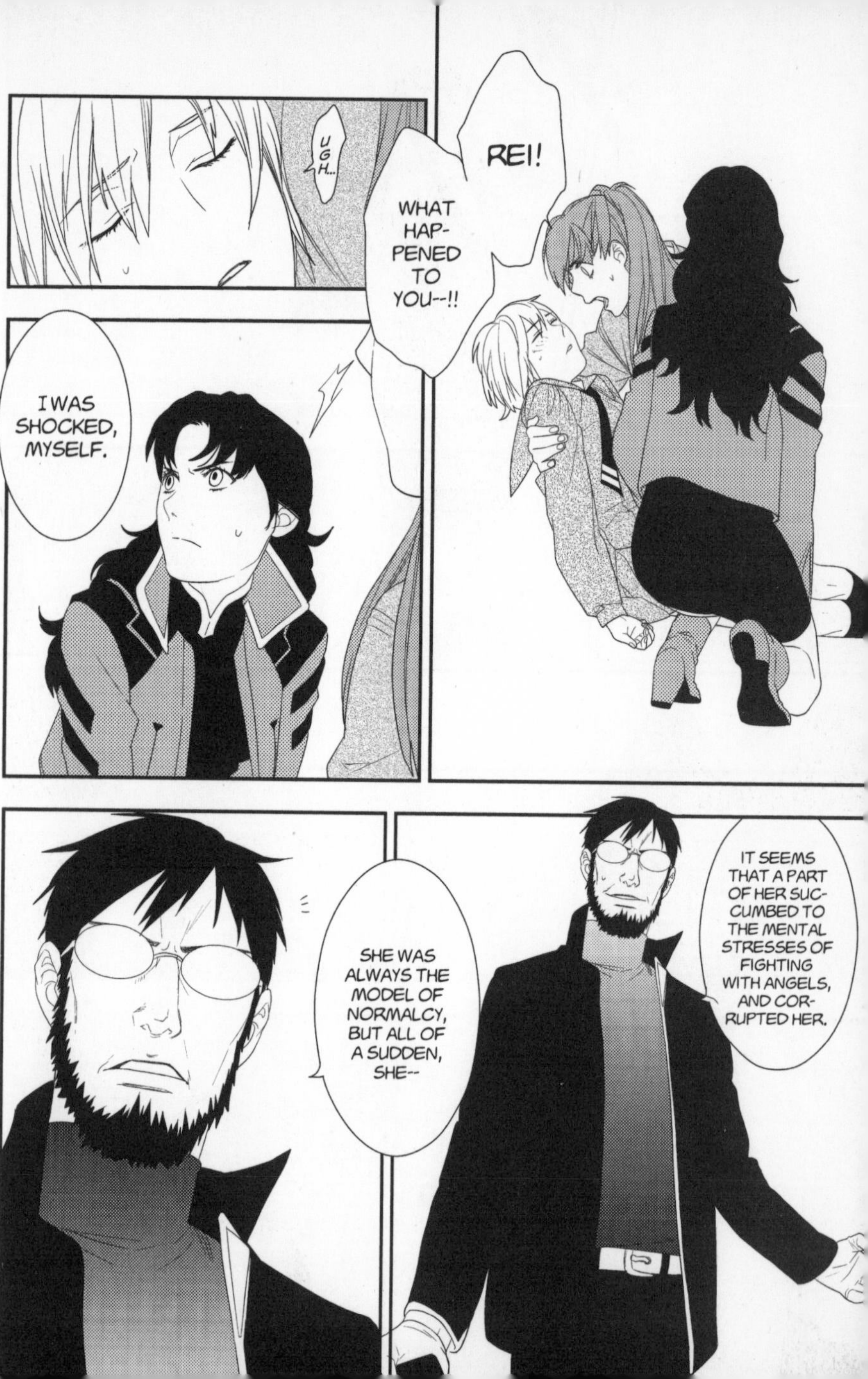
REI!
WHAT HAP-PENED TO YOU--!!
UGH...
I WAS SHOCKED, MYSELF.
IT SEEMS THAT A PART OF HER SUC-CUMBED TO THE MENTAL STRESSES OF FIGHTING WITH ANGELS, AND COR-RUPTED HER.
SHE WAS ALWAYS THE MODEL OF NORMALCY, BUT ALL OF A SUDDEN, SHE--

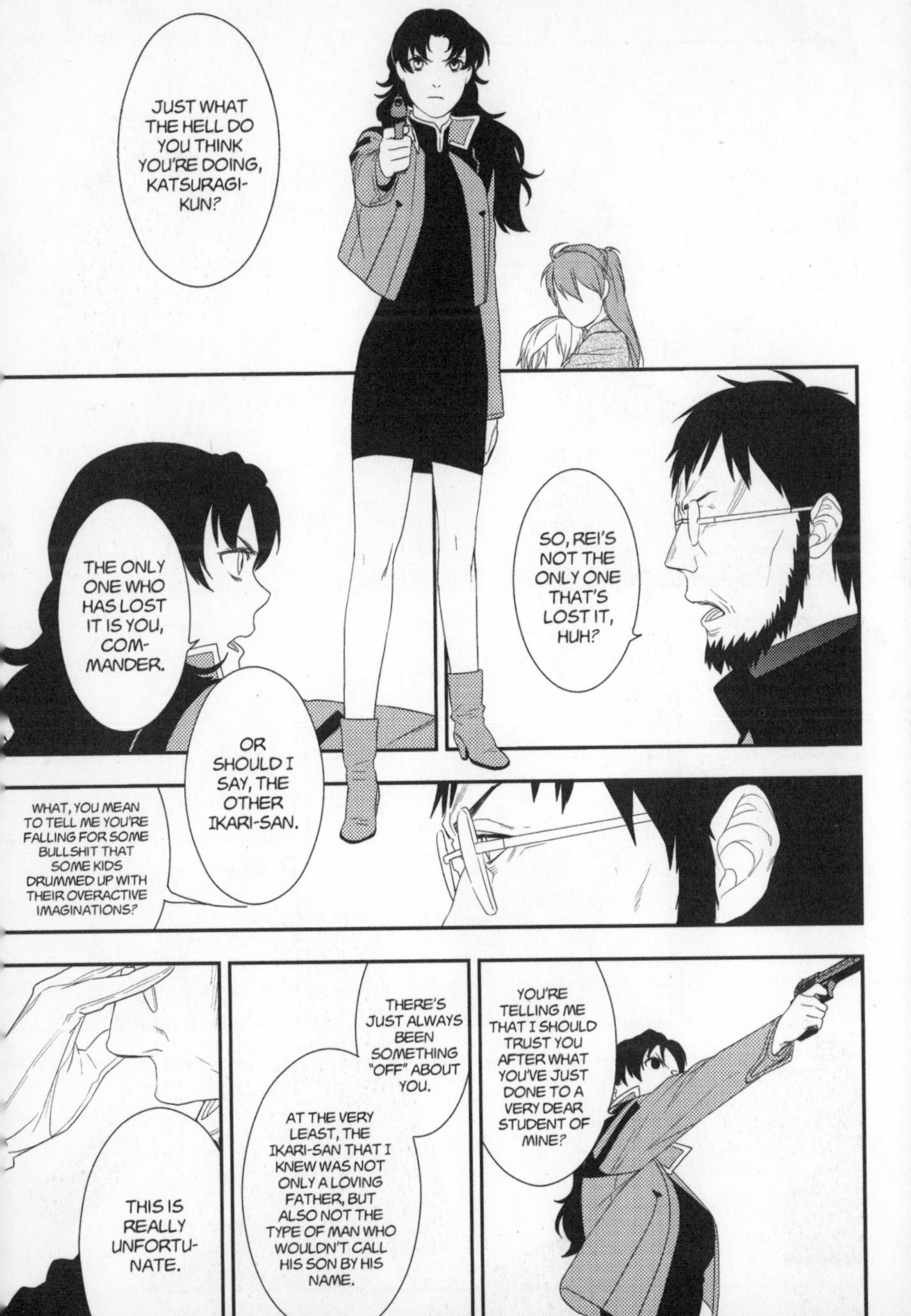
JUST WHAT THE HELL DO YOU THINK YOU'RE DOING, KATSURAGI-KUN?
SO, REI'S NOT THE ONLY ONE THAT'S LOST IT, HUH?
THE ONLY ONE WHO HAS LOST IT IS YOU, COM-MANDER.
OR SHOULD I SAY, THE OTHER IKARI-SAN.
WHAT, YOU MEAN TO TELL ME YOU'RE FALLING FOR SOME BULLSHIT THAT SOME KIDS DRUMMED UP WITH THEIR OVERACTIVE IMAGINATIONS?
YOU'RE TELLING ME THAT I SHOULD TRUST YOU AFTER WHAT YOU'VE JUST DONE TO A VERY DEAR STUDENT OF MINE?
THERE'S JUST ALWAYS BEEN SOMETHING "OFF" ABOUT YOU.
AT THE VERY LEAST, THE IKARI-SAN THAT I KNEW WAS NOT ONLY A LOVING FATHER, BUT ALSO NOT THE TYPE OF MAN WHO WOULDN'T CALL HIS SON BY HIS NAME.
THIS IS REALLY UNFORTU-NATE.

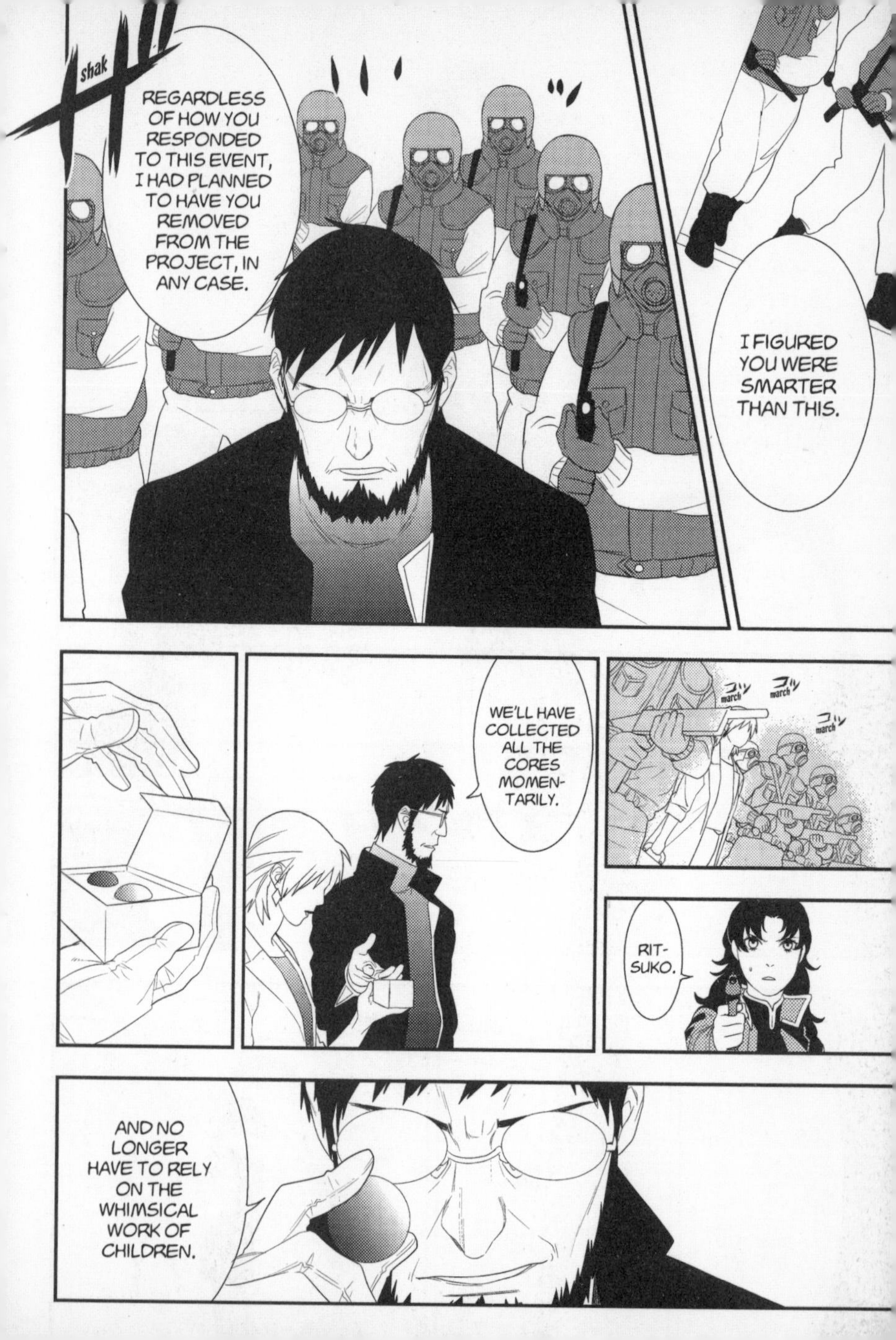
I FIGURED YOU WERE SMARTER THAN THIS.
shak
REGARDLESS OF HOW YOU RESPONDED TO THIS EVENT, I HAD PLANNED TO HAVE YOU REMOVED FROM THE PROJECT, IN ANY CASE.
コツ march
コツ march
コツ march
RIT-SUKO.
WE'LL HAVE COLLECTED ALL THE CORES MOMENTARILY.
AND NO LONGER HAVE TO RELY ON THE WHIMSICAL WORK OF CHILDREN.

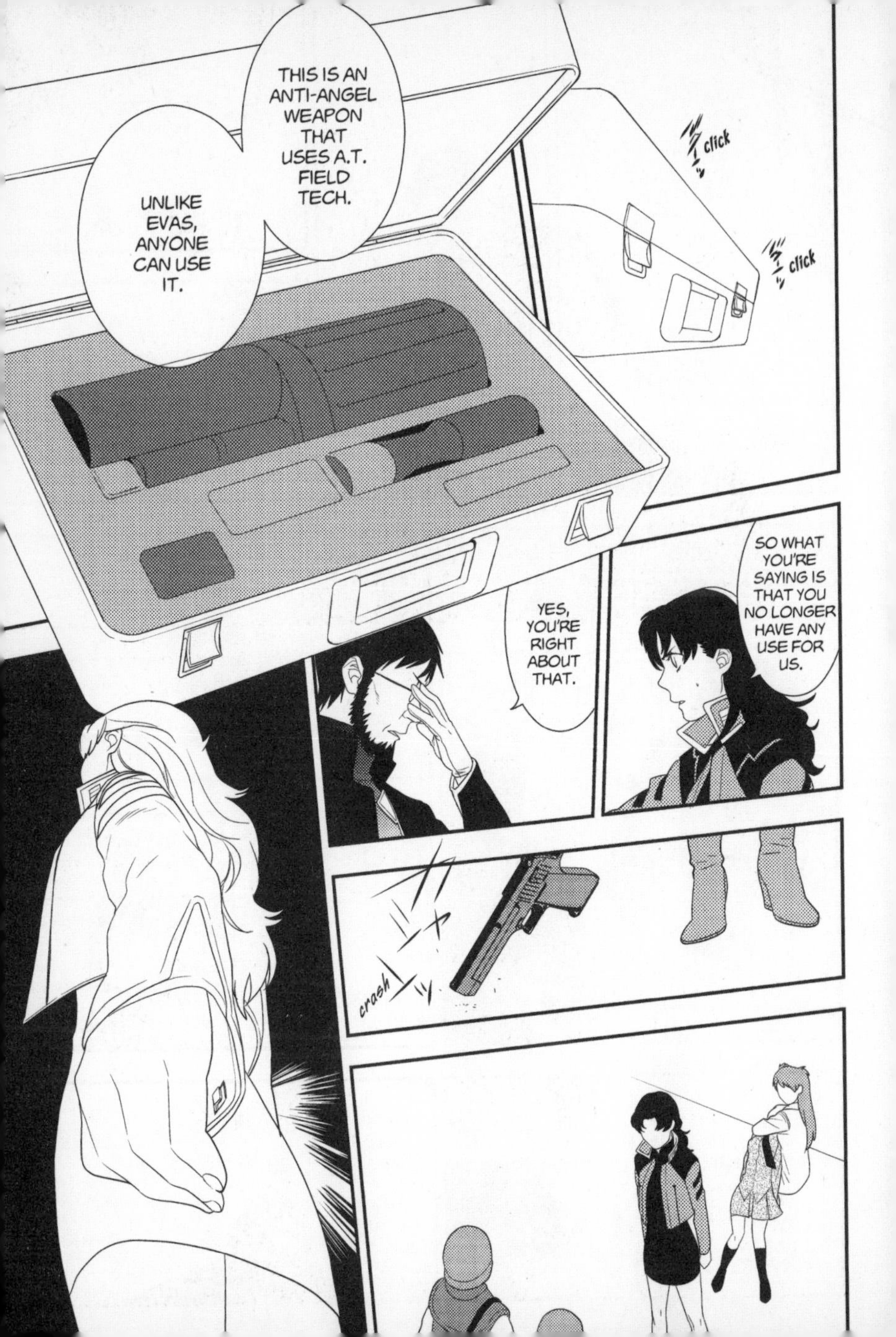
click
click
THIS IS AN ANTI-ANGEL WEAPON THAT USES A.T. FIELD TECH.
UNLIKE EVAS, ANYONE CAN USE IT.
SO WHAT YOU'RE SAYING IS THAT YOU NO LONGER HAVE ANY USE FOR US.
YES, YOU'RE RIGHT ABOUT THAT.
crash

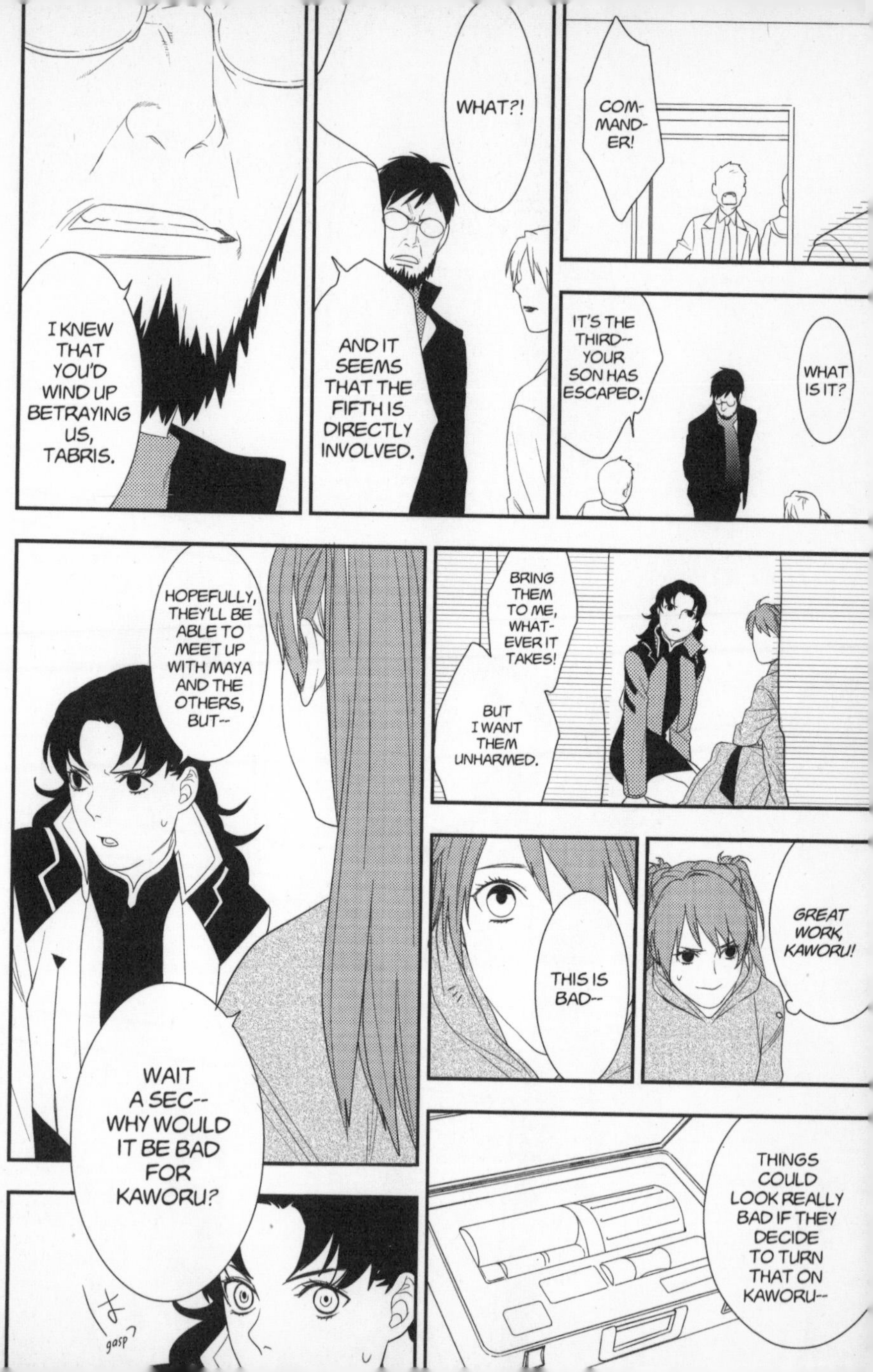
COMMANDER!
WHAT IS IT?
IT'S THE THIRD-- YOUR SON HAS ESCAPED.
WHAT?!
AND IT SEEMS THAT THE FIFTH IS DIRECTLY INVOLVED.
I KNEW THAT YOU'D WIND UP BETRAYING US, TABRIS.
BRING THEM TO ME, WHATEVER IT TAKES!
BUT I WANT THEM UNHARMED.
GREAT WORK, KAWORU!
THIS IS BAD--
HOPEFULLY, THEY'LL BE ABLE TO MEET UP WITH MAYA AND THE OTHERS, BUT--
WAIT A SEC-- WHY WOULD IT BE BAD FOR KAWORU?
THINGS COULD LOOK REALLY BAD IF THEY DECIDE TO TURN THAT ON KAWORU--
gasp

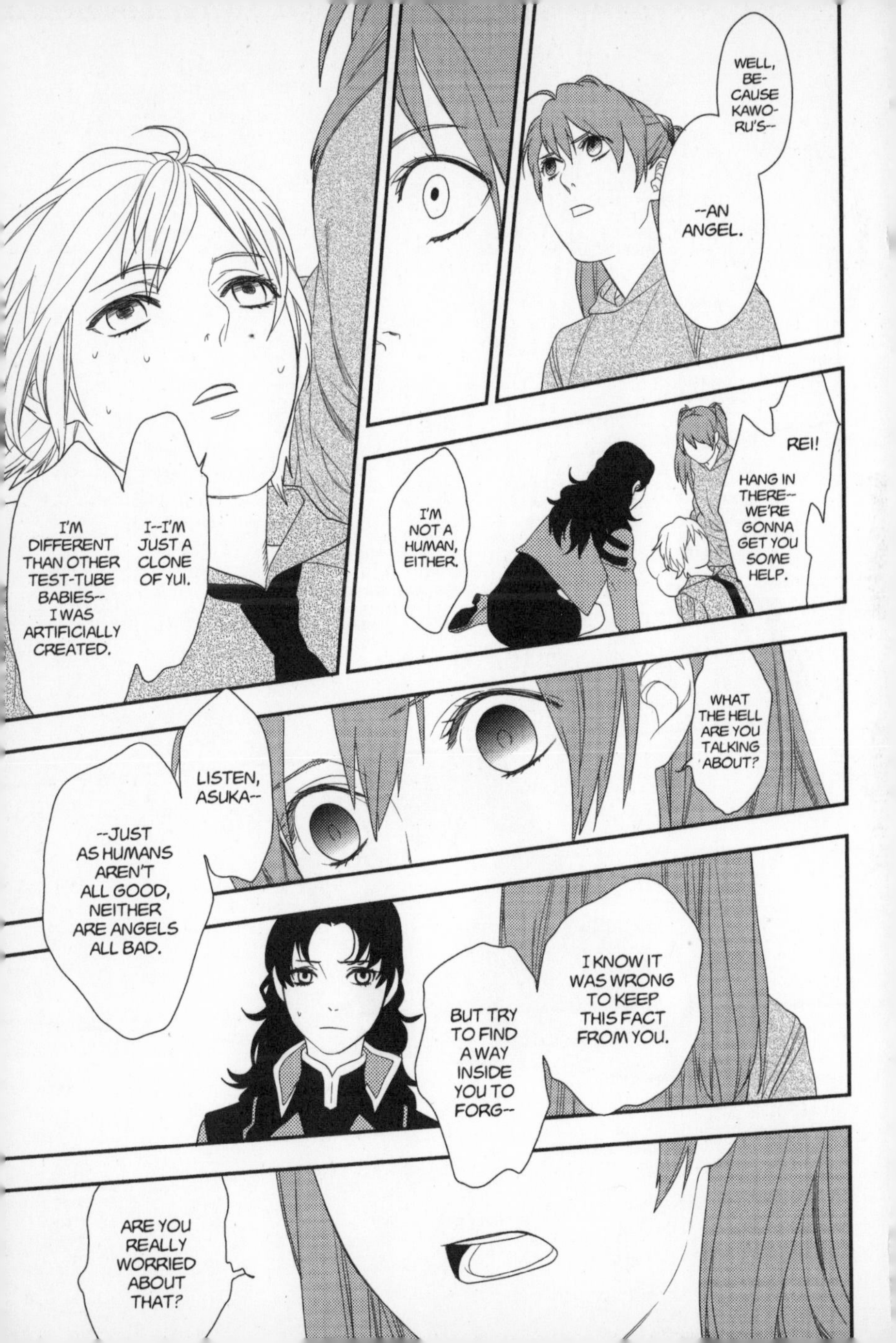
WELL, BE-CAUSE KAWO-RU'S--
--AN ANGEL.
REI!
HANG IN THERE-- WE'RE GONNA GET YOU SOME HELP.
I'M NOT A HUMAN, EITHER.
I--I'M JUST A CLONE OF YUI.
I'M DIFFERENT THAN OTHER TEST-TUBE BABIES-- I WAS ARTIFICIALLY CREATED.
WHAT THE HELL ARE YOU TALKING ABOUT?
LISTEN, ASUKA--
--JUST AS HUMANS AREN'T ALL GOOD, NEITHER ARE ANGELS ALL BAD.
I KNOW IT WAS WRONG TO KEEP THIS FACT FROM YOU.
BUT TRY TO FIND A WAY INSIDE YOU TO FORG--
ARE YOU REALLY WORRIED ABOUT THAT?

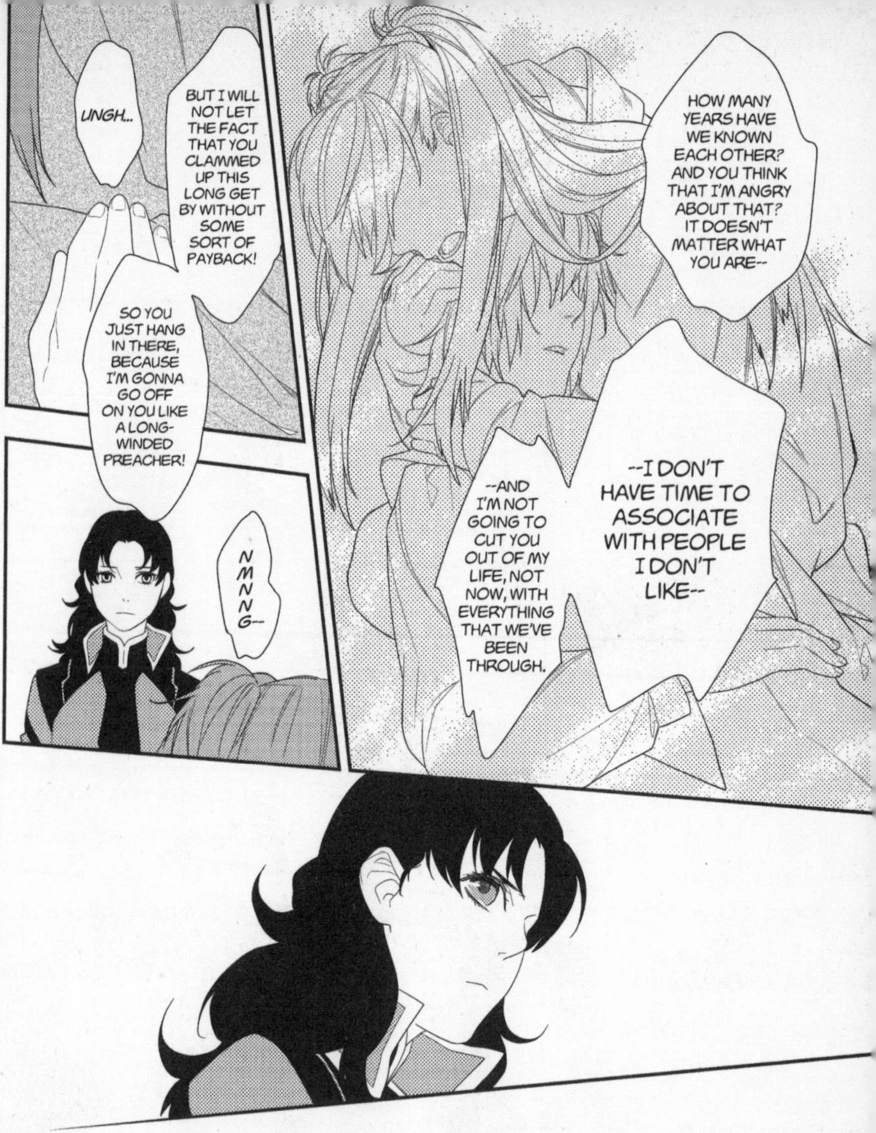
HOW MANY YEARS HAVE WE KNOWN EACH OTHER? AND YOU THINK THAT I'M ANGRY ABOUT THAT? IT DOESN'T MATTER WHAT YOU ARE--
--I DON'T HAVE TIME TO ASSOCIATE WITH PEOPLE I DON'T LIKE--
--AND I'M NOT GOING TO CUT YOU OUT OF MY LIFE, NOT NOW, WITH EVERYTHING THAT WE'VE BEEN THROUGH.
BUT I WILL NOT LET THE FACT THAT YOU CLAMMED UP THIS LONG GET BY WITHOUT SOME SORT OF PAYBACK!
UNGH...
SO YOU JUST HANG IN THERE, BECAUSE I'M GONNA GO OFF ON YOU LIKE A LONG-WINDED PREACHER!
NMNNG--
SHINJI-KUN...
KAWORU-KUN...

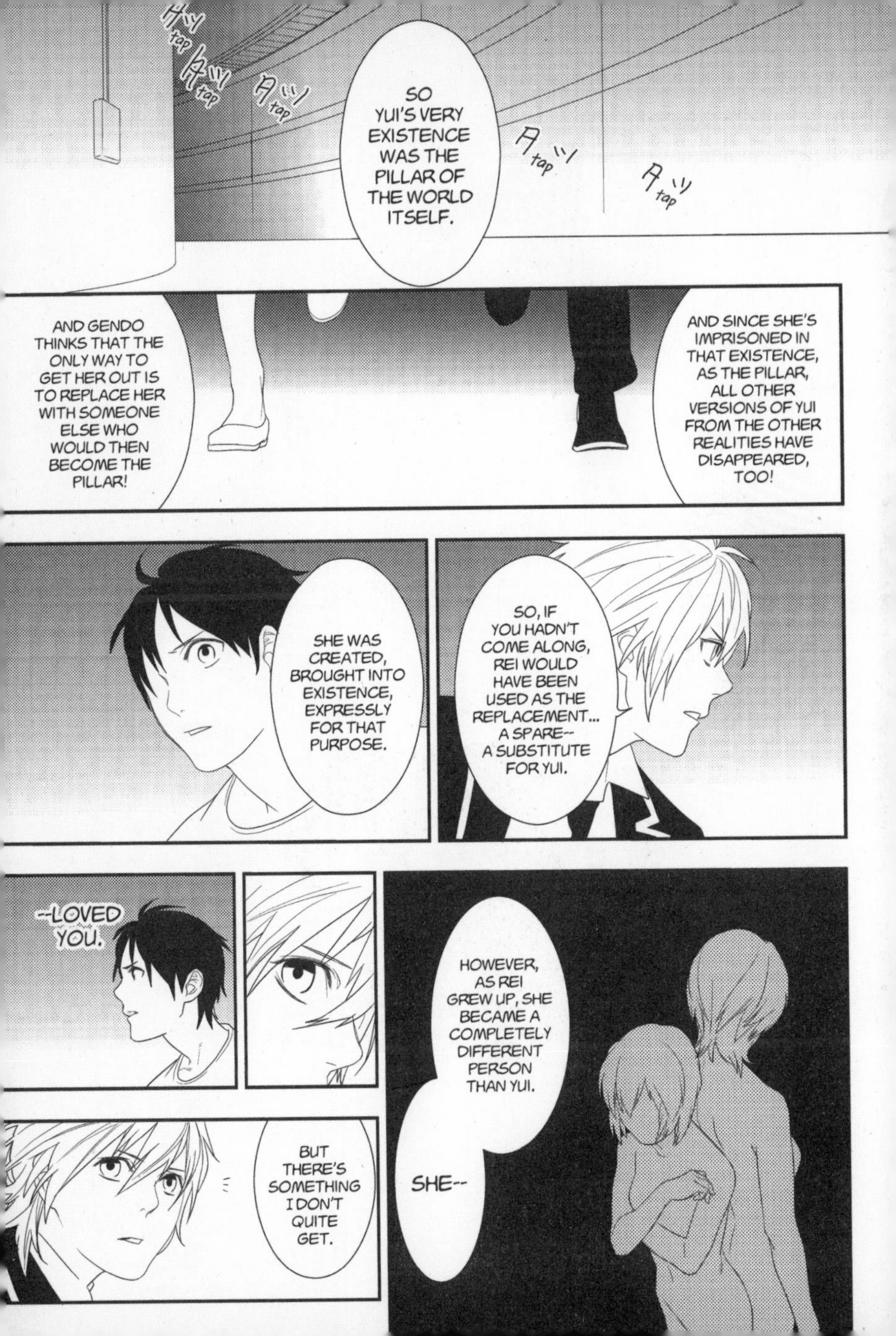

タッ tap
タッ tap
タッ tap
SO YUI'S VERY EXISTENCE WAS THE PILLAR OF THE WORLD ITSELF.
タッ tap
タッ tap
AND SINCE SHE'S IMPRISONED IN THAT EXISTENCE, AS THE PILLAR, ALL OTHER VERSIONS OF YUI FROM THE OTHER REALITIES HAVE DISAPPEARED, TOO!
AND GENDO THINKS THAT THE ONLY WAY TO GET HER OUT IS TO REPLACE HER WITH SOMEONE ELSE WHO WOULD THEN BECOME THE PILLAR!
SO, IF YOU HADN'T COME ALONG, REI WOULD HAVE BEEN USED AS THE REPLACEMENT... A SPARE-- A SUBSTITUTE FOR YUI.
SHE WAS CREATED, BROUGHT INTO EXISTENCE, EXPRESSLY FOR THAT PURPOSE.
HOWEVER, AS REI GREW UP, SHE BECAME A COMPLETELY DIFFERENT PERSON THAN YUI.
SHE--
--LOVED YOU.
BUT THERE'S SOMETHING I DON'T QUITE GET.

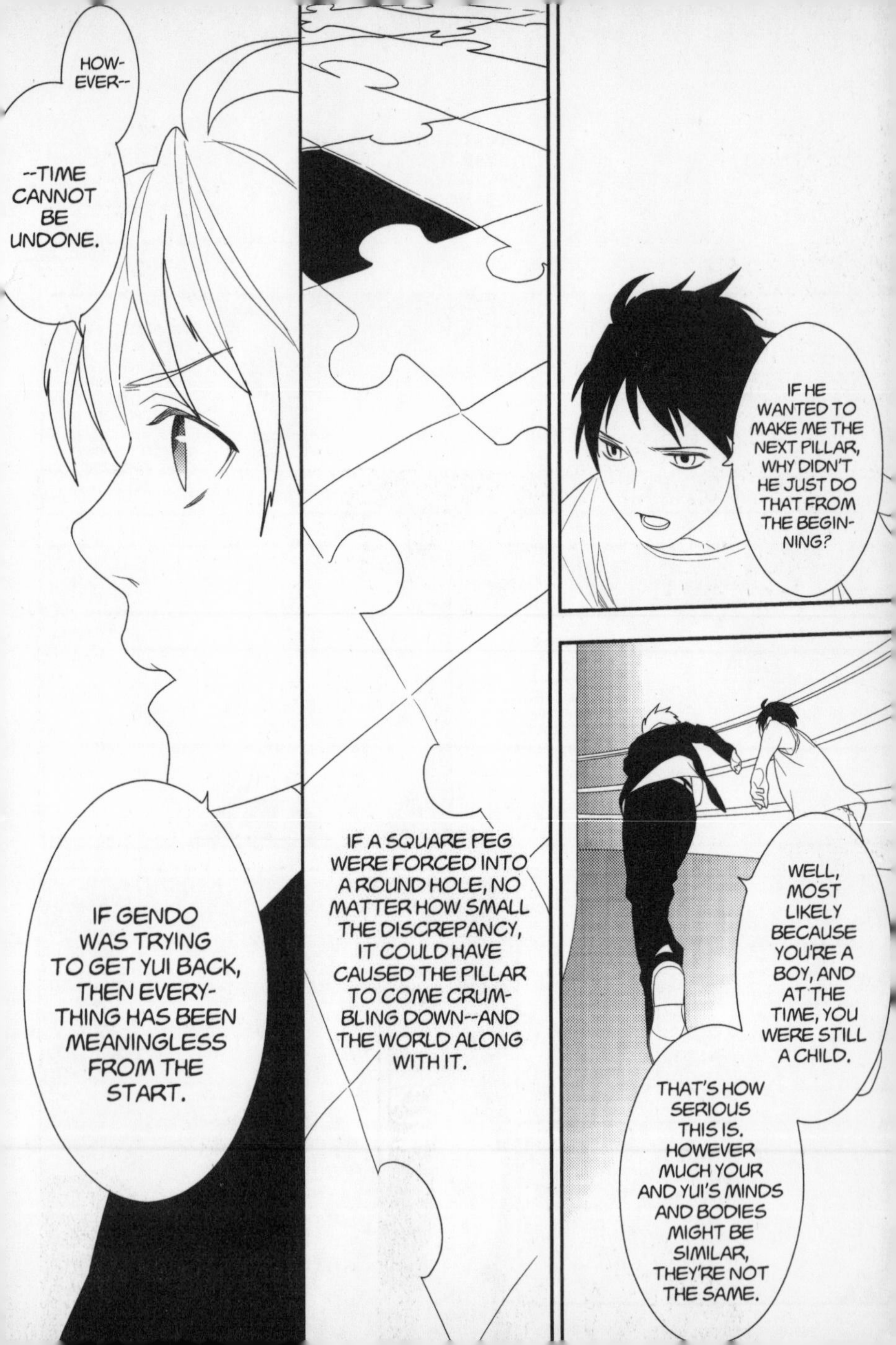
IF HE WANTED TO MAKE ME THE NEXT PILLAR, WHY DIDN'T HE JUST DO THAT FROM THE BEGIN- NING?
WELL, MOST LIKELY BECAUSE YOU'RE A BOY, AND AT THE TIME, YOU WERE STILL A CHILD.
THAT'S HOW SERIOUS THIS IS. HOWEVER MUCH YOUR AND YUI'S MINDS AND BODIES MIGHT BE SIMILAR, THEY'RE NOT THE SAME.
IF A SQUARE PEG WERE FORCED INTO A ROUND HOLE, NO MATTER HOW SMALL THE DISCREPANCY, IT COULD HAVE CAUSED THE PILLAR TO COME CRUM- BLING DOWN--AND THE WORLD ALONG WITH IT.
HOW- EVER--
--TIME CANNOT BE UNDONE.
IF GENDO WAS TRYING TO GET YUI BACK, THEN EVERY- THING HAS BEEN MEANINGLESS FROM THE START.

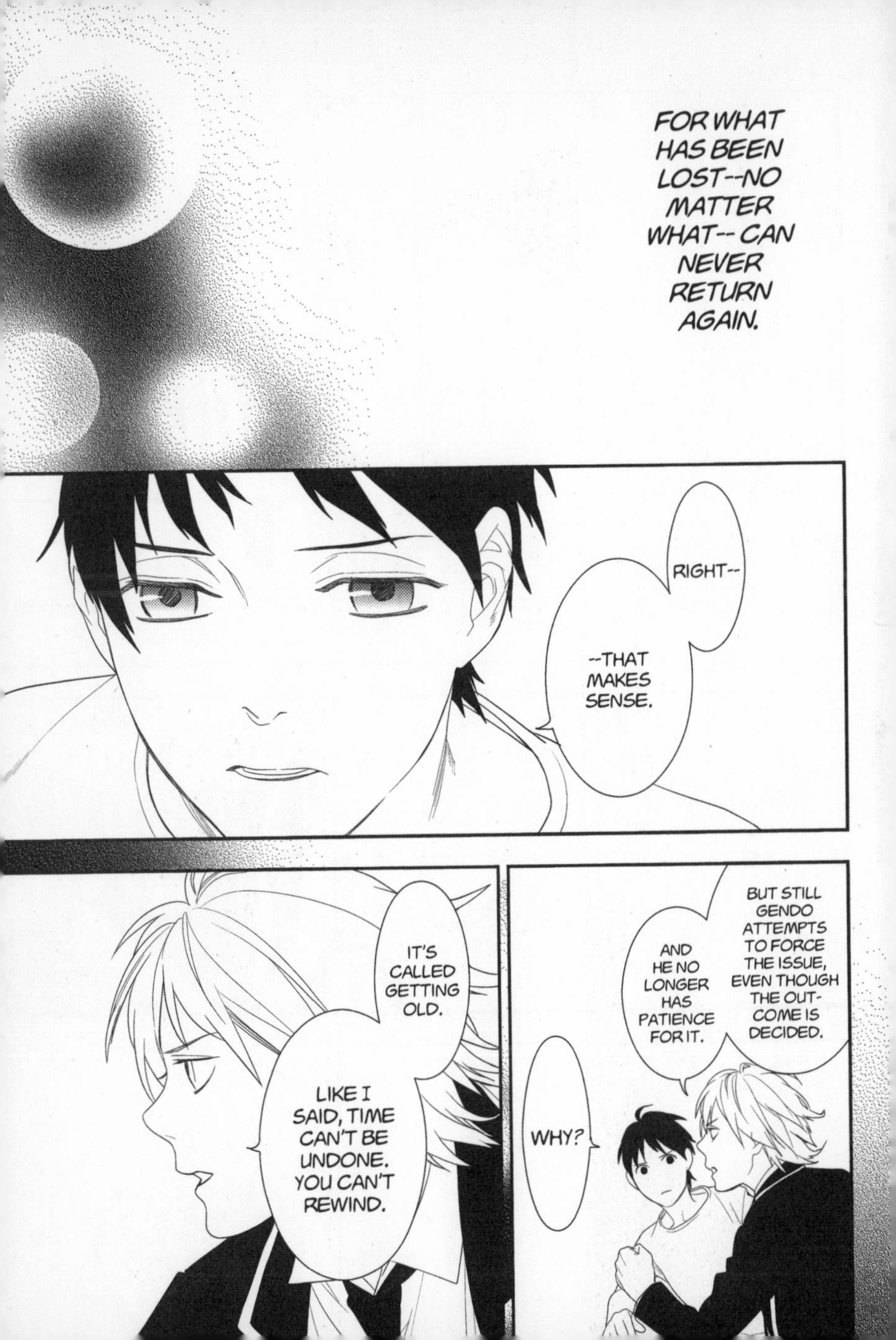
FOR WHAT HAS BEEN LOST--NO MATTER WHAT-- CAN NEVER RETURN AGAIN.
RIGHT--
--THAT MAKES SENSE.
BUT STILL GENDO ATTEMPTS TO FORCE THE ISSUE, EVEN THOUGH THE OUT-COME IS DECIDED.
AND HE NO LONGER HAS PATIENCE FOR IT.
WHY?
IT'S CALLED GETTING OLD.
LIKE I SAID, TIME CAN'T BE UNDONE. YOU CAN'T REWIND.

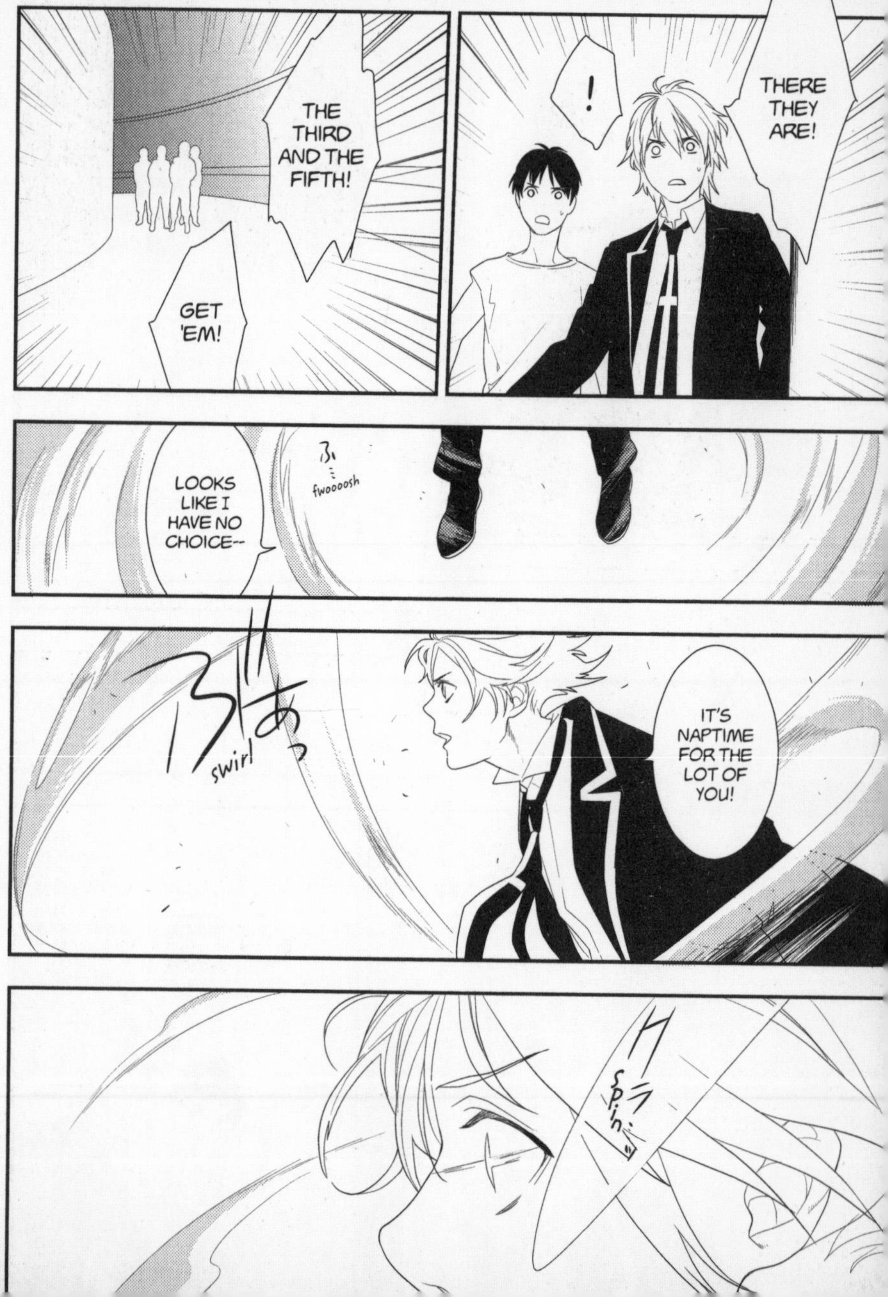
THERE THEY ARE!
!
THE THIRD AND THE FIFTH!
GET 'EM!
fwoooosh
LOOKS LIKE I HAVE NO CHOICE--
IT'S NAPTIME FOR THE LOT OF YOU!
swirl
spin

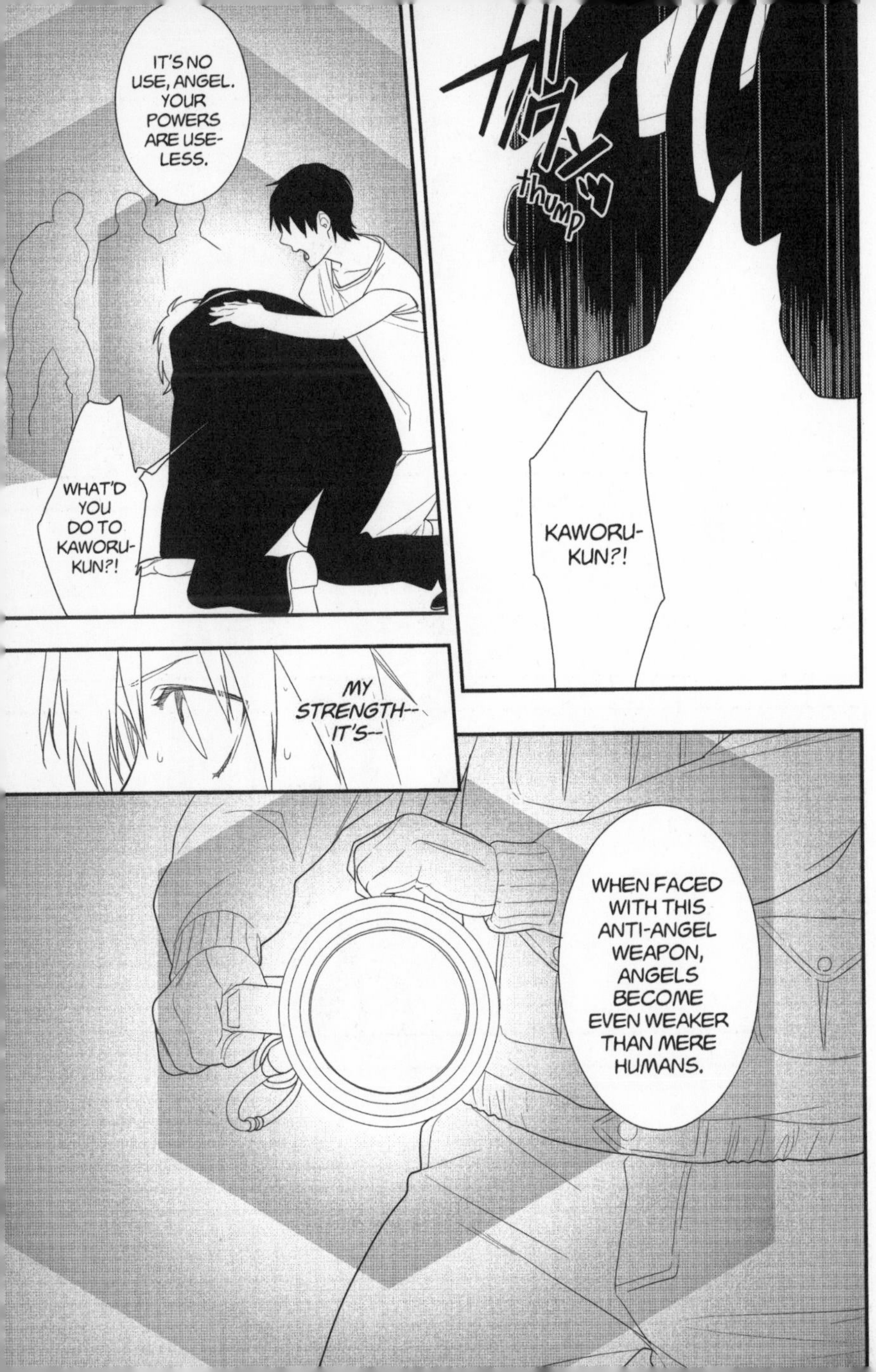
thump
KAWORU-KUN?!
IT'S NO USE, ANGEL. YOUR POWERS ARE USELESS.
WHAT'D YOU DO TO KAWORU-KUN?!
MY STRENGTH-- IT'S--
WHEN FACED WITH THIS ANTI-ANGEL WEAPON, ANGELS BECOME EVEN WEAKER THAN MERE HUMANS.

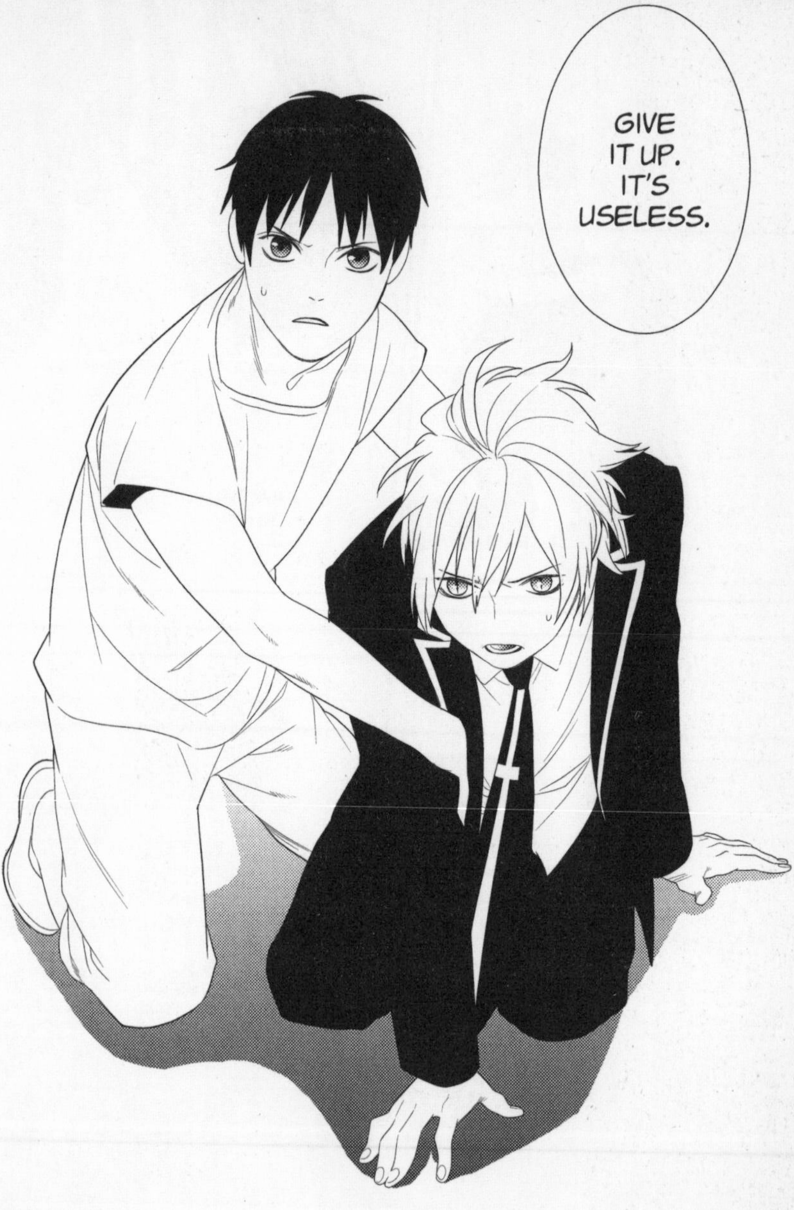
GIVE IT UP. IT'S USELESS.

END

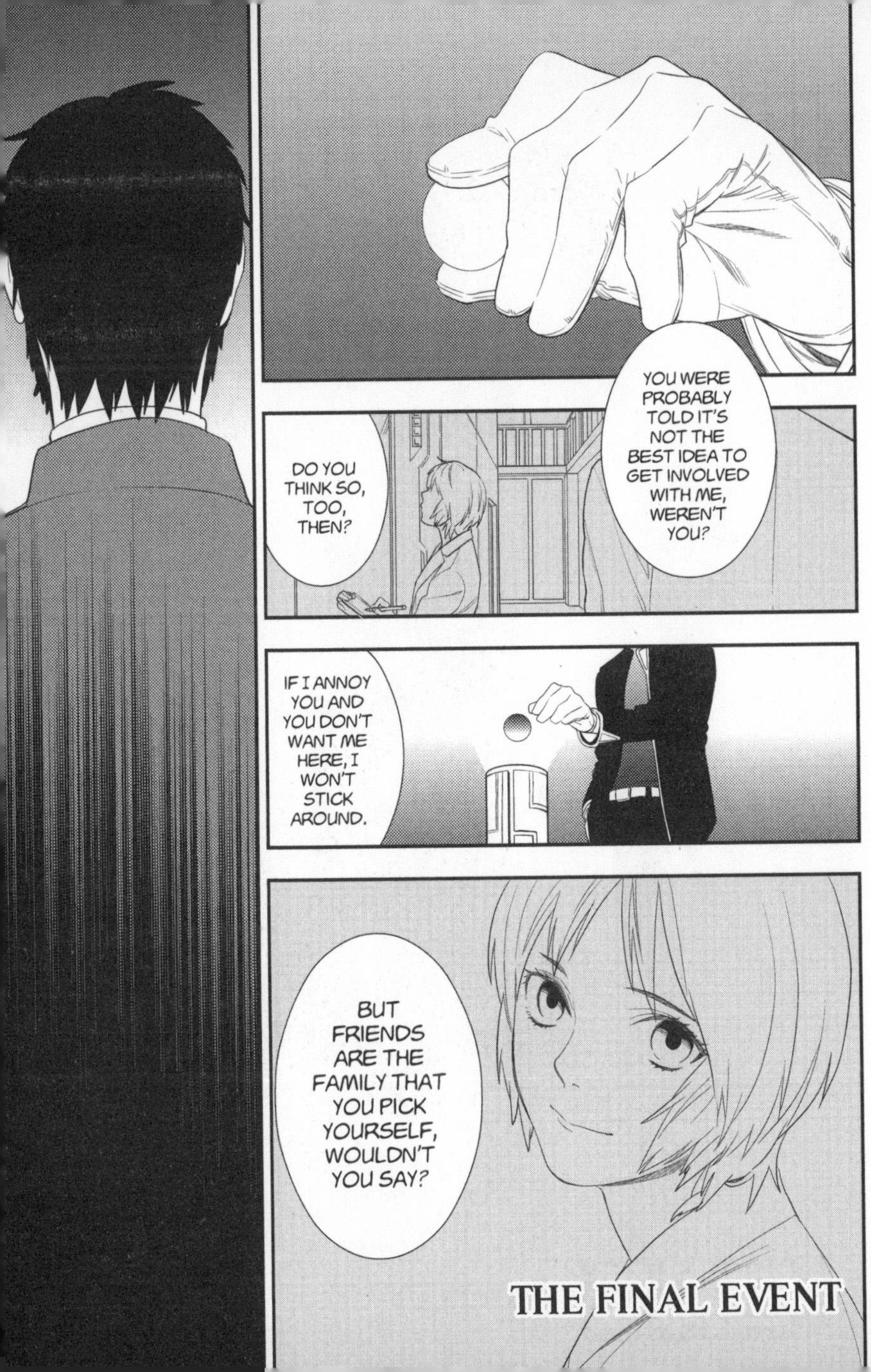
YOU WERE PROBABLY TOLD IT'S NOT THE BEST IDEA TO GET INVOLVED WITH ME, WEREN'T YOU?
DO YOU THINK SO, TOO, THEN?
IF I ANNOY YOU AND YOU DON'T WANT ME HERE, I WON'T STICK AROUND.
BUT FRIENDS ARE THE FAMILY THAT YOU PICK YOURSELF, WOULDN'T YOU SAY?
THE FINAL EVENT

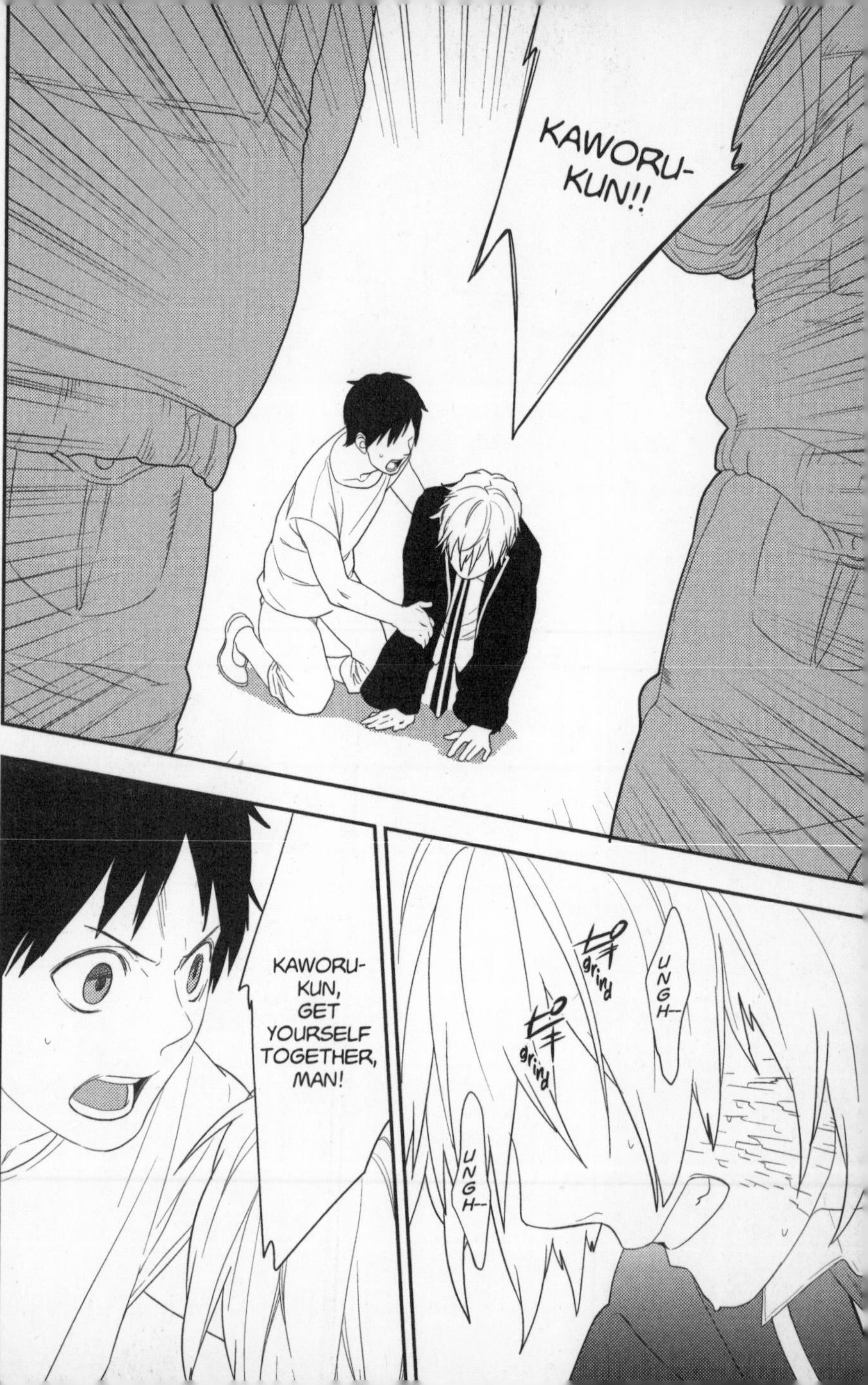
KAWORU-KUN!!
UNGH--
grind
grind
UNGH--
KAWORU-KUN, GET YOURSELF TOGETHER, MAN!

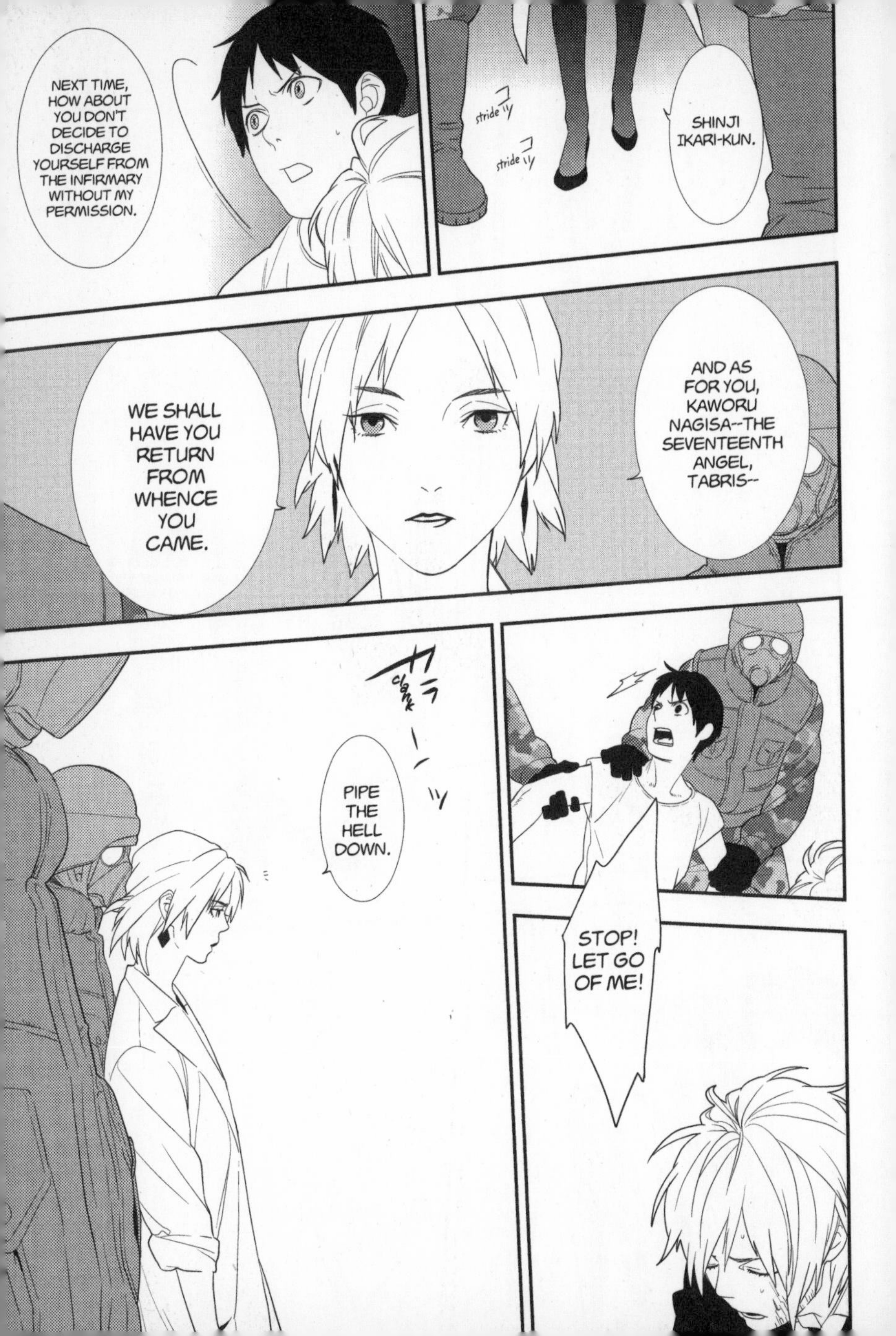
SHINJI IKARI-KUN.
stride
stride
NEXT TIME, HOW ABOUT YOU DON'T DECIDE TO DISCHARGE YOURSELF FROM THE INFIRMARY WITHOUT MY PERMISSION.
AND AS FOR YOU, KAWORU NAGISA--THE SEVENTEENTH ANGEL, TABRIS--
WE SHALL HAVE YOU RETURN FROM WHENCE YOU CAME.
STOP! LET GO OF ME!
clank
PIPE THE HELL DOWN.

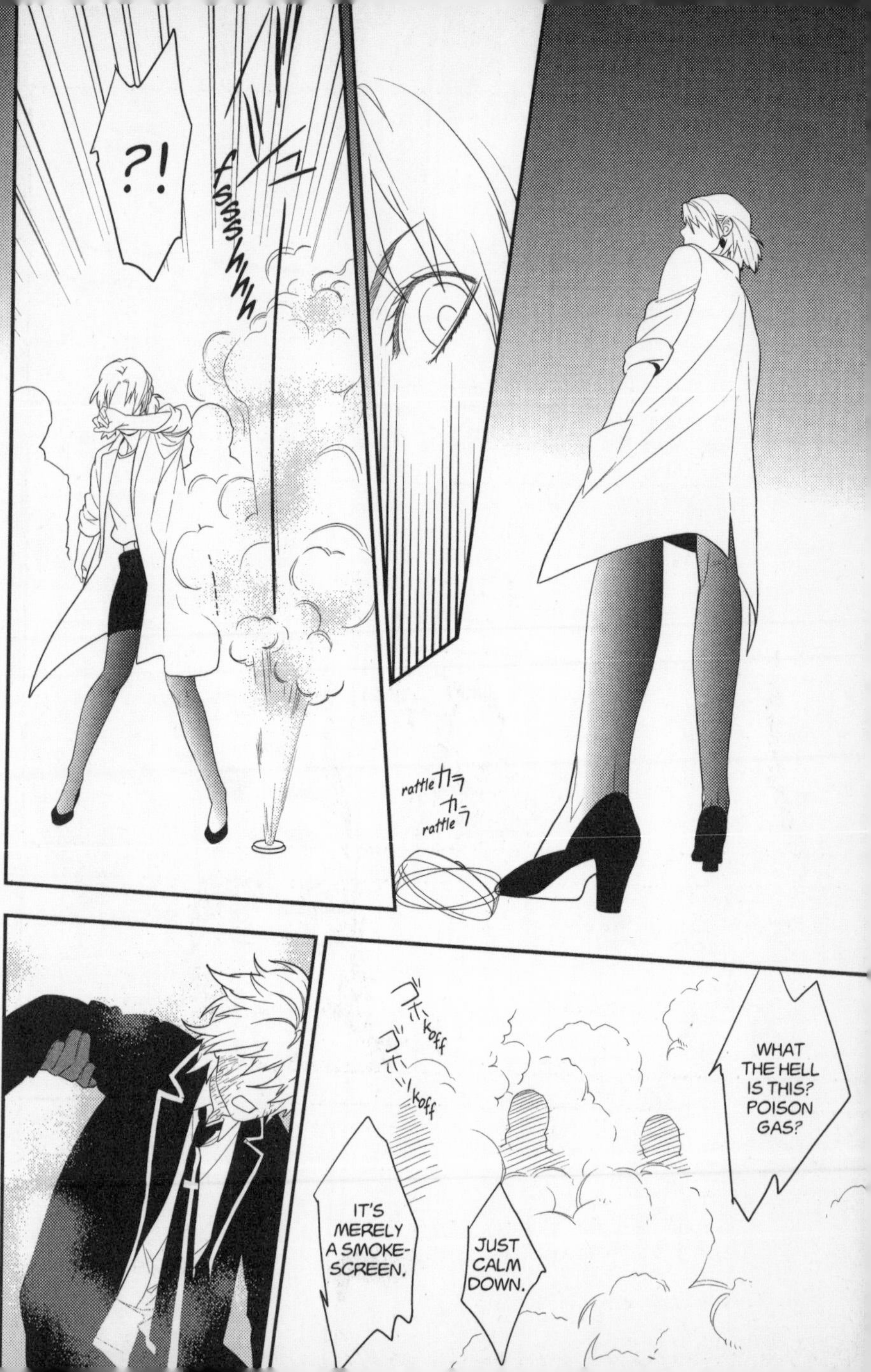
rattle カラ
カラ rattle
?!
fssshhhh
WHAT THE HELL IS THIS? POISON GAS?
ゴホ koff
ゴホッ koff
JUST CALM DOWN.
IT'S MERELY A SMOKE-SCREEN.

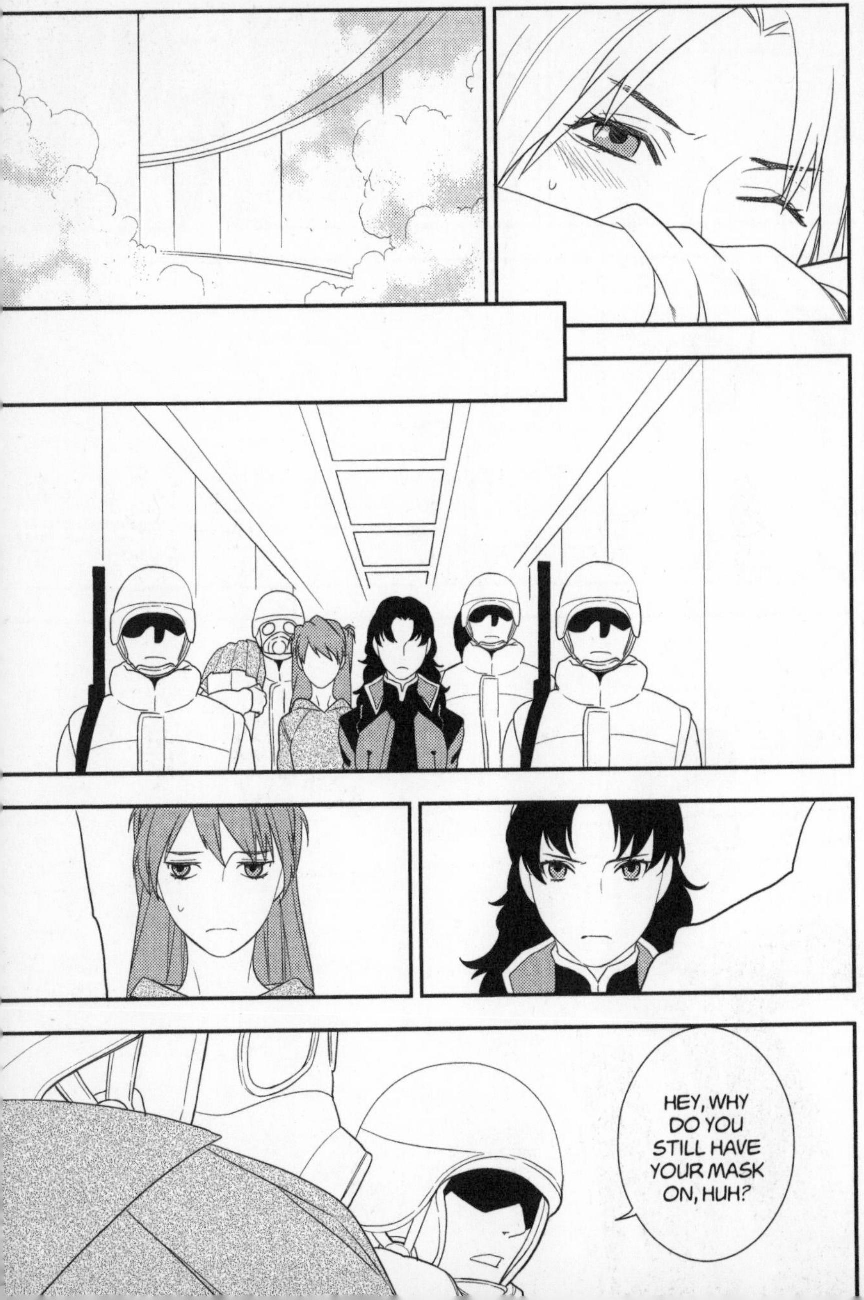
HEY, WHY DO YOU STILL HAVE YOUR MASK ON, HUH?

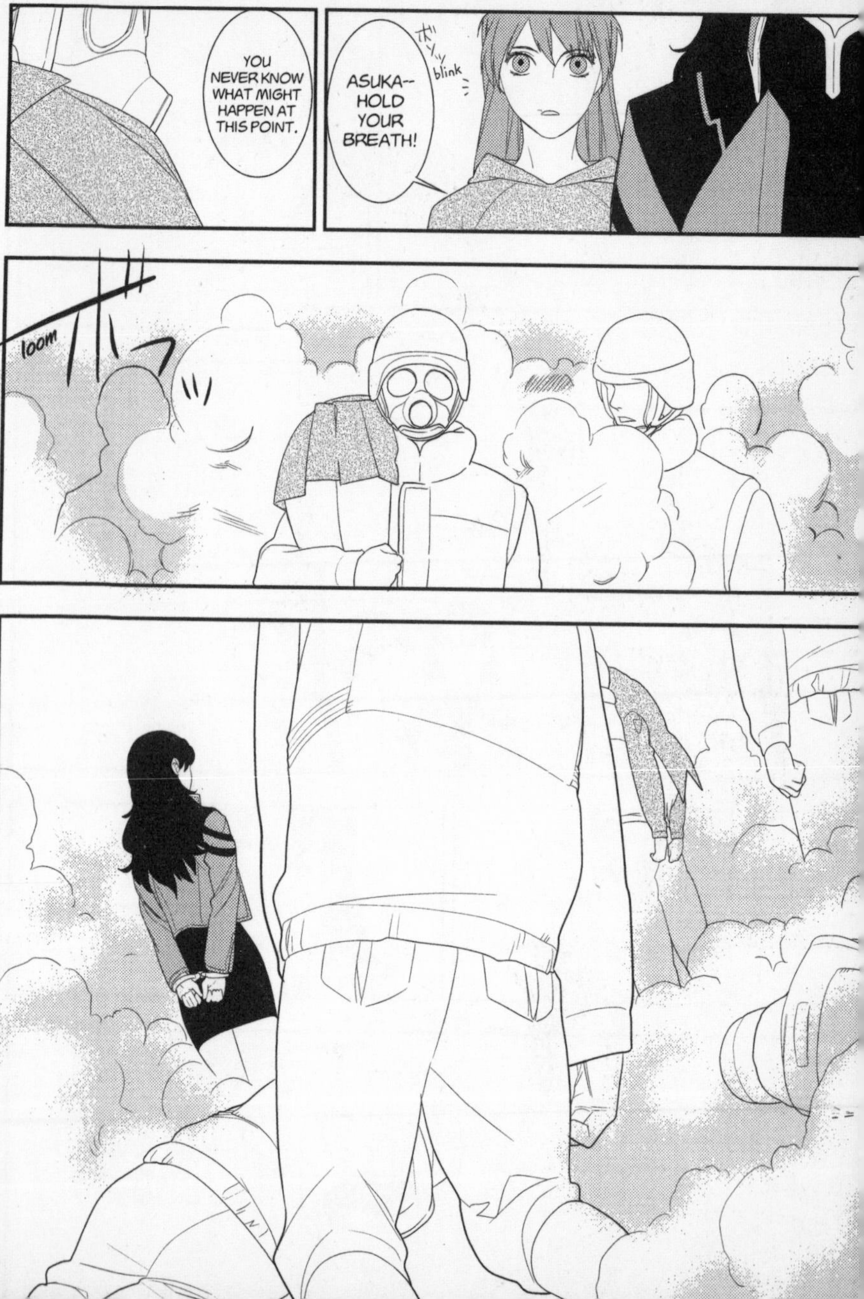
ASUKA-- HOLD YOUR BREATH!
blink
YOU NEVER KNOW WHAT MIGHT HAPPEN AT THIS POINT.
loom

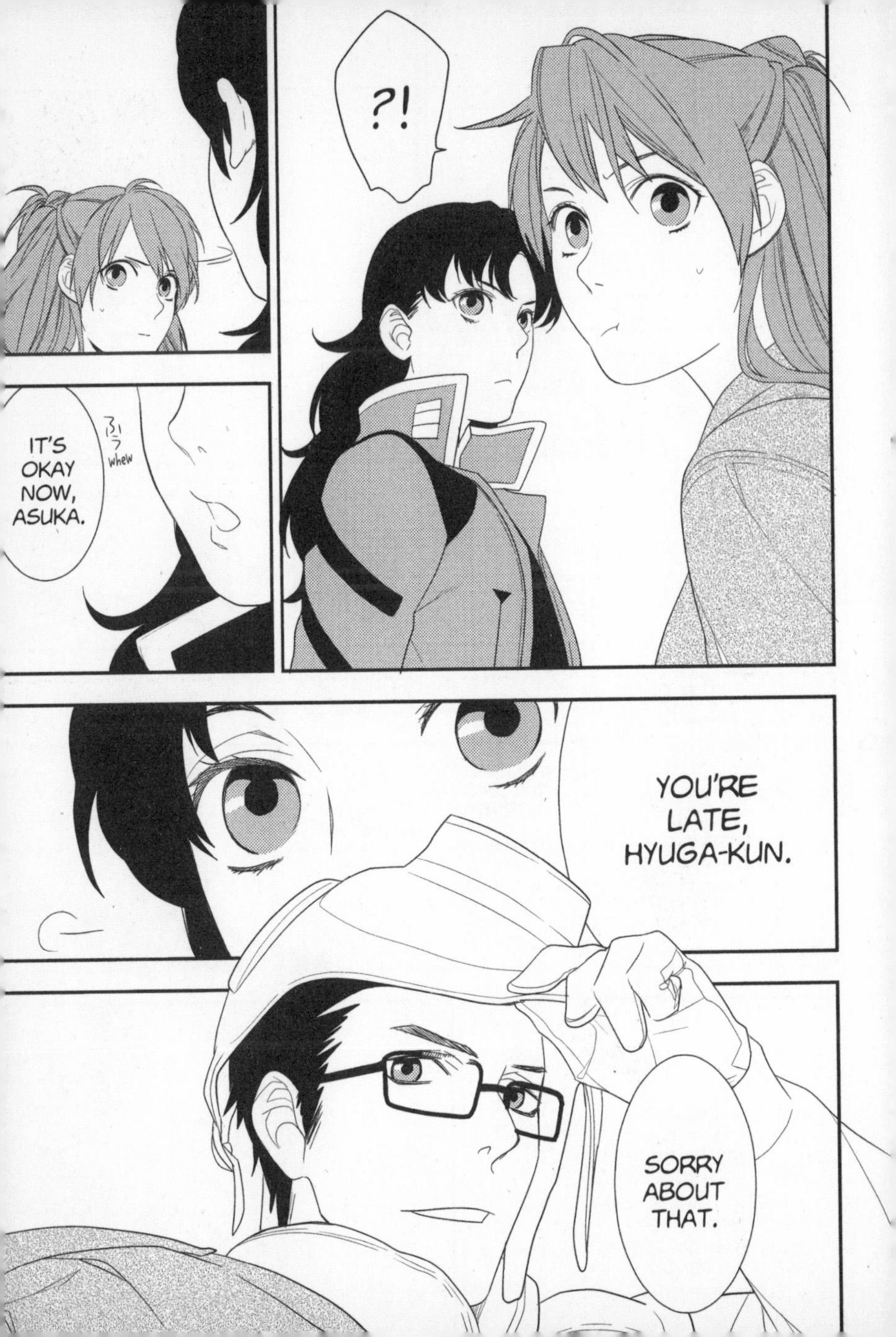
?!
ふぅ
whew
IT'S OKAY NOW, ASUKA.
YOU'RE LATE, HYUGA-KUN.
SORRY ABOUT THAT.

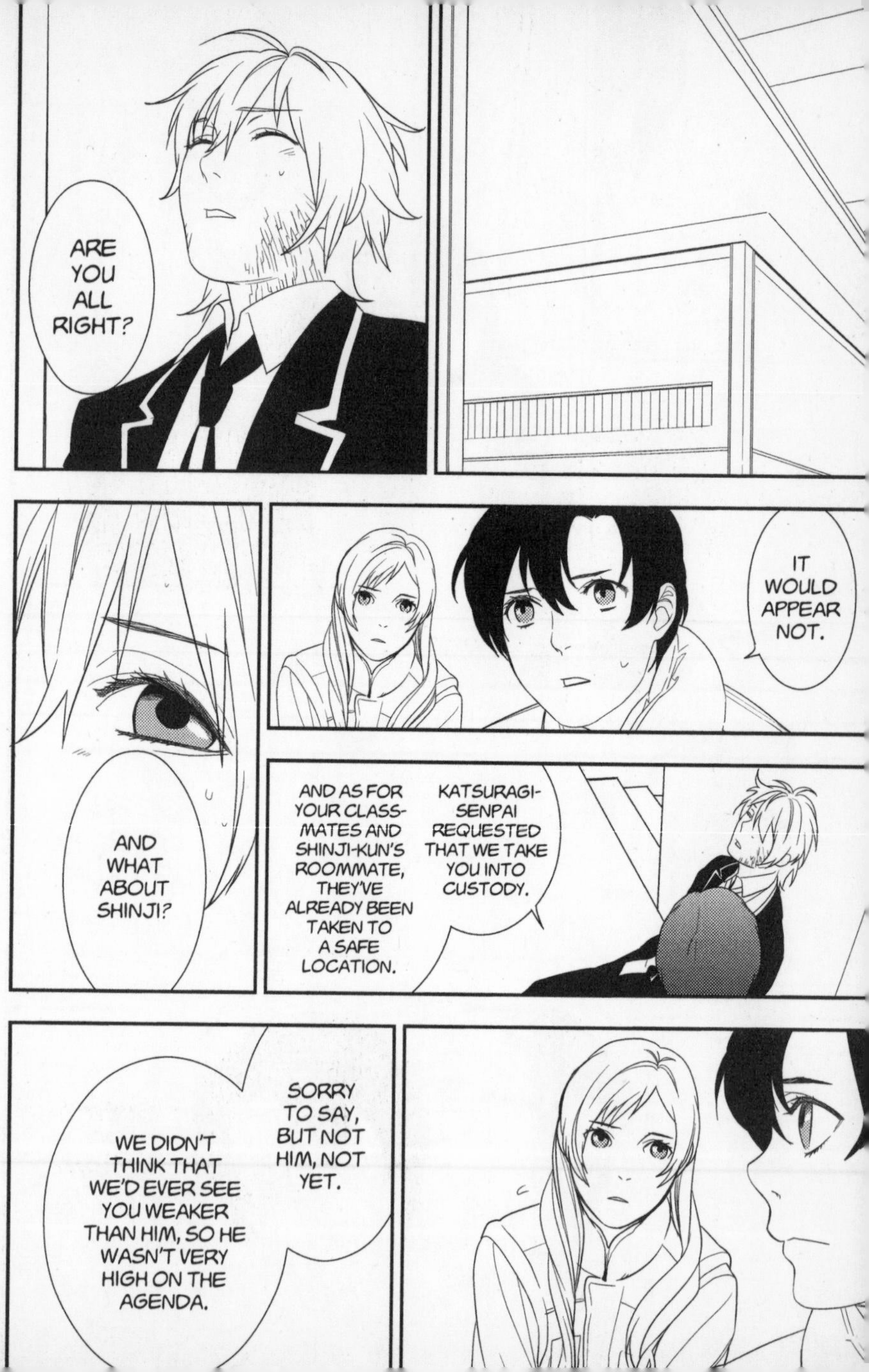
ARE YOU ALL RIGHT?
IT WOULD APPEAR NOT.
KATSURAGI-SENPAI REQUESTED THAT WE TAKE YOU INTO CUSTODY.
AND AS FOR YOUR CLASSMATES AND SHINJI-KUN'S ROOMMATE, THEY'VE ALREADY BEEN TAKEN TO A SAFE LOCATION.
AND WHAT ABOUT SHINJI?
SORRY TO SAY, BUT NOT HIM, NOT YET.
WE DIDN'T THINK THAT WE'D EVER SEE YOU WEAKER THAN HIM, SO HE WASN'T VERY HIGH ON THE AGENDA.

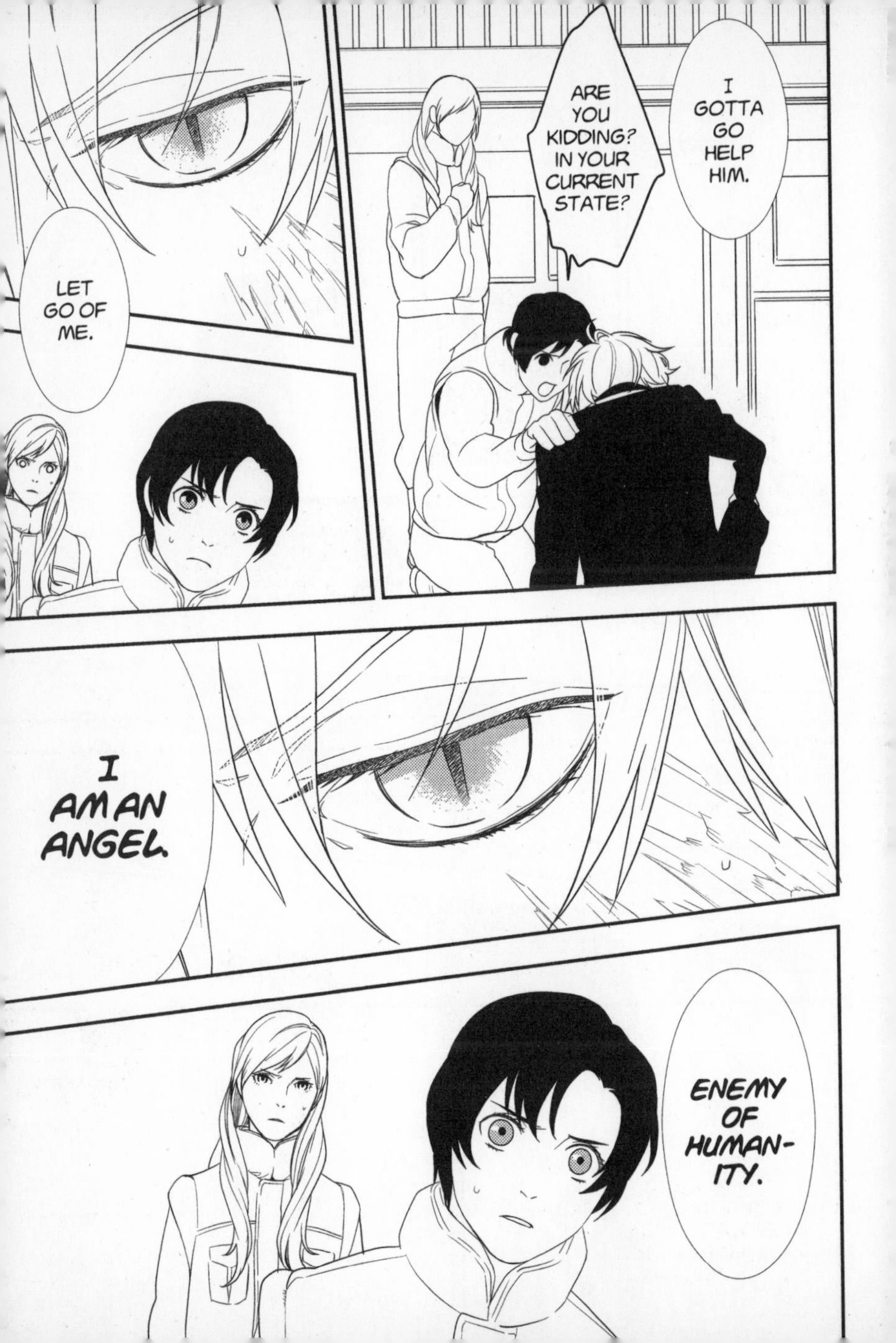
I GOTTA GO HELP HIM.
ARE YOU KIDDING? IN YOUR CURRENT STATE?
LET GO OF ME.
I AM AN ANGEL.
ENEMY OF HUMAN-ITY.

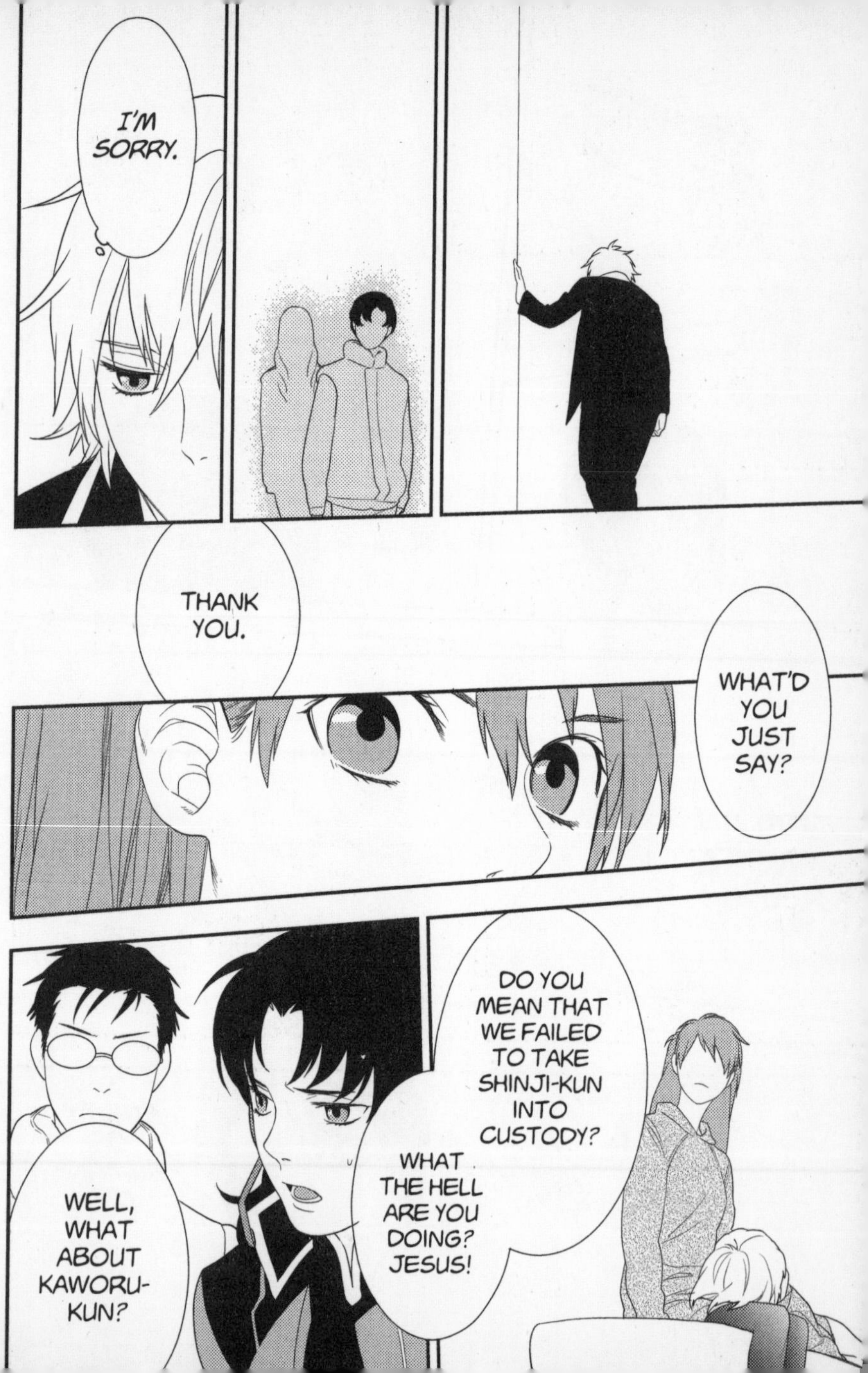
I'M SORRY.
THANK YOU.
WHAT'D YOU JUST SAY?
DO YOU MEAN THAT WE FAILED TO TAKE SHINJI-KUN INTO CUSTODY?
WHAT THE HELL ARE YOU DOING? JESUS!
WELL, WHAT ABOUT KAWORU-KUN?

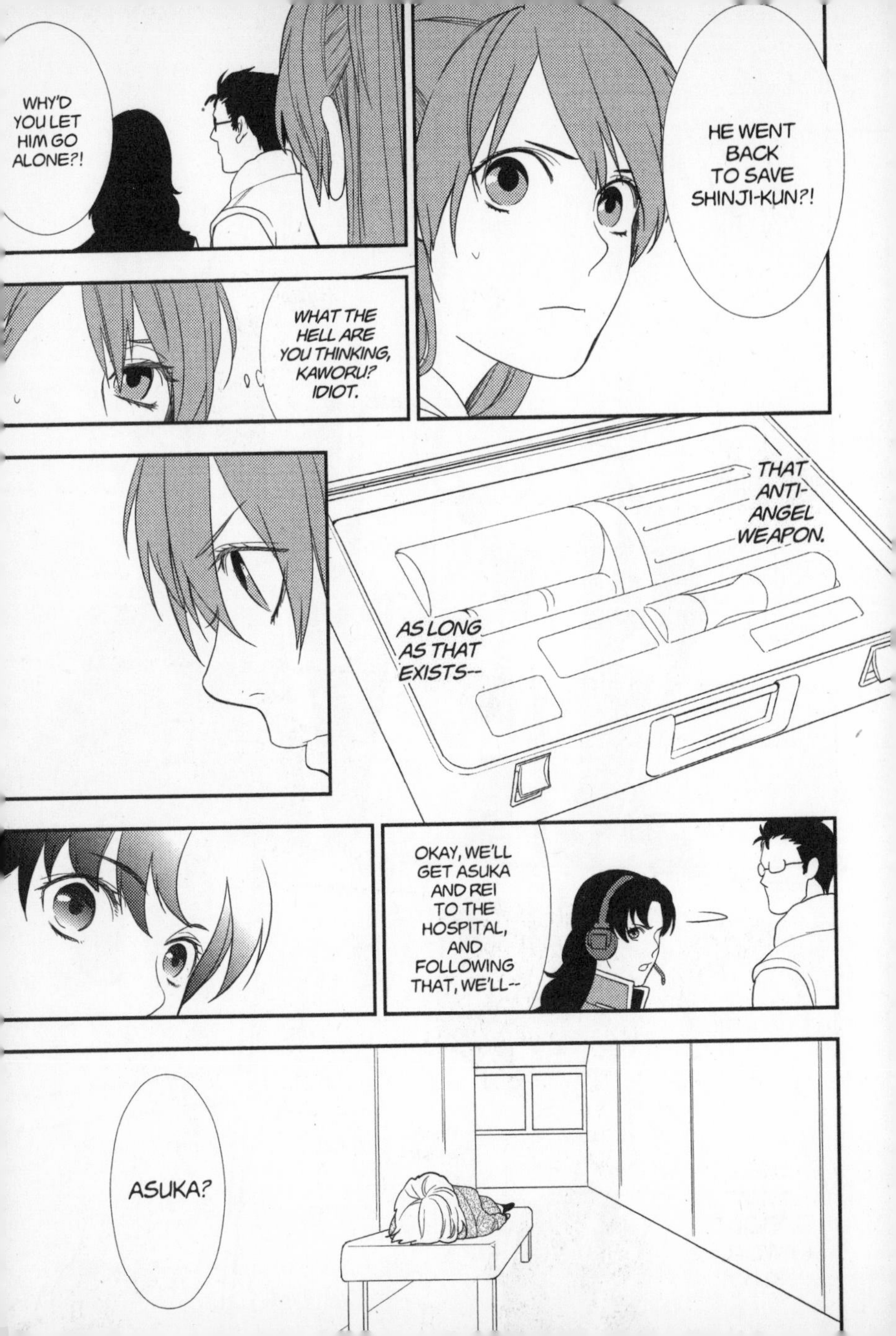
HE WENT BACK TO SAVE SHINJI-KUN?!
WHY'D YOU LET HIM GO ALONE?!
WHAT THE HELL ARE YOU THINKING, KAWORU? IDIOT.
THAT ANTI-ANGEL WEAPON.
AS LONG AS THAT EXISTS--
OKAY, WE'LL GET ASUKA AND REI TO THE HOSPITAL, AND FOLLOWING THAT, WE'LL--
ASUKA?

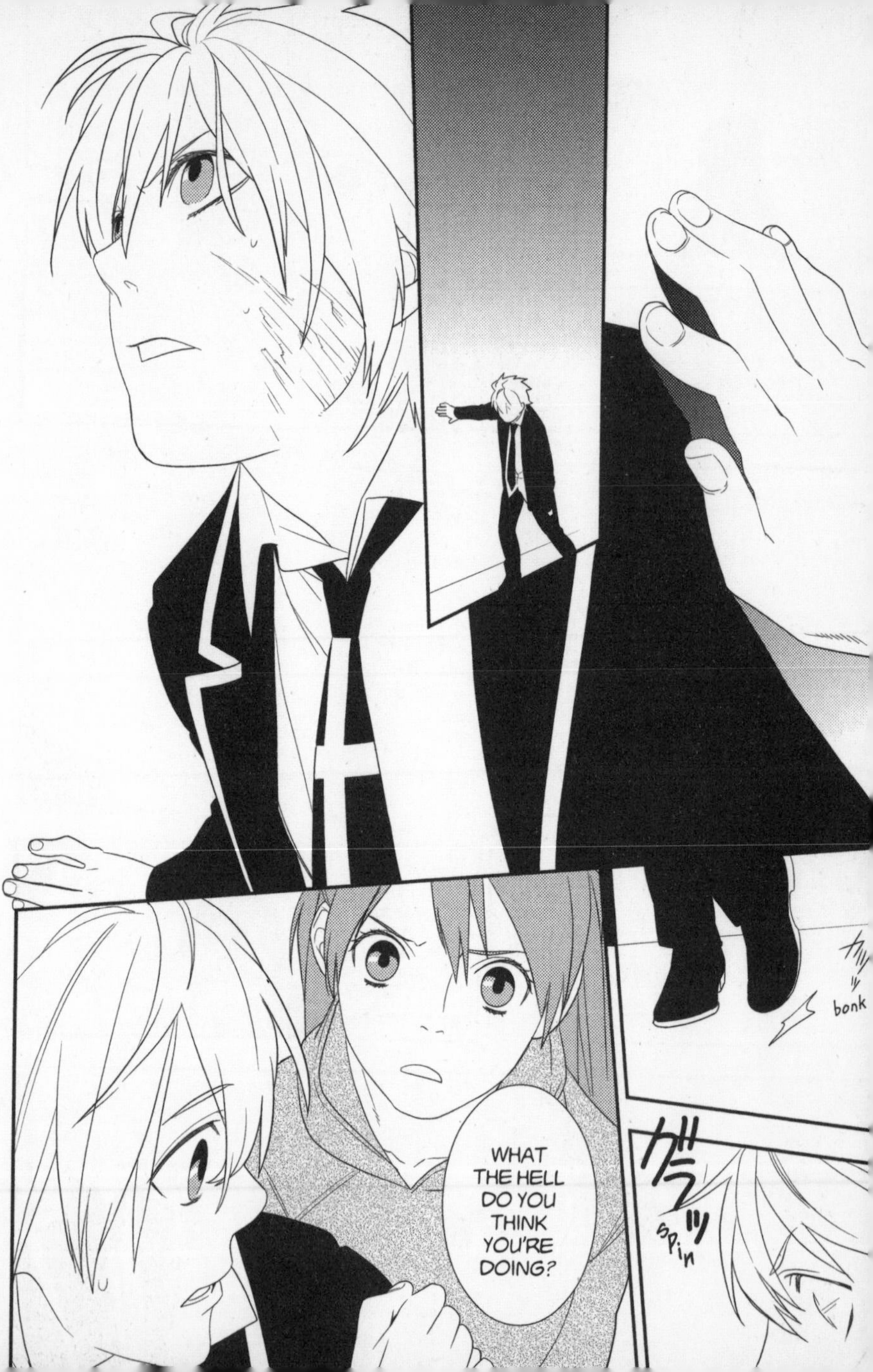
bonk
WHAT THE HELL DO YOU THINK YOU'RE DOING?
spin

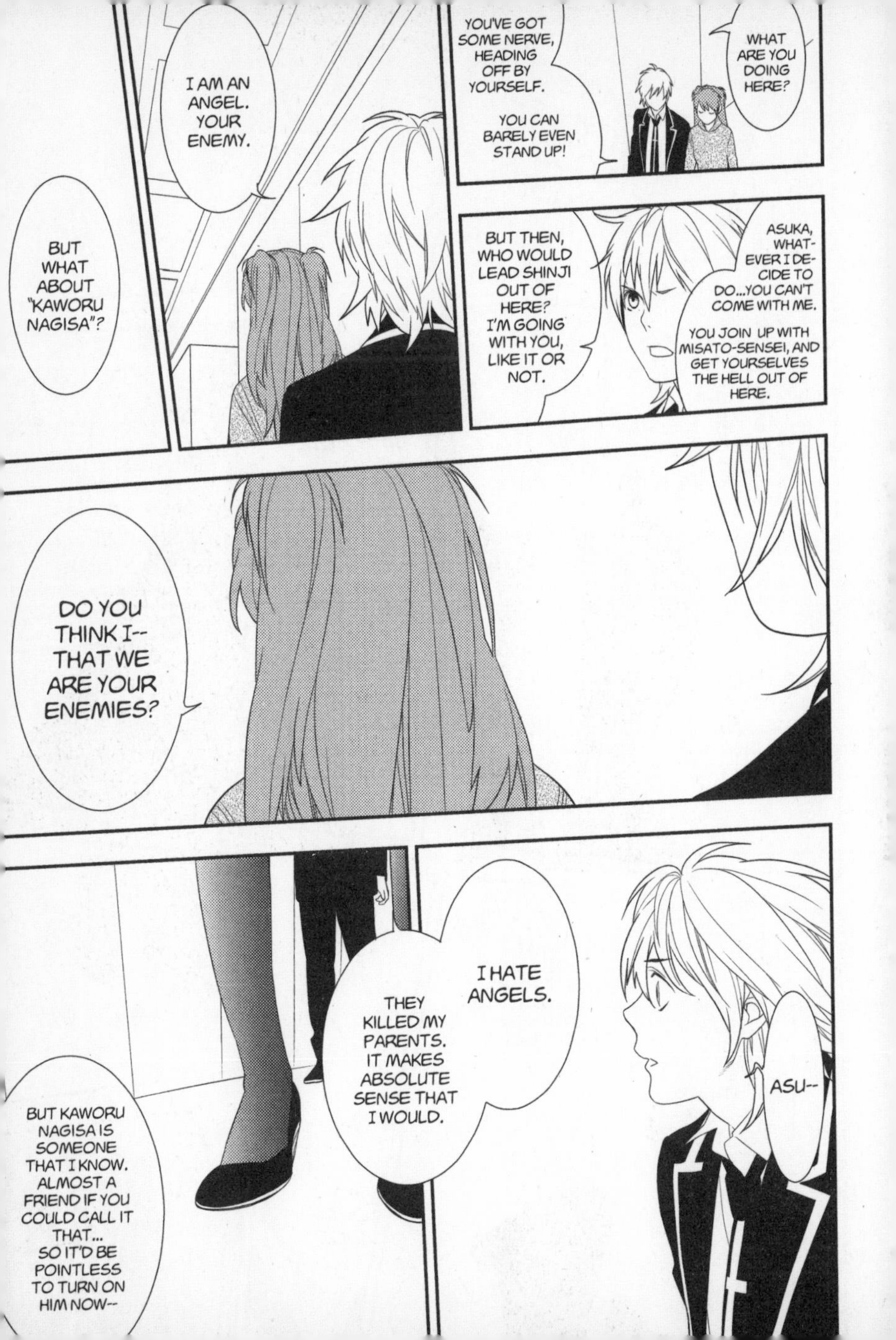
WHAT ARE YOU DOING HERE?
YOU'VE GOT SOME NERVE, HEADING OFF BY YOURSELF.
YOU CAN BARELY EVEN STAND UP!
ASUKA, WHAT-EVER I DE-CIDE TO DO...YOU CAN'T COME WITH ME.
YOU JOIN UP WITH MISATO-SENSEI, AND GET YOURSELVES THE HELL OUT OF HERE.
BUT THEN, WHO WOULD LEAD SHINJI OUT OF HERE? I'M GOING WITH YOU, LIKE IT OR NOT.
I AM AN ANGEL. YOUR ENEMY.
BUT WHAT ABOUT "KAWORU NAGISA"?
DO YOU THINK I-- THAT WE ARE YOUR ENEMIES?
ASU--
I HATE ANGELS.
THEY KILLED MY PARENTS. IT MAKES ABSOLUTE SENSE THAT I WOULD.
BUT KAWORU NAGISA IS SOMEONE THAT I KNOW. ALMOST A FRIEND IF YOU COULD CALL IT THAT... SO IT'D BE POINTLESS TO TURN ON HIM NOW--

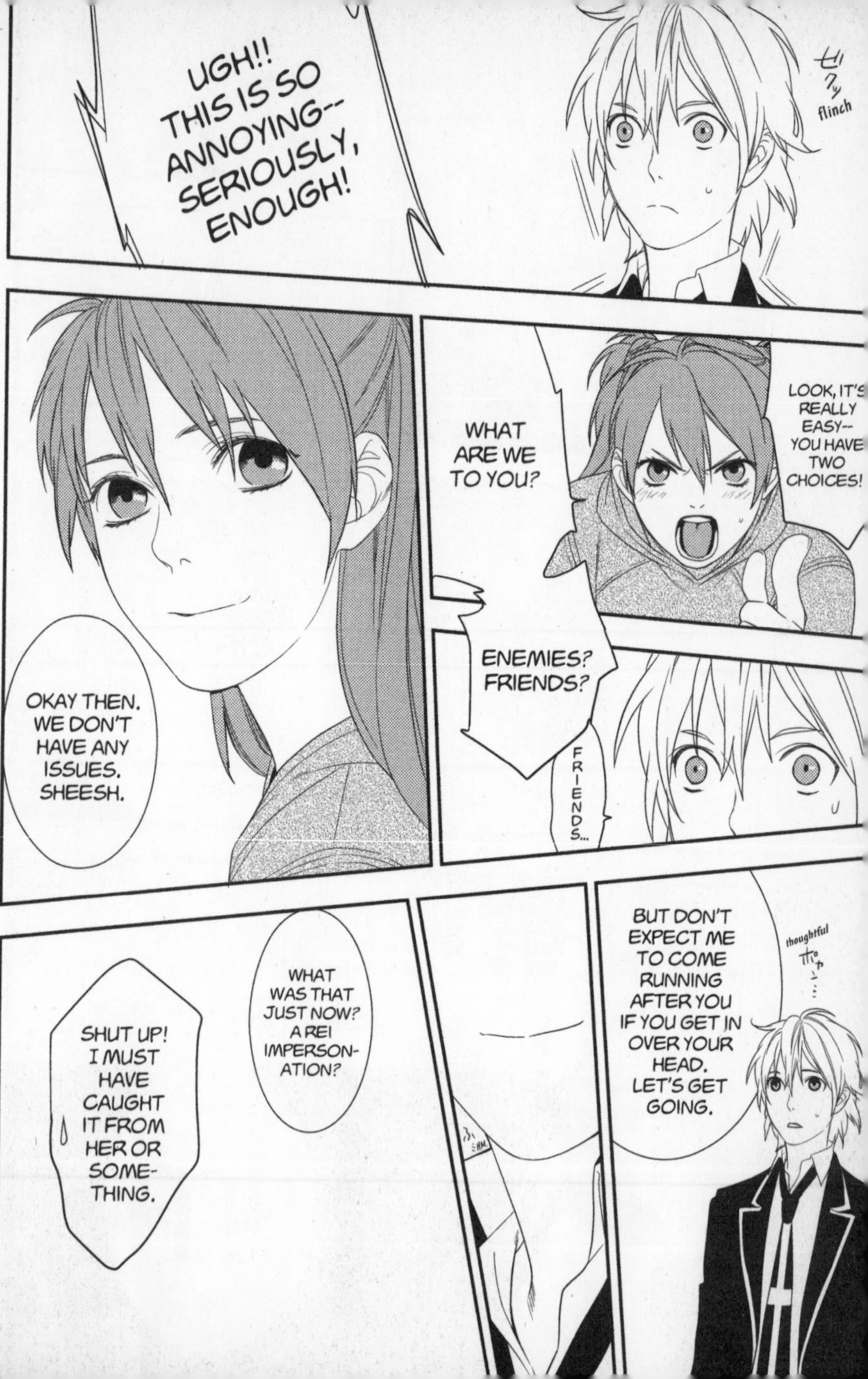
ビクッ
flinch
UGH!! THIS IS SO ANNOYING-- SERIOUSLY, ENOUGH!
LOOK, IT'S REALLY EASY-- YOU HAVE TWO CHOICES!
WHAT ARE WE TO YOU?
ENEMIES? FRIENDS?
FRIENDS...
OKAY THEN. WE DON'T HAVE ANY ISSUES. SHEESH.
thoughtful
BUT DON'T EXPECT ME TO COME RUNNING AFTER YOU IF YOU GET IN OVER YOUR HEAD. LET'S GET GOING.
WHAT WAS THAT JUST NOW? A REI IMPERSON-ATION?
SHUT UP! I MUST HAVE CAUGHT IT FROM HER OR SOME-THING.

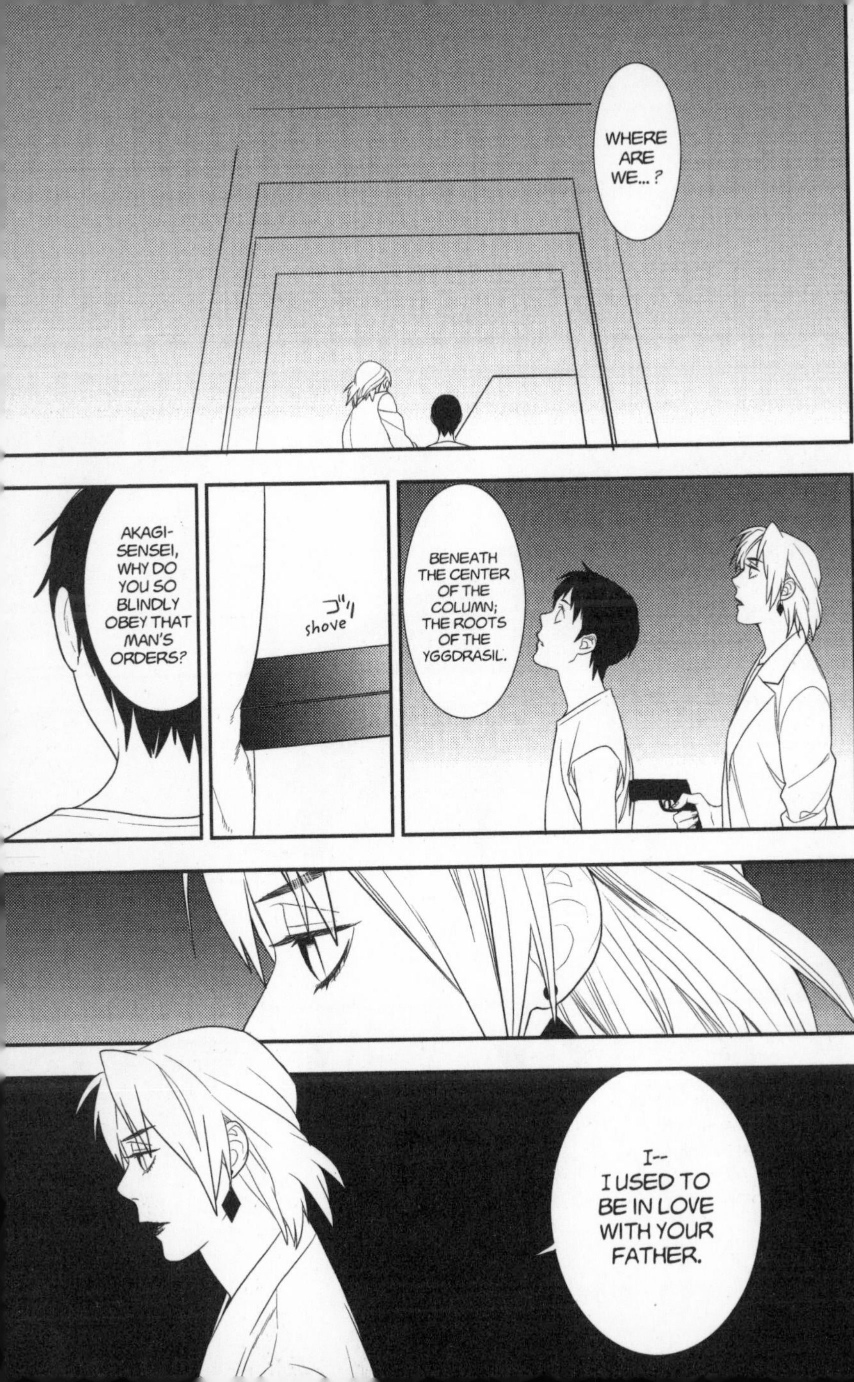
WHERE ARE WE...?
BENEATH THE CENTER OF THE COLUMN; THE ROOTS OF THE YGGDRASIL.
ゴリ
shove
AKAGI-SENSEI, WHY DO YOU SO BLINDLY OBEY THAT MAN'S ORDERS?
I-- I USED TO BE IN LOVE WITH YOUR FATHER.

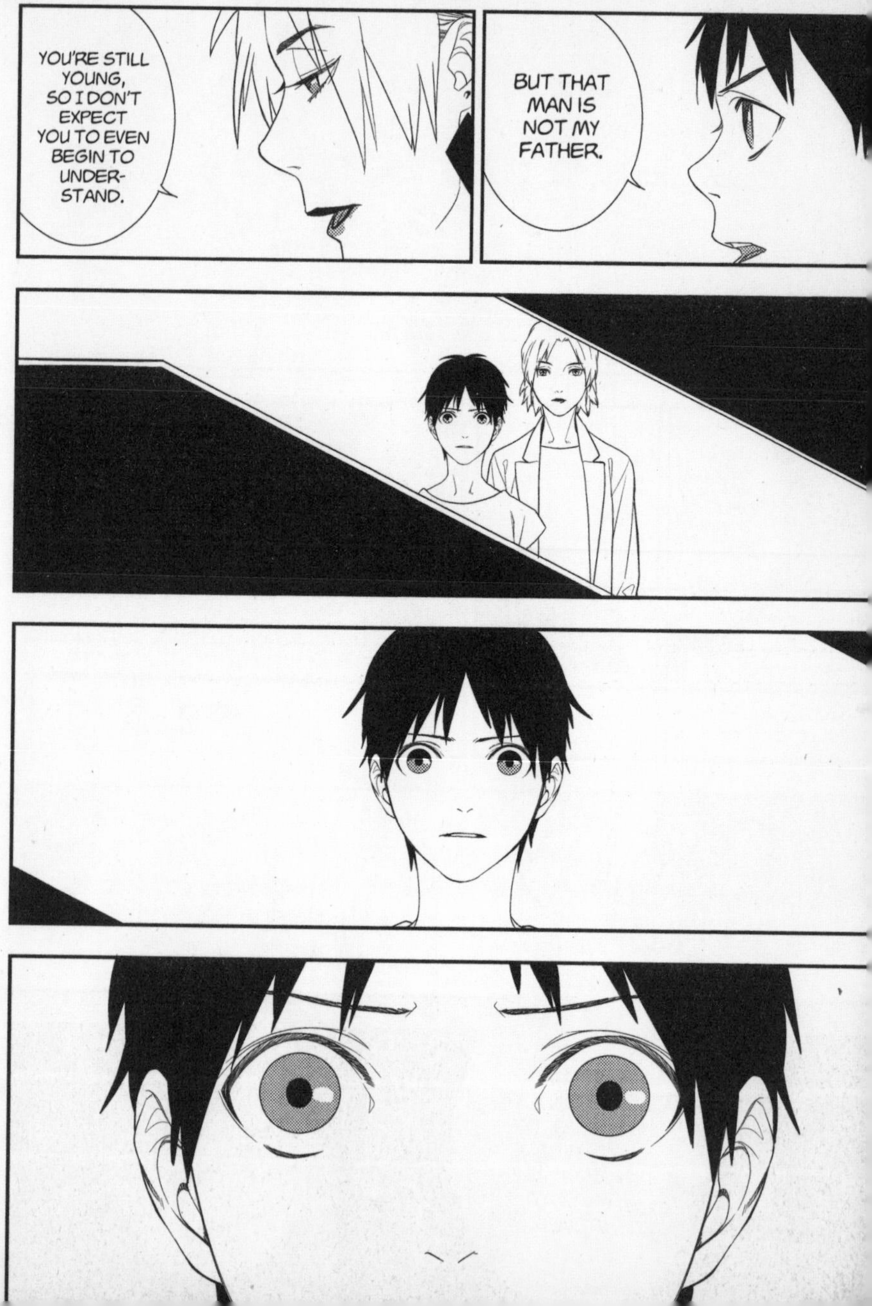
BUT THAT MAN IS NOT MY FATHER.
YOU'RE STILL YOUNG, SO I DON'T EXPECT YOU TO EVEN BEGIN TO UNDER-STAND.

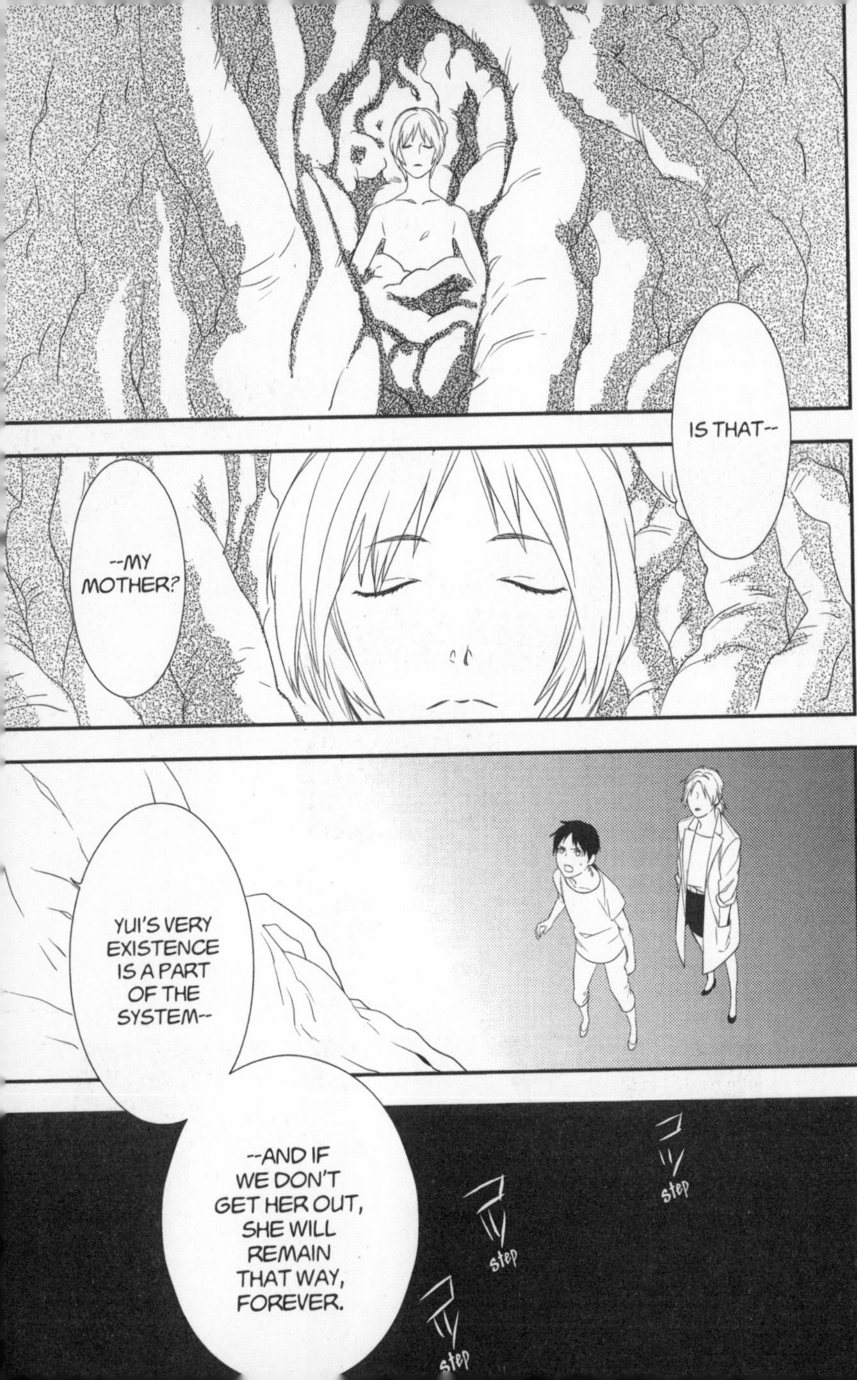
IS THAT--
--MY MOTHER?
YUI'S VERY EXISTENCE IS A PART OF THE SYSTEM--
--AND IF WE DON'T GET HER OUT, SHE WILL REMAIN THAT WAY, FOREVER.
コツ step
コツ step
コツ step

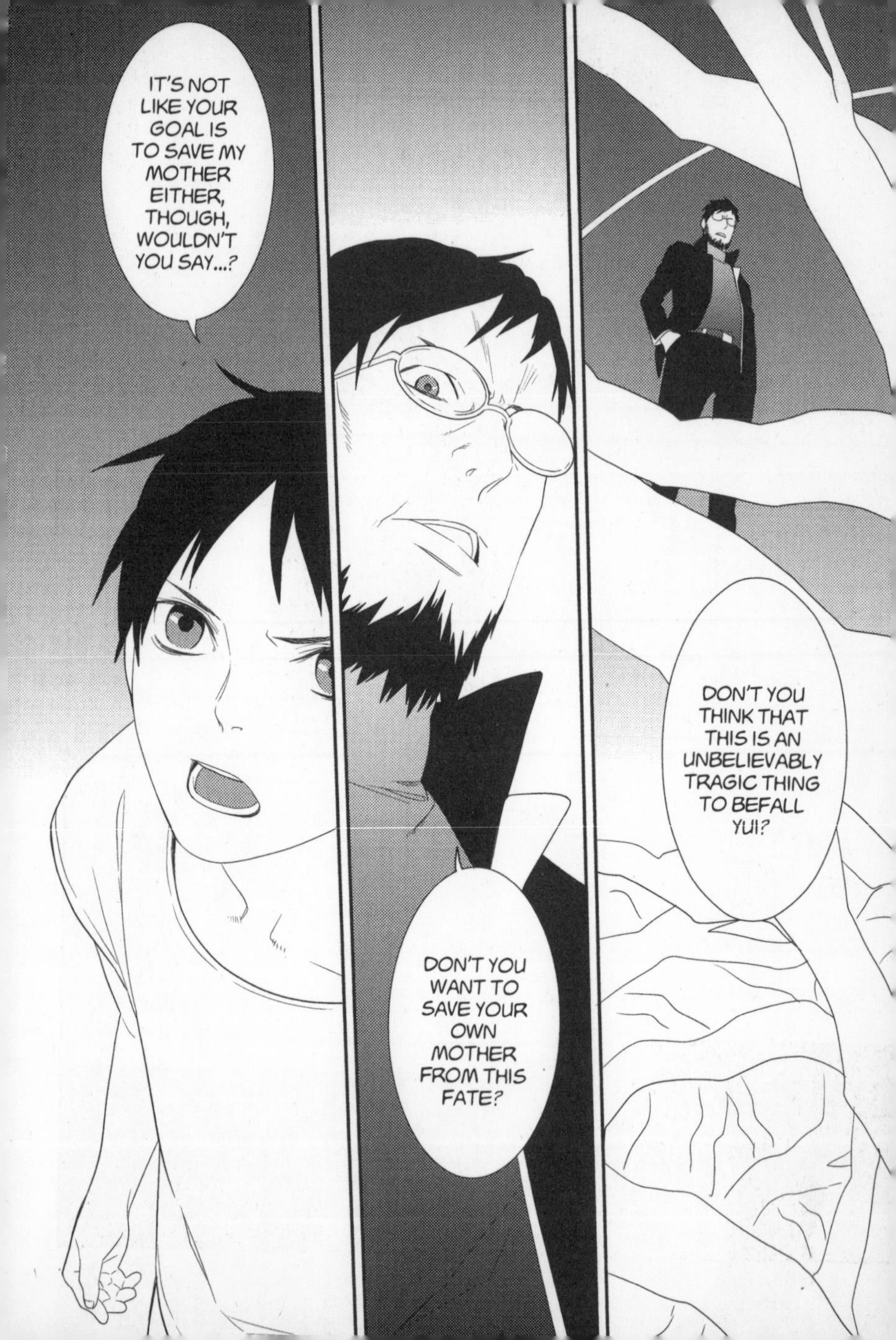
DON'T YOU THINK THAT THIS IS AN UNBELIEVABLY TRAGIC THING TO BEFALL YUI?
DON'T YOU WANT TO SAVE YOUR OWN MOTHER FROM THIS FATE?
IT'S NOT LIKE YOUR GOAL IS TO SAVE MY MOTHER EITHER, THOUGH, WOULDN'T YOU SAY...?

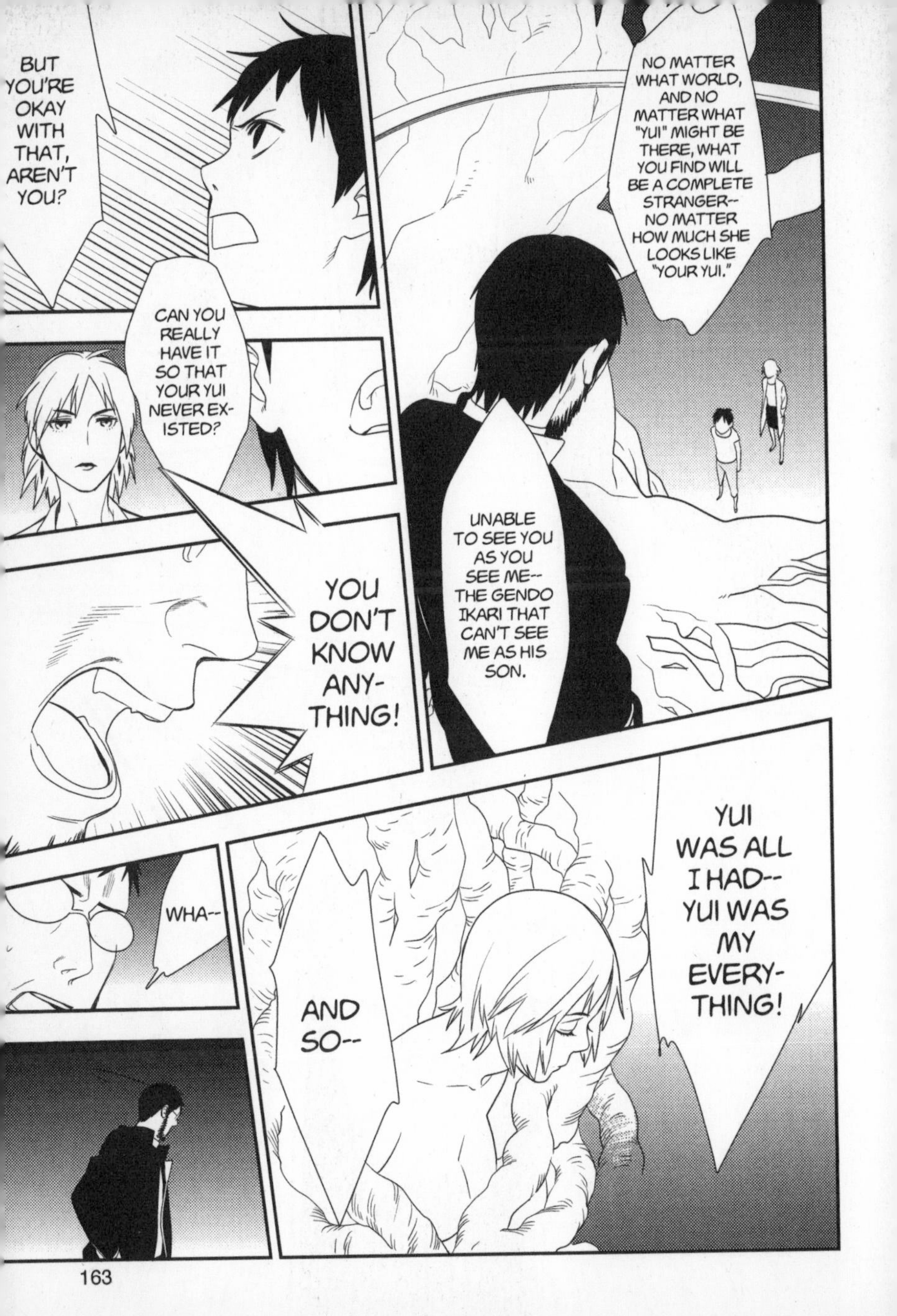
NO MATTER WHAT WORLD, AND NO MATTER WHAT "YUI" MIGHT BE THERE, WHAT YOU FIND WILL BE A COMPLETE STRANGER-- NO MATTER HOW MUCH SHE LOOKS LIKE "YOUR YUI."
UNABLE TO SEE YOU AS YOU SEE ME-- THE GENDO IKARI THAT CAN'T SEE ME AS HIS SON.
BUT YOU'RE OKAY WITH THAT, AREN'T YOU?
CAN YOU REALLY HAVE IT SO THAT YOUR YUI NEVER EX-ISTED?
YOU DON'T KNOW ANY-THING!
YUI WAS ALL I HAD-- YUI WAS MY EVERY-THING!
AND SO--
WHA--

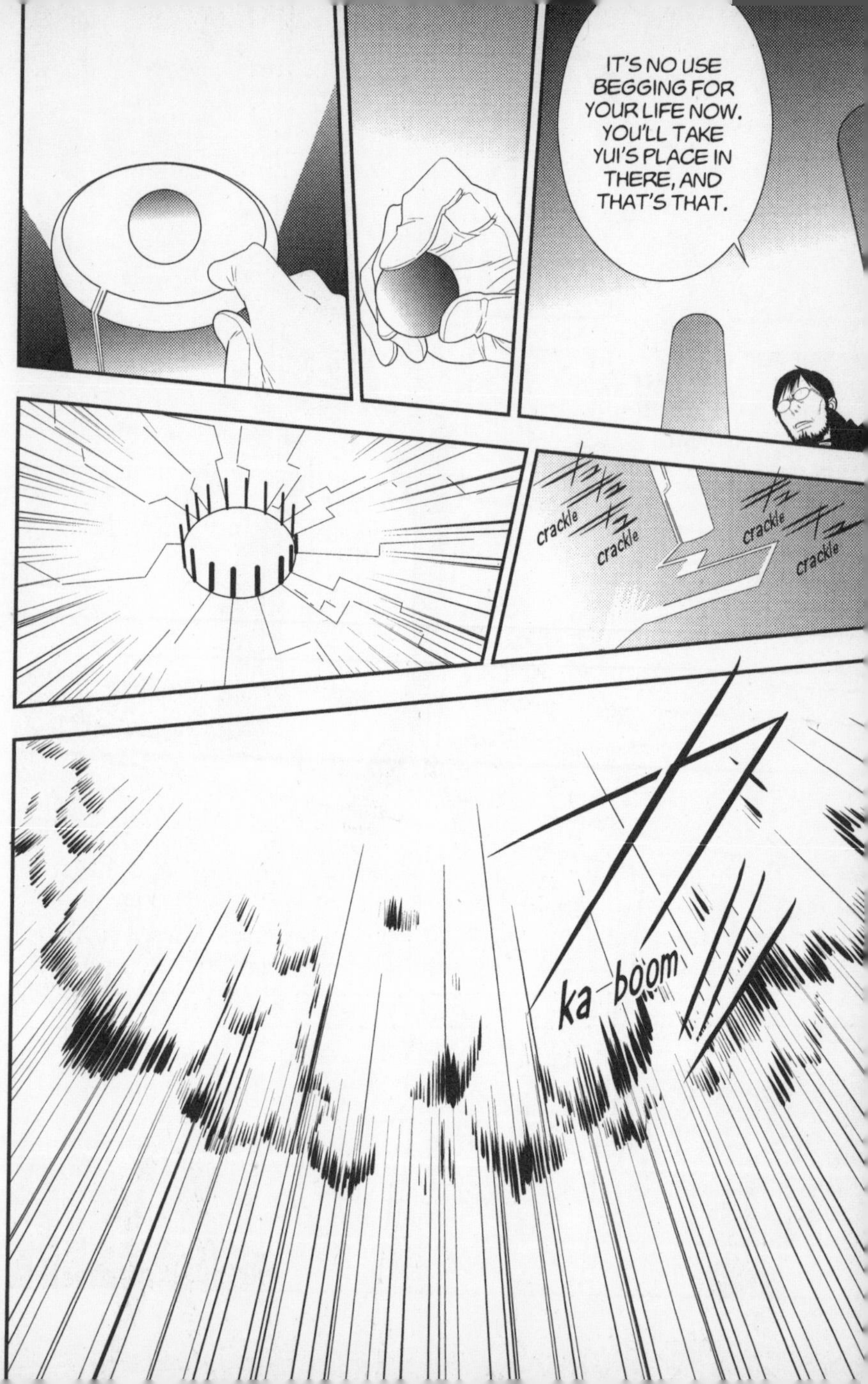
IT'S NO USE BEGGING FOR YOUR LIFE NOW. YOU'LL TAKE YUI'S PLACE IN THERE, AND THAT'S THAT.
crackle
crackle
crackle
crackle
ka-boom

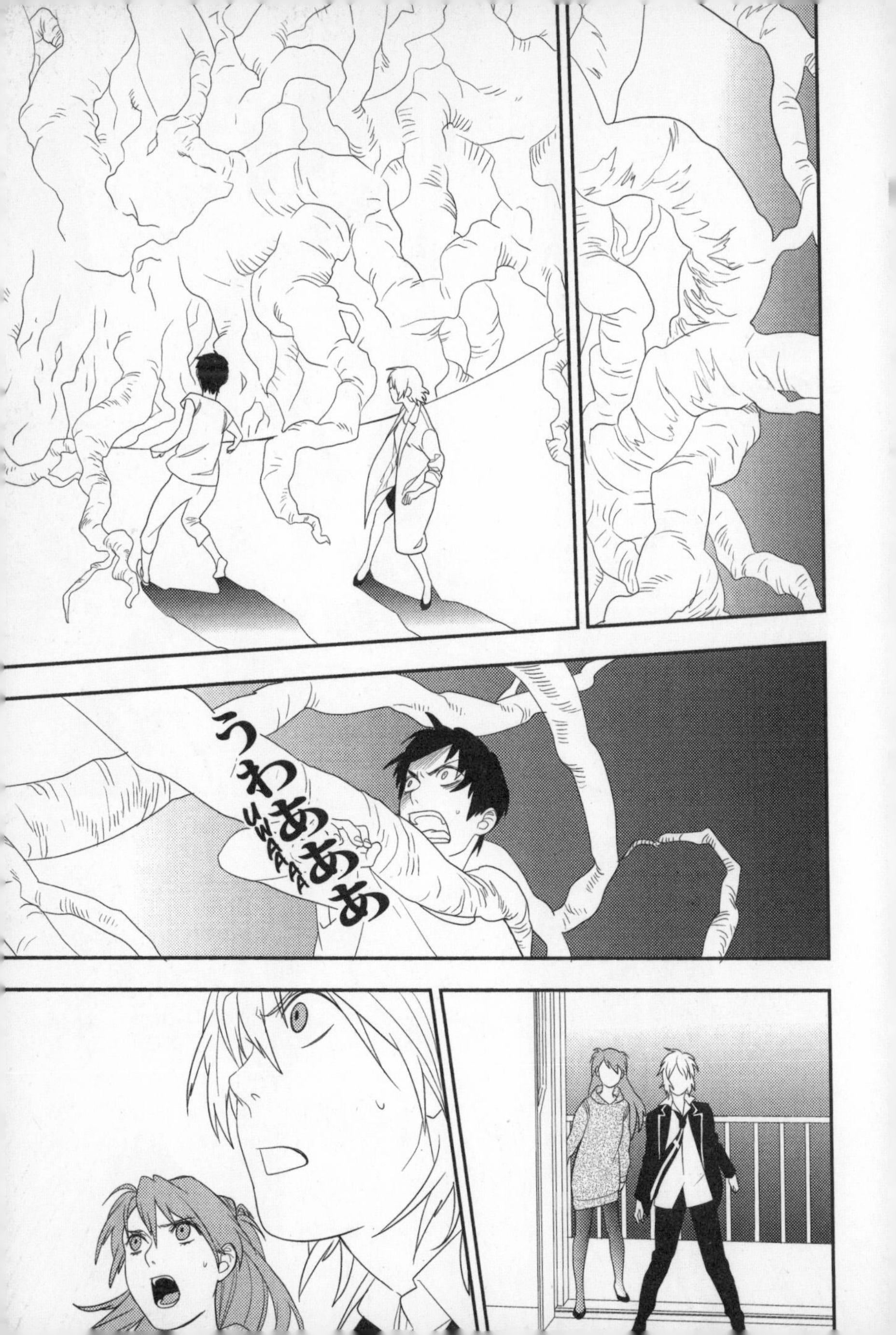
うわあああ
UWAAA

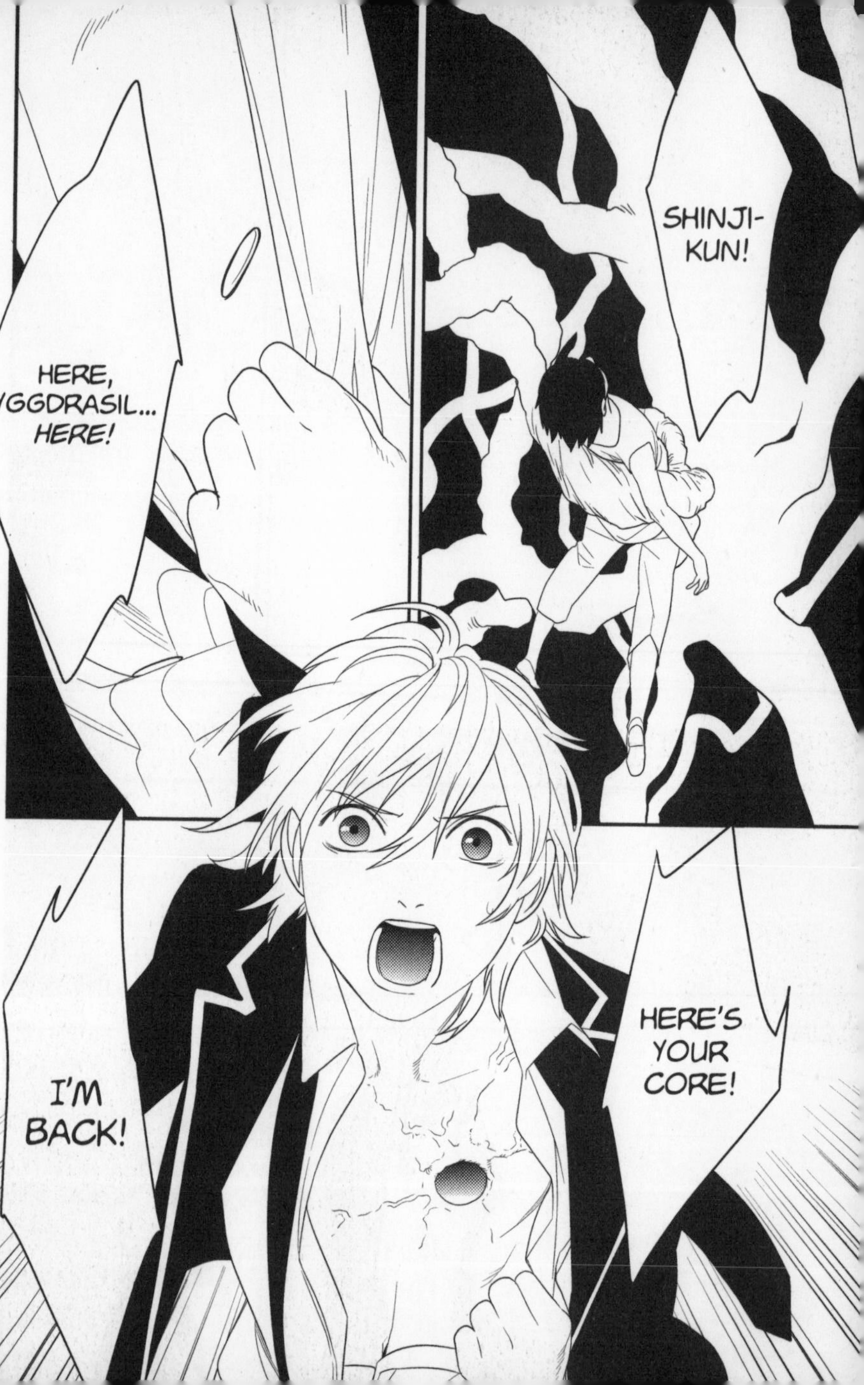
SHINJI-KUN!
HERE, YGGDRASIL... HERE!
HERE'S YOUR CORE!
I'M BACK!

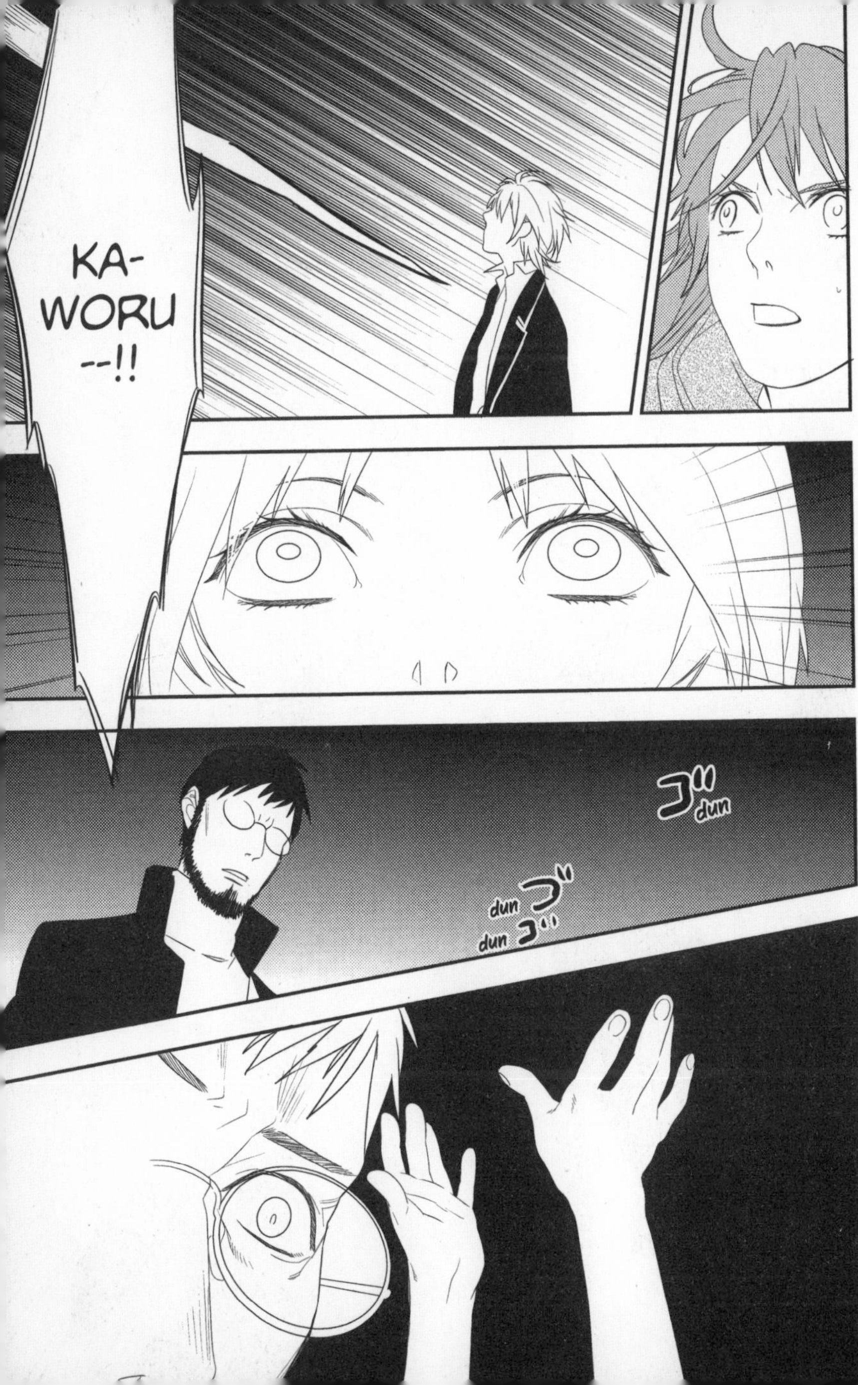
KA-
WORU
--!!
ゴ dun
ゴ dun
ゴ dun

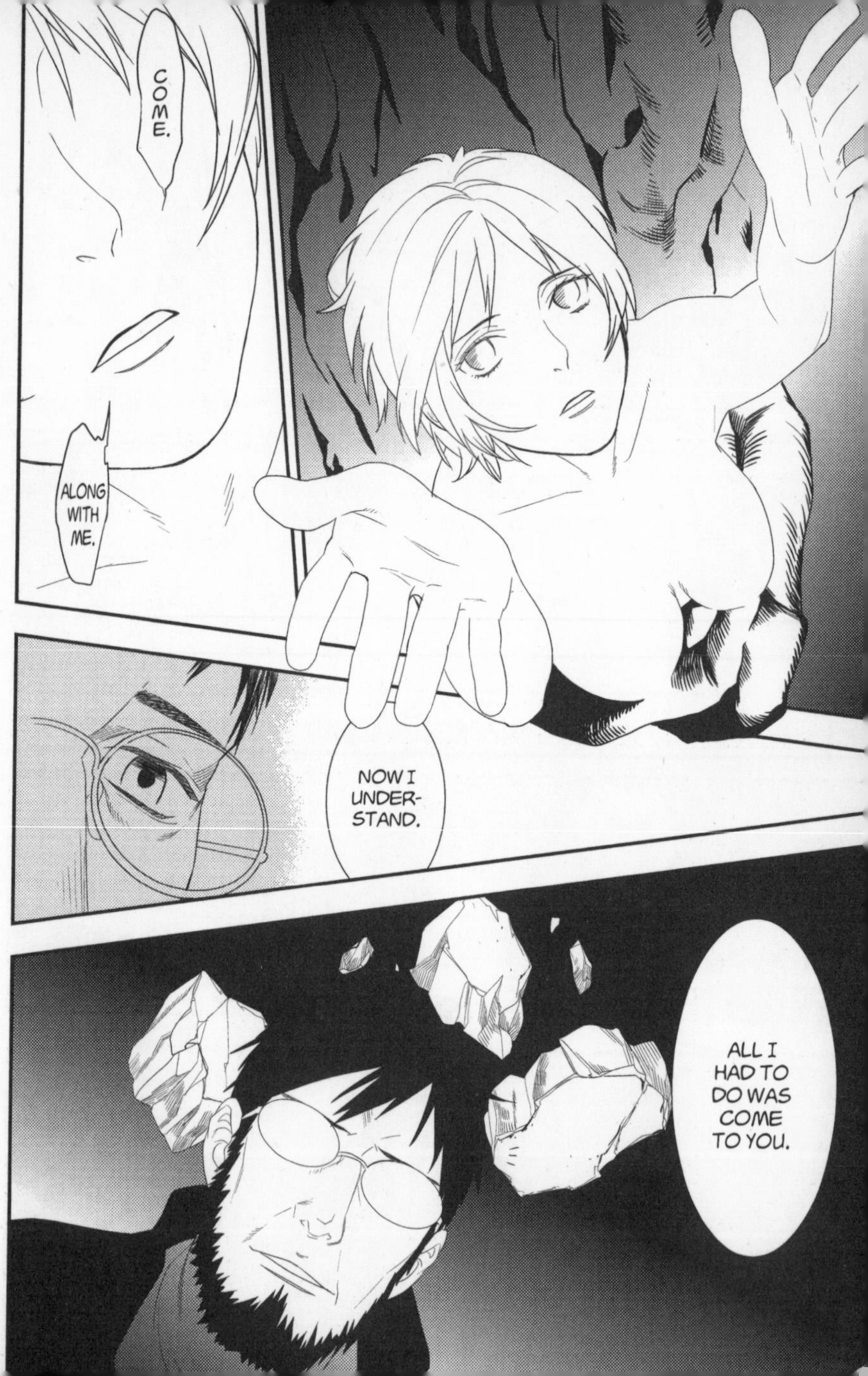
COME.
ALONG WITH ME.
NOW I UNDER-STAND.
ALL I HAD TO DO WAS COME TO YOU.

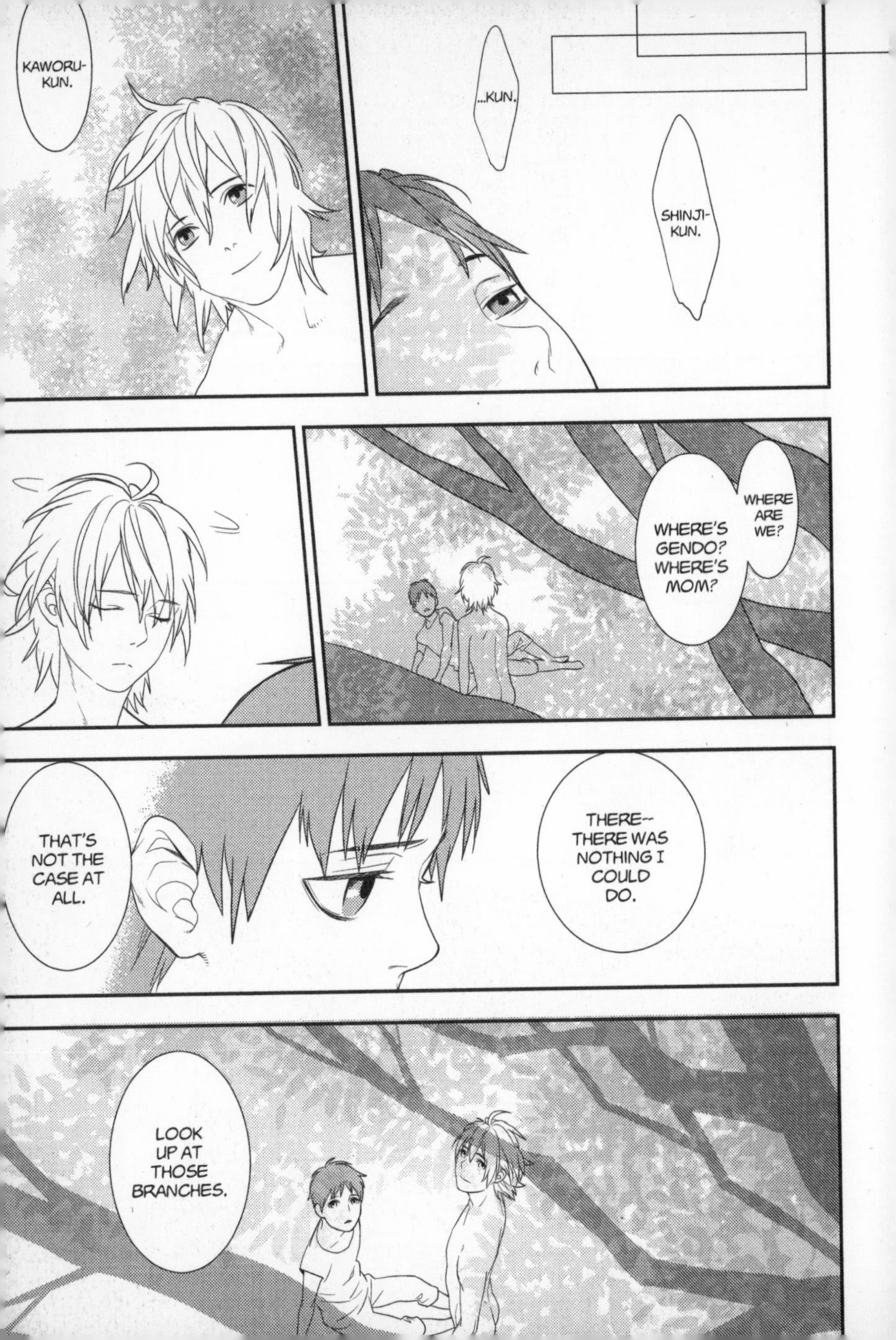
...KUN.
SHINJI-KUN.
KAWORU-KUN.
WHERE ARE WE?
WHERE'S GENDO? WHERE'S MOM?
THERE-- THERE WAS NOTHING I COULD DO.
THAT'S NOT THE CASE AT ALL.
LOOK UP AT THOSE BRANCHES.

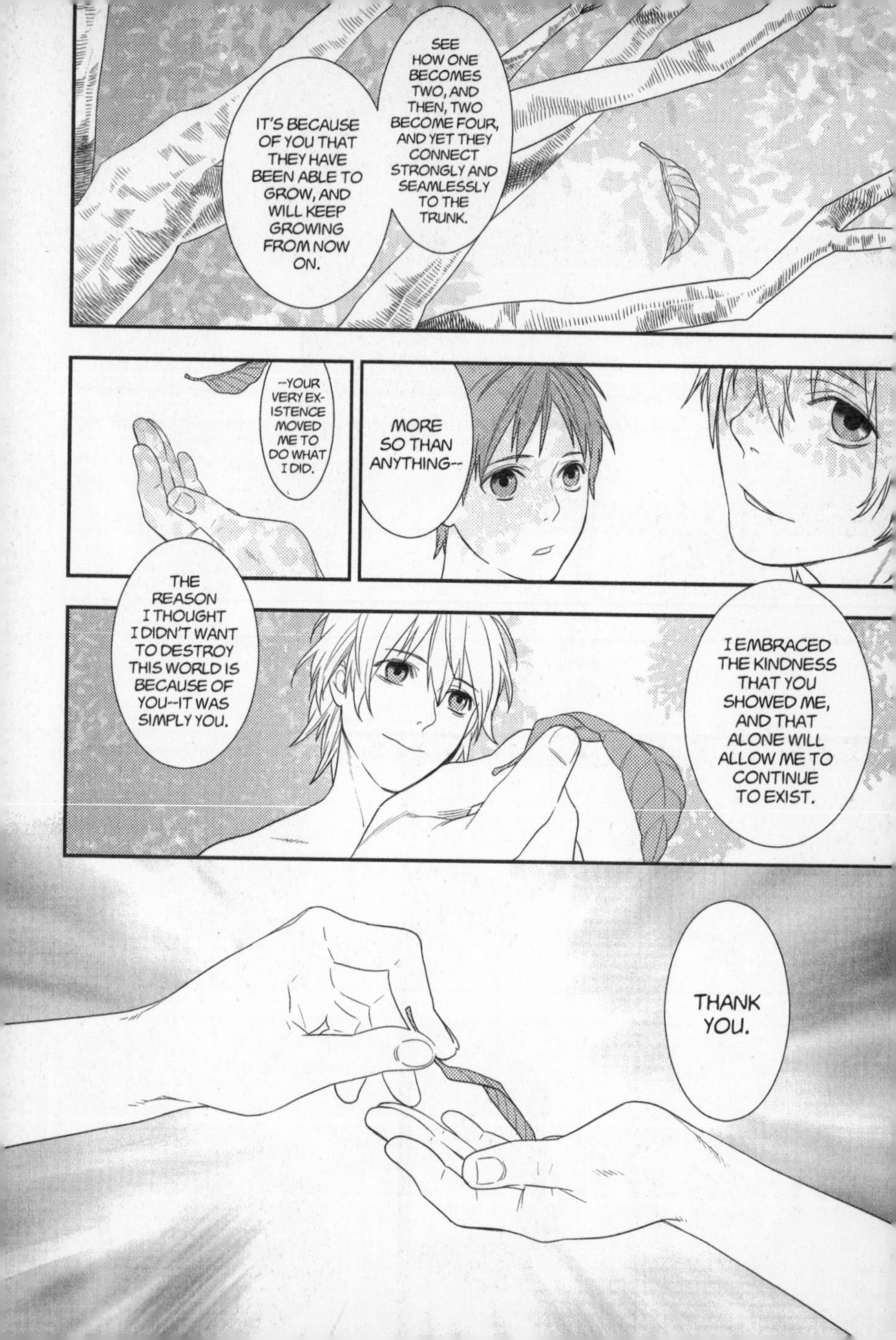
SEE HOW ONE BECOMES TWO, AND THEN, TWO BECOME FOUR, AND YET THEY CONNECT STRONGLY AND SEAMLESSLY TO THE TRUNK.
IT'S BECAUSE OF YOU THAT THEY HAVE BEEN ABLE TO GROW, AND WILL KEEP GROWING FROM NOW ON.
MORE SO THAN ANYTHING--
--YOUR VERY EXISTENCE MOVED ME TO DO WHAT I DID.
THE REASON I THOUGHT I DIDN'T WANT TO DESTROY THIS WORLD IS BECAUSE OF YOU--IT WAS SIMPLY YOU.
I EMBRACED THE KINDNESS THAT YOU SHOWED ME, AND THAT ALONE WILL ALLOW ME TO CONTINUE TO EXIST.
THANK YOU.

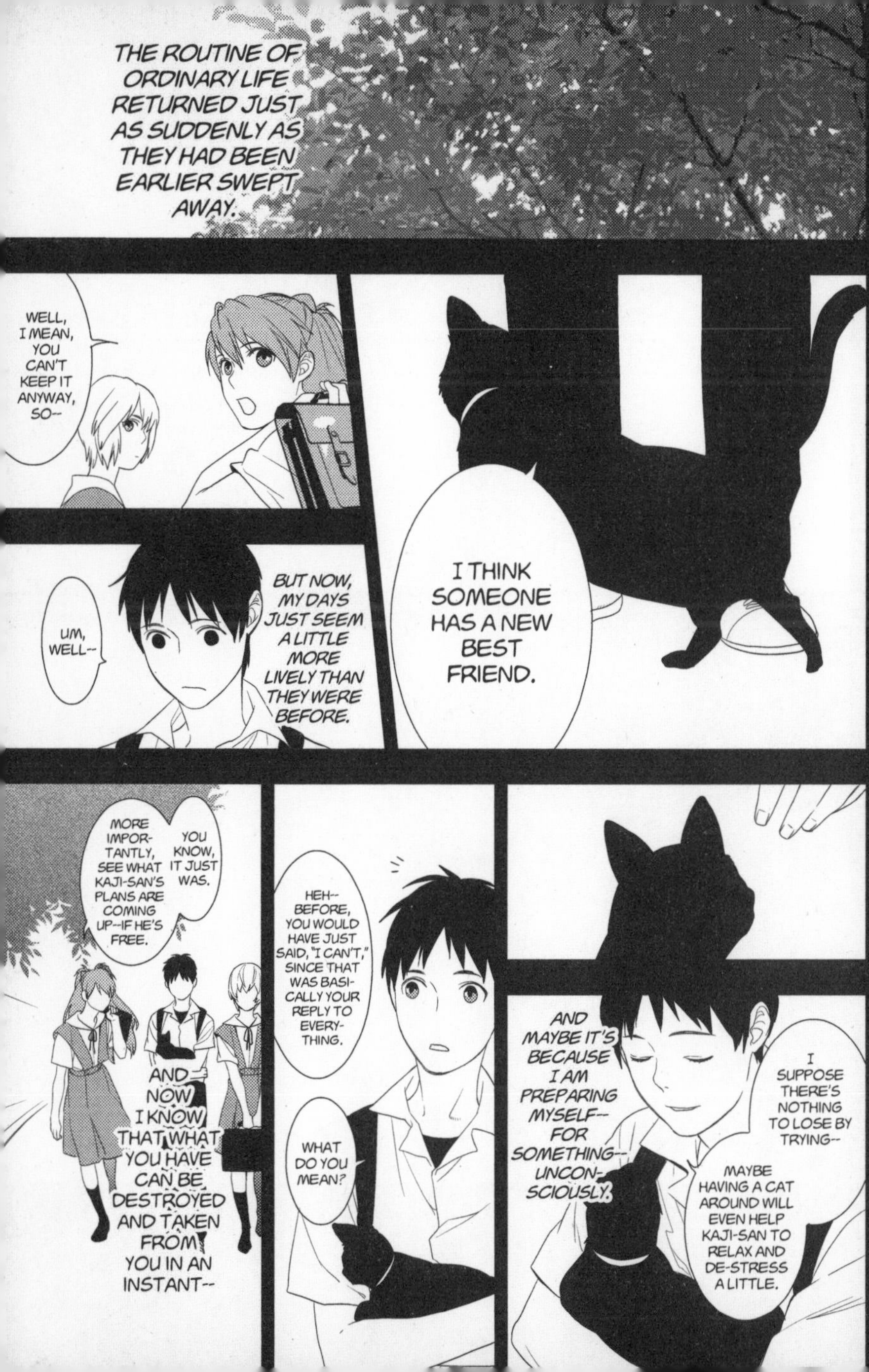
THE ROUTINE OF ORDINARY LIFE RETURNED JUST AS SUDDENLY AS THEY HAD BEEN EARLIER SWEPT AWAY.
I THINK SOMEONE HAS A NEW BEST FRIEND.
WELL, I MEAN, YOU CAN'T KEEP IT ANYWAY, SO--
BUT NOW, MY DAYS JUST SEEM A LITTLE MORE LIVELY THAN THEY WERE BEFORE.
UM, WELL--
I SUPPOSE THERE'S NOTHING TO LOSE BY TRYING--
MAYBE HAVING A CAT AROUND WILL EVEN HELP KAJI-SAN TO RELAX AND DE-STRESS A LITTLE.
AND MAYBE IT'S BECAUSE I AM PREPARING MYSELF--FOR SOMETHING--UNCONSCIOUSLY.
HEH--BEFORE, YOU WOULD HAVE JUST SAID, "I CAN'T," SINCE THAT WAS BASICALLY YOUR REPLY TO EVERYTHING.
WHAT DO YOU MEAN?
YOU KNOW, IT JUST WAS.
MORE IMPORTANTLY, SEE WHAT KAJI-SAN'S PLANS ARE COMING UP--IF HE'S FREE.
AND NOW I KNOW THAT WHAT YOU HAVE CAN BE DESTROYED AND TAKEN FROM YOU IN AN INSTANT--

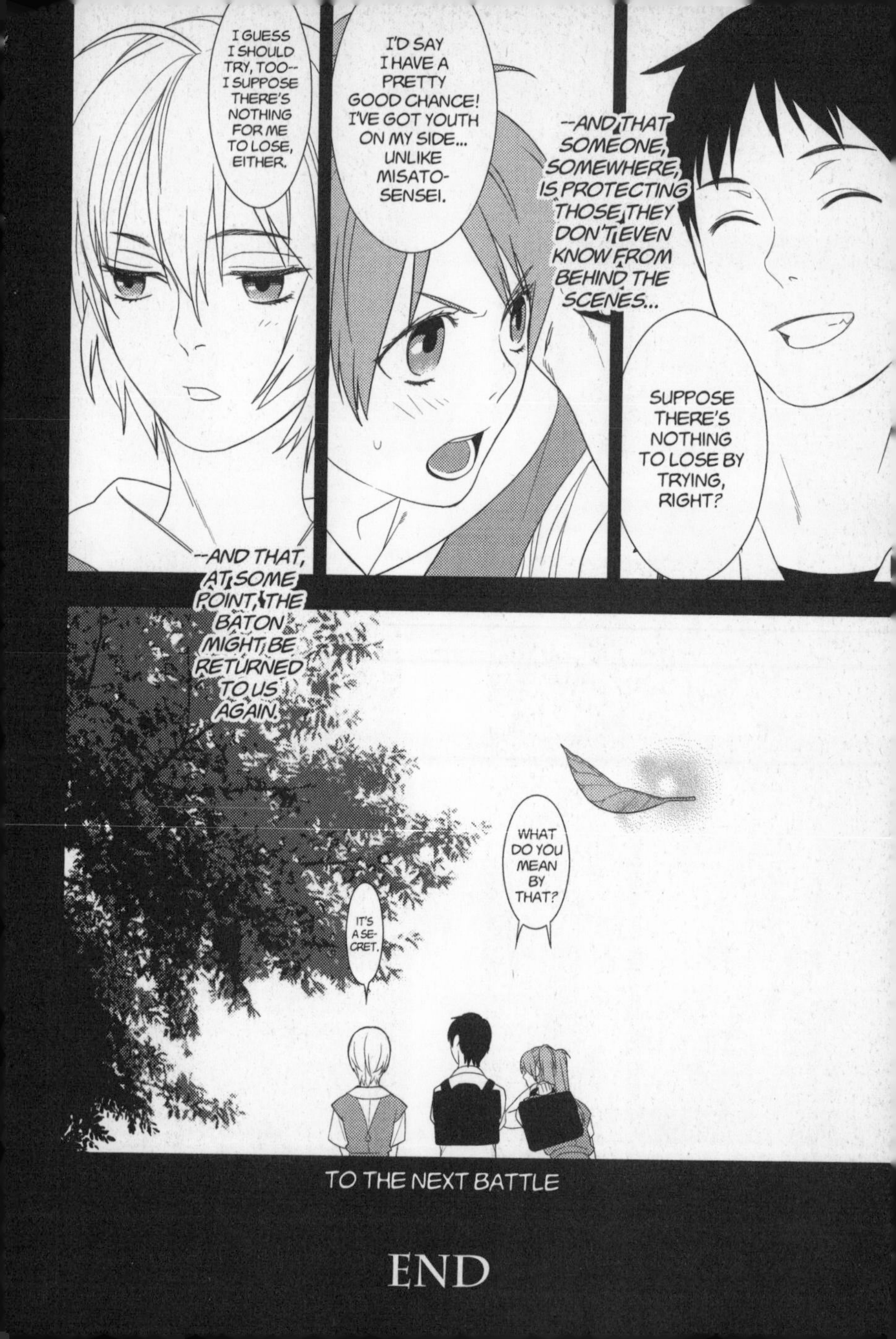
--AND THAT SOMEONE, SOMEWHERE, IS PROTECTING THOSE THEY DON'T EVEN KNOW FROM BEHIND THE SCENES...
SUPPOSE THERE'S NOTHING TO LOSE BY TRYING, RIGHT?
I'D SAY I HAVE A PRETTY GOOD CHANCE! I'VE GOT YOUTH ON MY SIDE... UNLIKE MISATO-SENSEI.
I GUESS I SHOULD TRY, TOO-- I SUPPOSE THERE'S NOTHING FOR ME TO LOSE, EITHER.
--AND THAT, AT SOME POINT, THE BATON MIGHT BE RETURNED TO US AGAIN.
WHAT DO YOU MEAN BY THAT?
IT'S A SE-CRET.

TO THE NEXT BATTLE

END

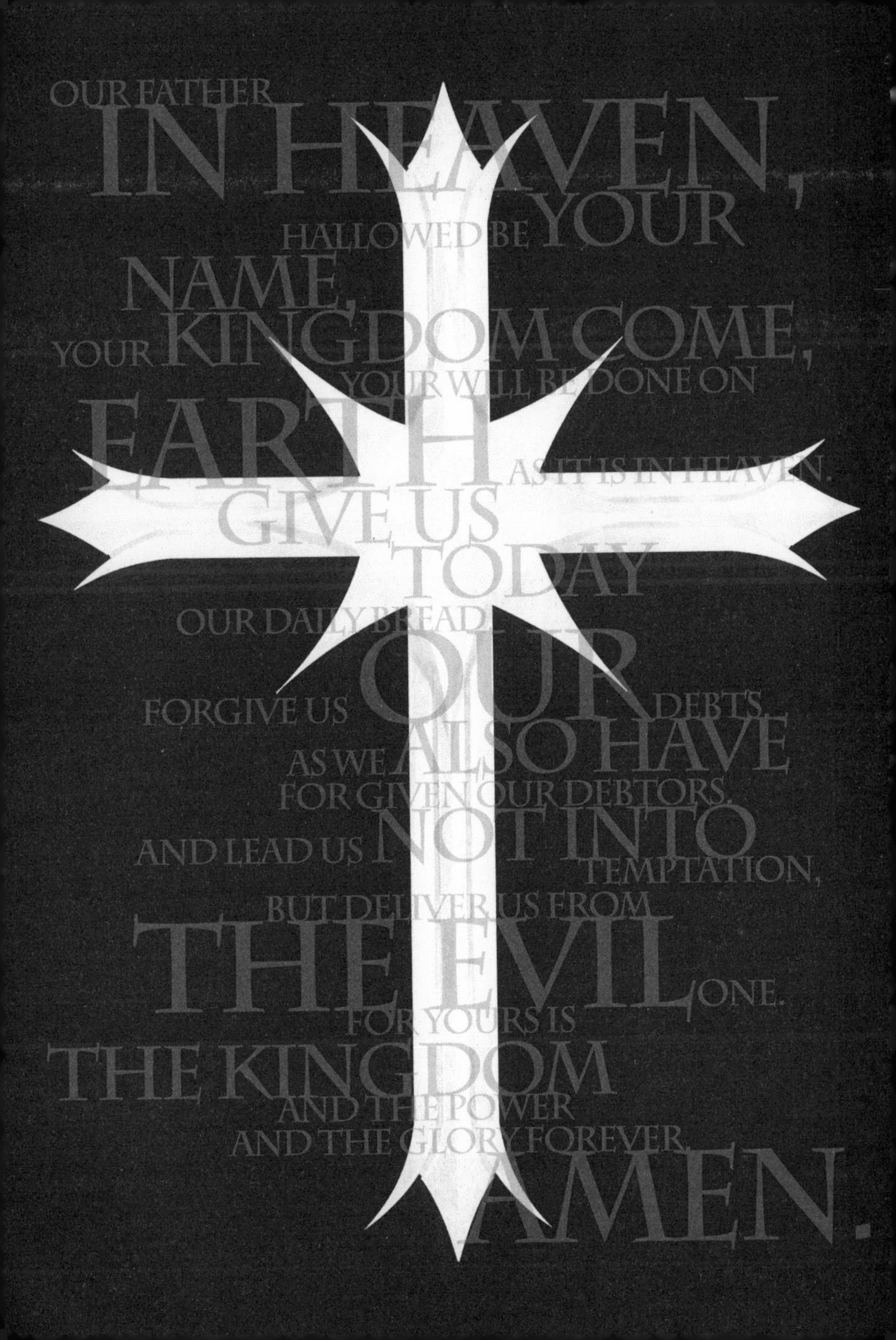
OUR FATHER
IN HEAVEN,
HALLOWED BE YOUR
NAME,
YOUR KINGDOM COME,
YOUR WILL BE DONE ON
EARTH AS IT IS IN HEAVEN.
GIVE US
TODAY
OUR DAILY BREAD.
FORGIVE US OUR DEBTS,
AS WE ALSO HAVE
FORGIVEN OUR DEBTORS.
AND LEAD US NOT INTO
TEMPTATION,
BUT DELIVER US FROM
THE EVIL ONE.
FOR YOURS IS
THE KINGDOM
AND THE POWER
AND THE GLORY FOREVER.
AMEN.

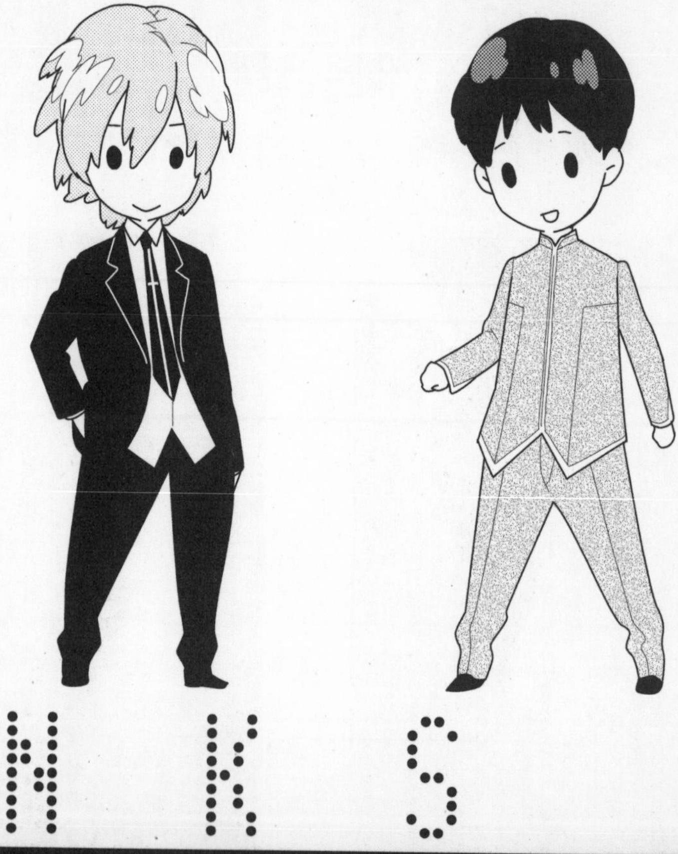
N K S

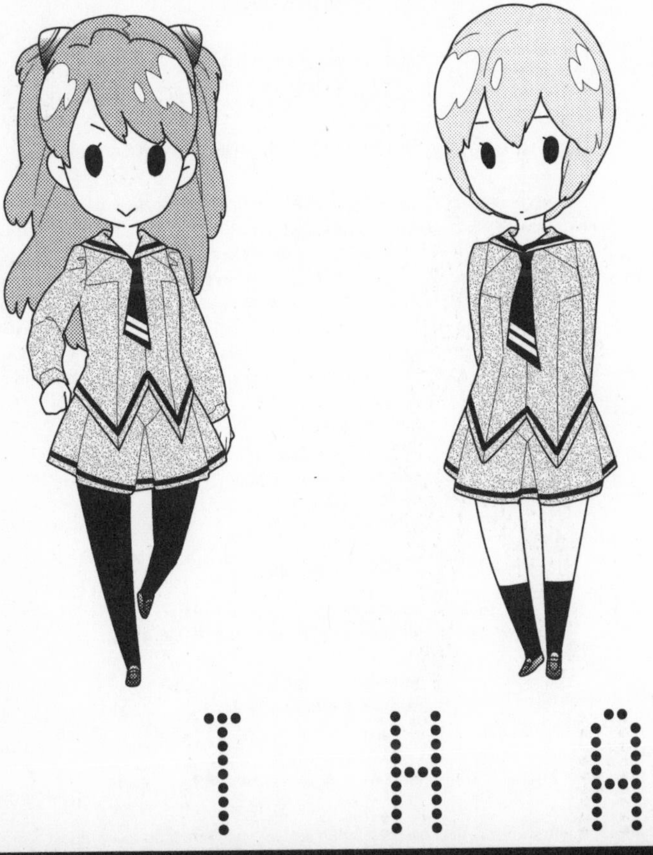
T H A

DESIGNER
STEPHEN REICHERT

EDITOR
JEMIAH JEFFERSON

PUBLISHER
MIKE RICHARDSON

DIGITAL PRODUCTION
IAN TUCKER

English-language version produced by **Dark Horse Comics**

NEON GENESIS EVANGELION CAMPUS APOCALYPSE Volume 4

Published by
Dark Horse Manga
A division of Dark Horse Comics, Inc.
10956 SE Main Street
Milwaukie, OR 97222

DarkHorse.com

**To find a comics shop in your area, call the
Comic Shop Locator Service toll-free at 1-888-266-4226.**

First edition: June 2011
ISBN 978-1-59582-689-3

1 3 5 7 9 10 8 6 4 2
Printed at Transcontinental Gagné, Louiseville, QC, Canada

MISATO'S FAN SERVICE CENTER

c/o Dark Horse Comics • 10956 SE Main Street • Milwaukie, OR 97222 • evangelion@darkhorse.com

Welcome to the final FSC for *Campus Apocalypse*! Yes, this four-volume series is now concluded—and wow, was that a humdinger of an ending or what? I always entertained the idea that maybe Gendo wasn't really the real Gendo; how could anybody be so cruel to and distant from his own son? Overlapping parallel realities have a way of making an already strained family relationship even more difficult for a kid to understand. Fortunately, Shinji has a different "family" made up of his classmates, teachers, and the perennially-unshaven Kaji, and they support him, even if they do tease him a lot. And in *Campus Apocalypse*, Shinji even believes that his adoptive family has his back, even when he suffers from doubt. I think it worked out well!

And now, a most excellent fan letter!

Dear Jemiah,

As a fan of the original TV series, I'm always a little bit wary of new spin-offs, but I've got to say that Campus Apocalypse *is a really fun re-imagining of the series. Can't wait for the next volume.*

I'm also loving the new movie rebuild so far, but I am apprehensive as to where Gainax will take it this time. I can't guess how it will end this time round, which is thrilling but also a little frightening. In that sense it feels like we've come full circle to the way it felt the first time the original series came out!

It's still an exciting time to be an Eva fan. In celebration of this fact, I'm sending some fan art of the original Eva pilots in their new Campus Apocalypse uniforms. Hope you like it!

Best wishes,
Ami Clark
P.S. My votes for fave characters are Shin-chan and Rei-chan! ˆoˆ

Thanks, Ami! Your splendid artwork is a fine addition to this volume.

In January, I was lucky enough to accompany fellow editor Carl Horn to a screening of *Evangelion 2.0: You Can (Not) Advance* at Portland's beautiful Living Room Theaters. Seeing *Evangelion* on the big screen is a delightful, incredible, overwhelming experience, especially in a crowd full of people who might not have known what *Evangelion* is all about (what must they have thought...?). All the colors, the violence, the superb music , Shinji's and Rei's strange passivity, the bizarre storyline, and a couple of sequences that are about as psychedelic as they come did a number on an unprepared audience. Nervous laughter broke out at times, but in general, the atmosphere was of reverent attention. The audience made a game attempt to "get it," and if they couldn't get it, they just sat back and let the images soak in.

Personally, I found myself experiencing the film as if for the first time, although I'd been lucky enough to see it on DVD in the summer of 2010.

Evangelion 2.0 is going to require repeated viewings to catch everything, and seeing it twice is nowhere near enough for me!

There are significant changes to the storyline—a good overview of some of them can be seen at http://www.imdb.com/title/tt0860906/trivia—including whole new characters, new battle outcomes, and even some changes to the characters' personalities and relationships. Needless to say, the *Rebuild* films are essential viewing for any *Evangelion* fan, and a great entry point for the uninitiated.

I'd love to hear some more fan reactions to *Evangelion 2.0*, even if they cannot happen in the pages of this series. Fortunately, Dark Horse

Manga has more *Evangelion* action ahead—our sister series, *The Shinji Ikari Raising Project*, isn't ending any time soon! Its eighth volume has just been completed, and there are plenty more where that came from. If you have Eva theories, fan art, rants, or just good ol' fashioned squee that you'd like to share, please do! Both *Evangelion* manga series share the same letters column address, and we're always delighted to hear from our readers.

It's been a pleasure working on this title. My thanks go out to all of you.

To the next battle,
—**Jemiah**

NEON GENESIS EVANGELION

Dark Horse Manga is proud to present two new original series based on the wildly popular *Neon Genesis Evangelion* manga and anime! Continuing the rich story lines and complex characters, these new visions of *Neon Genesis Evangelion* provide extra dimensions for understanding one of the greatest series ever made!

NEON GENESIS EVANGELION
THE SHINJI IKARI RAISING PROJECT

**STORY AND ART
BY OSAMU TAKAHASHI**

VOLUME 1
ISBN 978-1-59582-321-2 | $9.99

VOLUME 2
ISBN 978-1-59582-377-9 | $9.99

VOLUME 3
ISBN 978-1-59582-447-9 | $9.99

VOLUME 4
ISBN 978-1-59582-454-7 | $9.99

VOLUME 5
ISBN 978-1-59582-520-9 | $9.99

VOLUME 6
ISBN 978-1-59582-580-3 | $9.99

VOLUME 7
ISBN 978-1-59582-595-7 | $9.99

VOLUME 8
ISBN 978-1-59582-694-7 | $9.99

VOLUME 9
ISBN 978-1-59582-800-2 | $9.99

NEON GENESIS EVANGELION
Campus Apocalypse

**STORY AND ART
BY MINGMING**

VOLUME 1
ISBN 978-1-59582-530-8 | $10.99

VOLUME 2
ISBN 978-1-59582-661-9 | $10.99

VOLUME 3
ISBN 978-1-59582-680-0 | $10.99

VOLUME 4
ISBN 978-1-59582-689-3 | $10.99

**Each volume of *Neon Genesis Evangelion* features bonus color pages,
your *Evangelion* fan art and letters, and special reader giveaways!**

DARK HORSE MANGA
DarkHorse.com

AVAILABLE AT YOUR LOCAL COMICS SHOP OR BOOKSTORE
To find a comics shop in your area, call 1-888-266-4226 • For more information or to order direct: • On the web: darkhorse.com
E-mail: mailorder@darkhorse.com • Phone: 1-800-862-0052 Mon.–Fri. 9 AM to 5 PM Pacific Time.

NEON GENESIS EVANGELION IKARI-SHINJI IKUSEI KEIKAKU © OSAMU TAKAHASHI 2011. © GAINAX • khara. First published in Japan in 2006 by KADOKAWA
SHOTEN Publishing Co., Ltd., Tokyo. NEON GENESIS EVANGELION GAKUEN DATENROKU © MINGMING 2010 © GAINAX • khara. First published in Japan in 2008
by KADOKAWA SHOTEN Publishing Co., Ltd., Tokyo. English translation rights arranged with KADOKAWA SHOTEN Publishing Co., Ltd., Tokyo, through TOHAN
CORPORATION, Tokyo. Dark Horse Manga™ is a trademark of Dark Horse Comics, Inc. All rights reserved. (BL 7077)

Written by
Sankichi Meguro

Art by
Saki Okuse

Ghost Talker's Daydream tells the dark, sensual story of Misaki Saiki, a young woman with a troubled past, who is a professional dominatrix in one of Tokyo's most exclusive S&M clubs. However, her real money comes from something she likes even less than being a dominatrix. Ever since childhood, Misaki has had the ability to see and communicate with ghosts, and that talent is put to use by the Livelihood Protection Agency, which pairs Misaki with Souichiro Kadotake, a martial artist who happens to be deathly afraid of ghosts. Using her gifts, Misaki is able to help troubled departed spirits resolve what is troubling them and allow them to move on to the afterlife.

Volume One
ISBN 978-1-59307-950-5
Volume Two
ISBN 978-1-59582-186-7
Volume Three
ISBN 978-1-59582-234-5
Volume Four
ISBN 978-1-59582-260-4
Volume Five
ISBN 978-1-59582-666-4
Volume Six
ISBN 978-1-59582-715-9

$10.99 each

TEIZOKUREI DAYDREAM © SANKICHI MEGURO 2011 © SAKI OKUSE 2008 First published in Japan in 2002 by KADOKAWA SHOTEN Publishing Co., Ltd., Tokyo. English translation rights arranged with KADOKAWA SHOTEN Publishing Co., Ltd., Tokyo, through TOHAN CORPORATION, Tokyo. Dark Horse Books® and the Dark Horse logo are registered trademarks of Dark Horse Comics, Inc. (BL7071)

EDEN

It's an Endless World!

Volume 1
ISBN 978-1-59307-406-7

Volume 2
ISBN 978-1-59307-454-8

Volume 3
ISBN 978-1-59307-529-3

Volume 4
ISBN 978-1-59307-544-6

Volume 5
ISBN 978-1-59307-634-4

Volume 6
ISBN 978-1-59307-702-0

Volume 7
ISBN 978-1-59307-765-5

Volume 8
ISBN 978-1-59307-787-7

Volume 9
ISBN 978-1-59307-851-5

Volume 10
ISBN 978-1-59307-957-4

Volume 11
ISBN 978-1-59582-244-4

Volume 12
ISBN 978-1-59582-296-3

Volume 13
ISBN 978-1-59582-763-0

$12.99 each

BRIDE of the WATER GOD

When Soah's impoverished, desperate village decides to sacrifice her to the Water God Habaek to end a long drought, they believe that drowning one beautiful girl will save their entire community and bring much-needed rain. Not only is Soah surprised to be *rescued* by the Water God instead of killed; she never imagined she'd be a welcomed guest in Habaek's magical kingdom, where an exciting new life awaits her! Most surprising, however, is the Water God himself, and how very different he is from the monster Soah imagined . . .

Created by Mi-Kyung Yun, who received the "Best New Artist" award in 2004 from the esteemed *Dokja-manhwa-daesang* organization, *Bride of the Water God* was the top-selling *shoujo* manhwa in Korea in 2006!

Volume 1
ISBN 978-1-59307-849-2

Volume 2
ISBN 978-1-59307-883-6

Volume 3
ISBN 978-1-59582-305-2

Volume 4
ISBN 978-1-59582-378-6

Volume 5
ISBN 978-1-59582-445-5

Volume 6
ISBN 978-1-59582-605-3

Volume 7
ISBN 978-1-59582-668-8

Volume 8
ISBN 978-1-59582-687-9

$9.99 each

Previews for BRIDE OF THE WATER GOD and other DARK HORSE MANHWA titles can be found at darkhorse.com!

DARK HORSE MANHWA

HELLSING

VOLUME 1:
ISBN 978-1-59307-056-4

VOLUME 2:
ISBN 978-1-59307-057-1

VOLUME 3:
ISBN 978-1-59307-202-5

VOLUME 4:
ISBN 978-1-59307-259-9

VOLUME 5:
ISBN 978-1-59307-272-8

VOLUME 6:
ISBN 978-1-59307-302-2

VOLUME 7:
ISBN 978-1-59307-348-0

VOLUME 8:
ISBN 978-1-59307-780-8

VOLUME 9:
ISBN 978-1-59582-157-7

VOLUME 10:
ISBN 978-1-59582-498-1

$13.99 EACH

AVAILABLE AT YOUR LOCAL COMICS SHOP OR BOOKSTORE!
To find a comics shop in your area, call 1-888-266-4226.

For more information or to order direct visit darkhorse.com or call 1-800-862-0052
Mon.-Fri. 9 AM to 5 PM Pacific Time. Prices and availability subject to change without notice.

DMP
Digital Manga
Publishing

digitalmanga.com

DARK
HORSE
MANGA

darkhorse.com

STOP!

止まれ

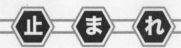

THIS IS THE BACK OF THE BOOK!

This manga collection is translated into English, but arranged in right-to-left reading format to maintain the artwork's visual orientation as originally drawn and published in Japan. If you've never read comics this way before, take a look at the diagram below to give yourself an idea of how to go about it. Basically, you'll be starting in the upper-right-hand corner, and will read each word balloon and panel moving right to left. It may take a little getting used to, but you should get the hang of it very quickly. Have fun! If this is the millionth manga you've read this way, never mind.

1
CAN WE SHOW YOU
huh ?
2
3
4
5
SHINJI-KUN...
...WASN'T IT?

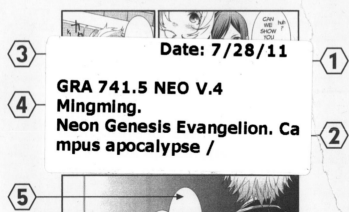

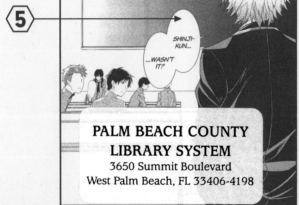